V&R

Novum Testamentum et Orbis Antiquus/ Studien zur Umwelt des Neuen Testaments

In cooperation with the "Bibel und Orient" foundation,
University of Fribourg/Switzerland.
Edited by Max Küchler (Fribourg), Peter Lampe,
Gerd Theißen (Heidelberg) and Jürgen Zangenberg (Leiden)

Volume 94

Vandenhoeck & Ruprecht

Colossae in Space and Time

Linking to an Ancient City

Edited by
Alan H. Cadwallader and Michael Trainor

Vandenhoeck & Ruprecht

with 67 figures

Bibliographic information published by the Deutsche Nationalbibliothek

The Deutsche Nationalbibliothek lists this publication
in the Deutsche Nationalbibliografie;
detailed bibliographic data available online: http://dnb.d-nb.de.

ISBN 978-3-525-53397-0
ISBN 978-3-647-53397-1 (e-book)

Typesetting by: textformart, Gottingen
Printed and bound in Germany by: ⊛ Hubert & Co, Göttingen

Printed on non-aging paper.

Contents

Preface

The demands of a university that encourages a heavy teaching load have meant that the time and energy needed to compile and edit this collection have too often lain at the horizon. However both Flinders University and the Australian Catholic University have provided funding and release for travel to distant places so that research could be pursued. The Australian Research Theology Foundation Inc has generously provided a grant also to assist various aspects of the project to proceed.

The need for a complete review of Colossae and its rich history has driven on the project and provided wells of patience to those who have contributed. To them we owe our thanks.

The editors of the series *Novum Testamentum et Orbis Antiquus* within Vandenhoeck and Ruprecht have likewise seen the importance of the project and have been supportive and encouraging of its completion.

Our thanks are also due to Umut Özgüç, Sarp Kaya and Ayse Ercan for their assistance in Turkish translations, amidst their own busy schedules.

There have also been numerous supporters, a chorus if you like, who have sung the right song at the right time, not least being our students who have eagerly sought out scraps of data, asked new questions and cultivated a momentum of interest.

Most of all, our labours have been welcomed by friends and colleagues in Turkey, keen to learn more of the heritage that is theirs. One family in particular has never flinched from the highest call of hospitality and have warmly welcomed their Australian visitors. So, to Ismail, Hafize, Onür and Özgür Iyilikçi, this book is dedicated.

Canberra, August 2011

Alan H. Cadwallader
Michael Trainor

Chapter 1

Colossae in Space and Time: Overcoming Dislocation, Dismemberment and Anachronicity

Alan H. Cadwallader / Michael Trainor

The recovery of the significance of the ancient city of Colossae has only now begun in any earnest or rigorous fashion. This is an ancient city whose reach spans from before the early bronze age to the present. Despite this length of time and the site's virtually continuous habitation of space Colossae has received little scholarly attention. The modern period has witnessed repeated calls for the excavation of the site but these have been matched by repeated failures in commitment to a project. The impasse is, in part, a product of its complex history and of presumptions guiding western scholarship. This is the guiding focus of this introductory essay which provides the rationale for the collection. The essays in this book cover the broadest span of the history of the site in its region that is possible to date. From the Achaemenid to the Byzantine periods, the records related to Colossae, both textual and artefactual, are sifted. Not only is new evidence presented for the first time but, perhaps more significantly, many new perspectives and insights have been extracted because of a detailed and rigorous re-examination of past foundations for study of the ancient site within its region. The results serve to contrast markedly from previous scholarship. At the same time, that scholarship itself needs forensic review not only to appreciate what the past has thus far yielded but also to understand why the study of Colossae has been so constricted.

There have been two long-term interruptions to the appreciation of the historical significance of the site. The first was the consequence of the final assertion of Seljuk control over the critical geopolitical pathway of the Lycus Valley east to Apameia (and beyond) late in the thirteenth century CE. The second was the result of the disappointment of European travellers at the apparently barren remains of the site. These travellers visited Colossae between the late seventeenth and early twentieth centuries and dismissed its long and rich past. These two factors meant that six hundred years passed when Colossae was more lost to enquiry than even the repeated cartographical confusion would suggest. It is this confusion that we first address.

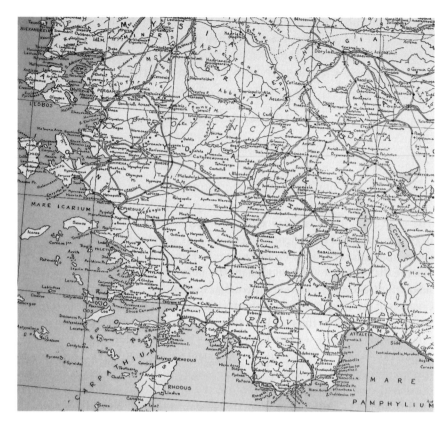

Fig. 1 Classical South-West Asia Minor with detail[1]

---

1 Detail from W.M. Calder/G.E. Bean, *A Classical Map of Asia Minor* (London: BIAA, 1958). Colossae and Chonai are to the right of centre.

The twelfth-thirteenth century writings of Nicetas Choniates and his brother Michael kept alive a literary connection between Colossae and Chonai.[2] Nicetas, for example, wrote that his native city, Chonai, was anciently known as Colossae, a repetition of a testimony from two hundred years earlier,[3] but for European eyes, this provided no trigonometric fix. Early western geographers and historians confidently identified Colossae with Denizli,[4] Honaz,[5] even a satellite village of Burdur[6] if it appeared at all. Indeed, as we shall see later, they also identified Colossae with the island of Rhodes off the south-western coast of Asia Minor.

Colossae's various positions on early maps confirmed the confusion over identity

Cartographers positioned Colossae to the west (rather than south-east) of Laodicea[7] or, as "Conos", between Laodicea to the north-west and Hierapolis to the north-east.[8] Or there was a tacit admission of ignorance in the omission of any adscriptions for the Lycus Valley, for example, in Sebastian Münster's famous *Cosmographica* (1544). "Laodichia" managed to claw its way onto Girolamo Ruscelli's "Natolia Nuova Tavola" included in his *Ptolemaeus La Geografia* (1561),

---

2 The memory of the connection made by Nicetas Choniates recurred. See, for example, W. F. Ainsworth, "A Memoir Illustrative of the Geography of the Anabasis of Xenophon", *The Classical Museum* 1 (1844) 170–85, on p.171.

3 Nicetas Choniates, *Chronicles* 178.19 (edition: Jan-Louis van Dieten (ed.), *Nicetae Choniatae Historia* (Berlin: Walter de Gruyter, 1975); Constantine VII Porphyrogenitus (emperor 913–959 CE), *De thematibus* 3.24 (edition: A. Pertusi, *De thematibus Introductione, testo critico, commento* (Città del Vaticano: Biblioteca apostolica vaticana, 1952), 68.32–40).

4 *Caledonian Mercury* April 11th, 1816, letter from the Reverend H. Lindsay, chaplain to the Levant Company in Constantinople, §III.

5 "Colossae, the ruins of which are called Khonas" [*sic*!] – H.I. Schmidt, *Course of Ancient Geography* (New York: Appleton and Co, 1861), 239; see also Louis Vincent de Saint-Marie, *Histoire des découvertes géographiques des nations Européennes dans les diverses parties du Monde* (3 vol.; Paris: Arthus-Bertrand, 1846), 3.512.

6 "Trimile – possibly a small town called (Colossa) May 10th": Memorandum Book II of the Reverend Edward T. Daniell for the inscription that was later published in T. A. B. Spratt/ E. Forbes, *Travels in Lycia, Milyas and the Cibyratis in Company with the late Rev. E. T. Daniell* (2 vol.; London: John van Voorst, 1847), 2.289 (= *CIG* III.4380k³). The first publication of the inscription removed Daniell's note, recognising his mistake and provided the correction that the woman named in the inscription, Aphiadis, was noted as a "Colossian" – that is, her birthplace was Colossae. She had married a man from a village near the cities of Balbura and Bubon, approximately 90 kilometres to the south of Colossae.

7 J. Bonfrere, *Onomasticon Urbium et Locorum Sacrae Scripturae* (Amsterdam: R & G Wetstein, 1711), map between pages 204 and 205.

8 G. Mercator, *Tabula I: Asiae* (1578) became part of his *Atlas sive Cosmographicae Meditationes de Fabrica Mundi et Fabricati Figura* (Duisburg: Albert Buys, 1595). Mercator included Chonai in spite of the absence of Colossae (the earlier name for Chonai) in Ptolemy's geography.

Fig. 2 The English schoolboy edition
of Cellarius' 1705 map of Colossae west
of Laodicea[9]

but the city had migrated north to the
Cayster River away from the Maeander
and Lycus Rivers *(Fig. 2)* and the Taurus
mountain range. Abraham Ortelius (1578)
repeated this transposition for "Laudichia",[10] although when it came to his map
of the "Peregrinationis Divi Pauli Typus Corographicus", Ortelius' concern to refine his accuracy saw both "Laodicea" and "Colosse" located in relation to one
another and the Maeander/Lycus rivers.[11]

---

9 Christopher Cellarius produced a number of maps, including that of Asia Minor, for
his *Notitiae Orbis Antiqui: Sive Geographia Plenior ... et Notitia Tabulis Geographicis* (1705/6)
which was published throughout Europe over the next ten years and was one of the most
popular works of ancient geography. A smaller version was turned into a school textbook by
the English schoolteacher, Samuel Patrick. The *Geographia Antiqua* (first issued in 1731), from
which this map is taken, was periodically re-issued into the nineteenth century, shaping perceptions of three generations of English scholars. See W. A. Goffart, *Historical Atlases: the first
three hundred years, 1570–1870* (London: University of Chicago Press, 2003), 231.

10 A. Ortelius, *Theatrum Orbis Terrarum* (Antwerp: 1570) map § 174 (van den Broecke/Ort
numbering).

11 *Parergon sive Veteris Geographiae Aliquot Tabulae* (Antwerp: Christopher Plantin, 1584)
map 1P (Ort/van den Broecke numbering system). The map was first published in 1579.

Fig. 3 Section of the map of the Mediterranean
from the voyages of Corneille de Bruin (1698),
showing the blank interior of Turkey

"Chonos" or some other guesstimation of the spelling of Honaz[12] sometimes
subsumed Colossae. Alternately, as in Salmon's 1756 map of Asia Minor, "Collo-
ses" stood alone of the Lycus Valley cities.[13] For those Europeans, like the Dutch
captain Corneille de Bruin, wanting to hug sea lanes and coastal ports, Colossae's distance from the Mediterranean (approximately 180 kilometres away)
meant that the entire Anatolian peninsula with very few exceptions was a blank
(Fig. 3).[14]

---

12 The spelling of Honaz remained insecure for centuries, partly due to the competition
between Arab, Greek and Turcoman renditions, partly due to the epidemic complications
attempted by Europeans: see A. H. Cadwallader, "The Reverend Dr. John Luke and the
Churches of Chonai", *GRBS* 48 (2008): 319–38 on p. 322. Philip Schaff's "Chronos" cannot be
excused by either however: P. Schaff, *A Dictionary of the Bible* (Philadelphia: American Sunday School Union, 4th Ed., 1887), 195.

13 Thomas Salmon, *The Modern Gazetteer: or a short view of the several nations of the world*
(London: S & E Ballard, 3rd Ed., 1756).

14 See C. de Bruin, "Tabula Geographica" in his *A Voyage to the Levant: or Travels in the
Principal Parts of Asia Minor, the Islands of Scio, Rhodes, Cyprus &c* translated by "W. J." (London: J. Tomson and T. Bennet, 1702 [1698 Dutch edition]).

Apart from the familiar and oft-repeated handful of literary references,[15] and inaccurate efforts to keep Colossae on the map, the site for the west had become lost to time and space. Colossae was literally dis-located. The above sampling that illustrates Colossae's geographic and cartographic displacement demonstrates how distant, malleable and unsecured Colossae had become. The days of a required stop-over on pilgrimage from Ephesus to the Holy Land had long gone.

The inhabitants of the immediate vicinity of the ancient site were shackled in bureaucratic tabulation for tax purposes to the town of Honaz. The compensation was that Colossae provided an opportunity for the continuation of the grand tradition of the Byzantines: it became little more than a quarry. The ancient city was distributed. It supplied polished marble veneer for the ancient khan (or caravanserai) built by Karasungur bin Abdullah in 1253–4 on the main road about six kilometres from Denizli. Building blocks and columns were extensively raided for the renovation of the early medieval fortress that had been initiated in the seventh-eighth century on the slopes of Honaz-dağ (Mt Cadmus) and which continued to be used into the eighteenth century. Column drums found their way to numerous houses for, *inter alia*, rolling down strips of land. Serendipitous discoveries of stone and other artefacts became items of exchange used to cement kinship and reinforce bonds of friendship and patronage in the social structure of the region.[16] And there was the continual demand for burial headstones.[17] All this was but a cockcrow before the Europeans began their competitive, acquisitive forays. Quite apart from the occasional deliberate damage from military conflict in the transition period to Ottoman control,[18] Colossae was, in a word, dis-membered.

Dislocation in the west and dismemberment in the east – these polarities characterise Colossae for the four hundred years between the Seljuk supremacy

---

15 Xenophon *Anab.* 1.2.6; Herodotos *Hist.* 7.30; Strabo *Geogr.* 8.8.16; Pliny *Nat.* 5.32.41, 31.2.20; Polyaenus *Strat.* 7.16; Diodorus Siculus 14.80.5; Ororios, 7.7.12; Eusebius *Chronicle* 210. The Letter to the Colossians also figured prominently in the recitation of sources. The story of St Michael the Archangel of Chonai, the other major text associated with Colossae, was ignored.

16 For the atavism of artefacts in Turkey, see M. Özdogan, "Ideology and Archaeology in Turkey", in L. Meskell (ed.), *Archaeology Under Fire: Nationalism, Politics and Heritage in the Eastern Mediterranean and Middle East* (London/New York: Routledge, 1988) 11–23, on p. 118.

17 See generally, M. Greenhalgh, "Spolia in Fortifications: Turkey, Syria and North Africa", in *Ideologie e pratiche del reimpiego nell'alto medioevo* (Spoleto: Centro Italiano di Studi sull'Alto Medioevo, 1999), 785–935.

18 For example, the church of St Michael at Chonai/Colossae was allegedly converted to a stable by the Turks under Sultan Alp Arslan in 1070 CE: John Scylitzes *Chron.* II. 686–87 (*PG* 122: 144–45A); it was plundered and burned by Theodore Mangaphas in 1189: Nicetas Choniates *Chron* 400.88 ff. The burning may however be of a church of St Michael at Aphrodisias. Certainly, Chonai's main church was sufficiently intact to be repaired in time for Pseudo-Alexis' ransacking in 1193: Nicetas Choniates *Chron.* 422.85 ff.

in the Lycus valley and the gradual relaxation of restriction on trade and travel inviting European representatives from bases at Constantinople and Smyrna. Deprecation from the west was to follow.

The Seljuk and Ottoman barrier to Colossae

Long before Chonai actually fell to final Seljuk control, the site – that "great pilgrim city"[19] – had held out as a Byzantine centre longer than many of its neighbours. Michael Choniates eulogised one bishop, named Nicetas, who moved into the metropolitanate of Chonai (c. 1143) unfazed by "the barbarians sequestering at the margins of his see"[20] – probably his evocation of the St Michael miracle story.[21] Nevertheless, Seljuk traders from "Kuniya" (Iconium) patronised the centre. These merchants joined the trade markets accompanying the festive throngs who gathered for the panegyric of the annual St Michael celebrations at Chonai (September 6th).[22] Security in the area was supplied by one of the largest and most strategically placed fortresses in the Maeander-Lycus valley. Chonai, or at least its upper reaches on the slope of Honaz-dağ, was *the* military garrison for the Thrakesion theme.[23] It protectively surveyed both east-west lines from Apameia to Ephesos and north-south lines from Synnada to Telmessos or Attaleia.[24] Of course this also made Chonai a prize spoil for contesting powers.[25]

---

19 M. Angold, *The Byzantine Empire, 1025–1204: a political history* (London/New York: Longman, 2nd Ed., 1997), 43. For a detailed overview of the importance of Chonai as a pilgrim site, see B. Kötting, *Peregrinatio religiosa: Wallfahrten in der Antike und das Pilgerwesen in der alten Kirche* (Munster: Antiquariat Th. Stenderhoff, 1980), 166–71.

20 Michael Choniates, *Encomium on Metropolitan Nicetas of Chonai* 44, (S. P. Lampros, Μιχαὴλ Ἀκομινάτου τοῦ Χωνιατοῦ τὰ σωζόμενα (2 vol.; Groningen: Bouma, 1968 [1879–80]), 1.38).

21 Anon., *Story of the Miracle of St Michael of Chonai*, §§ 9–10 (edition: M. Bonnet, *Narratio de Miraculo a Michaele Archangelo Chonis Patrato* (Paris: Librairie Hachette, 1890)), Sisinnius, *The Miracle of St Michael of Chonai*, § 11 (edition: J. Stiltingo/C. Suyskeno/J. Periero/J. Cleo (ed.), *Acta Sanctorum: September* (Paris/Rome: Victor Palmé, 1869 [1762]), 8.41C–47C)). The expression the "tents of the barbarians" had long become a Byzantine literary topos.

22 Michael Choniates, *Encom* 95 (Lampros, 1.56.12–18). For the importance of the fairs for celebrations of saints' lives, see S. Vryonis, "The Panegyris of the Byzantine Saint", in S. Hackel (ed.), *The Byzantine Saint* (London: Fellowship of St Alban and St Sergius, 1981), 196–226.

23 C. Foss, *Ephesus after Antiquity* (Cambridge: Cambridge University Press, 1979), 195–96, K. Belke/N. Mersich, *Phrygien und Pisidien* (Vienna: Österreichischen Akademie der Wissenschaft, 1990), 223. The Thrakesion theme was one of the fourteen administrative provinces of Byzantine control and, in the thirteenth century, housed 10,000 troops: see E. W. Brooks, "Arabic Lists of the Byzantine Themes", *JHS* 21 (1901), 67–77 on pp. 73–76.

24 See J. F. Haldon, *Warfare, State and Society in the Byzantine World 565–1204* (London: Routledge, 2003), 56.

25 P. Magdalino, *The Empire of Manuel I Komnenos, 1143–1180* (Cambridge: Cambridge University Press, 2002), 131.

The settling of Seljuk authority through south-western Anatolia and ultimately the formal establishment of Ottoman imperial bureaucratic control did
not spell the end of Christian presence in the area. After the final cementing
of Seljuk control in the fourteenth century, Chonai benefited from the familiarity wrought by trade connections and the subsequent determination of Sultan Mehmet II to preserve the Orthodox Patriarchate under Gennadius in 1454.
This ensured a measure of toleration for those Greeks and Armenians who were
content to forego some economic advantage in order to maintain their religious
commitment. Reports of "Greeks" present at Honaz dot European travel accounts from the seventeenth century on.[26] By "Greeks" was understood "Orthodox Christians", even though the Greek language had disappeared.[27]

However, the transfer of control of taxation through the two hundred years of
the passing from the Byzantine to the Ottoman eras had drastic consequences
for church authority. This was especially the case in those areas that continued a viable agricultural and value-added production in support of its local
population and beyond – such as we find at Chonai/Honaz.[28] Knowledge of
the actual areas that were previously strung together in a web of episcopal, archiepiscopal and metropolitical administration in the Eastern church now became extremely thin in the confused dispersion and administrative re-organi-
sation that followed.[29] The haphazard decisions of the fourteenth century that
asserted supposedly temporary, church oversight saw ecclesial control pass from
Colossae to Laodicea to Cotyaeum.[30] These decisions were as ineffective as they
were expedient, frequently designed "for reasons of sustenance" to support an *ex
loco* official.[31]

---

26 The reports of Greeks at Honaz vary from thirty families in 1669 ("The journals of the
Rev Dr John Luke chaplain to the Levant Co", BL Harl. 7021 f. 354a) to two hundred in 1832 in
J. A. Cramer, *A Geographical and Historical Description of Asia Minor* (2 vol.; Oxford: Oxford
University Press, 1832), 2.45.

27 There are some instances of Greek letters being retained as the form in which Turkish was written. The language of such texts (whether literary publications or inscriptions) are
called *karamanlidika*; see R. Clogg, "Some Karamanlidika Inscriptions from the Monastery
of the Zoodokhos Pigi, Balikli, Istanbul", *BMGS* 4 (1978): 55–67. Two inscriptions from Honaz
in karamanlidika are recorded, dating to 1853 and 1892; see G. Lampakis, Οἱ ἑπτὰ ἀστέρες τῆς
Ἀποκαλύψες (Athens: 1909) Κολοσαί.

28 See L. T. Erder/S. Faroqhi, "The Development of the Anatolian Urban Network during
the Sixteenth Century", *JESHO* 23 (1980) 265–303, on p. 273. On the mutation of the Greek
"Chonai" to the Arabic "Honaz", see Cadwallader, "The Reverend Dr. John Luke", 331.

29 See S. Vryonis, *The Decline of Medieval Hellenism in Asia Minor and the Process of
Islamization from the Eleventh through the Fifteenth Century* (Berkeley: University of California Press, 1971), 289.

30 See F. Miklosich/J. Müller, *Acta et diplomata graeca medii aevi sacra et profana* (6 vol.;
Vindobonae: C. Gerold, 1860–90), I.539, II.88, 210.

31 Vryonis, *Decline*, 297. Some Metropolitans did not gain a favourable European eye because of a reputed constant interest in money: see J. T. Bent (ed.), *Early Voyages and Travels in*

Some time during the fifteenth century, these once famous seats disappeared from episcopacy lists of the eastern church.[32] Later, Paul Rycaut, one seventeeth century English Ambassador at the Porte, reported that the Patriarch at Constantinople, nominally constituted some of the bishops under him in the district of Fener by "the ancient titles of Ephesus and Laodicea &c".[33] Similarly, sixty years later in 1739, Richard Pococke in one diary entry on his travels in Asia Minor reported that the Archbishop of Ephesos had once had 32 bishops under him, but by the time of Pococke's visit had none: "all the Province is his Diocese" he wrote.[34] Whether that "Province" included Colossae/Chonai is not stated.

Priests were very occasionally appointed to specific locations such as Colossae/Chonai, though the few who were available often pursued a wandering brief in order to maintain contact with Christians across the Ottoman empire.[35] An *epitropos* (steward) filled in necessary services of prayers and caretaking when no priest was present.[36] But the fact that priests do not seem to have been appointed by any set bishop demonstrates how piecemeal the contact and oversight had become[37] and how inconsequential the actual site of Chonai/Honaz was to Church authorities in the aftermath of its grand days. Of the ten churches that existed in Chonai at the time of the collapse of Byzantine control of the city, only two continued into the period of the renewal of European contact in the seventeenth century – the churches of the All-holy Virgin and of St. Constantine (the Great).[38] One western cleric visiting the area, the Reverend Dr Thomas Smith,

---

the Levant: 2. Extracts from the Diaries of Dr John Covell 1670–1679 (New York: Burt Franklin for the Hakluyt Society, 1893), 149.

32 J. Darrouzès, *Notitiae episcopatuum Ecclesiae Constantinopolitanae: Texte Critique, Introduction et Notes* (Paris: Institut Français d'Études Byzantines, 1981), 90.

33 P. Rycaut, *Account of the Greek and Armenian Churches* (London: 1679), 84.

34 Pococke to his mother, Letter XXXV, Dec 15th–26th 1739 BL Add 22998 f. 84b.

35 D. Goffman, *Izmir and the Levantine World* (Seattle/London: University of Washington Press, 1990), 150–52. See also John Fuller, *A Narrative of a Tour through Some Parts of the Turkish Empire* (London: Richard Taylor, 1829), 62.

36 For one unflattering account of the work (for financial remuneration) of an *epitropos*, see Dominic E. Colnaghi, "Travels in Levant 1852–59", *BL* Add 59502 f. 162.

37 Of the few notices from these centuries, Philadelphia and Cyprus both seem at one time or another to have supplied priests to serve at Honaz: see for Cyprus: A. Picenini, "Travel Diary, Asia Minor" (1705), *BL* Add 6269 f.48a, copied by Richard Chandler (with acknowledgement): *Travels in Asia Minor and Greece or An Account of a Tour made at the Expense of the Society of Dilettanti* (London: J. Booker, 1775), 113 – so also over a hundred years later: J. Hartley, *Researches in Greece and the Levant* (London: Seeley, 1833), 264; for Philadelphia: "The journals of the Rev Dr John Luke", *BL* Harl Ms. 7021 f. 354. Smyrna should probably be added to the group. It is likely that these were *ad hoc* arrangements though one should not rule out the legacy of long-standing contests between autocephalous churches: see M. Angold, "Byzantine 'Nationalism' and the Nicaean Empire", *BMGS* 1 (1975) 49–70 on pp. 59–61.

38 Cadwallader, "The Reverend Dr. John Luke", 331.

offered a jaundiced opinion of Colossae (1678) and denied its turkophone Greek population either church or priest.[39]

We know that at least one church or religious shrine was converted to a mosque as Christian identity gradually dissipated. The tradition that Sultan Murat II chose the chapel of St Archippos as site for a mosque (c. 1440) at least betrays the recognition that the St Michael miracle story and sacred healing spring exercised a powerful hold on the popular imagination, powerful enough for the Ottoman authorities to exert their authority over it architecturally and symbolically.[40] The Saint was associated with a legend in which the Archangel Michael responded to Archippos' plea that the ancient city be delivered from destruction by pagan hoards. The miraculous rescue underscored the power of the archangel, and his healing spring became a major site of devotion in the pilgrimage to Chonai. The conversion of *some* Christian site by Murat II no doubt appropriated a further Christian tradition and legend into long-term Muslim appreciation, as was our experience in 2005 when a local labourer showed us a spring that delivered healing from injury or disease after a threefold dipping.

Christian efforts to offset their loss of Colossae

For a time, alternatives to the loss of Colossae's mundane significance for Byzantine and Catholic Christianity were sought. The poetic genius of Manuel Philes (1280–1330) captured a false etymology that linked the name Colossae/Colossians with the Colossus of Rhodes.[41] The passage of time allowed Philes to de-

---

39 T. Smith, *Remarks upon the Manners, Religion and Government of the Turks. Together with a Survey of the Seven Churches of Asia as they now lye in their Ruines: and a Brief Description of Constantinople* (London: Moses Pitt, 1678), 249. This is repeated in/from Jerome Salter's earlier (?) travel journal: "A Brief Relation of the Travels of Jerom Salter" in the Bodleian Library, Eng. Msc. E. 218 f. 67. Salter was a "factor" (merchant) connected with Levant Company at Smyrna and made a number of expeditions along the coast and through the Maeander and Lycus Valleys during his years in Turkey.

40 There is considerable debate over which site actually holds the remains of the Murat Mosque. The claim for the building high up the slopes of Honazdağ inside the boundary walls of the medieval fortress may have merit: see M. Agir, *Honaz: doğa harikası* (İzmir: Nesa, 1994), 42–44. It certainly has the architectural characteristics of a Byzantine church and it is surrounded by mid-late Ottoman epitaphs. Richard Chandler had noted the church midway through the eighteenth century (*Travels*, 240). It was nominated as the Church of St Michael by one early tourist guidebook: Maj-Gen. Sir C. Wilson (ed.), *Handbooks for Travellers: Asia Minor* (London: John Murray, 1895), 105. A church of St Panteleimon has greater weight: Cadwallader, "The Reverend Dr John Luke", 325–26, but no claim at this stage is sure.

41 There has been an interesting revival of this etymology in recent times with the connection of place names beginning with "col-" with the notion of something which has been set up (as in a shrine or sacred place): see J-P. Vernant, *Myth and thought among the Greeks* (London: Routledge, 1983), 305 and the literature there cited. However, the dispute over the spell-

scribe this short-lived maritime edifice of the pre-Common Era in mythic pro-portions.[42] Philes wrote during the reign of the Byzantine Emperor Michael Paleologos. He sought to tie the awesome impact of the Colossus with the all-conquering apostle Paul. In a little epigram for "his [ie Paul's] Epistle to the Co-lassians" [sic], Philes sought to fuel a confidence in God's providence and pro-tection against the increasingly virulent threats of Turkish incursion. In typical Byzantine convolution, Philes stylistically wound together multiple traditions and punning allusions:

> The golden Paul conquered the bronze Colossos
> Having been taken from earth to the third heaven
> And he shatters the monstrous by the sling-shot of his words
> Setting the foundation stone in their midst.[43]

Long before the collapse of Constantinople in 1453, poetic license had collapsed into literalism, and the letter to the Colossians had metamorphosed into the let-ter to the Rhodians. The location of Colossae shifted across the Carpathian Sea, almost 200 kilometres to the south-west.[44] It helped considerably that Rhodes for a time remained more accessible to western travellers and inhabitants. The *Suda* or, more correctly, the huge dictionary by the eleventh century Byzan-tine lexicographer known as Suidas, stated quite baldly, "The Colossians are the Rhodians."[45] Sir John Mandeville (1300–1399), in his often-inventive *Travels*, claimed of "Collos" (=Rhodes) that "so call it the Turks yet."[46] This likely fabrica-tion was as much due to the increased assertion of western Christian presence on the island of Rhodes, as it was the legacy of Byzantine creativity.

---

ing of the ancient name of the city (Colassae as an alternative to Colossae) brought an earlier etymology, associated with κολάζω (punish): see W. Fleming, *A Gazetteer of the Old and New Testaments to which is added* … (Edinburgh: Edinburgh Printing and Publishing Co, 1838), 365. Vernant at least has the advantage of positing a pre-Hellenic form, though account must now be made of Hittite forebears: see Jacques Freu/Michel Mazoyer, *Les Hitties et leur histoire* (Kubaba: L'Harmattan, 2007), 81.

42 See Pliny *Nat.* 34.41; compare *Greek Anthology* 6.171. The Colossus of 33 metres height was finished in 290 BCE and destroyed by an earthquake some sixty years later. Pliny wrote, "Few people can make their arms meet round the thumb".

43 Epigram 44 (translation by Alan Cadwallader). For the text see E. Miller (ed.), *Manuelis Philae carmina ex codicibus Escurialensis, Florentinis, Parisinis et Vaticanis* (2 vol.; Paris: Im-perial Printers, 1855–1857), 1.23. Philes also wrote an extended epigram in honour of the mir-acle at Chona (2.236).

44 George Monachus *Short Chronicle* (*PG* 110.340B). Inscription (nick-)naming a citizen Colossos have created occasional confusion. Some have associated the bearer with the Phry-gian city: see L. Robert, *Noms indigènes dans l'Asie-Mineure gréco-romaine* (Amsterdam: Hakkert, 1963), 300–01.

45 Suidas sv. κολοσσαεύς. Other renowned Byzantine lexicographers or litterateurs such as Zonaras, Glycas and Eustathius propounded the same.

46 M.C. Seymour, *Mandeville's Travels* (Oxford: Oxford University Press, 1968 [1375]), 19.

Mandeville further alluded to the association of Colossae with Rhodes in his notice that the island was held (in his time) by the "Hospitallers". The dispute between Eastern and Western Christianity that had compounded the struggles of the Byzantines to hold their empire, was reflected in the unequal sharing of power on Rhodes. The "Knights of St John of Jerusalem, Hospitallers" established their own church, reputedly on the site of the base of the Colossus. They claimed the name "St John Colossensis" as patron.[47] Similarly, a Latin archdiocese of Rhodes was established in 1328, with the archbishop taking the same epithet – Colossensis – as a clear demarcation from the "Rhodiensis" of his Greek equivalent.

Accordingly many western authorities including the pilgrim notary Niccolò de Martoni and the priest-geographer Cristoforo Buondelmonti reinforced the conviction that the Rhodians were Paul's Colossians and, thereby, were the intended recipients of the prized letter.[48] Colossae itself, and even the Pauline letter were co-opted by ecclesiastics to assert a divine authorisation and position. Its geographical importance was inconsequential. It was not the first time that either the Colossus or Colossae had become divorced from geographical and temporal reality and re-married to "patterns of cultural perception and ways of thinking"[49] fashioned in the competition waged between groups, cities and/or state. In 1522, Suleyman the Great (or the Law-giver as he is wont to be named in Turkish histories) stifled such rivalries. He crushed Rhodian resistance to Ottoman imperial authority with a single withering siege. The intellectual parallel occurred in Europe. The Renaissance recovery of the classical heritage destroyed any support for the counterfeit claim that identified the island with the land-locked ancient city. Erasmus, Melanchthon and Davenant all resorted to the ancient texts (Xenophon, Strabo, Pliny and so on, ably corroborated by Eusebius and Ororios) to re-establish the position of Colossae as at least *not* on the island of Rhodes.[50] The ancient texts were collated to yield a relative

---

47 Otto Meinardus argues that the Templars, who came to Rhodes in 1309, were responsible for the name Colossi, having come to Rhodes from a province by that name in Cyprus: O. F. A. Meinardus "Colossus, Colossae, Colossi: Confusio Colossaea", *BA* 36 (1973) 33–36, on p. 35. "Coloso" is shown on Cyprus in Ortelius' map of Natolia (map § 174) and his map of Cyprus itself (map § 148, 1573 Dutch edition). The suggestion is not necessarily exclusive – the main point, that of ecclesiastical competition, remains.

48 J. P. A. van der Vin, *Travellers to Greece and Constantinople: Ancient Monuments and Old Traditions in Medieval Travellers' Tales* (Istanbul: Nederlands Historisch-Archaeologisch Instituut, 1980), 134.

49 L. I. Conrad, "The Arabs and the Colossus", *JRAS* 6 (1996) 165–87, on p. 181 *et passim*.

50 See T. J. Wengert, *Human Freedom, Christian Righteousness: Philip Melanchthon's exegetical dispute with Erasmus of Rotterdam* (Oxford/New York: Oxford University Press, 1998), 42, J. Allport, *An Exposition of the Epistle of St Paul to the Colossians by the Right Rev John Davenant, D.D* [1572–1641] (London: Hamilton, Adams & Co/Birmingham: Beilby, Knott and Beilby, 1831), lxxi.

but determinedly geographical place – Colossae was on the mainland, some-where in Phrygia, near Laodicea and Hierapolis. The Dutch geographer, Abra-ham Ortelius, went slightly further in an effort to explain the confusion. He introduced a nuanced compromise by arguing that *colossenses* belonged exclu-sively to the people of Colossae whereas *colassenses* attached to the inhabitants of Rhodes.[51]

Overall, it did mean that Colossae's wandering days were numbered, even though cartographers, into the eighteenth century, could not reach specific agreement about where to moor the Phrygian city or how to spell it. On some maps, "Colossos" was shifted from Rhodes back to Phrygia.[52] Resistance to the reassertion of an Anatolian homeland for Colossae continued for a time.[53] For example, the Roman Catholic church retained titular honorifics with bishops and archbishops still named *colossensis*, even if they were more often seated in Malta and Rome than at Rhodes. Nevertheless, St Paul's letter was being redi-rected towards a more secure address.

Geographers were now combining with classicists for a new appreciation and reclamation of the site. Ortelius is a good example of one who provided detailed texts to his maps frequently citing classical writers. Geography was for him the "eye of history".[54] Both disciplines were informed by and helped to foster a drive to discover anew this (and other) ancient sites and their more recent relatives. But the exploration of the interior of Asia Minor, unlike the coastline, could not be easily negotiated without Ottoman concession. Trade, ushered through two main ports, Smyrna and Constantinople (like Aleppo further east), provided the impulse. It would take time, centuries in fact, before geographers, explorers, classicists and traders gathered enough combined momentum and knowledge to broker a recovery of Colossae. Even in the mid-nineteenth century, one erstwhile English adventurer publicly acknowledged that many places had lost their his-tory and that he had often walked over a site only later to learn it had been one of the key ancient churches.[55] For a time, this was certainly true of Colossae. But

---

51 *Theatrum Orbis Terrarum*, text to map § 216 ("Insular Aliquot Aegaei Maris Antiqua Descrip.") (van den Broecke/Ort numbering system). The English edition, published after Ortelius' death in 1598, added Colossae was "now Chone, as Porphyrogennetas shows" (M. van den Brocke/D. van den Broecke-Günzburger "Cartographica Neerlandica" website: www.orteliusmaps.com, accessed December 2009). The debate over a vowel has revived in modern biblical analysis.

52 See, for example "Carte de la Grece Anciene et Moderne", in P. Claude Buffier, *Geogra-phie Universelle* (Paris: Giffart, 1759).

53 Petr Pokorný traces the Colossae-Rhodes connection as late as 1696 in the work of the geographer Vicenzo Coronelli: *Colossians: A Commentary* trans. S. S. Schatzmann (Massa-chusetts: Hendrickson, 1991), 19 n84.

54 From the title page of Ortelius, *Parergon*.

55 J. B. Simpson, "No Man's Land", in *The Glasgow Herald* 24th May, 1858.

then as one interruption to European appreciation of the historical significance of the site was slowly overcome, another conspired to take its place although for very different reasons. Even if the local inhabitants of Honaz continued to farm and trade during the later middle ages and renaissance in Europe, Colossae was still some way from confidently occupying space and time in western perceptions. To this we turn.

The reconnection of Europeans with
the ancient sites of Turkey

The burgeoning of general geographic interest in the area was frequently focussed on "Asia Minor". The sheer preference for the name "Asia Minor" over Turkey amongst geographers and historians, whilst not exclusive, betrayed a certain attitude to the Ottoman empire and its dominant Turkish demographic. Colossae, like many other cities on the peninsula land-mass, was recovered and disputes settled from classical sources rather than Arabic or Turkish ones. Xenophon, in particular, was mined repeatedly for the evidence that would identify the roadways, landmarks and great cities of the country. His "March of the Ten Thousand" went through constant, heavily annotated editions, chronological computations and cartographical representations, especially in publications in France and England,[56] the two European powers concerned to establish their position over against one another and with the Ottomans. Editions of Herodotos were not far behind. Derivatively, there were annotated publications of the places such authors mentioned, with a distinct bias towards the record of places mentioned in the Bible.

Initially, the combination of Renaissance rediscovery of classical writers and Ottoman restrictions (military and mercantile) on European movement through

---

56 See, for example, R. Amaseo, *Xenophontis de Cyri Minoris expeditione liber primus-septimus* (Bologna: J.B. Phaellus, 1534), J.J. Scaliger, *De Emendatione Temporum* (Frankfurt: Wechel, 1583), J. Bingham, *The Historie of Xenophon* (London: John Haviland, 1623), D. Petau, *The history of the world, or an Account of time compiled by the learned Dionisius Petavius and continued by others to the year of Our Lord 1659, together with a geographicall description of Europe, Asia, Africa and America* (London: J. Streater, 1659) (an English expansion of Petau's *Rationarium temporum in partes duas*, 1633), P. d'Ablancourt, *La Retraite des Dix Milles de Xenophon, ou l'Expédition de Cyrus contre Artaxerxes* (Paris: Camusat, 1648), J. Marsham, *Canon Chronicus: Aegyptiacus, Ebraicus, Graecus* (Leipzig: M. Birckner, 1676 [1672]), J.B.B. d'Anville, *Carte pour l'expédition de Cyrus le jeune et la retrait des dix-mille Grecs* (Paris: la Veuve Estienne, 1740), E. Spelman, *The Expedition of Cyrus into Persia; and the Retreat of the Ten Thousand Greeks* (2 vol.; Cambridge: Cambridge University Press, 1776), P-H. Larcher, *L'Expédtion de Cyrus dans l'Asie Supérieure et la Retraite des Dix Mille* (Paris: Debure, 1778), T. Hutchinson, *Xenophontis de Expeditione Cyri Minoris Commentarii e Recensione et cum notis selectis* (Oxford: Clarendon, 1787 [1742]).

Turkey encouraged the textual approach. However, even when travel reports filtered into anecdotal and published circulation, the classics remained the dominant means by which Colossae (and other ancient cities) were approached. This method is evident in nineteenth century exploration and tourism. European negotiation of the land of the Turk was classical and, where significant, Christian. It was as if the land would only yield its secrets to the west through western sources. European identity was firmly located in this arena of classics, and in a reflexive assumption, so too the land. And just as such sources were firmly held by European hands, the implied attitude was that the land would also be returned in some way to those same hands (whether by politics, cultural influence or trade).

At first, geographers and travellers were primarily concerned about matching ancient persons, places and times with different classical writers. Surety here was a mark of European exactitude, based mainly upon texts and characterised as having "hit upon the best method of reconciling the contradictory accounts" of the writers.[57]

Slowly such texts began to be supplemented by the reports of travellers, with the intent of improving and extending the knowledge culled from the classics.[58] Those more systematic in their preparation for travels digested the texts of ancient writers on Asia Minor. The Frankish (that is, European) libraries in Smyrna and on the island of Rhodes were stocked with classical writers, regarded as texts not only conducive to moral superiority but critical for the negotiation of the inland.[59]

Moreover, ambassadors and factors especially at Smyrna[60] developed *ad hoc* catalogues of places, routes, contacts and inscriptions which visitors were able to access (and add to) in connection with an expedition.[61] They arranged soirées

---

57 M. Freret, "Letter to the Author concerning the Chronology of his Work", in C.(A.) Ramsay, *The Travels of Cyrus* (Dublin: William Smith & Son, 9th Ed. 1763), 301.

58 W. M. Leake, *Journal of a Tour in Asia Minor with comparative remarks on the ancient and modern geography of that country* (London: John Murray, 1824), viii; J. MacD. Kinneir, *Journey through Asia Minor, Armenia and Koordistan in the years 1813 and 1814 with Remarks on the Marches of Alexander and Retreat of the Ten Thousand* (London: John Murray, 1818), *passim*.

59 The Reverend Edward T. Daniell, when he joined the Spratt-Forbes expedition as an "amateur epigrapher" at Smyrna, appears to have used the anchorage as an opportunity to prepare for the adventure, even though he did take some books with him: Spratt/Forbes, 1.viii, 2.9, 23.

60 At the beginning of the nineteenth century England, France, Russia, Holland, Austria and Spain were represented at Smyrna. England had 16–18 major businesses based at the port: J. O. Hanson, "Recollections of Smyrna", *BL* Add Ms 38591 ff. 50, 51.

61 See the many examples given in D. Whitehead, "From Smyrna to Stewartstown: A Numismatist's Epigraphic Notebook", *Proceedings of the Royal Irish Academy* (1999) 73–113; Colnaghi, "Travels", *BL* Add 59502 f. 145.

where travellers from different countries might gather and exchange observations[62] or share copies of inscriptions.[63] Sometimes, journals and catalogues were lent, not always gaining the expected honourable return![64] Houses in the European quarter were adorned with artefacts that had been taken from other sites,[65] from whence they passed to Europe: "Perhaps no place has contributed more than Smyrna to enrich the collections and cabinets of the curious in Europe."[66] Smyrna from the seventeenth into the nineteenth centuries was the prime point of departure into Turkey for trade and exploration: "the headquarters of the traveller".[67] The gaze, in this sense, was firmly set from the stand-point of the west and any phenomena were assessed accordingly *(Fig. 4)*.

Inevitably the tension between ancient and modern accounts was felt. The hold on the European imagination of Greek and Roman texts and their authors' indomitable self-belief meant that the sanctity of the ancient texts would not easily be sacrificed to modern challenges. This is well illustrated by such travellers as Richard Pococke who were still refining their means of recording routes and relevant annotations.[68] Robert Walpole in 1802 seems to have rued too much reliance on Pococke's Asia Minor journeys. He alleged, "he has been extremely negligent in noting bearings and distances; his narrative is very obscure and confused."[69]

---

62 At Rhodes, for example, Daniell was introduced to the naturalist Heinrich Loew and epigrapher Augustus Schönborn from Prussia. They covered similar territory and were able to hold a "delightful interview and conversation on the antiquities of Lycia" (Spratt/Forbes, 2.8). John Oliver Hanson reported that "Public Evenings" were held twice a week: "Recollections", *BL* Add Ms 38591 ff. 51, 52.

63 P. de Tournefort, *Relation d'un Voyage du Levant* (2 vol.; Paris: L'imprimerie Royale, 1717), 1.501.

64 It appears that Paul Rycaut's *Account of the Greek and Armenian Churches* (London: 1679), was indebted in part to a section of the journal kept by his chaplain, the Reverend Dr John Luke, a record he failed to return: see S. P. Anderson, *An English Consul in Turkey: Paul Rycaut at Smyrna 1667–1678* (Oxford: Clarendon Press, 1989), 218.

65 E. Chishull, *Travels in Turkey and Back to England* (London: W. Bowyer, 1747), vii, A. Schönborn, "Communication from Professor Schönborn of Posen relative to an important Monument recently discovered by him in Lycia", *Museum of Classical Antiquities* 1 (1851) 43.

66 Chandler, *Travels*, 72.

67 "Mahmouz Effendi", "Random Recollections of Smyrna", *The Era* 13th January, 1839. Smyrna became the recommended starting-point for the tourist: T. H. Usborne, *A New Guide to the Levant for the use of travellers in Greece, Egypt, Palestine, Syria and Asia Minor … also comprising the overland journey to India, the voyage from Suez to Bombay and the systems of dawk travelling in the three presidencies* (London: Craddock & Co, 1840), 311n.

68 See R. Pococke, *Description of the East and Some Other Countries* (2 vol.; London: W. Bowyer, 1745).

69 R. Walpole, *Memoirs Relating to European and Asiatic Turkey: edited from Manuscript Journals* (2 vol.; London: Longman, Hurst, Rees, Orme and Brown, 1817), 2.191.

Fig. 4 Sketch of Smyrna looking towards the bay[70]

Conciliation between old and new was the default position. This conviction grew through constant contact with the remnants of the civilisations that Europeans prized.[71] But this was frustrating as well. Walpole observed, "We know therefore little of the interior of the country, of its natural productions of the various remains of antiquity, of the situation of towns celebrated in Sacred and Profane history."[72] He was only too ready to blame local Turkish authorities for this gap in knowledge.

The triumph that came with the recovery of evidence for the location of an ancient site was palpable. The Reverend Edward T. Daniell, the epigrapher for Lieutenant T. A. B. Spratt and the naturalist Edward Forbes on their Lycian expeditions of 1841–42, could barely contain his excitement in a letter to England, "We can add to any map hitherto published the names of *eighteen* ancient cities,

---

70 Sketch of Smyrna by J. D. Harding reproduced in T. H. Horne, *Finden's Landscape Illustrations of the Bible, consisting of Views of the most remarkable places mentioned in the Old and New Testaments …* (London: John Murray, 1835), part xv.

71 See, for example, C. Texier, *Description de l'Asie Mineure* (3 vol.; Paris: L'Institut de France, 1839), 1.iii.

72 Walpole, *Memoirs*, 2.ix.

the sites of which we have unquestionably ascertained by inscriptions."[73] How-ever, the physical identification of an ancient site naturally led to the questioning of the authority of the ancients. The militarist turned archaeologist and antiqui-ties collector, William Leake, was among a number who criticised cartographi-cal forebears who "relied too much on the accuracy of their [Greek and Roman] texts."[74] Eventually, updated maps replaced their theologically and classically constrained progenitors. The maps of the Englishman Arrowsmith,[75] the Ger-man Kiepert and the detailed longitudinal computations of the Russian Wron-czenko[76] testify to this maturity in cartography. The transition however was slow to reach universal acceptance. Besides, these more geographically accu-rate maps emerged from a recognition of the importance of the classics and a conviction that Europe represented the 'fulfilment' of Greco-Roman aspira-tions. Such a conviction undergirded the ethos of the Society of Dilettanti. The Society financed Richard Chandler's explorations of Asia Minor (1740) so that the refined taste of Greek and Roman architecture (along with a few samples) might be transported back to England for replication.[77]

Smyrna's many benefits to European ambitions fulfilled another purpose. The long-term European inhabitants and the even longer reiteration of Euro-pean attitudes helped shape and direct the way in which the space and its in-habitants would be construed, what would be valued. The small Frank popula-tion in Smyrna[78] exercised a powerful socialising force on its visitors, its writers and through them, on general European attitudes. The constant references to coins, inscriptions, statuary, discoveries and monumental sketches were inter-woven with comments on Turkish administration and culture and on the condi-tion and character of the Greek population under Ottoman rule. Diaries, letters and publications clearly indicate the sorts of things that were actually seen and, more significantly, how perceptions were cultivated.[79]

---

73 Letter published in *The Athenaeum* July 23rd 1842, page 675 (italics original).

74 W. M. Leake, *On Some Disputed Questions of Ancient Geography* (London: John Murray, 1857), vii.

75 Arrowsmith's map was heavily dependent upon the map sketched by Colonel William Leake who had explored much of Turkey in 1800: Walpole, *Memoirs*, 2.ix.

76 H. Kiepert, *Karte von Kleinasien* (Berlin: Simon Schropp, 1843–45), which went through a number of corrected and updated editions; M. Wronczenko, *Travaux dans l'Asie Mineure, 1834–35* included in T. F. de Schubert (ed.), *Exposé des Travaux Astronomiques et Géodésiques executes en Russie 1855* (St Petersburg: Academy of Sciences, 1855).

77 Chandler, *Travels*, preface.

78 In 1825, the Reverend John Hartley estimated the European population in Smyrna was less than 1000 out of a total population of about 75,000 (45,000 Turks, 10,000 Greeks, 8,000 Armenians and 8000 Jews): *Researches,* 247.

79 The letters and journals of Richard Pococke provide frequent insights into the gather-ings of Europeans in consular or factor homes: see, for example, "Travels", *BL* Add 22998 ff.81, 82 (Letter dated Nov 5th – 16th, 1739).

This systemic influence at Smyrna on western inhabitants and visitors helps to explain two generalised, negative attitudes that dominate European analyses of Asia Minor from the sixteenth century. There were the pathetic, indisciplined collapse of the Greeks in the Ottoman empire and the corrupt deceit and culpable inefficiency of the "Musselman" Turk. Greeks were further judged as neglecting the treasures of their classical and Christian past. They needed Western imperial paternalism to "rescue" their country and heritage.

These criticisms of Greeks and Turks were highly prevalent in England. Several examples illustrate this.

- When Ortelius' Atlas was translated into English in 1606, a telling addition (here italicised) was made to the text describing "Natoliae" (Anatolia, Map 174): "If any one wants to know about the *miserable* state and condition of these countries …". This was not a novel descriptor intended to launch a revised attitude to the eastern 'other'. Rather it was an accommodation by Ortelius' successors-and-publishers to their English market.

- Elizabeth I's charter to allow the incorporation of "The Company of Merchants of the Levant" encouraged trade with a people (the Turks) considered to be different and inferior. Thomas Dallam, the organ builder aboard the ship delivering a present of a massive organ from the Queen of England to the Ottoman Sultan, wrote in his journal, "Heare yow maye se the base and covetus condition of these Rude and barbarus doged Turkes, and how litle they do Regard Christians."[80]

- The text accompanying John Speed's famous and much replicated map of "The Turkish Empire" with its adorning marginalia held, "The Turk is admired for nothing more than his sudden advancement to so great an Empire."[81]

- In the following century a similar criticism was directed to the Turks' approach to agriculture. In a book dedicated to the Anglican Archbishop of Canterbury, Patrick Gordon wrote, "much of the Inland Provinces lie uncultivated, a Thing too common in most countries subject to the Mahometan Yoke."[82]

- A final example illustrates how this English judgment about the Turks was also found in France. In 1835, the French poet and politician, Alphonse de Lamartine, exposed his delight at the slow, "providential" disintegration of the Ottoman empire. He exclaimed to his readers, "The stupid administration, or

---

80 Bent, *Early Voyages*, 39.

81 J. Speed, *A Prospect of the Most Famous Parts of the World* (London: George Humble, 1626/1627), sv.

82 P. Gordon (and R. Morden), *Geography Anatomiz'd or The Geographical Grammar: being a short and exact analysis of the whole body of modern geography* (London: printed by JR for Robert Mordern and Thomas Cockerill, 2nd Ed., 1702), 279; see also pages 184–96.

rather the destructive inertness, of the conquering race of Osman, has made a desert on all sides."[83]

These entrenched English and French attitudes began to change slowly. Boundary-breakers like Lord Byron in the early nineteenth century[84] and the actual experience of devoted travellers helped this movement. Edward Forbes reflected on this change of attitude towards the people that occurred in his fellow-traveller in Turkey, Edward Daniell,

Mr Daniell, like most European travellers, had commenced his journey prejudiced against the Mahometan part of the population: he concluded it with the strongest prepossessions in their favour. The disinterested attentions, frankness and courtesy we had met with from all ranks – from pacha to peasant; the good-faith and honesty of the Lycian Turks ... All that Sir Charles Fellows has said in favour of the Turks of Asia Minor[85] we can fully bear out.[86]

Even so, the Greeks did not emerge similarly exonerated. The phrase, "the clever knavery and selfishness of the Greek part of the population", belongs to the omission in the preceding quotation. It was a minor refrain for which the English blamed "enslavement" to the Turk, and became the justification for European intervention to remove Greece from Ottoman rule in 1832.[87]

European responses to the denuded höyük of Colossae *(Fig. 5)*

The above cursory overview of the transition from negligible European presence in the Turkish peninsula to a burgeoning amalgam of commerce, exploration and politics is the formative backdrop to the history of Colossae and Chonai. European presence in Constantinople and Smyrna had lead to tentative incursions into the artefact-saturated interior during the more benign seasons of

---

83 A. de Lamartine, *Travels in the East, including a Journey in the Holy Land* (2 vol.; Edinburgh: William and Robert Chambers, 1850 [from *Voyage en Orient*, 1835]), 2.305. Almost identical sentiments are expressed in W. McLeod, *The Geography of Palestine or the Holy Land including Phoenicia and Philistia, with a Description of the Towns and Places in Asia Minor visited by the Apostles...* (London: Longman, Brown, Green and Longmans, 1847), 89. The charge had become a monotonous stereotype.

84 M. Sharafuddin, *Islam and Romantic Orientalism: Literary Encounters with the Orient* (London/New York: I. B. Tauris, 1994).

85 A reference to C. Fellows, *A Journal Written During an Excursion in Asia Minor* (London: John Murray, 1838), v.

86 Spratt/Forbes, 2.5–6.

87 See, for example, H. Christmas, *The Shores and Islands of the Mediterranean, including a visit to the Seven Churches for Asia* (3 vol.; London: R. Bentley, 1851), 2.249, 287.

Fig. 5 View of the Colossae höyük and necropolis behind (below farmhouse)

Fig. 6 The caricature of a Levant Company chaplain from
the magazine "Vanity Fair" 5th September, 1874.

spring or autumn. Frequently, the second-best resource for such expeditions was the chaplaincy attached to ambassadors or discrete entities, most notably the Levant Company. (The best resource, as most were to discover but few were to acknowledge, was the local population.) The chaplains' classical and ecclesiastical training combined with the prejudices shaped by European self-belief directed their endeavours *(Fig. 6)*. The Seven Churches tour quickly established itself as a favourite pastime, besides the requisite collecting of coins, inscriptions and portable artefacts.[88]

The first European publication that speaks of the search for Colossae on the ground rather than in text was that of the Reverend Doctor Thomas ("Tograi") Smith. He acknowledged that previous travellers had laid out the schema before him, though he was one of few who brought knowledge of Turkish and Arabic as well:[89]

Gentlemen who live in Smyrna, out of a pious zeal and a justly commendable curiosity, some few years since were the first who made a voyage thither [to the "Seven Churches"] to see the remainders of that magnificence, for which those Cities were so renowned in the Histories of ancient times.[90]

His rendition of Colossae set the tone if not the expansion of knowledge for the next two centuries.

Colosse, by the Turks called Chonos, is situated very high upon a hill, the plains under it very pleasant; but we were no sooner entered into it, but we thought it fit to leave it; the inhabitants being a vile sort of people so that we doubted of our safety among them. There still remain some poor Christians notwithstanding those horrid abuses they are forced to endure: but without any Church or Priest: poor miserable Greeks, who amidst that ignorance and oppression they labour under still, though they have forgotten their own language and speak only Turkish.

Here we see, in miniature, the six key elements governing the re-engagement with Colossae after Ottoman restrictions were relaxed:
– the reference to past classical times
– the collation of Colossae with "the Seven Churches of Asia Minor" and the three Lycus Valley cities

---

88 In a letter to his mother, Richard Pococke is concerned that artefacts that he has sent 'home' be protected from the thieving eyes of others: Pococke, "Travels", *BL* Add 22998 f. 87b (Letter dated Feb 28th – Mar 16th 1739–40 [*sic*]). He mentions 'medals' in a letter of Apr 12th – 23rd 1740 (f. 88b).

89 Ewa Siemieniec-Golas, "Turkish Words in Smith's Epistolae Quatuor (1674)", *Studia Turcologica Cracoviensia* 1 (1995) 125–49 notes that Smith provides a crucial record of the transition between the language of Old Ottoman and New Ottoman.

90 Smith, *Seven churches of Asia*, 206. Smith published his first edition in Latin.

- the confusion over the relationship between Colossae and Chonai
- the desire for material evidence of a bygone magnificence, both viewable and collectible
- the difficulties that Europeans found in negotiating their way around Colossae and Chonai and the infrequency of visits.
- the uncritical perception of Turk and Greek.

We shall touch on each of these points briefly.

The classical texts established a connection between Colossae, the river Lycus and the neighbouring cities of Laodicea and Hierapolis. Because the volume of classical testimonia for these cities was considerably more than for Colossae, comparative generalisations based on Laodicea and Hierapolis were applied to Colossae. Whilst a measure of regional cultural similarity can be admitted,[91] identity cannot be assumed and gaps in knowledge supplied (inductively and deductively) must be treated with requisite circumspection. Frequently however, such methodological reserve was absent.

The most blatant example of this tendency comes with a little help from Eusebius: that of the devastating earthquake that hit Laodicea in 61 CE. Eusebius surmised that each member of the Lycus Valley trio was similarly hit.[92] But here an odd break with the regional generalisation occurred: the early modern era was quick to conclude that the evidence that testified to Laodicea's rebuilding[93] was *not* transferable to Colossae. This was doubtless fostered by contemporary travellers' accounts that marvelled at the quality of the ruins preserved at Laodicea, with "three theatres of white Marble, and a stately Circus, all so entire as yet, that they would seem to be only of a modern Date".[94] By contrast, dismay greeted the perceived barrenness of Colossae or negative reactions festered at the inhospitable welcome or dangers experienced at Honaz. Edwin Davis even managed to incorporate into his disappointment at the site, the stock disdain for agricultural productivity in complete ignorance of the fertility of the region,

---

91 Following L. Robert "Inscriptions", in J. des Gagniers *et al* (ed.), *Laodicée du Lycos: le Nymphée, Campagnes 1961–1963* (Quebec: L'Université Laval, 1969) 247–389, on p. 328.

92 Eusebius *Chronicon* § 210. The triune collation in earthquake devastation has become an axiom of modern scholarship in different disciplines, even if the date remains unsettled: see Bo Reicke, "The Historical Setting of Colossians", *RevExp* 70 (1973) 429–38, on pp. 430, 432, L. Piccardi, "The AD 60 Denizli Basin earthquake and the apparition of Archangel Michael at Colossae (Aegean Turkey)", in L. Piccardi/W.B. Masse (ed.), *Myth and Geology* (London: Geological Society, 2007) 95–115, on pp. 95, 97, J. Murphy-O'Connor, "Colossians", in J. Barton/J. Muddiman (ed.), *The Oxford Bible Commentary* (Oxford: Oxford University Press, 2001) 1191–98, on p. 1191.

93 Tacitus *Ann.* 14.27. Tacitus makes no mention of Colossae in regard to the earthquake or the rebuilding.

94 Gordon, *Geography Anatomiz'd*, 280.

Nothing appears to be left of the town ... We saw no remains of a city wall, no theatre and apparently no public buildings of any importance ... In this poor upland valley, with a barren soil and far out of the route of traffic, Colossae could never have been a place of much importance.[95]

Colossae may have begun to be located again but any sense of its strategic and creative significance in space and time was overcome by the absence of any positive visible evidence. For some archaeologists, travellers and geographers, a direct anachronistic line was tracked between the skeletal detail of an earthquake and the region about Honaz. The development of Chonai became the compensation for the decline of Colossae.

Initially, in the first two centuries of European efforts to recover sites meaningful to their classical and Christian cultural heritage, Honaz and Colossae were still equated because of the testimonia of Constantine Porphyrogennitus, Nicetas Choniates and the ecclesiastical gazette of Michael Le Quien.[96] Pitton de Tournefort clearly considered the fortress on Honazdağ (still massive and in use in the eighteenth century) as the ancient site, labelling it "Chonac or Couleisar" *(Fig. 7)*.[97]

When Francis Arundell's sketch of Honaz appeared in 1834, the town had descended from the mountain heights but it was similarly labelled, albeit after the fashion of Nicetas Choniates: "Chonas, ... anciently Colossae".[98] Arundell's sketches[99] became the templates for two generations,[100] even when Chonai (Honaz) and Colossae began to be thought of as separate entities *(Fig. 8)*.

---

95 E. J. Davis, *Anatolica; or The Journal of a Visit to some of the Ancient Ruined Cities of Caria, Phrygia, Lycia and Pisidia* (London: Grant, 1874), 116; similarly, L. de Laborde, *Voyage de l'Asie Mineure* (2 vol.; Paris: Firmin Didot, 1861 [1838]), 102.

96 *Oriens Christianus in quatuor Patriarchatus digestus; quo exhibentur Ecclesiae, Patriarchae, caeterique Praesules totius Orientis ... Opus posthumum* (3 vol.; Paris: Ex Typographia Regia, 1740), 1.813–16.

97 De Tournefort, *Voyage du Levant*, sketch facing 1.320.

98 F. V. J. Arundell, *Discoveries in Asia Minor* (2 vol.; London: R.Bentley, 1834), sketch facing 2.164.

99 The second sketch of Chonai (featuring the Greek church at Honaz?) was not included in Arundell's publications but surfaced in *Finden's Landscape Illustrations*, part 23 (1835).

100 The first sketch is repeated in J. Kitto, *The Pictorial Bible being the Old and New Testaments* (Oxford: Oxford University Press, 1856), 493 and W. Smith (ed.), *A Concise Dictionary of the Bible* (London: Little, Brown and Co, 1865), 169. The left centre section of the second sketch found its way into J. R. Beard, *The People's Dictionary of the Bible* (London: Simpkin, Marshall, 3rd Ed., 1850), 1.383. All these went through multiple editions; all these tied Colossae and "Chonas" together at either the town of Honaz or the fortress above it. The equation (albeit by way of the succession of one over the other) remained in W. S. W. Vaux, *Greek Cities and Islands of Asia Minor* (London: SPCK, 1877), 142 and J. Eadie (ed.), *A Biblical Cyclopedia* (London: Charles Griffin, 20th Ed., 1878 [1848]), sv. Colossae.

Fig. 7 Pitton de Tournefort's designation of Colossae/Chonai
located at the mountain fortress.

The question was whether Honaz and Colossae were to be equated or separated
and whether the contemporary Honaz was the means to pinpoint the ancient and
Byzantine site. Some maps, such as that of Richard Pococke, clearly separated
them, albeit, in Pococke's case, with "Konous" to the east-nor'east of Colossae.[101]
The problem stemmed from a reliance on the testimony of Herodotos, for whom
the prime identification was the river Lycus. When Richard Chandler felt sufficiently under local threat in 1740 to forestall any search for Colossae, he endeav-
oured to "supply the deficiency, by giving as clear an account as I can, of the ancient geography of that region".[102] This "clear account" was nothing more than a
repetition of Herodotos' fantastic tale of the Lycus river disappearing down a
chasm, there to emerge five stadia (slightly less than a kilometer) later.[103]

In 1829, John Williams was confident "that in the subterranean current and
re-appearance of the Lycus, we have a certain guide for the discovery of the
site of Colossae" even if an earthquake may have damaged the landmark.[104]

---

101 Pococke, *Description*, 2.33, plate 43. This must qualify Chandler's criticism that Pococke
did not distinguish the two places (*Travels*, 240–41).

102 Chandler, *Travels*, 243, 272.

103 Herodotos *Hist.* 7.30.

104 J. Williams, *Two essays on the geography of ancient Asia: intended partly to illustrate the
campaigns of Alexander, and the Anabasis of Xenophon* (London: John Murray, 1829), 85.

CHONAS,—anciently COLOSSE.

KHONOS, THE ANCIENT COLOSSAE.

Fig. 8 Francis Arundell's sketches of Honaz

It was not that such geological curiosities were unknown in Turkey.[105] It was simply that the endeavour to cement the site of Colossae (and the reliability of Herodotos) by finding such a phenomenon was an abject failure. The höyük (artificial mound) that is so much the focus of modern tourism was insufficient to pinpoint the place.[106] The necropolis, in the absence of an ethnonym locking in the name of the city, was little more than evidence of *some* ancient site *(Fig. 9)*.[107] Because of the testimony of the ancients, the Lycus River remained the prime determinant of Colossae in European minds even into the second half of the nineteenth century.

William Hamilton became the one credited with the separation of Colossae from Chonai with the former's location at the mound three kilometres to the north of Honaz.[108] But the need to authenticate Herodotos remained.[109] Hamilton defied geological reality by claiming that a travertine encrustation had formed a platform over the river of the dimensions mentioned by the "father of history". Again, an earthquake was provided as the required explanation for the demise of the geophysical curiosity and the salvaging of Herodotos' reputation.

---

105 Spratt and Forbes report just such a credited occurrence amongst villagers in the vicinity of lake "Avelan Gule" (289).

106 The mound was dismissed by the British soldier-explorers, Capt. C. Irby/Capt. J. Mangles, *Travels in Egypt and Nubia, Syria and Asia Minor during the years 1817 and 1818* (London: T. White, 1823), 522. They surmised that the many such mounds dotting the valleys of Turkey were ancient fortresses (p. 508).

107 "… even now it [the city] lacks the confirmation of any inscription found *in situ* and giving the name." See J. B. Lightfoot, *Saint Paul's Epistles to the Colossians and Philemon* (London: Macmillan, 9th Ed, 1890 [1875]), 13–14. A premature effort was made in C. Boeckh's monumental *Corpus Inscriptionum Graecarum* to supply this lack by building an over-ambitious reconstruction (§ 3956) on a fragmentary inscription recorded by Francis Arundell: see A. Cadwallader, "A New Inscription [=Two New Inscriptions], A Correction and a Confirmed Sighting from Colossae", *EA* 40 (2007) 109–18, on pp. 114–15.

108 W. J. Hamilton, "Extracts from Notes made on a Journey in Asia Minor in 1836", *JRGS* 7 (1837) 34–61, on p. 56; *Researches in Asia Minor. Pontus and Armenia* (2 vol.; London: J. Murray, 1842), 1.508. Hamilton was repeatedly lauded as the discoverer of Colossae (quite against the evidence): see W. F. Ainsworth, *Travels in the Track of the Ten Thousand Greeks; being a Geographical and Descriptive Account of the Expedition of Cyrus and of the Retreat of the Ten Thousand Greeks as related by Xenophon* (London: John W. Parker, 1844), 17. G. Long, "Colossae", in W. Smith, *Dictionary of Greek and Roman Geography* (2 vol.; London: Walton and Maberly, 1854), 1.648, Davis, *Anatolica*, 117, J. M'Clintock/J. Strong, *Cyclopedia of Biblical, Theological and Ecclesiastical Literature* (New York: Harper, 1868), 2.420, A. H. Smith/W. M. Ramsay, "Notes on a Tour in Asia Minor", *JHS* 8 (1887) 222–67, on p. 225. Infra-European competition in discoveries in "the East" showed itself in the French desire to support "their" discoverer of Colossae, Leon de Laborde: see E. Renan, *Histoire des origines du Christianisme* (6 vol.; Paris: Michel Lévy Frères, 1863–79), 3.357. Compare this with de Saint-Marie, *Histoire des découvertes géographiques*, 3.512.

109 This was recognised by William Mitchell Ramsay when he finally distanced himself from Hamilton's explanation: "only the supposed necessity of explaining Herodotos…". See his "Antiquities of Southern Phrygia and the Border Lands I", *AJA* 3 (1887) 344–68, on p. 358.

Fig. 9   A sketch of a tomb stone by Edwin Davis, 1874.[110]

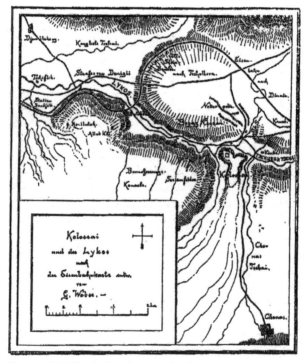

Fig. 10   G. Weber's sketch-map of Colossae in its immediate
surrounds of waterways, villages roads and railway.[111]

---

110 Davis, *Anatolica*, sketch facing page 115.
111 Weber, "Lauf des Lykos", 195.

Not until the incisive analysis of G. Weber was the European need to preserve the integrity of its abrogated heritage finally relinquished – at least in this small instance. Weber also attempted to give an accurate cartographical section of Colossae in relation to "Chonas" and the rivers dissecting the site *(Fig. 10)*.[112]

Two photographs of the "Ruines de Colosses" and "Chonas" by Henri Carmignac published towards the end of the nineteenth century finally eliminated the concordant visualisation of the places that had been the legacy of Arundell *(Fig. 11)*.[113]

With Ramsay's insistence on the separation of Colossae from Chonai,[114] the latter replacing the former in geography and population, Colossae's location had been secured finally. European satisfaction however came at the cost of separating it in time and space from Chonai.

A considerable period of time spanned the European "discovery" of Colossae. There are four main reasons for this.

- In part, the infrequency of European visitors to this part of the Lycus Valley contributed to the imprecision governing the identification and location of the site. Repetition of previous accounts rather than new insights frequently filled the publications. "Want of time and the obstacles thrown in our way, prevented that accurate investigation of the country which would have been requisite," pleaded John Hartley,[115] a missionary cleric combining antiquarian fascination with zeal for "a population … reposing in death".[116]
- European arrogance and local Turkish politics stalled a number of European attempts to explore the region.[117] The Frankish expectation that papers signed by the *cadi* or *pasha* (governor) in Smyrna[118] would hold authority throughout the Maeander and Lycus valleys often led to disappointment when their bearers failed to receive the proper dignity and respect from authorities in the areas.
- Rivalries between towns and their respective dignitaries were particularly in evidence in the eighteenth century. Denizli and Honaz maintained a suspicious distance from each other, a tension that came to a head with the revolt of Soley Bey Ogle in the 1730s. The fortress on Honaz-dağ overlooking Honaz

---

112 G. Weber's meticulous analysis: "Der unterirdische Lauf des Lykos bei Kolossai", *Ath. Mitt.* 16 (1891) 194–99.

113 E. le Camus, "Colosses", in F. Vigouroux (ed.), *Dictionnaire de la Bible* (Paris: Letouzey et Ané, 1899), 2.862, 864.

114 W. M. Ramsay, *The Historical Geography of Asia Minor* (London: John Murray, 1890), 134–35.

115 Reported from Hartley's magazine journal contribution by Thomas Milner, *History of the Seven Churches of Asia: their Rise, Progress and Decline with notices of the Churches of Tralles, Magnesia, Colosse, Hierapolis, Lyons and Vienne; designed to show the fulfilment of Scripture Prophecy* (London: Holdsworth and Ball, 1832), 358 n399.

116 Hartley, *Researches*, 11.

117 See, for example, Chandler, *Travels*, 243, Arundell, *A Visit to the Seven Churches of Asia Minor with an excursion into Pisidia* (London: John Rodwell, 1828), 96.

118 See Usborne, *A New Guide*, 311n.

326. — Ruines de Colosses. D'après une photographie de M. Henri Cambournac.

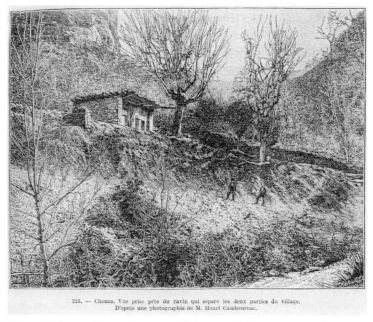

325. — Chonas. Vue prise près du ravin qui sépare les deux parties du village.
D'après une photographie de M. Henri Cambournac.

Fig. 11 Lithograph reproductions of photographs by Henri Cambournac.
Above, the distant Honaz-dağ looms above the Colossae mound;
below shows the ravine at Honaz.[119]

---

119 So far we have been unable to locate or ascertain the exact date of the original photographs or plates on which these reproductions were based.

township and commanding a sweeping view of Colossae and the Lycus valley maintained 4000 of the rebel aga's troops. He was reported to have installed eleven cannons in its still manifestly secure walls before 40,000 troops were sent from the Grand Signor to strangle the insurgency.[120]

- The dangers of the mysterious east were made a dominant motif in European texts[121] and media reports. The recommendation to undeterred European visitors was to stay at a more tranquil Denizli[122] (in spite of the memory of a devastating earthquake in 1713).[123] The result was that day trips by horseback to Honaz and attempts to explore (for) Colossae were reduced to a few hours at best, given that the outward ride from Denizli took around 4 hours. This established the pattern almost through to the present. William Calder's epigraphical forage in 1933 that lead to a doubling of published inscriptions from Colossae[124] included only one half day's visit to the site itself.[125] It was a far greater haul than the equally brief and ultimately fruitless visit by Harold Mare in 1975.[126] The same brief *ad hoc* engagement has governed the encounter with pottery from James Mellaart's cursory sweep in 1953[127] to a small gathering of a few samples of pottery and glass fragments in 1963.[128] And Clive Foss' concern that the medieval fortresses of Asia Minor be thoroughly mapped has similarly left Colossae/Chonai with little more than a note.[129]

---

120 Pococke, *Description*, 69, Chandler, *Travels*, 239.

121 See C. Wilkinson, *A Tour through Asia Minor and the Greek Islands, with an Account of their Inhabitants ... and curiosities for the Instruction and Amusement of Youth* (London: Darton and Harvey, 1806), preface; Leake, *Tour in Asia Minor*, iv–v.

122 P. Lucas, *Voyage du Sieur Paul Lucas, fait en 1714 ... dans la Turquie, l'Asie, Sourie, Palestine, Haute e Basse-Égypte, ...* (3 vol.; Rouen: R. Machuel, 1719), 1.232; Hartley, *Researches*, 261.

123 Arundell's party did reach an accommodation, physical and diplomatic, with the Honaz population: *Description*, 163–69.

124 W.H. Buckler/W.M. Calder, *Monumenta Asiae Minoris Antiqua VI: Monuments and Documents from Phrygia and Caria* (Manchester: Manchester University Press, 1939).

125 See A.H. Cadwallader, "Revisiting Calder on Colossae", *AS* 56 (2006) 103–11, on p. 104.

126 W.H. Mare, "Archeological Prospects at Colossae", *Publication of the Near East Archeological Society* 7 (1976) 39–59.

127 J. Mellaart, "Preliminary Report on a Survey of Pre-Classical Remains in Southern Turkey", *AS* 4 (1954) 175–240, on pp. 192, 230–31.

128 The small 'harvest' of 24 pieces of pottery and one piece of glass was deposited (by "J.M.B.") in the pottery room of the British Institute at Ankara. No documentation accompanies the finds. The collection was probably part of the project conducting piecemeal surveys of a number of sites in the Burdur-Antalya-Denizli area with funding provided by the University of Sydney. See T. Özgüç et al, "Recent Archaeological Research in Turkey", *AS* 14 (1964) 21–37.

129 See C. Foss, "The Survey of Medieval Castles of Anatolia, 1982–1984", in R. Matthews (ed.), *Ancient Anatolia* (London: BIAA, 1998), 359–66, on p. 363, "Chonai", in A.P. Kazhdan (ed.), *The Oxford Dictionary of Byzantium* (New York/Oxford: Oxford University Press, 1991), 427 and generally C. Foss, *Byzantine fortifications: an introduction* (Pretoria: University of South Africa, 1986), H. Barnes/M. Whittow, "The Survey of Medieval Castles of Anatolia (1992–96)", in Matthews (ed.), *Ancient Anatolia*, 347–58.

In summary, Colossae has suffered from a lack of concerted attention. The reasons are not hard to find.

Those who visited Colossae were struck by the lack of visible evidence of a monumental past. After the grandeur of Ephesus, Laodicea or any other of the sites of the seven churches of Asia that had become the requisite and dutiful goal of European travel, Colossae was quite simply a disappointment. Only a cavea remained of the theatre, and even that was not always recognised. The pottery sherds that littered the site attracted no more than ancillary observation, the stones that remained were singularly uninteresting, the inscriptions so few, buildings completely absent, the gravestones so odd – little, it seemed, survived to invite either touristic or scientific interest. Even the clamour for ancient coins to fill European cabinets became muted because of a dearth of supply.[130] Almost as quickly as Colossae had been recovered for western dissection it was dropped. The "practically nothing to see" of Macmillan's 1908 tour guidebook to Asia Minor sounded the death knell.[131]

As one nineteenth century writer put it, in prophetic as well as historic terms, "it might have been forgotten, but for its place in the early history of the Christian church".[132] Indeed, Colossae's early Church connections have dominated European calibration of the site, impacting upon the interpretation of its history and significance. Colossae's Christian connection has overshadowed any appreciation of its Hittite, Persian and Hellenistic past,[133] caused its supposed demise in the first century and offered little attention to its later Roman and regional life. The Byzantine period has been occasionally visited but with little analysis of the significance of a second crucial textual witness: the story of the miracle of St Michael the Archangel.[134]

Biblical interpreters linked Colossae to Laodicea through their study of the New Testament letter to the Colossians (2:1, 4:13,15–16). They considered that what threatened Laodicea in the Book of Revelation also applied to Colossae. The removal of candlesticks in Rev 2:5 – the evocative apocalyptic threat to the survival of the seven churches, was extended to include Colossae because of its biblical association with Laodicea, the more devastating because not even its ruins

---

130 Davis, *Anatolica*, 121.

131 Macmillan & Co., *Guide to Greece, the Archipelago, Constantinople, the Coasts of Asia Minor, Crete and Cyprus* (London: Macmillan, 1908), 195.

132 H. I. Smith, *The Course of Ancient Geography* (New York: D. Appleton, 1861), 239.

133 But see F. Cornélius, *Geschichte der Hethiter* (Darmstadt: Wissenschaftliche Buchgesellschaft, 1973), N. Sekunda, "Achaemenid Settlement in Caria, Lycia and Greater Phrygia", in H. Sancisi-Weerdenburg and A. Kuhrt (ed.), *Achaemenid History VI: Asia Minor and Egypt: Old Cultures in a New Empire* (Leiden: Nederlands Instituut voor het Nabije Oosten, 1991) 175–96, on p. 208, Freu/Mazoyer, *Les Hitties*, 81.

134 The notable exception is Glenn Peers, *Subtle Bodies, Representing Angels in Byzantium* (Berkeley: University of California Press, 2001). See also D. Duran, "The Cult of the Archangel Michael in Byzantine Asia Minor", MA thesis, Koç University, June 2007.

remained.[135] Just as classics had become history, so also had theology – with Colossae itself the victim and the earthquake taken as the instrument of judgment. The three hundred year European search for Colossae had effectively resulted in another interruption; the enquiry had become a blockage, as effective as the early Ottoman shutdown to the Franks of the south-western interior of Turkey. The presuppositions that sponsored the efforts to situate Colossae in space and time had ultimately denied their achievement.

The repeated twentieth century observation that Colossae awaited excavation and required immediate attention[136] sounds hollow. As we have shown, despite the lack of obvious attention to the site, Colossae has held great significance across a long period (see the Chronology included in this collection). From Hittite attestation to Byzantine approbation, Colossae has held a unique position in south-west Turkey.[137] Indeed neither of these period designations ought to be seen as the parameters of the significance of the site. Colossae cannot be reduced to a figurative construct posturing as a backdrop for a Pauline letter, however important that text has been to European determination to "capture" the city.

Our intention through this collection of essays is to help in the task of restoring Colossae to time and space, to recognise something of the chronological span and regional influence that the city held and to gather together a critical appraisal of the existing evidence as a provision for future investigation.

Bibliography

d'Ablancourt, P., *La Retraite des Dix Milles de Xenophon, ou l'Expédition de Cyrus contre Artaxerxes* (Paris: Camusat, 1648).

Agir, M., *Honaz: doğa harikası* (İzmir: Nesa, 1994).

Ainsworth, W.F. "A Memoir Illustrative of the Geography of the Anabasis of Xenophon", *The Classical Museum* 1 (1844) 170–85, 299–317.

- *Travels in the Track of the Ten Thousand Greeks; being a Geographical and Descriptive Account of the Expedition of Cyrus and of the Retreat of the Ten Thousand Greeks as related by Xenophon* (London: John W. Parker, 1844).

---

135 Lightfoot, *St Paul's Epistles*, 41, 70.

136 See Buckler and Calder, xi, N.T. Wright, *Judas and the Gospel of Jesus* (Grand Rapids, Mich.: Baker, 2006), 1, B. Witherington, *The letters to Philemon, the Colossians and the Ephesians: a socio-rhetorical commentary on the captivity Epistles* (Grand Rapids, Mich.: Eerdmans, 2007), 19, M.R. Cosby, *Apostle on the Edge: an Inductive Approach to Paul* (Louisville, KY: Westminster John Knox Press, 2009), 238.

137 See P. Briant, *Antigone le Borgne: Les débuts de sa Carrière et les problèmes de l'assembleè macedonienne* (Paris: Les Belles Lettres, 1973), 78, P. Debord, "Les routes royales en Asie Mineure Occidentale", in P. Briant (ed.), *Dans les pas des Dix-Mille: Peuples et pays du Proche Orient vus par un Grec* (Pallas 43) (Toulouse: Presses Universitaires du Mirail, 1995) 89–97, on pp. 93–94.

Allport, J., *An Exposition of the Epistle of St Paul to the Colossians by the Right Rev John Davenant, D.D* [1572–1641] (London: Hamilton, Adams & Co/Birmingham: Beilby, Knott and Beilby, 1831).

Amaseo, R., *Xenophontis de Cyri Minoris expeditione liber primus-septimus* (Bologna: J. B. Phaellus, 1534).

Anderson, S. P., *An English Consul in Turkey: Paul Rycaut at Smyrna 1667–1678* (Oxford: Clarendon Press, 1989).

Angold, M., "Byzantine 'Nationalism' and the Nicaean Empire", *BMGS* 1 (1975) 49–70.

d'Anville, J. B. B., *Carte pour l'expédition de Cyrus le jeune et la retrait des dix-mille Grecs* (Paris: la Veuve Estienne, 1740).

Arundell, F. V. J., *A Visit to the Seven Churches of Asia Minor with an excursion into Pisidia* (London: John Rodwell, 1828).

– *Discoveries in Asia Minor* (2 vol.; London: R. Bentley, 1834).

Barnes, H./M. Whittow, "The Survey of Medieval Castles of Anatolia (1992–96)", in R. Matthews (ed.), *Ancient Anatolia* (London: BIAA, 1998) 347–58.

Beard, J. R., *The People's Dictionary of the Bible* (London: Simpkin, Marshall, 3rd Ed., 1850).

Belke, K./N. Mersich, *Tabula Imperii Byzantini Bd 7: Phrygien und Pisidien* (Vienna: Österreichischen Akademie der Wissenschaft, 1990).

Bent, J. T. (ed.), *Early Voyages and Travels in the Levant: 2. Extracts from the Diaries of Dr John Covell 1670–1679* (New York: Burt Franklin for the Hakluyt Society, 1893).

Bingham, J., *The Historie of Xenophon* (London: John Haviland, 1623).

Bonfrere, J., *Onomasticon Urbium et Locorum Sacrae Scripturae* (Amsterdam: R. & G. Wetstein, 1711).

Bonnet, M., *Narratio de Miraculo a Michaele Archangelo Chonis Patrato* (Paris: Librairie Hachette, 1890).

Briant, P., *Antigone le Borgne: Les débuts de sa Carrière et les problèmes de l'assembleè macedonienne* (Paris: Les Belles Lettres, 1973).

Brooks, E. W., "Arabic Lists of the Byzantine Themes", *JHS* 21 (1901) 67–77.

de Bruin, C., "Tabula Geographica" in his *A Voyage to the Levant: or Travels in the Principal Parts of Asia Minor, the Islands of Scio, Rhodes, Cyprus &c* translated by "W. J." (London: J. Tomson and T. Bennet, 1702).

Buckler, W. H./W. M. Calder, *Monumenta Asiae Minoris Antiqua VI: Monuments and Documents from Phrygia and Caria* (Manchester: Manchester University Press, 1939).

Buffier, P. C., *Geographie Universelle* (Paris: Giffart, 1759).

Cadwallader, A. H., "Revisiting Calder on Colossae", *AS* 56 (2006) 103–11.

– "A New Inscription [=Two New Inscriptions], A Correction and a Confirmed Sighting from Colossae", *EA* 40 (2007) 109–118.

– "The Reverend Dr. John Luke and the Churches of Chonai", *GRBS* 48 (2008) 319–38.

Calder, W. M./G. E. Bean, *A Classical Map of Asia Minor* (London: BIAA, 1958).

Chandler, R., *Travels in Asia Minor and Greece or An Account of a Tour made at the Expense of the Society of Dilettanti* (London: J. Booker, 1775).

Chishull, E., *Travels in Turkey and Back to England* (London: W. Bowyer, 1747).

Christmas, H., *The Shores and Islands of the Mediterranean, including a visit to the Seven Churches for Asia* (3 vol.; London: R. Bentley, 1851).

Clogg, R., "Some Karamanlidika Inscriptions from the Monastery of the Zoodokhos Pigi, Balikli, Istanbul", *BMGS* 4 (1978) 55–67.

Conrad, L. I., "The Arabs and the Colossus", *JRAS* 6 (1996) 165–87.

Cornélius, F., *Geschichte der Hethiter* (Darmstadt: Wissenschaftliche Buchgeselschaft, 1973).

Cosby, M. R., *Apostle on the Edge: an Inductive Approach to Paul* (Louisville, KY: Westminster John Knox Press, 2009).

Cramer, J. A., *A Geographical and Historical Description of Asia Minor* (2 vol.; Oxford: Oxford University Press, 1832).

Darrouzès, J., *Notitiae episcopatuum Ecclesiae Constantinopolitanae: Texte Critique, Introduction et Notes* (Paris: Institut Français d'Études Byzantines, 1981).

Davis, E. J., *Anatolica; or The Journal of a Visit to some of the Ancient Ruined Cities of Caria, Phrygia, Lycia and Pisidia* (London: Grant, 1874).

Debord, P., "Les routes royales en Asie Mineure Occidentale", in P. Briant (ed.), *Dans les pas des Dix-Mille: Peuples et pays du Proche Orient vus par un Grec* (Pallas 43; Toulouse: Presses Universitaires du Mirail, 1995) 89–97.

van Dieten, J-L. (ed.), *Nicetae Choniatae Historia* (Berlin: Walter de Gruyter, 1975).

Duran, D., "The Cult of the Archangel Michael in Byzantine Asia Minor", MA thesis, Koç University, June 2007.

Eadie, J. (ed.), *A Biblical Cyclopedia* (London: Charles Griffin, 20th Ed., 1878 [1848]).

Erder, L. T./S. Faroqhi, "The Development of the Anatolian Urban Network during the Sixteenth Century", *JESHO* 23 (1980) 265–303.

Fellows, C., *A Journal Written During an Excursion in Asia Minor* (London: John Murray, 1838).

Fleming, W., *A Gazetteer of the Old and New Testaments to which is added …* (Edinburgh: Edinburgh Printing and Publishing Co, 1838).

Foss, C., *Ephesus after Antiquity* (Cambridge: Cambridge University Press, 1979).

– *Byzantine fortifications: an introduction* (Pretoria: University of South Africa, 1986).

– "The Survey of Medieval Castles of Anatolia, 1982–1984", in R. Matthews (ed.), *Ancient Anatolia* (London: BIAA, 1998) 359–66.

Freu, J./Michel Mazoyer, *Les Hitties et leur histoire* (Kubaba: L'Harmattan, 2007).

Fuller, J., *A Narrative of a Tour through Some Parts of the Turkish Empire* (London: Richard Taylor, 1829).

des Gagniers, J. et al (ed.), *Laodicée du Lycos: le Nymphée, Campagnes 1961–1963* (Quebec: L'Université Laval, 1969).

Goffart, W. A., *Historical Atlases: the first three hundred years, 1570–1870* (London: University of Chicago Press, 2003).

Goffman, D., *Izmir and the Levantine World* (Seattle/London: University of Washington Press, 1990).

Gordon, P. (and R. Morden), *Geography Anatomiz'd or The Geographical Grammar: being a short and exact analysis of the whole body of modern geography* (London: printed by JR for Robert Mordern and Thomas Cockerill, 2nd Ed., 1702).

Greenhalgh, M., "Spolia in Fortifications: Turkey, Syria and North Africa", in *Ideologie e pratiche del reimpiego nell'alto medioevo* (Spoleto: Centro Italiano di Studi sull'Alto Medioevo, 1999) 785–935.

Haldon, J. F., *Warfare, State and Society in the Byzantine World 565–1204* (London: Routledge, 2003).

Hamilton, W. J., "Extracts from Notes made on a Journey in Asia Minor in 1836", *JRGS* 7 (1837) 34–61.

– *Researches in Asia Minor. Pontus and Armenia* (2 vol.; London: J. Murray, 1842).

Hartley, J., *Researches in Greece and the Levant* (London: Seeley, 1833).

Horne, T.H., *Finden's Landscape Illustrations of the Bible, consisting of Views of the most remarkable places mentioned in the Old and New Testaments* ... (London: John Murray, 1835).

Hutchinson, T., *Xenophontis de Expeditione Cyri Minoris Commentarii e Recensione et cum notis selectis* (Oxford: Clarendon, 1787 [1742]).

Irby, Capt. C./Capt. J. Mangles, *Travels in Egypt and Nubia, Syria and Asia Minor during the years 1817 and 1818* (London: T. White, 1823).

Kazhdan, A.P. (ed.), *The Oxford Dictionary of Byzantium* (New York/Oxford: Oxford University Press, 1991).

Kiepert, H. *Karte von Kleinasien* (Berlin: Simon Schropp, 1843–45).

Kinneir, J. MacD., *Journey through Asia Minor, Armenia and Koordistan in the years 1813 and 1814 with Remarks on the Marches of Alexander and Retreat of the Ten Thousand* (London: John Murray, 1818).

Kitto, J., *The Pictorial Bible being the Old and New Testaments* (Oxford: Oxford University Press, 1856).

de Laborde, L., *Voyage de l'Asie Mineure* (Paris: Firmin Didot, 2 vols, 1861 [1838]).

de Lamartine, A., *Travels in the East, including a Journey in the Holy Land* (Edinburgh: William and Robert Chambers, 1850).

Lampakis, G., Οἱ ἑπτὰ ἀστέρες τῆς Ἀποκαλύψεως (Athens: 1909).

Lampros, S.P., Μιχαὴλ Ἀκομινάτου τοῦ Χωνιατοῦ τὰ σῳζόμενα (2 vol.; Groningen: Bouma, 1968 [1879–80]).

Larcher, P-H., *L'Expédtion de Cyrus dans l'Asie Supérieure et la Retraite des Dix Mille* (Paris: Debure, 1778).

Le Quien, M., *Oriens Christianus in quatuor Patriarchatus digestus; quo exhibentur Ecclesiae, Patriarchae, caeterique Praesules totius Orientis* ... *Opus posthumum* (3 vol.; Paris: Ex Typographia Regia, 1740).

Leake, W.M., *Journal of a Tour in Asia Minor with comparative remarks on the ancient and modern geography of that country* (London: John Murray, 1824).

– *On Some Disputed Questions of Ancient Geography* (London: John Murray, 1857).

Lightfoot, J.B., *Saint Paul's Epistles to the Colossians and Philemon* (London: Macmillan, 9th Ed, 1890 [1875]).

Lucas, P., *Voyage du Sieur Paul Lucas, fait en 1714 ... dans la Turquie, l'Asie, Sourie, Palestine, Haute e Basse-Égypte, ...* (3 vol.; Rouen: R. Machuel, 1719).

Macmillan & Co., *Guide to Greece, the Archipelago, Constantinople, the Coasts of Asia Minor, Crete and Cyprus* (London: Macmillan, 1908).

Magdalino, P., *The Empire of Manuel I Komnenos, 1143–1180* (Cambridge: Cambridge University Press, 2002).

Mare, W.H., "Archeological Prospects at Colossae", *Publication of the Near East Archeological Society* 7 (1976) 39–59.

Marsham, J., *Canon Chronicus: Aegyptiacus, Ebraicus, Graecus* (Leipzig: M. Birckner, 1676 [1672]).

McLeod, W., *The Geography of Palestine or the Holy Land including Phoenicia and Philistia, with a Description of the Towns and Places in Asia Minor visited by the Apostles...* (London: Longman, Brown, Green and Longmans, 1847).

M'Clintock, J./J. Strong, *Cyclopedia of Biblical, Theological and Ecclesiastical Literature* (New York: Harper, 1868).

Meinardus. O. F. A., "Colossus, Colossae, Colossi: Confusio Colossaea", *BA* 36 (1973) 33–36.

Mellaart, J., "Preliminary Report on a Survey of Pre-Classical Remains in Southern Turkey", *AS* 4 (1954) 175–240.

Mercator, G., *Atlas sive Cosmographicae Meditationes de Fabrica Mundi et Fabricati Figura* (Duisburg: Albert Buys, 1595).

Miklosich, F./J. Müller, *Acta et diplomata graeca medii aevi sacra et profana* (Vindobonae: C. Gerold, 6 vols, 1860–90).

Miller, E. (ed.), *Manuelis Philae carmina ex codicibus Escurialensis, Florentinis, Parisinis et Vaticanis* (2 vol.; Paris: Imperial Printers, 1855–1857).

Milner, T., *History of the Seven Churches of Asia: their Rise, Progress and Decline with notices of the Churches of Tralles, Magnesia, Colosse, Hierapolis, Lyons and Vienne; designed to show the fulfilment of Scripture Prophecy* (London: Holdsworth and Ball, 1832).

Murphy-O'Connor, J., "Colossians" in J. Barton/J. Muddiman (ed.), *The Oxford Bible Commentary* (Oxford: Oxford University Press, 2001) 1191–98.

Ortelius, A., *Theatrum Orbis Terrarum* (Antwerp: 1570).

– *Parergon sive Veteris Geographiae Aliquot Tabulae* (Antwerp: Christopher Plantin, 1584).

Özdogan, M., "Ideology and Archaeology in Turkey", in L. Meskell (ed.), *Archaeology Under Fire: Nationalism, Politics and Heritage in the Eastern Mediterranean and Middle East* (London/New York: Routledge, 1988) 111–23.

Özgüç, T., *et al*, "Recent Archaeological Research in Turkey", *AS* 14 (1964) 21–37.

Peers, G., *Subtle Bodies, Representing Angels in Byzantium* (Berkeley: University of California Press, 2001).

Pertusi, A., *De thematibus Introductione, testo critico, commento* (Città del Vaticano: Biblioteca apostolica vaticana, 1952).

Petau, D., *The history of the world, or an Account of time compiled by the learned Dionisius Petavius and continued by others to the year of Our Lord 1659, together with a geographicall description of Europe, Asia, Africa and America* (London: J. Streater, 1659).

Piccardi, L., "The AD 60 Denizli Basin earthquake and the apparition of Archangel Michael at Colossae (Aegean Turkey)", in L. Piccardi/W. B. Masse (ed.), *Myth and Geology* (London: Geological Society, 2007) 95–115.

Pococke, R., *Description of the East and Some Other Countries* (2 vol.; London: W. Bowyer, 1745).

Pokorný, P., *Colossians: A Commentary* translated by S. S. Schatzmann (Peabody, Mass: Hendrickson, 1991).

Ramsay, C.(A.), *The Travels of Cyrus* (Dublin: William Smith & Son, 9th Ed. 1763).

Ramsay, W. M., "Antiquities of Southern Phrygia and the Border Lands I", *AJA* 3 (1887) 344–68.

– *The Historical Geography of Asia Minor* (London: John Murray, 1890).

Reicke, B., "The Historical Setting of Colossians", *RevExp* 70 (1973) 429–38.

Renan, E., *Histoire des origines du Christianisme* (6 vol.; Paris: Michel Lévy Frères, 1863–79).

Robert, L., *Noms indigènes dans l'Asie-Mineure gréco-romaine* (Amsterdam: Hakkert, 1963).

Rycaut, P., *Account of the Greek and Armenian Churches* (London: 1679).

de Saint-Marie, L. V. *Histoire des découvertes géographiques des nations Européennes dans les diverses parties du Monde* (Paris: Arthus-Bertrand, 1846).

Salmon, T., *The Modern Gazetteer: or a short view of the several nations of the world* (London: S & E Ballard, 3rd Ed., 1756).

Scaliger, J. J., *De Emendatione Temporum* (Frankfurt: Wechel, 1583).

Schaff, P., *A Dictionary of the Bible* (Philadelphia: American Sunday School Union, 4th Ed., 1887).

Schmidt, H. I., *Course of Ancient Geography* (New York: Appleton and Co, 1861).

Schönborn, A., "Communication from Professor Schönborn of Posen relative to an important Monument recently discovered by him in Lycia", *Museum of Classical Antiquities* 1 (1851) 43.

de Schubert, T. F. (ed.), *Exposé des Travaux Astronomiques et Géodésiques executes en Russie 1855* (St Petersburg: Academy of Sciences, 1855).

Sekunda, N., "Achaemenid Settlement in Caria, Lycia and Greater Phrygia", in H. Sancisi-Weerdenburg/A. Kuhrt (ed.), *Achaemenid History VI: Asia Minor and Egypt: Old Cultures in a New Empire* (Leiden: Nederlands Instituut voor het Nabije Oosten, 1991) 175–96.

Siemieniec-Golas, E., "Turkish Words in Smith's Epistolae Quatuor (1674)", *Studia Turcologica Cracoviensia* 1 (1995) 125–49.

Seymour, M. C., *Mandeville's Travels* (Oxford: Oxford University Press, 1968 [1375]).

Sharafuddin, M., *Islam and Romantic Orientalism: Literary Encounters with the Orient* (London/New York: I. B. Tauris, 1994).

Smith, A. H./W. M. Ramsay, "Notes on a Tour in Asia Minor", *JHS* 8 (1887) 222–67.

Smith, H. I., *The Course of Ancient Geography* (New York: D. Appleton, 1861).

Smith, T., *Remarks upon the Manners, Religion and Government of the Turks. Together with a Survey of the Seven Churches of Asia as they now lye in their Ruines: and a Brief Description of Constantinople* (London: Moses Pitt, 1678).

Smith, W. (ed.), *Dictionary of Greek and Roman Geography* (2 vol.; London: Walton and Maberly, 1854).

– *A Concise Dictionary of the Bible* (London: Little, Brown and Co, 1865).

Speed, J., *A Prospect of the Most Famous Parts of the World* (London: George Humble, 1626/1627).

Spelman, E., *The Expedition of Cyrus into Persia; and the Retreat of the Ten Thousand Greeks* (2 vol.; Cambridge: Cambridge University Press, 1776).

Spratt, T. A. B./E. Forbes, *Travels in Lycia, Milyas and the Cibyratis in Company with the late Rev. E. T. Daniell* (2 vol.; London: John van Voorst, 1847).

Stiltingo, J./C. Suyskeno/J. Periero/J. Cleo (ed.), *Acta Sanctorum: September* (Paris/Rome: Victor Palmé, vol. 8, 1869 [1762]).

de Tournefort, P. *Relation d'un Voyage du Levant* (2 vol.; Paris: L'imprimerie Royale, 1717).

Texier, C., *Description de l'Asie Mineure* (3 vol.; Paris: L'Institut de France, 1839).

Usborne, T. H., *A New Guide to the Levant for the use of travellers in Greece, Egypt, Palestine, Syria and Asia Minor ... also comprising the overland journey to India, the voyage from Suez to Bombay and the systems of dawk travelling in the three presidencies* (London: Craddock & Co, 1840).

Vaux, W. S. W., *Greek Cities and Islands of Asia Minor* (London: SPCK, 1877).

Vernant, J-P., *Myth and thought among the Greeks* (London: Routledge, 1983).

Vigouroux, F. (ed.), *Dictionnaire de la Bible* (Paris: Letouzey et Ané, 1899).

van der Vin, J.P.A., *Travellers to Greece and Constantinople: Ancient Monuments and Old Traditions in Medieval Travellers' Tales* (Istanbul: Nederlands Historisch-Archaeologisch Instituut, 1980).

Vryonis, S., "The Panegyris of the Byzantine Saint", in S. Hackel (ed.), *The Byzantine Saint* (London: Fellowship of St Alban and St Sergius, 1981) 196–226.

– *The Decline of Medieval Hellenism in Asia Minor and the Process of Islamization from the Eleventh through the Fifteenth Century* (Berkeley: University of California Press, 1971).

Walpole, R., *Memoirs Relating to European and Asiatic Turkey: edited from Manuscript Journals* (2 vol., London: Longman, Hurst, Rees, Orme and Brown, 1817).

Weber, G., "Der unterirdische Lauf des Lykos bei Kolossai", *Ath.Mitt.* 16 (1891) 194–99.

Wengert, T. J., *Human Freedom, Christian Righteousness: Philip Melanchthon's exegetical dispute with Erasmus of Rotterdam* (Oxford/New York: Oxford University Press, 1998).

Whitehead, D., "From Smyrna to Stewartstown: A Numismatist's Epigraphic Notebook", *Proceedings of the Royal Irish Academy* (1999) 73–113.

Wilkinson, C., *A Tour through Asia Minor and the Greek Islands, with an Account of their Inhabitants ... and curiosities for the Instruction and Amusement of Youth* (London: Darton and Harvey, 1806).

Williams, J., *Two essays on the geography of ancient Asia: intended partly to illustrate the campaigns of Alexander, and the Anabasis of Xenophon* (London: John Murray, 1829).

Wilson, Maj-Gen. Sir C. (ed.), *Handbooks for Travellers: Asia Minor* (London: John Murray, 1895).

Witherington, B., *The letters to Philemon, the Colossians and the Ephesians: a socio-rhetorical commentary on the captivity Epistles* (Grand Rapids, Mich: Eerdmans, 2007).

Wright, N. T., *Judas and the Gospel of Jesus* (Grand Rapids, Mich: Baker, 2006).

Chapter 2

Changing Patterns of Land-Holding in the South-Western Border Lands of Greater Phrygia in the Achaemenid and Hellenistic Periods

Nicholas Sekunda

Obviously for the purposes of this volume it would be ideal to concentrate our enquiries on the hinterland of the later city of Colossae alone, but, given the extent of the evidence, this is not possible. The evidence for the city of Colossae is insufficient in itself to give a comprehensive picture of changes in settlement in the wider region. Instead I have used the wider term "south-western border lands of Greater Phrygia". To the ancients, Hellespontine Phrygia was the region of Anatolia lying to the south-east of the Hellespont, while Greater Phrygia lay in central Anatolia, the two regions being separated from one another by Lydia. This will enable the literary evidence for Kelainai in particular to be taken into account, against the background of the literary and epigraphic evidence for the wider area too. A comparative study of this nature yields significant advantages for the understanding of Colossae in the Achaemenid period by elucidating the place of the ancient city in the sometimes contentious allocation of royal, satrapal and noble estates, along with their settlement, in south-west Asia Minor.

This essay necessarily involves a considerable repetition of material I have dealt with previously.[1] I have, however, taken the opportunity to add new evidence which has come to my attention, for example the extremely important archaeological evidence from the Tatarlı tumulus, and to refine my interpretation of the evidence at certain points.

---

1 See N. V. Sekunda, "Achaemenid Settlement in Caria, Lycia and Greater Phrygia", in H. Sancisi-Weerdenburg/A. Kuhrt (ed.), *Achaemenid History VI. Asia Minor and Egypt: Old Cultures in a New Empire. Proceedings of the Groningen 1988 Achaemenid History Workshop* (Leiden: Nederlands Instituut voor het Nabije Oosten, 1991) 83–143; "The Aribazoi: A Family in Seleucid Service", in E. Dąbrowa/M. Dzielska/M. Salamon/S. Sprawski (ed.), *Donum Centenarium. Księga pamiątkowa ku czci profesora Józefa Wolskiego w setną rocznicę urodzin* (Kraków: Towarzystwo Wydawnicze "Historia Iagiellonica", 2010) 219–27.

The Lydian Period

The fifth century BCE historian, Herodotos, reports that Xerxes and the army passed from Kelainai by "the city of the Phrygians called Anaua and the lake from which the salt comes and came to a great city in Phrygia called Colossae. In it the river Lycus descends into a pit in the ground and vanishes, and afterwards, reappearing some five stades further on, it issues too, into the Maeander. From Colossae the army set out towards the bounds of Phrygia and Lydia and came to the city of Kydrara, where there stands a pillar set up by Kroisos, declaring, in its inscription, the boundary" (Herodotos *Hist.* 7.30).[2]

The exact route which Xerxes followed to arrive at Kelainai, and that which he took after Sardis, have been the subject of some debate, but his route from Kelainai through Colossae to Kydrara is precisely described, and is therefore beyond dispute, and so need not detain us here.[3]

The Lydian Royal Inheritance – Pythes the Lydian

Herodotos tells us (*Hist.* 7.27) that before Xerxes arrived at Colossae (in 481 BCE), he first marched to Kelainai in Phrygia, where he was received by Pythios, the son of Atys, a Lydian. This Pythios, according to Herodotos, was the wealthiest man in the empire after Xerxes himself.

Pythes (otherwise Pythios: in either form the name is connected with the worship of Apollo at Delphi) was the son of Atys the Lydian, in turn grandson of Kroisos, the last king of Lydia. Atys was the only son of Kroisos (Herodotos *Hist.* 1.38, but *cf* 85). He died in a hunting accident, which took place very soon after his wedding (1.43). Kroisos made an accommodation with Cyrus after the Persian conquest of Lydia, and, it seems, handed his estates on to his grandson Pythes. The conventional date for the fall of Sardis is 546 BCE, but it is perhaps more likely that it took place between 539 and 530.[4]

These estates included a city in Caria which was given the name Pythopolis, perhaps a foundation of Pythes himself. Thus Stephanus Byzantinus *s.v.*

Pythopolis, a city of Caria, which later was called Nysa. Pythopolis is formed from 'Pythoū', marked with a circumflex on the last accent (περισπωμένος), as Hormou-

---

2 D. Grene (trans.), *The History of Herodotus* (Chicago/London: University of Chicago Press, 1987), 481.

3 Probably the most recent treatment is that of D. Müller, *Topographischer Bildkommentar zu den Historien Herodots. Kleinasien* (Tübingen: E. Wasmuth, 1997), 163–65.

4 See N. Ehrhardt, "Die Ionier und ihr Verhätnis zu den Phrygern und Lydern", in E. Schwertheim and E. Winter (ed.), *Neue Forschungen zu Ionien* (*Asia Minor Studien* 53; Bonn: Habelt, 2005) 93–111, on p. 106 n108.

polis is formed from 'Hermoū', the genitive. And this Pythes was so very much the richest of men, that when he entertained Xerxes he provided for every one of his soldiers six golden darics each. The citizen is called a 'Pythopolites' like a 'Hermopolites', and there is another Pythopolis in Mysia.

Plutarch (*Mor.* 262d–263a; repeated in Polyaenus *Strat.* 8.42) records that when gold was found, Pythes put all the citizens of the city to work digging and washing the gold until his wife intervened in their favour.

It seems that Pythes accompanied Xerxes and the army as far as Sardis. There he came before the king immediately upon his departure for Europe and begged that the eldest of his five sons be spared from service with the army to take care of him and his possessions. Xerxes was angered by the request, and ordered Pythes' eldest son to be cut in two, and the army to march out through the two halves of the body (Herodotos *Hist.* 7.38–9; Plutarch *Mor.* 263a–b; Seneca *De ira* 3.16.4). According to Plutarch (*Mor.* 263b–c) Pythes later starved himself to death at Pythopolis.

The story rewards closer investigation. Herodotos (*Hist.* 7.27) details that Pythes, on the arrival of Xerxes at Kelainai, "entertained the entire army of the King with every sort of hospitality, and Xerxes as well".[5] From this reference it would be reasonable to conclude that Pythes owned considerable property at Kelainai. Indeed many have been led to suggest that Pythes was once based at Kelainai.[6] Pythes was most likely "based" at Pythopolis, the city in Caria he had presumably founded, and which was later named Nysa; but that he also owned property at Kelainai is clear. It is also likely that the lands owned by Pythes had once been part of the estate owned by Kroisos as King of Lydia, land which Pythes had inherited.

Part of the Lydian "Royal Estate" may well have been taken by Cyrus upon the conquest of the Lydian Kingdom; part may have been voluntarily alienated by Kroisos at some later date; but part was in turn inherited by Pythes, it seems. Significantly, the family did not participate in the Lydian revolt led by Paktyas against Cyrus. So it would be reasonable to assume, in my view, that Pythes held extensive lands throughout the former Lydian Kingdom, as well as at Pythopolis and Kelainai.

Pythes offered to give all his wealth to Xerxes, which amounted to 2,000 talents of silver and 3,993,000 golden Daric staters. This extraordinary largesse was to help in the war against Greece. Pythes himself, in Herodotos' retelling, provides the reason: "for me the livelihood from my slaves and my estates

---

5 Grene, 480.

6 See J. M. Balcer, *Sparda by the Bitter Sea: Imperial Interaction in Western Anatolia* (Chico: Scholars Press, 1984), 202.

(ἀνδραπόδων καὶ γεωπέδων) will suffice" (Herodotos *Hist.* 7.28).[7] So the bulk of Pythes' land-holdings would have been in rural estates run by slaves.

It would also be reasonable to assume that much of this land originally belonging to the Lydian Crown had been acquired by conquest when the Lydian state was expanding. Kelainai, of course, lay outside the traditional borders of Lydia, and had once belonged to the Phrygian Kingdom. It seems that the Phrygian Kingdom was severely weakened by successive Kimmerian invasions from the north which took place in the first half of the seventh century BCE, with the consequence that Phrygian lands in the west were incorporated by the expanding Lydian kingdom up to the Halys River, that flows out from the eastern Anatolian plateau. It would be reasonable to assume that it was during this course of events that extensive property in and around Kelainai first came into the possession of the Mermand Dynasty (approximately 680–547 BCE).

The Lydian crown held other lands outside the traditional borders of Lydia, and one example can be cited. Strabo (13.1.17) mentions a royal hunting-ground on the Peirossos mountain near Zeleia, which was laid out by the Lydians, and again, later by the Persians. Hunting was an activity of prime importance to the Persian nobility, and, it seems, to the Lydians who came before them. Hence the importance of these hunting-grounds to both societies.

The Achaemenid Period

Xenophon (*Anab.* 1.2.6) gives us an account of the route taken by the Cyrean mercenaries towards the east in 401 BCE. This group of (mainly) Greek mercenaries, otherwise known as the "Ten Thousand", was raised by Cyrus the Younger to aid in his revolt against his older brother Artaxerxes II. They set out from Sardis and marched through Lydia to the Maeander river, and then marched through Phrygia to Colossae "a city occupied and prosperous and large" (πολὶν οἰκουμένην καὶ εὐδαίμονα καὶ μεγάλην). There they remained seven days, presumably waiting for the arrival of Menon the Thessalian together with a further 1000 hoplites and 500 peltasts. Later the army marched on to Kelainai, and Xenophon provides the following description of the city (*Anab.* 1.2.7–9). It is to be noted that the patterns of ownership are quite different from what they were some eighty years previously. Xenophon reports that Cyrus the Younger possessed a palace and a *paradeisos* full of wild animals there, through the middle of which flowed the Maeander River, and a second palace belonging to the Great King, which Xerxes had built during his withdrawal through the city after his defeat in Greece.

It would be difficult to avoid the conclusion that Xerxes had built his palace at Kelainai on property he had taken from Pythes. The anonymous, fragmentary

---

7 Grene, 480.

history of the period, the *Hellenica Oxyrhyncha* (12 (7).3), tells us that Kelainai was the largest city in Phrygia, and it seems reasonable to assume that the city was the capital of the Greater Phrygian satrapy during the Achaemenid period.[8] Perhaps the palace from which the satrapy was normally governed was this first palace built by Xerxes. Plutarch gives us the impression that after his fall from favour, Pythes retired to Pythopolis to starve himself to death, after which his wife exercised the rule admirably (*Mor.* 263c). So it seems that Pythes and his remaining family retained government in Pythopolis, but perhaps this was not the case throughout the whole of his extensive estates. Pythes may have ceded some of them to Xerxes in an attempt to buy favour with the King for his surviving sons.

Pythes' base of wealth was his rural "slaves and estates" and it may also have been at this point that Xerxes allocated rural estates in the south-western border lands of Greater Phrygia to some of the Persian nobles in his train as a reward for their services. A number of literary references may be used to support this contention, which, although equivocal and inconclusive individually, seem to point towards a pattern of noble settlement in the South-West border lands of Greater Phrygia, which we find repeated in other areas of "Lower Asia" west of the Halys river in the period of Achaemenid occupation too.

Plutarch (*Cimon* 9.2–4) mentions that when Cimon captured some Persians in Sestos and Byzantium their friends and kinsmen came down from Phrygia and Lydia to ransom them. Unfortunately we are not told whether in this case Phrygia means Hellespontine Phrygia or Greater Phrygia. It is possible that both areas are meant.

At a slightly earlier date, during the Ionian revolt (499 BCE), Herodotos (*Hist.* 5.98) tells us that some of the Paeonians who had been settled in Phrygia remained where they were, but the rest moved back to the west, and as they retreated they were pursued by a large body of Persian cavalry. It is most unfortunate that we do not know where in Phrygia these Paeonians had been settled, but I think it is reasonable to presume that we are dealing with Greater Phrygia, probably in some district not too remote from the coast. It is also reasonable to presume that the Persian cavalry in question had been raised from Persian landholders settled within the satrapy of Phrygia. These may also have comprised an element of the Persians having *nomoi*, that is, designated districts, "within the Halys" (Herodotos *Hist.* 5.102) who came to the rescue after the sack of Sardis in 498 BCE. If this interpretation is correct, it necessarily indicates that the first settlement of Persians occurred before the main settlement, which I have suggested occurred after the downfall of Pythes some twenty years later.

The first century historian, Curtius (4.12.11), mentions that regiments of Phrygians, Cataonians, Cappadocians and Syrians, presumably cavalry, fought

---

8 Compare P. Briant, *Antigone le Borgne* (Paris: Les Belles Lettres, 1973), 52.

on the wings of the Persian army at Gaugamela (331 BCE). These troops were presumably recruited from Iranian noble families settled in these provinces in former times. It is unlikely that they were mercenaries, as at this time the areas in question would have been overrun by the Macedonian army, and so would not be available to the king for the recruitment of mercenaries. Therefore I think it is reasonable to assume that these regiments were, in fact, the usual satrapal cavalry regiments raised from Persian land-holders settled in the four satrapies named.

This constitutes all the evidence available in the literary sources, but given that one would expect the evidence for Phrygia to be sparse anyway, I think it is sufficient to warrant an assumption that the satrapy was subject to the same pattern of noble settlement as the other satrapies lying further west, namely Hellespontine Phrygia, Lydia and Caria. In fact the Iranian influence on Phrygia seems to have been quite considerable.

The *chōra* of Tithraustes

A papyrus fragment (*FGrH* 105, 4 ed. Jacoby) has survived which has been very plausibly connected with the historical incident mentioned by Diodorus (16.22. 1–2) when in 356/5 BCE the Athenian general Chares gave military aid to the satrap Artabazos who had rebelled against the Persian King, and who was fighting against the satraps. The subject of the sentence, probably Chares, "... joining in attacking Phrygia, ravaged the estate of Tithraustes" (καὶ συνεμβα|λὼν εἰς Φρυγίαν ἐπόρθει τὴν Τιθραύσ|του χώραν). If we take this passage literally, Tithraustes' estate (*chora*) would have lain somewhere in the western borderlands of Phrygia. It seems reasonable to assume that Chares would have been attacking eastwards from Sardis and Lydia, and it seems quite possible that the axis of the attack may have run along the road systems passing through Colossae and Kelainai. This cannot be taken as certain, as it is possible that the attack may have taken place further to the north. On the other hand, the story of the earlier Tithraustes (presuming him to be related to the younger Tithraustes) and Ariaios, as collaborating in the despatching of Tissaphernes, does suggest regional proximity.

Modern scholars are divided as to the status of Tithraustes. Simon Hornblower has discussed the problem, calling him a "private" Persian, presumably indicating by this that Tithraustes was principally motivated to defend his own property.[9] Olmstead calls Tithraustes "a loyal satrap" and also calls him "the younger Tithraustes" in contrast to the Tithraustes sent down to Asia some

---

9 S. Hornblower, *Mausolus* (Oxford: Clarendon, 1982), 144 n57.

forty years before with an assassination brief.[10] A scholion on Demosthenes' *First Philippic* (4.19) mentions a force "of 20,000 Persians, the majority of them cavalry under the command of Tithraustes" (δισμυρίους Περσῶν καὶ πλεῖστον αὐτὸν ἱππικὸν ὑπὸ Τιθραύστον στρατηγούμενον).[11] From this passage it is clear that the status of Tithraustes must be greater than that of a local land-holder, even though the papyrus, in referring to the ravaging of his *chora*, demonstrates beyond doubt that he was a local landholder.

In 395 BCE, King Artaxerxes had sent down one Tithraustes to Lower Asia (Xenophon *Hell.* 3.4.25). Tithraustes had previously held the extremely important office of *chiliarchos*, the most important post in the Empire next to that of King (Nepos 9.3.2). According to Diodorus (14.80.7–8), the King had appointed Tithraustes *hegemon* of satraps. Polyaenus (*Strat.* 7.16.1) adds that he arrived in Lower Asia with a letter from King Artaxerxes ordering Ariaios to join in arresting Tissaphernes. Ariaios invited Tissaphernes to join him at Colossae, where Ariaios overpowered Tissaphernes and handed him over to Tithraustes, transporting him in a covered wagon to Kelainai where he was beheaded.

A third individual called Tithraustes, a bastard son of Xerxes (Diodorus 11.60.5), is attested earlier in our texts. He served as commander of the royal fleets at Eurymedon in about 467 BCE, — the exact date of the battle is disputed (Plutarch *Cimon* 12.4). At about this time, it seems that the satrap of Greater Phrygia was one Epixyes (the satrap of "Upper Phrygia" in Plutarch *Them.* 30.1), whom Plutarch connects with the return of Themistocles from the Persian court to Lower Asia. The chronology of this is uncertain, but it must have occurred at about the same time as the assassination of Xerxes in 465 BCE.

Epixyes was later succeeded by a certain Arsames. Polyaenus (*Strat.* 7.28) relates two anecdotes concerning Arsames. In the first he tells us that Arsames captured Barce in Cyrenaica. This siege seems to belong to the 450's when Egypt, and presumably Cyrenaica with it, managed to break loose from Persian rule temporarily. Soon after both were re-subjugated. A series of satrapal revolts, principally led by Megabyzus, followed. In the second anecdote Polyaenus tells us that Arsames revolted from the king, ruled Greater Phrygia, and managed to foil a plot by his hipparch and some of his cavalry to betray him to his enemy. Some of this cavalry probably consisted of Persian land-holders from the satrapy. The date of this incident is uncertain, and it is always possible that Polyaenus has listed the exploits of two different individuals called Arsames in the same chapter. Nevertheless I would like to suggest that following the collapse of this revolt Tithraustes replaced Arsames as satrap of Greater Phrygia, and that the

---

10 A. T. Olmstead, *History of the Persian Empire* (Chicago/London: University of Chicago Press, 1948), 428.

11 W. Dindorf, *Demosthenes VIII. Scholia Graeca ex Codicibus aucta et Emendata* (Oxford: E Typographeo Academico, 1851), 154 ad 4.45.

office, with the lands, was inherited by later generations of the same family, including the Tithraustes (II) of the 390's, who was presumably his grandson, and the Tithraustes (III) of the 350's, who may have been his grandson's grandson. Even if the first Tithraustes was not appointed satrap of Greater Phrygia in the mid-fourth century, it seems highly probable that the *chora* of the family lay near Kelainai. If this supposition is correct it throws some new light on the campaign of the Athenian general Chares, and the rather exaggerated claims made as to its success, for if Chares had, in fact, reached Kelainai and plundered the lands around it, he would have advanced further into southern Phrygia than Agesilaus managed in 395, for Agesilaus had turned back before reaching Colossae, let alone Kelainai, the capital of the satrapy *(Hell. Oxyrh.* 12 [7].4). To Greeks of the middle of the fourth century, before the time of Alexander, Agesilaus had had the greatest successes in opposing the Persians, and it is into this context that the achievement of Chares needs to be placed.

In 1969 local villagers raided a tumulus at Tatarlı, situated 30 kilometres to the north west of Kelainai on the road running to the old Phrygian capital at Gordion. The tumulus was subsequently excavated by Afyon Museum. The tomb chamber buried beneath the tumulus constitutes the latest example in a long tradition of Phrygian timber-lined chamber tombs.[12] Four of the painted beams coming from the tomb are now in Munich. The beams are decorated in Achaemenid style, showing, among other scenes, battles between Persians and warriors in nomadic dress, typical for Scythians. Carbon 14 examination of the beams first indicated a date of around 451 BCE±22. Subsequent dendrochronological examination proved that the beams were cut around 478 BCE.[13] These dates would not be too early to contradict the supposition that the South East borderlands of Phrygia were settled from confiscated land originally belonging to Pythes the Lydian, which had subsequently entered the possession of the Persian king Xerxes following his fall from favour. It is possible that the tomb in Tatarlı had once belonged to the first Tithraustes himself, but other explanations (and occupants) must surely not be excluded, especially if the first Tithraustes had replaced a previous important landholder, such as Arsames or Epixyes.

In summary, three historical individuals bearing the name Tithraustes are known, and there are good reasons for locating at least two of them in the "southwestern border lands of Greater Phrygia", that is, in the region encompassing Colossae.

---

12 L. Summerer, "Picturing Persian Victory: The Painted Battle Scene on the Munich Wood", in A. Ivantchik/V. Licheli (ed.), *Achaemenid Culture and Local Traditions in Anatolia, Southern Caucasus and Iran. New Discoveries* (Leiden/Boston: Brill, 2007) 3–30, on p. 4.

13 L. Summerer, "From Tatarlı to Munich: The Recovery of a Painted Wooden Tomb Chamber in Phrygia", in İ. Delemen (ed.), *The Achaemenid Impact on Local Populations and Cultures in Anatolia (Sixth-Fourth Centuries B. C.)* (Istanbul: Türk Eskicag Bilimleri Enstitusu Yayinlari, 2007) 131–58, on pp. 145–46.

The Estate of Ariaios

In the lexicon compiled by Suidas, under the entry "Ariaios" comes the information that it is simply "a personal name" (Ἀριανός. Ὄνομα κύριον). The personal
name probably means "the Aryan", that is, belonging to the racial group, rather
than "the Arian", that is coming from the Iranian province called Aria (which
would probably be Haraiva- in Old Persian).[14]

The only bearer of the name, apart from a mythological king of Arabia (Diod.
2.1.5) was an individual living in Lower Asia in antiquity.[15] Ariaios had been a
hyparchos (Xenophon *Anab.* 1.8.5) and a faithful friend (Ctesias 53) of Cyrus the
Younger and had commanded the left wing of his army at Cunaxa, during which
battle he deserted the body of Cyrus (Xenophon *Oec.* 4.19). After the collapse
of the revolt he had been pardoned by the king. He does not participate in the
defence of Lower Asia against the Lakedaemonians, and he only reappears on
the scene when Tithraustes has been sent down. As has been stated previously,
he helped Tithraustes to capture Tissaphernes by inviting him to visit Colossae.

Therefore, Ariaios may have been based at that city. At Colossae, he overpowered Tissaphernes "with the aid of his servants" (μετὰ τῶν θεραπευτήρων
Polyaenus *Strat.* 7.16.1) and handed him over to Tithraustes. The "servants"
mentioned in the passage could have been Ariaios' subordinate land-holders,
but they do not have to be. Likewise, the passage could be taken to imply that
Tithraustes and Ariaios were in a "feudal" relationship, but this is not necessarily the case. When Tissaphernes had been killed, Tithraustes put Ariaios and one
Pasiphernes in charge of operations *(Hell. Oxyrh.* 19 (14).3), and Ariaios is later
found at Sardis (Xenophon *Hell.* 4.1.27). Pasiphernes may also have been one of
the "dukes" of Greater Phrygia under Tithraustes. By this term I mean an Iranian land-holder settled in a satrapy, of inferior social status to the satrap (generally an office inherited from one generation of a family to the next) but commanding loyalty from a number of heads of families settled in a given area — in
which case Pasiphernes could have held lands in any of the other areas of noble
settlement in Phrygia. However, it is equally possible that Pasiphernes was an
officer of the king who had come down to lower Asia with Tithraustes.

Therefore there seems to be sufficient evidence in the literary sources to support a hypothesis that there were at least two areas of noble settlement in Greater
Phrygia. One, around Kelainai, supported the family of Tithraustes and depend-
ants and included the *chora* of the dynasty. A second, around Colossae, supported the family of Ariaios. However, there is also evidence for a third family of
prime importance in the area. It seems to me that each of these "ducal" families

---

14 R. Schmitt, *Die iranier-Namen bei Aischylos* (Vienna: Österreichische Akademie der
Wissenschaften, 1978), 43 n57, *cf* p. 31).

15 W. Judeich, "Ariaios (2)", *RE* 2,1, (1895), 811.

would be able in turn to command the services of a number of other families settled in the immediate area. In this context we are able to cite by way of comparison that at the turn of the fifth and fourth centuries, the "duke" Spithridates had at his disposal 200 cavalry (Xenophon *Ages.* 3.3; Plutarch *Ages.* 8.3) with which he deserted to Agesilaus, leaving the satrap Pharnabazus with 400 (Xenophon *Hell.* 4.1.17). So, based on these figures, if there were two or three comparable "ducal" families settled in the south-west border lands of Greater Phrygia, they would each be able to call on the support of a couple of hundred "retainers". These would not all be heads of families settled on a couple of hundred individual estates. One rather imagines a dozen or so estate-holders able to mobilize a dozen or so members of their immediate family and associated individuals.[16]

Aribazos

There is evidence for a Hellenistic family based in Lower Asia which used the personal name Aribazos (Ἀρίβαζος). The name is clearly the Old Persian **Aryabazu* meaning "Arm of the Iranians" or the like.[17] Only one certainly Iranian individual is mentioned in the ancient sources as bearing this name, a Hyrcanian who led a plot to kill Darius (Aelian *Var. Hist.* 6.14). When the plot failed, those involved in it were spared but were sent to the most distant borders of the Empire. The name could, then, be Hyrcania, and there is some evidence for Hyrcanian settlement in Lydia in Achaemenid times, for a part of the Hermos valley was called the Hyrcanian Plain, which can be located thanks to the existence of a later town there called Hyrcanis.[18]

The first individual using the name Aribazos we know of from the Hellenistic period is an individual mentioned in a papyrus dealing with the opening phases of the Third Syrian War of 246–241 BCE (*PPetrie* II.45; III.144 = *FGrH* 160).[19]

---

16 Compare N. V. Sekunda, "Persian Settlement in Hellespontine Phrygia", in A. Kuhrt/ H. Sancisi-Weerdenburg (ed.), *Achaemenid History III: Method and Theory. Proceedings of the Fifth Achaemenid History Workshop* (Leiden: Nederlands Instituut voor het Nabije Oosten 1988) 175–96, on pp. 182–7.

17 F. Justi, *Iranisches Namenbuch* (Marburg: N. G. Elwert'sche Verlagsbuchhandlung, 1895), 25 *sv.* "arischen (starken) Arm habend"; A. H. M. Stonecipher, *Graeco-Persian Names* (NY: American Book Co, 1918), 20 *sv.*; E. Benveniste, *Titres et noms propres en iranien ancien* (Paris: Librairie C. Klincksieck, 1966), 115–117; W. Hinz, *Altiranisches Sprachgut der Nebenüberlieferungen* (Wiesbaden: Harrassowitz, 1975), 39.

18 L. Robert, *Hellenica VI* (Paris: Adrien-Maisonneuve, 1948), 16–22; N. Sekunda, "Achaemenid Colonization in Lydia", *REA* 87 (1985) 7–30, on p. 20.

19 R. S. Bagnall/P. Derow, *Greek Historical Documents: The Hellenistic Period* (Chico: Scholars Press, 1981), 50–52, no. 27 (with earlier literature); M. M. Austen, *The Hellenistic World from Alexander to the Roman Conquest: A Selection of Ancient Sources in translation* (Cambridge: Cambridge University Press, 1981), 63–64, no. 220 for English translations.

Aribazos is mentioned there as the Seleucid στρατ[ηγός] (that is, Satrap) of Cilicia, who was killed by the local population as he passed through the Taurus Mountains trying to escape from the forces of Ptolemy III. Modern writers who have commented on this passage have assumed Aribazos to have been an Iranian.[20] Indeed Ivana Savalli-Lestrade remarks on the peculiar position of Aribazos as an oriental holding the position of *strategos* so early on in the history of the Seleucid Empire.[21]

A second Aribazos is mentioned by Polybius, firstly as commander[22] of the city of Sardis under the rebel Seleucid king, Achaios, at the time of the capture of the lower city in 214 BCE (7.17.9, 7.18.4,7). His precise title and status are unknown, but he was obviously a key figure in the administration of Achaios. Following the capture of Achaios in 212 BCE, the remaining defenders of the citadel were divided into supporters of his wife, Laodike, and supporters of Aribazos. Thus divided, however, they soon surrendered the citadel to Antiochus III. In a third passage (8.21.9) the name appears as Ἀριόβαζος in the manuscripts. We hear nothing further of Aribazos. In this case too the general opinion of modern scholars is that Aribazos is an Iranian.[23]

Leaving aside the problem of the ethnicity of these two individuals, it seems reasonable to conclude, given the rarity of the name, that they were related. Grainger has suggested that the relationship was father and son.[24] This is quite reasonable given that some thirty-odd years separate the two incidents, but it could possibly have been a grandfather-grandson relationship. Whatever the relationship, we seem to have two members of the same family in Seleucid service, the first as governor of Cilicia and the second as commander of the city of Sardis.

Achaios was a cousin of Antiochus III, who, in 233 BCE, had accompanied the expedition of Seleukos III to recover the lands of the Seleucid kingdom in Asia Minor beyond the Taurus Mountains that had been lost to Attalos I of Pergamon. On the death of Seleukos III, he was appointed as governor of Asia Minor beyond the Tauros by his successor Antiochus III. For reasons that are not clear Achaios took power in the region in 220, and maintained his independence down to his capture.[25] One might argue that the younger Aribazos was probably

20 For example, E. R. Bevan, *The House of Seleucus* (2 vol.; London: Edward Arnold, 1902), 1.291; M. Launey, *Recherches sur les armées hellénistiques* (2 vol.; Paris: de Boccard, 1949), 1.565–66; L. Capdetrey, *Le pouvoir seleucide. Territoirs, adminstration, finances d'un royaume hellénistique (312–129 avant J-C.)* (Rennes: Presses Universitaires de Rennes, 2007), 245.

21 I. Savalli-Lestrade, *Les Philoi royaux dans l'Asie hellénistiques* (Geneva: Droz, 1998), 227, A6.

22 J. Ma, *Antiochus III and the Cities of Western Asia Minor* (Oxford: Oxford University Press, 1999), 57: "governor".

23 Bevan, 1.291; Launey, 1.567; *cf* F. W. Walbank, *An Historical Commentary on Polybius Vol ii* (Oxford: Oxford University Press, 1967), 66.

24 J. D. Grainger, *A Seleukid Prosopography and Gazetteer* (Leiden: Brill, 1997), 81.

25 Ma, 54–57.

from a family with estates in Lower Asia who found himself involved in the revolt of Achaios, since, being local, he could not extricate himself from it. This is not an argument that carries any great conviction, however, and we must seek further evidence.

A third piece of evidence from the literary sources pertaining to the family of Aribazos, further obfuscates, rather than clarifies both the question of the ethnicity and of the place of residence of the Aribazoi. Two anonymous epigrams in the *Greek Anthology* (12.61 and 62) are written in praise of a youth called Aribazos.[26]

> Look! Consume not all Cnidus utterly, Aribazus:
> The very stone is softened and is vanishing.

> Ye Persian mothers, beautiful, yea beautiful are the children ye bear,
> But Aribazus is to me a thing more beautiful than beauty.

These two, separate, epigrams redound with interpretative difficulties. Although the two epigrams are listed as anonymous, Gow and Page ascribe both poems to the *Stephanos* collection of Meleager, compiled in the early first century BCE.[27] The reasons for this ascription are not clearly stated, but the two anonymous fragments lie in the manuscript between two epigrams both specifically ascribed to Meleager, and the clearly homoerotic character of the two epigrams would be suitable for that author. They do not necessarily have to be written by the same author. Gow and Page noted that the second couplet could have been composed by Meleager or another late poet, but inspired by the first.

So we have two separate epigrams to an Aribazos — not necessarily the same individual. The second epigram perhaps being a purely artificial literary device inspired by the first. The ascription to Meleager is quite uncertain, and so, therefore, is the date. Furthermore the setting of the poem in Knidos does not necessarily imply that the family was based there. The father of this young Aribazos may have been occupying a post in the Seleucid administration at Knidos, and so only temporarily resident there.

How about the apparently clear statement concerning the Persian (not Hyrcanian) ethnicity of Aribazos? Gow and Page further note, "The second couplet, which asserts that Persian boys are καλοί but Aribazus is κάλλιον τὸ καλόν might mean that καλός as an epithet does not do him justice ("more beautiful than beauty itself"), but it is also compatible with the meaning that despite his Persian name he is not in fact a Persian". So the author of the second couplet may have assumed Aribazos to be Persian merely from the name, writing years after

---

26 Loeb translation of W. R. Paton.

27 A. S. F. Gow/D. L. Page, *The Greek Anthology: Hellenistic Epigrams* (2 vol.; Cambridge: Cambridge University Press, 1965), 1.xvi, 2.568.

the author of the first couplet, and with no knowledge at all of the true ethnicity of Aribazos. Nevertheless, if we take the second couplet at face value, Aribazos was ethnically Persian.

My faith in the validity of applying evidence derived from fine literature to the solution of historical problems is low, so let us now turn to the potentially more reliable fragments of epigraphic evidence.

The Personal Name Aribazos at Athens

The tombstone of a Laodicean citizen called Ariabazos son of Apollonios has been recovered in Athens (*IG*² ii.9162). The tombstone is in the form of a column stele and so clearly postdates the sumptuary reforms of Demetrius of Phaleron that it must be Hellenistic in date. The present whereabouts of this stone is not known, so a closer date cannot be suggested from the letter forms. The deceased individual could be from any one of a number of cities called Laodicea, but Robert is probably correct to suggest that the Phrygian city of Laodicea on Lycus is the most likely.[28]

I cannot explain why the personal name is spelt Ariabazos in this inscription, instead of the form Aribazos which we have encountered in the literary texts so far, or the alternative form Ariobazos which the manuscripts of Polybius supply. According to Alvin Stonecipher the former form is a "Variant of Ἀριόβαζος (q.v.)".[29] It seems to be simply a further variant form of the Old Persian *Aryabazu*, but closer to the original Iranian form in sound. Once again, given the extreme rarity of the name, it seems most attractive to connect this individual with the other Aribazoi mentioned in the literary texts.

The next individual to hold this unusual name is one Aribazos (Ἀρίβαζος) son of Seleucus, an Athenian citizen with the demotic Peiraios. This individual figures in a number of second-century inscriptions from Athens, dated by the editors of *LGPN* 2 to 148–120 BCE.[30] He is first mentioned in a catalogue of *hieropoioi* for the *Romaia* festival (*IG* ii².1938, 12) dated to the archonate of Lysiades (148 BCE). In an inscription (*IG* ii².1331 + Add. p. 673) dated to around 130 BCE Aribazos is honoured by a decree of the Dionysiac *technitai*. Finally he is listed in a catalogue of *epimeletes* of the Peiraios honoured by the *boule* in a decree (*IG* ii².1939, 14) dated to the decade 130–120 BCE. According to Marie-Françoise Baslez, the royal patronymic of Ariobazos son of Seleucus may perhaps betray

---

28 L. Robert, "Inscriptions", in J. des Gagniers/P. Devambez/L. Kahl/R. Ginouves, *Laodicée du Lycos: Le Nymphée. Campagnes 1961–63* (Quebec: L'Université Laval, 1969) 247–389, on p. 334 n3.

29 Stonecipher, 19 sv.

30 This same individual is listed as number 161990 in John S. Traill, *Persons of Ancient Athens Volume 3* (Toronto: Athenians, 1995), 26.

the servile origins of this individual.[31] Walther Judeich, to the contrary, saw in the personal name given to this individual evidence for the "political" adoption of personal names, and connected this Athenian individual with the Seleucid Aribazos.[32] By this term, Judeich wished to imply that the Athenian individual was of approximate equal status to the Anatolian family in Seleucid service, and had adopted the name into their family thanks to their close links with them (one thinks primarily of guest-friendship in this context) and as a way of paying a compliment to them.

The name later occurs in a single Athenian inscription (*IG* ii².10742) of the Imperial period, a funerary monument in the form of a simple column commemorating one Aribazos son of Aribazos. The name is listed without any demotic, but is taken to belong to a citizen.[33]

A further individual with the name Ἀρίβαζος is found in an inscription from Miletus.[34] This inscription, perhaps dating to the second century BCE on the grounds of the letter forms, consists of a list of names of non-Milesians, who are presumably awarded Milesian citizenship. The name in the inscription (which is not illustrated) is published as Ἀρίβαζος the son of Andreas, a Syracusan. In a note to the line, however, the editors remark that a reading of Ἄμβατος cannot be ruled out from the squeezes ("nach dem Abklatsch nicht ausgeschlossen"). So this reading seems uncertain. The name Ambatos is rare, but thanks to Pape and Benseler's lexicon,[35] can be found listed by Phlegon of Tralles (*FGrH* 257 F 37) as belonging to an inhabitant of the city of Interamnia. Without seeing the inscription, certainty is impossible.

As far as I am aware, the only other certain occurrence of the name Aribazos in the literary and archaeological record comes in an inscription of the Roman Imperial period from Sebaste, where it occurs in a list of gerousiasts of the city as the patronymic of an individual named Theudas.[36] The city of Sebaste was from its very name evidently an Augustan foundation, although it is possible that it was preceded by a Hellenistic city of unknown name.[37] It lay on the road from

---

31 M.-F. Baslez, "Présence et traditions iraniennes dans les cites de l'Egée", *REA* 87 (1985) 137–55, on p. 52.

32 W. Judeich, "Politische Namengebung in Athen", in M. San Nicolò (ed.), *ETITYMBION Heinrich Swoboda dargebracht* (Reichenburg: 1927) 99–106, on p. 104.

33 *LGPN* 2, 50; Traill, 26, nos 161980, 161985.

34 *LGPN* 3A, 54 citing an inscription contained in G. Kawerau/A. Rehm, *Das Delphinion in Milet* (Th. Wiegand, *Milet I*, Heft III; Berlin: Georg Reimer, 1914), 92, no. 79, 8.

35 W. Pape/G. E. Benseler, *Wörterbuch der griechischen Eigennamen* (Braunschweig: F. Vieweg, 1862–70), 63.

36 P. Paris, "Inscriptions de Sebaste", *BCH* 7 (1883) 448–57, on p. 454; L. Robert, "Malédictions funéraires grecques III. – Une Malédiction funéraire dans la Plaine de Karayük", *CRAI* (1978) 277–86, on pp. 284–85 n63.

37 D. Magie, *Roman Rule in Asia Minor to the End of the Third Century after Christ* (2 vol.; Princeton: Princeton University Press, 1950), 1.471–72, 2.1334 n14.

Akmonia to Eumeneia, sixty-four kilometres north-west of Apameia, and so a little further from Laodicea on Lycus, near the site of the modern village of Selgikler.[38]

Although the greatest caution has to be exercised in the interpretation of a family using Iranian name-forms in the post-Achaemenid period in Lower Asia, perhaps the family of the Aribazoi, given the rarity of the name, is an example of an Iranian family which managed to maintain its social position after the fall of the Achaemenid Empire. Notwithstanding the difficulties of interpretation, the two couplets in the *Palatine Anthology,* taken at face value and with the support of the epigraphic evidence, argue for the Iranian ancestry of the young Aribazos mentioned there. The location of Knidos given by the first couplet is not necessarily to be taken as the place of residence of the family. The father of the young Aribazos mentioned there may have been resident in Knidos whilst on service for his Seleucid ruler.

As the personal name Aribazos also occurs at Sebaste and the variant form Ariabazos at Laodicea probably on Lycus, a city founded by Antiochus II (261–248 BCE), it would seem appropriate to locate the estates of this prominent family in Seleucid service somewhere in the region. The rarity of the name cannot be stressed too greatly. The two "Phrygian" individuals bearing this name do not necessarily have to be members of the noble family of the Aribazoi: their families could have adopted the name of a local prominent noble family for any one of a number of reasons, and once adopted it may have been handed down over the generations to survive into Roman times at Sebaste.

Given that there seems to be a concentration of Achaemenid Iranian noble settlement in western Phrygia around the cities of Kelainai and Colossae, it is possible that an Iranian noble family using the name Aribazos was given lands in this region. They need not necessarily be descended from the Hyrcanian Aribazos who plotted against Darius, although this is always possible. After the fall of the Achaemenid Empire, the family entered Seleucid service.

How did the name spread to Athens? Is it possible that the Ariabazos son of Apollonios of Laodicea on Lycus is to be identified with Aribazos II, who was in fact the homonymous grandson of the Aribazos I who died in the Taurus Mountains in 246 BCE, and that the family itself had been awarded the citizenship of Laodicea on Lycus? If the family also used the name Apollonios is it possible that other bearers of the name Apollonios known to be in Seleucid service may have been members of this family? Is it further possible that following the collapse of the revolt of Achaios, although the life of Aribazos was spared, he decided to transport himself to Athens? The more one studies the Hellenistic period, the more one gains the impression that at that time Athens was a cosmopolitan place

---

38 K. Belke/N. Mersich, *Tabula Imperii Byzantini Bd 7: Phrygien und Pisidien* (Vienna: Österreichischen Akademie der Wissenschaft, 1990), 376–78.

of refuge, perhaps to be compared with Paris during the later nineteenth and earlier twentieth centuries. Is it possible that he and his descendants were awarded Athenian citizenship, and is it then possible that the Athenian citizen Aribazos son of Seleukos of Peiraios known to be active 148–120 BCE was a descendant, and also the Athenian citizen Aribazos son of Aribazos who lived in the city in the Roman period?

As enticing as these highly speculative questions are, the answer to all of them is likely to be "no". Aribazos son of Apollonios died as a Laodicean in Athens, and so was not awarded Athenian citizenship. For chronological reasons Aribazos II is likely to have been the son of Aribazos I, as Grainger suggests, not the grandson. The chronology would work to make the Athenian Aribazos son of Seleukos, prominent in 148–120, the grandson of Aribazos II, but it seems more probable that both these "Seleucid" names were borrowed into an Athenian family as "political" names, just as Judeich suggested. Perhaps the ancestors of the family had entered into Seleucid service, either under Aribazos I or Aribazos II, and had adopted the personal names Seleukos and Aribazos into their family naming systems then, at some point during the third century. It is possible, though, that the Aribazos son of Aribazos commemorated in an Imperial tombstone is a descendent of this individual.

The Downfall of Persian Land-Holding
in the South-Western Border Lands of Greater Phrygia

An interesting passage in Plutarch (*Eum.* 8.5) tells us that the army of Eumenes was once wintering in the area of Kelainai in the post-Alexander succession crisis that ushered in the First War of the Diadochoi (320–319 BCE).[39] In order to raise pay, he sold to the various officers in the army the homesteads and castles (ἐπαύλεις καὶ τετραπυργίας) in the surrounding countryside, which were full of slaves and flocks. One presumes from this passage, and by inference from the celebrated passage describing the castle of Asidates in the Kaikos valley (Xenophon *Anab.* 7.8.12–14), that these "homesteads and castles" will have belonged to Persian land-holders of lesser status than the family of Tithraustes, that is, of Persian "knights" under the "dukes" of the Tithraustid dynasty.

Pierre Briant has discussed this passage in detail, and has demonstrated that these estates were auctioned for pillaging and for temporary occupation, rather than permanently alienated as regards ownership.[40] Therefore actual ownership

---

39 R. A. Billows, *Antigonos the One-Eyed and the Creation of the Hellenistic State* (Berkeley/Los Angeles/London: University of California Press, 1990), p. 74, has the army of Eumenes winter in Cappadocia.

40 P. Briant, *Rois, tributs et paysans: études sur les formations tributaires du Moyen-Orient ancien* (Paris: Presses Universitaire Franche-Comté, 1982), 56–62.

of the lands will not have been transferred. Nevertheless the destruction and loss of wealth, future revenues, and possibly of life, among the owners of these estates may well have been considerable. It is possible, therefore, that the Persian land-owning nobility settled around Kelainai never fully recovered from the devastation suffered at this time. It is possible, furthermore, that many of these lands may have been confiscated from their original Persian owners during the years immediately following the Macedonian invasion of Phrygia, when Antigonus was based at Kelainai, and when, as has been suggested above, the Persian nobility of Phrygia was serving in the cavalry on the wings of the Persian army at Gaugamela (331 BCE). The political situation would have been further complicated by the Persian counter-offensive in Phrygia that took place after the battle of Issus (333 BCE). During this period, apart from their obvious hostility to the Macedonian invaders, the Persian nobles serving with the Persian forces could technically be considered traitors by Alexander, who had already assumed rule of Asia.

"Iranian" Survivals in Post-Achaemenid Times

Consequently I believe it is perfectly possible that very few Persians remained in Kelainai by the end of the fourth century, perhaps none at all. Indeed, in the turmoil which followed in the wake of the Macedonian invasion and the subsequent Persian counter-offensive, it is difficult to believe that other than a handful of local inhabitants of Iranian origin retained their former status as land-holders.

In this respect it is important to realize that the occurrence of Iranian names in the local onomasticon can be explained in a variety of ways other than the survival of families of Iranian origin passing their names on over the generations. Baslez stressed the practice of former slaves of oriental origin adopting, on emancipation, Iranian names with royal or noble associations. Iranian names could be adopted by non-Iranian local families through the mechanisms of guest-friendship or intermarriage. The best example of this seems to be a Lydian family, who adopted the name Artapates during the Achaemenid period, and subsequently retained the name alternating with another name Tleptolemos during the Hellenistic period, where it distinguished itself in Ptolemaic service.[41]

---

41 Sekunda, "Achaemenid Settlement", 98–100.

Surviving 'Iranian' Names at Apameia

Kelainai was re-founded as Apameia by Antiochus I around 275 BCE, and named after Apame, his Bactrian mother, the wife of Seleucus I.[42] It has been suggested that Antiochus was influenced in his choice of name for the new city by the existence of a flourishing Iranian element in the area of Kelainai.[43] I believe that this inference is unsound. A huge number of Seleucid cities were called Apameia: Seleucus founded at least three, and his son Antiochus many more.[44]

Apameia has furnished a considerable number of later inscriptions mentioning one Tiberius Claudius Mithridates, father of Ti. Cl. Piso Mithridatianus, and president of the *Koinon* of Asia about 128 CE (*IGR* IV.780, 787, 788, 790 = *MAMA* VI.109, 110, 180, 182). I do not believe it is safe to use the names Mithridates and Mithradatianus to prove any Iranian connections in the family. The former name is too widespread in the Imperial period to be used for this evidential purpose.

The only other Iranian name attested at Apameia is that of a moneyer with the name Maiphernes. It occurs on autonomous bronze coinage issued by the city in the Roman period.[45] This name belongs to a group of Iranian names formed from an initial *Mai-* element, which seems to have an original meaning of "moon".[46] This group of names is not confined to Cappadocia: for example a Maiphorres is attested in the Avroman parchments.[47] Louis Robert, however, notes the very heavy concentration of such names in Cappadocia.[48] Therefore one should at least consider the possibility that the original Maiphernes was a Cappadocian who became established at Apameia some time in the first century BCE through the influence of the Cappadocian royal house.

Therefore, unless a large amount of evidence for the survival of Iranian names comes to light at Apameia some time in the future, which cannot be explained in any of the ways outlined above, I conclude that the Persian noble population settled around Kelainai in the Achaemenid period had become displaced by the end of the fourth century BCE. Even if further Iranian names come to light

---

42 L. Robert, "Documents d'Asie Mineure XXIII–XXVIII", *BCH* 107 (1983) 497–599, on p. 504.

43 J.Robert/L. Robert, *Fouilles d'Amyzon en Carie, I: Exploration, histoire, monnaies et inscriptions* (Paris: de Boccard, 1983), 117; compare P. Briant, "Les iraniens d'Asie Mineure après la chute de l'Empire achemenide", *DHA* 11 (1985) 167–95, on p. 174.

44 Bevan, 1.31 n4.

45 L. Robert, *Noms indigènes dans l'Asie mineure gréco-romaine* (Paris: Maisonneuve, 1963), 349.

46 Compare Benveniste, 105 with references.

47 E.H. Minns, *Scythians and Greeks in South Russia* (Cambridge: Cambridge University Press, 1915), 22 ff.

48 Robert, "Documents d'Asie Mineure", 514 ff.

at Apameia, the possibility that Iranians in Seleucid service were among those established in the new city, as may have happened at Laodicea, needs to be considered.

Mardonios of Apollonia

Further to the west of Kelainai/Apameia lay the later city of Apollonia on the Maeander. An inscription dating to the early third century BCE, previously attributed to Apollonia in Lycia,[49] mentions one Mardonios son of Aristomachos, a *kalos kagathos* living in the region of Apollonia and performing services for the city, but who was not a citizen. Robert, attributing the inscription to Apollonia on the Maeander, has pointed out that the name Mardonios occurs on imperial coins from Hypaipa, and it may be that Mardonios came from a Hypaipan family.[50]

This is a very attractive suggestion, for it seems that Hypaipa and the adjacent Kilbanian plain was an area of Persian noble settlement, and we do know that the "Lydo-Persians" continued to worship at Hypaipa and Hierakome in Pausanias' time.[51] I presume that these "Lydo-Persians" were the descendants of Persian noble families settled around Hypaipa, who continued to administer the temple into the imperial period. The family of Mardonios could be one of these families. We are, however, some quite considerable distance from Hypaipa. Perhaps, then, the name Mardonios may have been used by more than one of the Persian noble families settled in Lower Asia, or had spread from the Hypaipan family to that of Aristomachus. If so, we could see Mardonios as a local landowner having estates in the region of Colossae. A final compromise possibility might be that the one family owned estates both near Hypaipa and Colossae. Whichever is the correct interpretation, the early date of this inscription suggests that the family of Mardonios may have been settled in Lower Asia during the Achaemenid period.

The use of alternating Greek and Iranian names in the family is interesting. This should not necessarily be interpreted as suggesting that the family is a local one who adopted Iranian names. Mardonios' grandfather, who may also have been called Mardonios, may have given his son Aristomachos a Greek name as a "political" act in the early years following the conquest of Alexander. There is no reason why the "political" adoption of foreign names might not have worked both ways.

---

49 L. Robert, *Villes d'Asie Mineure* (Paris: de Boccard, 2nd Ed, 1962), 56–57 n3.
50 Robert, "Documents d'Asie Mineure", 498–505.
51 Sekunda, "Achaemenid Colonization", 14, 23–24.

So, in conclusion, although the probability is that the huge majority of Iranian families holding estates in the Achaemenid Period probably lost their lands with the coming of the Macedonians, the family of Mardonios may have been one that did not.

Iranian Names at Laodicea on Lycus

The Laodicean citizen named Aribazos son of Apollonios buried at Athens has already been mentioned. The tombstone of a second Laodicean citizen called Menoitas son of Mithridates (*IG²* ii.9180) has been recovered in Athens, and again Robert was probably correct to suggest that the Phrygian city of Laodicea on Lycos is the most likely candidate for the city of origin.[52] The name Mithridates is not of any great significance, given its popularity during post-Achaemenid times, but it is possible that the name was adopted into the local repertoire of family naming-systems in use in the region of Laodicea on Lycos due to the presence of Iranians in the same area during the Achaemenid Period.

An epitaph from Athens (*IG²* ii.9187) dating to the first century BCE, records the inscription Πέρσης Θεμίσωνος Λαοδικεύς. It is sometimes assumed that Perses was a slave, belonging to one Themison of Laodicea, that he was of Iranian origin and had been given the slave ethnonym Perses in consequence.[53] A more straightforward interpretation, however, might be simply to regard the epitaph as being to one Perses son of Themison of Laodicea. The name Perses is a perfectly respectable Greek name and there need be no Iranian connection whatsoever.

A number of other Laodicean citizens with Iranian personal names are attested in later inscriptions.[54] A list of singers from Laodicea for 150 CE, in an unedited inscription of Claros, includes one Arsakes son of Athenodorus.[55] The survival of this Iranian name in a family settled in the area some six hundred years earlier is obviously possible, but there are alternative explanations. Arsakes is one of the Iranian names preserved in Lycian inscriptions, with three occurrences in Lycia, and a fourth example from north Pisidia. It is possible that the single example of Arsakes from Laodicea had spread from Lycia in post-Achaemenid times through intermarriage. The original reason for the name being adopted was that it is a name with royal associations — the throne name of the Parthian kings being Arsakes.

A late Hellenistic list of names, of uncertain purpose, from Laodicea includes one Mithres son of Mithres.[56] As has been noted before, the popularity and

---

52 Robert, "Inscriptions", 334 n3.
53 Compare Baslez, 147 n83.
54 Robert, "Inscriptions", 333–34.
55 *Ibid*, 333.
56 *Ibid*, 334 no 3, l.3.

ubiquity of this Greek diminutive form of Mithridates prevents its use as a certain indicator of Achaemenid survivals.

To this list should be added a further name, late Hellenistic and recovered from near Laodicea, that is, Mithraboges/Mithrabogos.[57] Given the late Hellenistic date, and the great rarity of the name, there would seem to be more grounds for suggesting that this name may reflect Persian settlement in the area during the Achaemenid period, than has been the case in most of the examples discussed previously. Having said this however, it does not necessarily follow that the family of Mithraboges is of Iranian ethnic origin. The name could have been adopted by a local family through intermarriage or as a "political" act during the Achaemenid period, and retained in the family naming-system into the Hellenistic period. Even so, granted the possibility that an Iranian family could have established itself in the area in the Hellenistic period, this inscription could well point to the presence of a Persian family using the name Mithraboges in the Colossae district during the Achaemenid period.

Therefore there seems to be a considerable concentration of Iranian names in the area of Laodicea on Lycus. Furthermore many of these names are not ones of the common sort, such as Mithridates or Mithres, which were popular in the Hellenistic and Imperial periods, and which seem to have been widely adopted by persons with no Iranian connections. However it is very difficult to decide whether these Iranian names arrived in the area thanks to Achaemenid settlement around Colossae, or thanks to Seleucid settlement associated with Laodicea. In no single case can any firm connection be made with any Laodicean family using an Iranian name and any Iranian present in the west during the Seleucid hegemony. Nevertheless, the suspicion remains that a number of these Iranian names may have been brought to the area by the foundation of Laodicea on Lycus.

The Name Oumanios

An inscription from Aphrodisias referring to events of 39 or 38 BCE mentions one Pythes son of Oumanios, who was almost certainly an inhabitant of Laodicea, though Robert thought he might have moved there from Aphrodisias.[58] Robert demonstrates that the name Oumanios is Iranian, and is the same as that lying behind the name Omanes[59] occurring in an inscription of Smyrna (OGIS 229, ll. 104–5). This inscription dates to the mid third-century, probably to

---

57 H. Malay/R. Schmitt, "An Inscription recording a new Persian name: Mithrabogesor Mithrabogos", *EA* 5 (1985) 27–29.

58 Robert, "Documents d'Asie Mineure", 506–8.

59 On which see R. Schmitt, "Einige iranische Namen auf Inschriften oder Papyri", *ZPE* 17 (1975) 15–24, on pp. 23–24.

the early years of the reign of Seleucus Kallinikos (246–222 BCE), though its precise date is uncertain. It records certain privileges, including *politeia*, awarded to "Omanes and to the Persians placed under his orders". Omanes seems to be the Iranian commander of a body of troops in the Seleucid army, which had presumably been raised in the east of the empire, and were now stationed in the vicinity of Smyrna. It is possible that Omanes and his men remained in the west after completion of their service, and were settled there as Seleucid colonists. It is highly unlikely, as is frequently suggested, that the troops of Omanes were raised from Persian colonists in Lydia. It would be tempting to suggest a family connection between this individual and the Oumanios of the Aphrodisias inscription, and to suggest that this particular name was brought to the west during the Hellenistic period. It is rather unlikely, however, that the name, though the same in its Iranian form, would be used with such variation in the Greek if it was being used within a single family, and yet, Greek inscriptions record a range of variations on a root name; see, for example, *MAMA* VI.46 with Buckler and Calder's reconstruction of the brothers Apollonios and Apollonides. Further, and more importantly, the same root name also occurs, this time in the form Omaneas, in a table of expenses of the Delian *hieropoioi* (*IG* xi.2.287 A ll.78–9) for 251 BCE, telling us that one Omaneas and those under him were paid 17 drachmas and 3 obols for cleaning the Nymphaion. The Delian Omaneas is obviously a person of low social status, and can have no connection with either Omanes or Oumanios, unless the name had been adopted by Omaneas on account of its noble associations. Thus doubt is cast on the reliability of connecting names in this way.

There remains, obviously, the possibility that the name Oumanios came to the west during the Achaemenid period. At least the relatively early date of this inscription restricts the possibilities to the Achaemenid or Hellenistic periods. Again the purpose of this discussion has not been to attempt to prove any family or other connections for the Seleucid period, but simply to demonstrate, for Laodicea on Lycus at least, that such suggestions can be advanced as easily for the Seleucid period as for the Achaemenid.

Aphrodisias

Some distance to the south-west of Colossae lies the site of the later city of Aphrodisias, which has furnished a further two Iranian names.[60] One inscription, which is probably anterior to the imperial period, mentions Aba, the daughter of Artapates, wife of Athenagoras, son of Menedotos. A second, of imperial date, mentions one Mithridates, son of Athenagoras, a *kalos kagathos*. Both individuals presumably belong to the same family.

---

60 Robert, "Documents d'Asie Mineure", 505–9.

The naming-practices of this last family are of great interest. Aba, which might be thought of as a Semitic name at first glance, is, in fact, Anatolian. The name Aba, or Abba, with a masculine form Abbas, is certainly an indigenous one, as has been pointed out by Robert, who collects the Anatolian evidence.[61] Robert lists one example at Stratonikeia in Caria, two from Pisidia, one example of Abba from an indeterminate location, but with a father called Mogetasis, a name common in Lydia and the Kibyratis. Further examples are listed by Zgusta, who includes an example of Aba from Lycia.[62] These names would seem to be connected with the Carian place-name Aba, mentioned by Stephanus Byzantinus (sv. Ἄβαι ... Ἄβα πόλις Καρίας).[63] Thus names of this group seem to be concentrated in south-western Anatolia, in the general area of ancient Caria and Lydia. The most distinguished bearer of the name was one Aba daughter of the Carian dynast Hyssaldomos, father of Hekatomnos. Hornblower has rightly pointed out that she may have been only a half-sister to Hekatomnos, rather than full-sister.[64]

Furthermore, we can perhaps connect the wife of the Athenagoras of the first inscription, the daughter of one Artapates, either with the family using the name Artapates at Tabai, or with one of the noble families using this name in Lycia.

The Tabai Region

Another group of Persian name forms comes from the south-east of Caria, towards the borders of Greater Phrygia and Lycia. The Tabai region alone has furnished a considerable number of Persian names; Artapates, Mithres and Mithridates at Tabai itself, Artabazos and Mithres at Herakleia Salbake, and Artabazos and Mithres at Sebastopolis.[65] There could be some connection between the repetition of the names Artabazes and Mithres at both Herakleia and Sebastopolis.

It was the view of Louis Robert that the Tabai district had been settled by Iranians during the Achaemenid period, and this may well be the case. Perhaps, though, it might be better to regard the Tabai region as dependent on Colossae, which lay within easy travelling distance some 20–30 kilometres to the northeast. In the Achaemenid period, therefore, the Tabai region may have lain within Greater Phrygia rather than Caria.

---

61 Robert, *Noms indigènes*, 504–8.

62 L. Zgusta, *Kleinasiatische Personennamen* (Prague: Tsche. Akad. Wissenschaft, 1964), 43–4.

63 Compare K. Buresch, *Aus Lydien: epigrafisch-geografische Reisefrüchte* O. Ribbeck (ed.) (Leipzig: Teubner, 1878), 123.

64 Hornblower, 36 n8, *cf* 149 n161.

65 J. Robert/L. Robert, *La Carie* II (Paris: Adrien-Maisonneuve, 1954), 79; Robert, "Malédictions funèraires", 285; Robert, *Études anatoliennes* (Paris: de Boccard, 1937), 353–4; "Inscriptions", 334 n1.

Hellenistic Colossae

There is no evidence for the preservation of Iranian personal names in the on-omasticon of later Colossae itself, and indeed even general information about the city is very limited. Pliny (*Nat.* 5.41.145) recites a list of most famous (*cele-berrima*) Phrygian towns, which includes Colossae, with no further informa-tion. The fact that the list also includes Kelainai instead of Apameia, led Magie to suggest that this list was compiled from an old source.[66] It is perhaps signif-icant that elsewhere in the same book (5.105–6) when Pliny lists the *conventi* (juridical centres) of Phrygia and the *civitates* belonging to them, Apameia/Kel-ainai is mentioned as a *conventus*, and he then names six peoples belonging to it, and nine remaining tribes of no note: Colossae is not mentioned. Strabo (12.8.13) lists Colossae in a lacunose passage, which first mentions that Apameia and Laodicea are the largest Phrygian cities, and in their neighbourhood are situated towns (πολίσματα and then, after the *lacuna*, goes on to list Aphrodisias, Colos-sae, Themisonium, Saunaus, Metropolis and Apollonias. As Magie has pointed out,[67] it is inaccurate to infer from this that Colossae was a πόλισμα, as the inter-vening lacuna makes this uncertain. Also, the other cities in the list were by no means negligible, and so any inference that Colossae "had greatly diminished in size and importance" is unwarranted. In fact, Strabo (*Geogr.* 12.8.16) mentions that the countryside around Laodicea produces sheep which are famous for pro-ducing wool, which is superior to Milesian in its softness, but also from its black-ness, and that the Κολοσσηνοί derive a splendid revenue from the wool which they produce as neighbours of the Laodikeians. Pliny (*Nat.* 21.27.51) elsewhere refers to the colour of this wool as *colossinus*. So we may infer that in the Augus-tan period when Strabo was writing the city was prosperous.

Colossae definitely retained the status of an independent *polis* throughout the Hellenistic period. This is clear from inscriptions listing the ethnic. An ep-itaph from Smyrna (*IK* 23.440) was dedicated to the memory of Diodotos "a Kolossean" (Κολοσηνός), a student (φιλόλογος) who had died there. Smyrna not Ephesus is the provenance of the Diodotos inscription. The ethnic is also at-tested to a woman named Arphias from a village near Balboura (*CIG* 3.4380k[3]). The normal array of city officials we would expect of a thriving Phrygian city of Greek culture are attested in the Imperial inscriptions. The citizen body of the city was the *demos* itself, which elected a council (*boulē*) (*MAMA* VI.39). Other inscriptions mention a *boularchos* (*IGR* IV.870). Other liturgical offices attested in the epigraphic record include that of ἀγονοθέτης διὰ βίου (*MAMA* VI.40).

It would be more accurate to take the view that during the Hellenistic pe-riod the south-western border region of Greater Phrygia experienced a period of

---

66 Magie, 2.986 n22.
67 *Ibid.*

urbanization and growth in trade which enabled the area to support many more cities than the original two, Kelainai and Colossae, which we find in the region during the Achaemenid period. The major new city was Laodicea "on the Lycus", evidently founded by Antiochus II and named after his wife Laodike before their divorce in 253 BCE.[68] This city lay very close to Colossae. Indeed Colossae seems to have suffered something of an eclipse as a city in the Hellenistic period, thanks to the establishment of a number of royal and other foundations in the area.

Conclusion

Before their inclusion in the territories under the control of Rome, changes in the patterns of land ownership in the "south-western border lands of Greater Phrygia" can be detected in the (fragmentary) historical record. The first preserved historian to deal with the local situation was Herodotos. We can deduce from his writings that a large proportion of the most valuable land was in the possession of the kings of Lydia. Before that time, they could have passed into royal ownership upon the fall of the Phrygian kingdom, but certainty escapes us. It seems that these estates remained under the control of the Mermand Dynasty, the last ruling monarch of which was Croesus, down to the time of the second Persian invasion of Greece. It was as a result of the fall from favour of Pythes, that these lands fell out of Lydian control, at first passing into the ownership of the Persian king Xerxes. It seems that these lands in turn were given to individuals favoured by the Persian monarch. One of them may have been his illegitimate son Tithraustes, who founded a dynasty which controlled lands in the local area for several generations. Other important individuals who probably received lands in this way, were the predecessors of families who later used the names Ariaios and Artabazos. It seems that the majority of Persian land-holders lost their estates during the Macedonian, but one exception to this was possibly the family of Aribazos, and another may have been the family of Mardonios. These cases, it seems, would be very much the exception rather than the rule. All this time Colossae functioned as an important city of the region, second only to Kelainai. With the coming of the Hellenistic period, however, numerous royal foundations partially eclipsed its importance. It nevertheless remained an important and autonomous city, with its own ethnic.

---

68 Magie, 2.986 n23.

Map of places mentioned in the chapter

© by Dorota Sakowicz

Bibliography

Austen, M. M., *The Hellenistic World from Alexander to the Roman Conquest: A Selection of Ancient Sources in translation* (Cambridge: Cambridge University Press, 1981).

Bagnall, R. S./P. Derow, *Greek Historical Documents: The Hellenistic Period* (Chico: Scholars Press, 1981).

Balcer, J. M., *Sparda by the Bitter Sea: Imperial Interaction in Western Anatolia* (Chico: Scholars Press, 1984).

Baslez, M-F. "Présence et traditions iraniennes dans les cites de l'Egée", *REA* 87 (1985) 137–55.

Belke, K./N. Mersich, *Tabula Imperii Byzantini Bd 7: Phrygien und Pisidien* (Vienna: Österreichische Akademie der Wissenschaft, 1990).

Benveniste, E., *Titres et noms propres en iranien ancien* (Paris: Librairie C. Klincksieck, 1966).

Bevan, E. R., *The House of Seleucus* (2 vol.; London: Edward Arnold, 1902).

Billows, R. A., *Antigonos the One-Eyed and the Creation of the Hellenistic State* (Berkeley/Los Angeles/London: University of California Press, 1990).

Briant, P., *Antigone le Borgne: Les débuts de sa Carrière et les problèmes de l'assembleè macedonienne* (Paris: Les Belles Lettres, 1973).

– *Rois, tributs et paysans: études sur les formations tributaires du Moyen-Orient ancien* (Paris: Presses Universitaire Franche-Comté, 1982).

– "Les iraniens d'Asie Mineure après la chute de l'Empire achemenide", *DHA* 11 (1985) 167–95.

Buresch, K., *Aus Lydien: epigrafisch-geografische Reisefrüchte* O. Ribbeck (ed.) (Leipzig: Teubner, 1878).

Capdetrey, L., *Le pouvoir seleucide. Territoirs, adminstration, finances d'un royaume hellénistique (312–129 avant J-C.)* (Rennes: Presses Universitaires de Rennes, 2007).

Dindorf, W., *Demosthenes VIII. Scholia Graeca ex Codicibus aucta et Emendata* (Oxford: E Typographeo Academico, 1851).

Gow, A. S. F./D. L. Page, *The Greek Anthology: Hellenistic Epigrams* (2 vol.; Cambridge: Cambridge University Press, 1965).

Grene, D. (trans.), *The History of Herodotus* (Chicago, London: University of Chicago Press, 1987).

Ehrhardt, N., "Die Ionier und ihr Verhätnis zu den Phrygern und Lydern", in E. Schwertheim/E. Winter (ed.), *Neue Forschungen zu Ionien* (Asia Minor Studien 53; Bonn: Habelt, 2005) 93–111.

Grainger, J. D., *A Seleukid Prosopography and Gazetteer* (Leiden: Brill, 1997).

Hinz, W., *Altiranisches Sprachgut der Nebenuberlieferungen* (Wiesbaden: Harrassowitz, 1975).

Hornblower, S., *Mausolus* (Oxford: Clarendon, 1982).

Judeich, W., "Ariaios (2)" *RE* 2,1, (1895) 811.

– "Politische Namengebung in Athen", in M. San Nicolò (ed.), *ETITYMBION Heinrich Swoboda dargebracht* (Reichenburg: 1927) 99–106.

Justi, F., *Iranisches Namenbuch* (Marburg: N. G. Elwert'sche Verlagsbuchhandlung, 1895).

Kawerau, G./A. Rehm, *Das Delphinion in Milet* (Th. Wiegand, Milet I, Heft III; Berlin: Georg Reimer, 1914).

Launey, M., *Recherches sur les armées hellénistiques* (2 vol.; Paris: de Boccard, 1949).

Ma, J., *Antiochus III and the Cities of Western Asia Minor* (Oxford: Oxford University Press, 1999).

Magie, D., *Roman Rule in Asia Minor to the End of the Third Century after Christ* (2 vol.; Princeton: Princeton University Press, 1950).

Malay, H./R. Schmitt, "An Inscription recording a new Persian name: Mithraboges or Mithrabogos", *EA* 5 (1985) 27–29.

Minns, E. H., *Scythians and Greeks in South Russia* (Cambridge: Cambridge University Press, 1915).

Müller, D., *Topographische Bildkommentar zu den Historien Herodots. Kleinasien* (Tübingen: E. Wasmuth, 1997).

Olmstead, A. T., *History of the Persian Empire* (Chicago/London: University of Chicago Press, 1948).

Pape, W./G. E. Benseler, *Wörterbuch der griechischen Eigennamen* (Braunschweig: F. Vieweg), 1862–70.

Paris, P. "Inscriptions de Sebaste", *BCH* 7 (1883) 448–57.

Ramsay, W. M., *The Cities and Bishoprics of Phrygia* (2 vol.; Oxford: Clarendon Press, 1897).

Robert, L., *Études anatoliennes* (Paris: de Boccard, 1937).

– *Hellenica VI* (Paris: Adrien-Maisonneuve, 1948).

– *Noms indigènes dans l'Asie mineure gréco-romaine* (Paris: Maisonneuve, 1963).

– "Inscriptions", in J. des Gagniers/P. Devambez/L. Kahl/R. Ginouves, *Laodicée du Lycos: Le Nymphée. Campagnes 1961–63* (Quebec: L'Université Laval, 1969) 247–389.

– "Malédictions funéraires grecques III. – Une Malédiction funéraire dans la Plaine de Karayük", *CRAI* (1978) 277–86.

– "Documents d'Asie Mineure XXIII–XXVIII", *BCH* 107 (1983) 497–599.

Robert, J./L. Robert, *La Carie II* (Paris: Adrien-Maisonneuve, 1954).

– *Fouilles d'Amyzon en Carie, I: Exploration, histoire, monnaies et inscriptions* (Paris: de Boccard, 1983).

Savalli-Lestrade, I., *Les Philoi royaux dans l'Asie hellénistiques* (Geneva: Droz, 1998).

Schmitt, R., "Einige iranische Namen auf Inschriften oder Papyri", *ZPE* 17 (1975) 15–24.

– *Die iranier-Namen bei Aischylos* (Vienna: Österreichische Akademie der Wissenschaften), 1978.

Sekunda, N. V., "Achaemenid Colonization in Lydia", *REA* 87 (1985) 7–30.

– "Persian Settlement in Hellespontine Phrygia", in A. Kuhrt/H. Sancisi-Weerdenburg (ed.), *Achaemenid History III: Method and Theory. Proceedings of the Fifth Achaemenid History Workshop* (Leiden: Nederlands Instituut voor het Nabije Oosten, 1988) 175–96.

– "Achaemenid Settlement in Caria, Lycia and Greater Phrygia", in H. Sancisi-Weerdenburg/A. Kuhrt (ed.), *Achaemenid History VI: Asia Minor and Egypt: Old Cultures in a New Empire* (Leiden: Nederlands Instituut voor het Nabije Oosten, 1991), 83–143.

– "Arianos (Polyb. 8.16–20): an Iranian or Cretan Mercenary at Sardeis in 214 BC?", *Electrum* 10 (2005) 53–58.

– "The Aribazoi: A Family in Seleucid Service", in E. Dąbrowa/M. Dzielska/M. Salamon/S. Sprawski (ed.), *Donum Centenarium. Księga pamiątkowa ku czci profesora*

Józefa Wolskiego w setną rocznicę urodzin (Kraków: Towarzystwo Wydawnicze "Historia Iagiellonica", 2010) 219–227.

Stonecipher, A. H. M., *Graeco-Persian Names* (NY: American Book Co, 1918).

Summerer, L., "Picturing Persian Victory: The Painted Battle Scene on the Munich Wood", in A. Ivantchik/V. Licheli (ed.), *Achaemenid Culture and Local Traditions in Anatolia, Southern Caucasus and Iran. New Discoveries* (Leiden/Boston: Brill, 2007) 3–30.

– "From Tatarlı to Munich: The Recovery of a Painted Wooden Tomb Chamber in Phrygia", in İ. Delemen (ed.), *The Achaemenid Impact on Local Populations and Cultures in Anatolia (Sixth-Fourth Centuries B. C.)* (Istanbul: Türk Eskicag Bilimleri Enstitusu Yayinlari, 2007) 131–58.

Walbank, F. W., *An Historical Commentary on Polybius Vol ii* (Oxford: Oxford University Press, 1967).

Zgusta, L., *Kleinasiatische Personennamen* (Prague: Tschechische Akadademie der Wissenschaften, 1964).

Chapter 3

The Languages of the Lycus Valley

Rick Strelan

This essay aims to reconstruct, with the aid of some speculation, the language world of the Lycus Valley in the period of the first century of Christian presence there. I include "some speculation" because I am very conscious of the scarcity of hard evidence available for such a reconstruction and of the methodological issues that flow from building with a scarcity of data. To plunge *in medias res* with one question: if on a tomb in Colossae I read a Greek epitaph, how would I know if the deceased spoke Greek or not? Could I confidently conclude that the living, who obviously had the inscription done, *spoke* Greek? And if they did, does a funerary inscription tell me the extent of their Greek usage? And in any case, just what does "Greek" mean, given that there were more than twenty dialects of that language, and that, in addition, there were various localized forms of Greek such as "Phrygian Greek"? And can I tell anything at all from the surviving inscriptions about how the Greek was pronounced, or whether the Greek was in any way influenced by a vernacular? I also intend to explore whether or not there is any evidence that vernacular languages survived the dominating presence of Greek and Latin. Were the latter "killer languages"? How great, and how rapid, was language death in the face of Hellenization? Is there evidence of language assimilation and of bi- or multi-lingualism in the undoubtedly hellenised Lycus?

I am very conscious that comparisons have an odor that is not always pleasant and that parallelomania is not always a healthy state of mind; but drawing on language survival in Australia raises some relevant questions, at least, for the linguistic climate of the Lycus. In Australia, there are 231 languages spoken today in a population of about 20 million; most Australians would not know that fact, and most could probably not name more than twenty of those languages, even when pushed. Even fewer Australians would know that there are some 25 indigenous/aboriginal languages still being widely spoken and some 100+ others known in written form or still "alive" in the heads of the elderly. Most are also unaware that language death has occurred over the past two hundred years — the death possibly of some 200 aboriginal languages. For all that language death (or murder, *Sprachmord* as the Germans say), the fact is that some indigenous languages still survive despite being non-written languages, despite contact with the dominant English language, despite deliberate politi-

cal policies of language assimilation into the mainstream, despite the lack of ed-
ucational, political and financial support for these languages. I mention this for
no other reason than to make the parallel with the language map of the Imperial period. As will be shown, the language world of Asia Minor was complex
and only basically understood by those who, like Herodotos, Strabo and Pausanias, made any attempt at all to describe it. Most Greeks and Romans of the
literate and educated variety knew very little about the languages of the "barbarian" world around them, and it would appear very few cared to know. But if
there is one thing that is clear even from them it is that their world was bewil-
deringly polyglot.

   If I may push an Australian parallel further: traditionally, Australian abori-
gines, being illiterate, did not mark graves with inscriptions, but in the modern
era it is not unknown that traditional languages are used on gravestones, nearly
always in the form of Scripture verses or Christian hymns. Some inscriptions
are bi-lingual, but the majority is in English, and it is the use of that language
that is often misleading. For example, the famous aboriginal Australian artist, Albert Namatjira, is buried in a grave that has an inscription in English. He
himself was a native Arrente speaker (Arrente existed as a written language by
his death) and his own English was quite "broken". It would be mistaken to conclude that because the dominant colonial language, English, is used on his gravestone, that he himself or his relatives spoke English to any significant degree,
let alone as their dominant language. We actually know that not to be the case
and so we would have to explain the use of English on his gravestone in some
other way.

   To add to the complexity: can we really tell a person's ability to converse
and speak in a language from their ability to write in the language? I can
write in German more fluently than I can speak the language. Many bilin-
guals today are very conscious of their deficiencies when speaking a language
not that of their mothers. It seems to be an ancient phenomenon as well. Cicero suggests that Attic Greeks held other forms of Greek (including his) in
some disdain as being less erudite and a lesser form of language (*ad Attic.*
1.19). Paul could be quite persuasive when he wrote in Greek, but there is a
hint that his spoken Greek was nowhere near as convincing, at least to the
Greek-speakers of Corinth (2 Cor 10:10). Josephus wrote/translated his writings into Greek but was self-conscious of his accent when speaking the language
(*Ant.* 20.263; *Vita* 40). The Greek of the New Testament writers is commonly
criticized for its "Semitisms", and Revelation is almost ridiculed for its "bad"
Greek. This is not a modern criticism. Many Church fathers were sensitive to
criticisms of the quality of the Greek of their authoritative Scriptures. It clearly
was not the Greek of the educated – was it a form of Greek that second-lan-
guage users could understand? Were many of the addressees literate only in
"biblical Greek"?

My point is quite simple even if the substance is very complex: because Greek is found on so many inscriptions, funerary and otherwise, in the Lycus and elsewhere, it is not sufficient evidence that it was the dominant language of those honored or of those who paid for the stones and their inscriptions.

Inscriptions as Language Evidence

Our evidence for language usage in the Hellenistic world is dependent on two sources: inscriptions, and observations and comments in literature. I will discuss the latter shortly. As for the inscriptional evidence, this is believed in some quarters to present the "facts" of the matter in a way that the literature does not and possibly cannot. Inscriptions are seen to offer the "raw stuff" of history. But do they? On what grounds do they offer better data than the historians and geographers of the day? Do inscriptions really present unproblematic, objective data?

It is very common to reach certain conclusions about language usage on the basis of the evidence of the inscriptions. For example, van der Horst argues that because, of the 1600 known Jewish funerary inscriptions collected from the Roman world between 300BCE and 500CE, 70% are in Greek, 12% in Latin and 18% in Hebrew, this is evidence that Jews spoke Greek; and because 40% of the first century inscriptions in Palestine are in Greek, this is evidence that Jews in that region at that time were Hellenized.[1] But is this evidence of the people's (living or dead) spoken ability in Greek? Can it really be used to conclude that Greek was used in other contexts beside that of remembering the dead? Is it really any different from deciding the language of choice of Namatjira and his relatives because his epitaph is in English?

The choice of language and the stylized conventional form of so many inscriptions make implicit statements that belie their apparent agenda-less words. In many funerary and honorific inscriptions the form is so conventional that the only distinctive feature in many of them is the name! In any case, like all texts, they provide a dialogue; they are "saying something" via the medium of the words and the style. The style and the choice of language (Greek, for example) indicated the language of status and power, of kinship and family, of gender and class, of memory and of desire. Inscriptions are meant for the living and for future generations. They are part of constructing memory, part of the desire strong in the Graeco-Roman world to be remembered, and to be remembered with honour. Three things might be noted: first, the relation between memory and reality is not always as close as it might appear; secondly, from a language-selection point of view, if one wanted to be remembered, then writ-

---

1 P. van der Horst, "Jewish Funerary Inscriptions—Most Are in Greek", *BARev* 18 (1992) 46–57.

ing would be a significant factor. And obviously, language choice was limited to those languages that had a script and an alphabet; it was also determined to some significant degree by recognizing the language of the future, the target and dominant language of the day. Greek satisfied all of these conditions in much the same way as English satisfied the conditions and expectations of those who wanted Albert Namatjira to be remembered. My third observation is that people in the Lycus Valley had language choice in some, maybe even in most, language contexts. They could choose what language to use in whatever context. It is clear that Greek was the dominant language *in certain linguistic domains or contexts*. It would appear that in the Lycus, as elsewhere, the language of memorial was Greek, and the language of status and honor was Greek. But there is clear evidence that in other contexts, another language might have been used. For example, Latin military inscriptions have been found in Laodicea and Apameia, suggesting that Latin was the selected language especially in the context of announcing or acknowledging military honors. It was also the language used for road mileage markers and in legal dealings. In other contexts, especially those of a less formal nature, I suggest another, different, language was a viable option.

Along with language selection on the basis of social context, there is the matter of finances. There is some discussion, even debate, as to whether inscriptions of any kind were limited to those who could afford to have them produced. It might appear obvious, but it is worth noting that inscriptions *did* cost and so did the material on which they were made – stone, and in many cases marble. It is true that in the case of some rural areas of Anatolia, access to waste marble was reasonably easy and therefore more affordable (in contrast to places like Rome);[2] but even then those who would claim that inscriptions were limited to those who could afford it, have a valid argument. John Durand claimed that "The poor could not afford inscribed stones. The illiterate peasantry would have been the last to be honored by inscriptions".[3] And Steven Friesen reminds us that only about 1–3% of the population of the empire could be classified as rich and that the vast majority of early Christians were poor – that is, living near, at or below subsistence levels.[4] It is worth stressing that epitaphs and tombs and memorials were all part of giving honor; those whose lives were not deemed honorable therefore did not receive such marks of remembrance. It is true on the other hand that many people belonged to *collegia* or guilds whose duty it was to provide the

---

2 T. Drew-Bear/C. Thomas/M. Yoeldoesteran, *Phrygian Votive Steles* (Turkey: Museum of Anatolian Civilizations, 1999), 13.

3 J. Durand, "Mortality Estimates from Roman Tombstone Inscriptions", *AJS* 65 (1960) 365–73, on p. 366.

4 S. Friesen, "Prospects for a Demography of the Pauline Mission: Corinth among the Churches", in S. J. Friesen/D. Schowalter (ed.), *Urban Religion and Roman Corinth: Interdisciplinary Approaches* (Cambridge, Mass: Harvard University Press, 2005) 351–70.

necessary funds for a burial – so even the very poor could assume a burial that provided them with a smooth transition into the underworld. If *collegia* were responsible for burials, then they presumably were also responsible for any inscription and for the language of that inscription. That also assumes, of course, that the majority of people *had* some inscription to mark their burial place. The majority of the poor were simply buried with little to identify them apart from, at best, a marker or stele indicating the presence of a grave. Many *stelae* were made of wood which of course deteriorated relatively quickly. It is also quite understandable that an archaeologist is going to be more excited about a tomb or *stele* with inscriptions containing some detail than ones that were plain, unadorned, or simply markers identifying the dead. The fact is that many died unmarked and so unremembered. Are there funerary inscriptions for the 1100 buried in the cemetery of Qumran, for example? Most Jewish funerary inscriptions have been found on ossuaries and they in turn have been found in fairly large family "plots" and these all suggest wealth. The discovery in Rome in the 19th century of 75 mass burial pits just outside and north of the Esquiline Gate is further evidence that many were buried with very little honor and with no identification. These pits contained between 500–800 bodies in each, and they clearly are the burial sites of the poor and indigent.[5] Horace knew of the potter's field in which bodies were unceremoniously dumped (*Sat.* 8.8.1–16); Rome issued laws about the dumping of corpses in the streets.[6] This is all a reminder that grave inscriptions do not tell the full story!

There are those who reject the argument that only the elite and wealthy could afford grave inscriptions on the grounds of the inscriptional evidence itself. Kaimio, for example, thinks "in many cases it seems as if the lower social classes were particularly eager to leave a lasting linguistic monument of themselves, usually an epitaph".[7] If he is right, then the matter of the language of the deceased and/or of the living is clouded even more. Funerary inscriptions were closely related in style and genre to other honorific inscriptions because that is precisely what they were – indicators of lasting honor to the deceased. It is quite possible that it was a bestowal of an honor that might not have been given in the deceased's life-time! The language – and the material on which the language appeared – naturally fitted the honor, prestige, status and memory they were meant to convey. Greek words inscribed on stones, preferably marble, was the way to go! How indicative these were of the deceased's actual language proficiency (or that of the commemorators) is quite another question.

---

5 J. Bodel, "Dealing With the Dead: Undertakers, Executioners, and Potter's Fields in Ancient Rome", in E. Marshall/V. Hope (ed.), *Death and Disease in the Ancient City* (London/New York: Routledge, 2000) 128–50, on p. 131.

6 D. Kyle, *Spectacles of Death in Ancient Rome* (London: Routledge, 2001), 162–70.

7 J. Kaimio, *The Romans and the Greek Language* (Helsinki: Societas Scientiarum Fennica, 1979), 19.

Before leaving the evidence of the inscriptions, one other factor is of some significance and that is the role of the carver or inscriber. After all, the actual words that appear, their form and their style, in the end also reflect the language ability of the inscriber. The inscription process theoretically required three people: a *scriptor* to write a draft to the customer's specifications; an *ordinator* to draw the guidelines and capital letters on the stone; and a *sculptor* to do the actual chiseling. No doubt, in poorer workshops (such as one might find in the country) these jobs may have been combined, and it might well have happened that the actual cutter wrote on the basis of what he heard rather than what he saw. In any case, he would spell either by convention or according to his own hearing or reading of the words given to him to inscribe. In the matter of spelling especially, the influence of the inscriber's own first language might be expected to appear. Many modern geneaologists, professional and amateur, will be familiar with scribes of earlier times writing down unfamiliar (often foreign) names, for example, according to patterns of sounds that they were familiar with. The issue of the literacy and illiteracy levels of stone-cutters is very complex and it includes judgments such as whether the spelling (for example) is "wrong" or whether so-called "mistakes" reflect peculiar first-language patterns, pronunciation and so on.[8] Signs of illiteracy or incompetency in a language might include inconsistency of spelling, a change in vowels (although often that probably reflects pronunciation issues), mal-formation of letters or the inclusion of "foreign" letters. Some of these will be mentioned again below when looking at Phrygian inscriptions particularly.

The Language World according to the ancient writers

Price believes the weight given to inscriptional evidence is a distortion:

In particular, the nature of the sources for the imperial period has led some scholars to over-emphasize the prevalence of Greek language and culture. This simple picture of pervasive Hellenism is too dependent on the testimony of Greek inscriptions and neglects the dynamics of Greek culture.[9]

To repeat the obvious: if the only evidence of language usage available to us was that from inscriptions, then we would probably have to conclude that the Lycus and the whole Roman empire was dominated by Greek and Latin, no matter what the language context. At the very most, we would have to construct a bi-lingual

---

8 See L. Curchin, "Literacy in the Roman Provinces: Qualitative and Quantitative Data from Central Spain", *AJP* 116 (1995) 461–476; Drew-Bear, *Phrygian Votive Steles*, 44.

9 S. Price, *Rituals and Power: The Roman imperial cult in Asia Minor* (New York: Cambridge University Press, 1984), 91.

world. On the other hand, even the inscriptions themselves on closer examination reveal the influence, even if only to a small degree, of living, local languages.

But inscriptions are not the only evidence we have; there is the evidence of the literature.

This evidence is almost totally restricted to Greek and Latin authors (Herodotos, Cicero, Strabo, Ovid, Pliny, Pausanias for example). They were not linguists or writing language histories; and most of them clearly have a cultural perspective on language that is problematic. The New Testament also occasionally shows glimpses of a multi-lingual world. According to Acts 2, over a dozen living language groups were represented at the Pentecost festival in Jerusalem, including that of Phrygian Jews. I suggest that this episode indicates language groups that Luke knew had heard the Gospel – and by possible implication continued to hear it – in their own languages. Phrygian Jews most likely came from or had a deal of contact with the Lycus Valley. The surface reading of Acts 2 suggests Phrygian Jews spoke an ἴδιος διάλεκτος (2:8–10). In addition, Luke is aware of the use of a Lycaonian language in the Roman colonized Lystra (Acts 14:11). In this incident, it is possible that language selection is in play. The locals believe the gods have come into their presence, and so they choose to speak the language they used in cultic contexts, and that was a traditional and possibly aboriginal language rather than the modern, contemporary language of Greek. When Paul was shipwrecked on Melite, the "barbarians" (οἱ βάρβαροι) showed him kindness; presumably, they did not use Greek as their first language (Acts 28: 2, 4). The polyglot nature of the world is also known to the visionary of Revelation (10:11; 17:15).

The New Testament simply reflects its near-contemporary literature in depicting the Graeco-Roman world as multilingual. Cicero says,

Few of our people know Greek and few likewise are the Greeks who know Latin. Thus we are deaf to their language and they to ours. Similarly, we are all deaf to those languages – and they are innumerable [quae sunt innumerabilis] – which we do not understand (Tusc. 5.116).

Over two hundred years later, little had changed. Sextus Empiricus, who lived in Alexandria and in Athens, wrote: "All men do not understand the speech of all – Greeks that of barbarians and barbarians that of Greeks, or Greeks that of Greeks or barbarians that of barbarians" (Math. 1.37). Even dialectical differences were numerous: "Both the Dorian and the Attic dialects are numerous" (1.89) with variations in pitch and tone.

Diodorus Siculus (1st BCE) speaks of the "present existence of every conceivable kind of language" (1.8.4), and Pliny the Elder speaks of "a small matter to tell of but one of measureless extent if pondered on, is the number of national languages and dialects and varieties of speech" (Nat. 7.1.7). Mithridates was said to have learned 20–25 of the languages of Asia Minor so that he could speak to his subjects without an interpreter (Valerius Maximus 8.7.16). This might exaggerate his linguistic skills, but it probably reflects with at least a modicum of accuracy the number of languages in the region.

Strabo is also aware of the hundreds and hundreds of spoken languages. Around the Black Sea and northern parts of Asia Minor among the Caucasii alone he claims there were over seventy languages spoken (*Geogr.* 11.4.6). Strabo also implies he himself knew of Phrygian language survival especially in a cultic context. He notes that some Athenians in the time of Demosthenes used the language of the Phrygians in a Phrygian ritual: "*êvoe saboe*", and "*hyês attês, attês hyês*", and it appears that Strabo himself knows this language because he adds, "for these words are in the ritual of Sabazius and the Mother" (*Geogr.* 10.3.18). As will be seen, Phrygian was the dominant traditional language of the Lycus.

In recent times, the claim is made that the "evidence relating to bilingualism in antiquity is immense and the subject is underexploited".[10] More frequently, modern commentators are at least acknowledging the multilingual nature of the Empire. Kaimio writes conservatively:

We must assume that most language communities of the Roman Empire were diglot or even polyglot and quite a few of their members in one way or another bilingual or multilingual. Even if they were unilingual, they had a certain language choice: for the purposes of communication, they could use the only language they knew, they could refer to an interpreter, or they could choose to say nothing. But for the others, there was a real choice between languages …[11]

A further significant factor is the argument of Price that there was a marked distinction between cities and rural life in relation to Hellenism in general and to the imperial cult in particular. He claims that the cults of the rural, non-Greek gods remained strong and virtually unaffected by Hellenism.[12] The survival of the traditional cults in Phrygia was highlighted earlier by scholars like Ramsay who saw their survival as an explanation for the use of a Phrygian language in some tombstone inscriptions:

Moritz Schmidt rightly recognised in some barbarous formulas appended to Greek sepulchral inscriptions of the Roman period, a curse in the native tongue against violators of the tomb. Why should this one part of the inscription be in the native tongue, and the rest in Greek? Either the belief was that the old Phrygian tongue was more holy, and more efficacious with the gods of Phrygia, or the fact was that the Phrygian

---

10 J.N. Adams/S. Swain, "Introduction", in J.N. Adams/M. Janse/S. Swain (ed.), *Bilingualism in Ancient Society: Language Contact and the Written Text* (Oxford: Oxford University Press, 2002) 1–22, on p. 1.

11 Kaimio, 14.

12 Price, 91–100.

language was more generally intelligible than Greek. Either alternative shows the strength of the old native feeling in the country; in spite of Graeco-Roman dress and foreign language, the Phrygian character is not hidden.[13]

Of course, it might also have been a case of "both ... and" rather than Ramsay's "either... or". In Ramsay's opinion, "Phrygia was the least Hellenised part in all the Province; as a whole, it still spoke the native tongue, and was little affected by Greek manners."[14]

And he insisted,

It is no longer a matter of doubt that the native languages of Phrygia, Pisidia, Lycaonia, Cappodocia, Lycia etc persisted in common use far longer than was believed. It was only in the cities that Greek was much used, while the rustic populations continued to speak their native languages.[15]

This might not surprise when one considers the demography of the Lycus Valley. Most inhabitants lived in small towns (κωμοπόλεις, Strabo *Geogr.* 12.2.6; 12.6.1) and on large estates or in very small rural villages. According to Brixhe, colonial land-owners in Phrygia were rare; and landlords and the local aristocracy were largely absent.[16] For those living in communities at Laodicea, Hierapolis or Colossae, language contact intruded into virtually every aspect of life from the courts to trade to religion to the army. We know from Pliny, Juvenal and Martial that Rome, for example, was filled with the sounds of barbarian voices speaking in their own languages or using a pidgin form of Greek or Latin. Ovid also complains loud and long about the mixing of languages that is so pervasive in Tomis where he was exiled that he is deeply worried about falling into the same language patterns as those he bemoans (*Tristia* 3.14.43–52). Of course on a smaller scale, the same thing would have been the case in the Lycus – people came into contact with other languages in the towns. Laodicea in particular, lying as it did in a knot of significant trade and travel routes, must have heard the languages of many peoples. Colossae further east would understandably have heard more eastern dialects, being more closely linked as it was with places like Apameia and Pisidian Antioch. But the Lycus in general was not a heavily populated, thoroughly urbanized valley, and there were undoubtedly some in the surrounds

---

13 W. M. Ramsay, "Sepulchral customs in Ancient Phrygia", *JHS* 5 (1884) 241–63, on pp. 249–50.

14 Ramsay, *The Letters to the Seven Churches of Asia and Their Place in the Plan of The Apocalypse* (Grand Rapids, Mich.: Kregel, 2003 [1904]), 415.

15 Ramsay, *Historical Commentary on Galatians* (Grand Rapids, Mich.: Kregel, 1997 [1899]), 288.

16 C. Brixhe, "Interactions between Greek and Phrygian under the Roman Empire", in *Bilingualism in Ancient Society* 246–66, on p. 255.

of the valley, especially in the more hilly regions) who had very little language contact with others.

The Phrygians were agriculturalists and viticulturalists as well as being renowned for their horse-breeding, and these industries and others involved them in trade. Traders often followed the route down the Maeander which brought them into regular contact with western Asia Minor towns like Miletus, Ephesus and Smyrna already in the sixth century BCE (Hipponax *fr.* 36). Hipponax makes an interesting observation about their use of a trading language: "And if they catch the Phrygians, who come down to Miletus to put their barley on the market, bargaining in pidgin-lingo, they sell them for slaves" (καὶ τοὺς σολοίκους ἦν λάβωσι περνᾶσιν Φρύγας μὲν ἐς Μίλητον ἀλφιτεύσοντας) (Hipponax *fr.* 27). Ramsay, who had a good sense for social realities in Anatolia, comments:

The Ephesian poet used phrases and terms caught from the lingua franca (σολοίκους Φρύγας) in which business was done, at the markets of Miletus and Ephesus, a mixed "pigeon-Greek" containing Lydian and Greek and Phrygian words mixed probably with some old Anatolian (that ancient language "of the gods" as Homer sometimes called it).[17]

The Lycus, in particular, was known for a variety of qualities and colours of wool, and so the people who produced that wool would want to trade, as would the dyers, the weavers and the rug-makers who manufactured with it. There are Greek inscriptions in Hierapolis and Laodicea, for example, indicating the presence of guilds of wool-workers, weavers and dyers.[18] Coppersmiths and stone-masons were also in guilds there; and the leather-worker referred to in an inscription from Colossae (*MAMA* VI.44) presumably also belonged to an association or guild in that city. Smiths and masons in particular might have been quite itinerant having to look for work where it might be found. The shepherds and the shearers, probably living away from urban settlements most of the time, probably retained their vernacular and knew little Greek because they had little need for it except in trading and business contexts. Even the traders might well have had a limited vocabulary in Greek and were "poor" in their grammar but they knew enough to be understood. Many people in their business dealings knew enough Greek "to get by". Despite the fact that Greek inscriptions have also been found in more remote areas, the old view of Jones that there were "islets of civilization in a barbarian ocean" in my opinion still stands. Jones elaborated:

There seems to have been a sharp cultural cleavage between the upper classes, who had not only received a literary education in Latin and Greek, but probably spoke one or

---

17 Ramsay, *Asianic Elements in Greek Civilisation 1915–1916* (London: Murray, 1927), 144.

18 P. Harland, *Assocations, Synagogues and Congregations: Claiming a Place in Ancient Mediterranean Society* (Minneapolis: Fortress Press, 2003), 207–10.

other of these languages, and the mass of the people, who were not only illiterate, but spoke in a different tongue. It is clear that many of the common people, not only peasants but townspeople, had no knowledge of Greek or Latin.[19]

Within these small *poleis*, it was not uncommon for people to live among people of their own professional, tribal and language background. Paul was typical of such itinerants who found accommodation and employment among residents from their own linguistic and religious background. In this way, he simply followed the common practice noted by Mitchell:

It is perfectly clear that many communities in the Empire contained distinct population groups within them, whose members belonged to separate organisations. This is as true of the Greek East, with its groups of Romans, Jews, Thracians and others who maintained their identity within Greek cities, as it is of the West, where we encounter Roman citizens forming *vici, pagi, conventus* and the like inside native communities.[20]

In the towns of the Lycus there were Jewish communities and Christian communities, many of them with distinct language groupings as well. The reference to "Greek, Jew … barbarian, Scythian" in Col 3:11 might be indicative of these divisions. Trying to determine language usage outside of the towns is almost impossible because the hard data are even less available. It is almost totally limited to inscriptions and the vast majority of them were in Greek (or Latin) for reasons previously mentioned. It is in this regard that we have little alternative but to turn to the references in the literature. Justin, for example, is aware of Christians in rural areas who were "uneducated and barbarous in their speech" (*1 Apology* 60) which almost certainly indicates a distinct lack of proficiency in Greek. He also claims with some hyperbole, "there is not one single race of men, whether barbarians or Greeks, or whatever they may be called, nomads, or vagrants, or herdsmen living in tents, among whom prayers and thanksgiving are not offered through the name of the crucified Jesus" (*Dial.* 117). He suggests that they did so in their own languages. Clement of Alexandria observes that "men confess that prayers uttered in a barbarian tongue are more powerful" (*Strom.* 1.21).

Irenaeus implies that native languages were used to communicate the Gospel tradition orally:

To which course many nations of those barbarians who believe in Christ do assent, having salvation written in their hearts by the Spirit, without paper or ink, and, carefully preserving the ancient tradition, believing in one God … Those who, in the absence of written documents, have believed this faith, are barbarians, so far as regards

---

19 A. H. M. Jones, *The Later Roman Empire* (Oxford: Basil Blackwell 1964), 995.

20 S. Mitchell, "Iconium and Ninica: Two Double Communities in Roman Asia Minor", *Historia: Zeitschrift für Alte Geschichte* 28 (1979) 409–38, on p. 416.

our language ... If any one were to preach to these men the inventions of the heretics, speaking to them in their own language, they would at once stop their ears ...
(*Haer.* 3.4.2–4).

Even centuries later, Chrysostom says of John's Gospel,

Are not these things [Greek philosophies] with good cause extinct, and vanished
utterly? ... But not so the words of him [John] who was ignorant and unlettered; for
Syrians, and Egyptians, and Indians, and Persians, and Ethiopians, and ten thousand
other nations, *translating into their own tongues* the doctrines introduced by him, barbarians though they be, have learned to philosophize (*Hom. Jo.* 2.5).

Theodoret, a fifth century bishop of Cyrrhus, writes similarly,

Every country that is under the sun is full of these words and the Hebrew tongue is
turned not only into the language of the Grecians, but also of the Romans, and Egyptians, and Persians, and Indians, and Armenians, and Scythians, and Sauromatians,
and briefly into all the languages that any nation uses (*Affect.* 5.66).

We know the Lycus was settled by various groups in its long history. Of course,
there were Phrygians, and for a period they dominated the region. The Persians,
Lydians and Attalids also ruled the Lycus, as did eventually the Romans. So,
from the east there were Syrians and Jews, from the west there were Greeks and
Romans, from the closer regions there were Carians and Lydians. There is no
doubt about the cultural and language mix of the valley; nor is there doubt about
the ability of local vernaculars to survive hellenization.

It is something corroborated more recently by the Turkish scholar, Recai
Tekoglu, who says:

The Ionian, Aeolian, Dorian and Pamphylian dialects of ancient Greek have special
forms peculiar to Anatolia. However, it must be stressed that the dialects other than
the Pamphylian one were isolated in Anatolia. For all these three dialects it must be
mentioned that their contacts with the native Anatolian peoples remained very weak.
... When we look at the Ionian and Aeolian dialects, we see that they were surrounded
with crowded and large populations of Sfardia (=Lydia), Caria and Phrygia, and we
infer that these Hellenic dialects did not have any contacts with these bigger civilisations in the "language field". ... There exist languages, whose linguistic beings are
known to us, but which are not represented epigraphically, for example, the Cappadocian and Lycaonian languages. Thus, the condition that a linguistic being be identified
epigraphically does not hold a priority.[21]

Over the years, those who have endeavored to draw the language map of Asia
Minor and elsewhere have come to the same conclusion: Despite the lack of

---

21 Ş. Recai Tekoğlu, "Corpus Project for Inscriptions in the Pamphylian Dialect, and the
Sidetian and Pisidian Languages in the Antalya and Side Museums: 2005", *Anmed* 4 (2006)
75–81, on pp. 77–78.

epigraphic evidence in most cases, a significant number of languages survived the presence of Greek and Latin. In some cases, that survival was the result of languages developing their own alphabets and so their own literature. Holl provided sufficient evidence to suggest that at least the following languages were still living languages well into the Christian era: Cappodocian, Celtic, Isaurian, Lycaonian, Mysian and Phrygian.[22] More recently, Ramsay MacMullen has noted especially the surviving strength of Syriac in a Greek cultured world of the elite.[23] He has argued that Syriac and Coptic and Celtic are examples of languages that had survived in oral forms and then "suddenly" developed written form and provided a literature in imitation of the Greeks and Latins. The Armenian and Georgian translations of Scriptures (and of the Church fathers) by the fifth century might also be added to this list as examples of old languages becoming literary languages. According to Strabo, the Armenians came from Thessaly, Phrygia and Mesopotamia (*Geogr.* 11.4.8). The influence of Phrygian on Armenian is quite likely.

How "koine" was Greek

Deissmann claimed that by the turn of the Era, "men no longer spoke dialects of Greek. The world had become unified and men spoke... a *single* Greek international language, one *common* tongue".[24] This is simply not the case; and Deissmann's distinction between colloquial and literary Greek is far too simplistic. Babel continued well into the Christian era.

It is generally agreed that at no time was there a systematic attempt to enforce Greek (or Latin) on the barbarians or to obliterate their languages. The bottom line is that the majority of people spoke Greek as a second language and used it only in specific linguistic domains. The inscriptional evidence might not suggest this, but the other evidence does. So the domination of Greek, including so-called *koine* Greek, is questionable. For me, even the term *koine* is today problematic. To whom or for whom was it "common"? Was it common in all language contexts? There is more than ample evidence that it was not. Instead, code-switching and dialect-switching probably took place – people could switch between Greek and their own language or even between Greek dialects within the one conversation; and all speakers made language choices dependent on the

---

22 K. Holl, "Das Fortleben der Volkssprachen in Kleinasien in nachchristlicher Zeit", *Hermes* 43 (1908) 240–54.

23 R. MacMullen, "Provincial Languages in the Roman Empire", *The American Journal of Philology* 87 (1966) 1–17.

24 G.A. Deissmann, *Light from the Ancient East Or the New Testament Illustrated by Recently Discovered Texts of the Graeco-Roman World* (Grand Rapids, Mich.: Kregel, 2003 [1908]), 66, italics his.

language domain. Language register is also a factor – people speak a certain kind of language (vocabulary, grammar, tone, volume) to certain people and in certain social contexts. Sextus Empiricus said that orators would simply not speak the way they do in law-court oratory when conversing with their friends – unless they wanted to be laughed at. He also notes that speakers should use a certain register when speaking to slaves (*Math.* 2.58; 1.234–235).

The complexity, variety and fluidity of Greek language usage are used by Tatian at the end of the second century for his own agenda when he says:

> ... the way of speaking among the Dorians is not the same as that of the inhabitants of Attica, nor do the Aeolians speak like the Ionians. And, since such a discrepancy exists where it ought not to be, I am at a loss whom to call a Greek. And, what is strangest of all, you hold in honour expressions not of native growth, and by the intermixture of barbaric words (βαρβαρικαὶς φωναίς) have made your language (διάλεκτον) a medley (*Orat.* 1).

The New Testament is said to be written in Koine, but there is some doubt as to how *koine* it really was because of its significant Semitic influence: "it becomes plain that the New Testament cannot be taken as a reliable representative of spoken Greek in Greece in the first century CE, but only as one branch of *Koine* Greek, one that represented Semitic influence."[25] If that is true, then what about Greek written or spoken anywhere else, such as in the Lycus Valley, spoken and written under different influences? It should not be simply assumed that the audiences of the letter, *Colossians*, spoke the same kind of Greek as the writer. Relevant is S. Recai Tekoğlu's general comment that "to the ears of an educated person, a speaker of the lower *koine* mispronounced almost every other word".[26]

Language elitism is as striking among modern scholars as it was in Dionysius Halicarnassus, for example. It is well-represented by Caragounis who believes that Atticism, which he calls "the noble instrument", had been reduced to "a panhellenic means of communication (the Koine) after it had been contaminated with elements from the other dialects ... Worse still, on the lips of the barbarians, Attic lost its charm and the result was a language with little resemblance to its past".[27] Not surprisingly, then, it is common to talk about "bad Greek" or "tortured Greek". The author of Revelation receives heavy criticism in this regard. Moule says he "writes like a person just learning to write in Greek. He is capable of horrifying grammatical blunders and patently Semitic idioms".[28] Ramsay

---

25 C. Caragounis, *The Development of Greek and the New Testament: Morphology, syntax, phonology, and textual transmission* (Tübingen: Mohr-Siebeck, 2004), 123.

26 R. Drews, *The Greco-Roman World from Alexander to Hadrian*, (ebook) chapter 5: http://sitemason.vanderbilt.edu/classics/drews/COURSEBOOK accessed 27th July, 2010.

27 Caragounis, 569–70.

28 C. F. D. Moule, *An Idiom Book of New Testament Greek* (Cambridge: Cambridge University Press, 1963), 3.

talks of "barbarous (sometimes unintelligible) Greek" found on inscriptions in the central districts of Asia.[29] And Larsen also talks about the "tortured Greek" of the Phrygian inscriptions which he puts it down to the fact that Phrygia was not very deeply Hellenized.[30]

What the so-called "bad Greek" and "misspellings" often indicate is that the language is being used by a non-first language speaker. Writers (and especially also speakers) used Greek with the grammatical structures and with the phonetic idiosyncracies of their first language. This was also true in the Lycus Valley, with the result that one can detect what is rightly called a "Phrygian Greek", that is, a Greek identifiable as Greek but marked by vocabulary, grammar, phonetics, and pronunciation distinctly showing Phrygian language elements and influence.[31]

There is one other piece of evidence to suggest that Greek (and Latin) were not universally understood, even among the elite, and that is the references to interpreters. The literary evidence for the use of *hermeneis* or *interpretes* is relatively abundant. But of special relevance to this essay is the reference to such roles in the epigraphic material. Cadwallader has drawn attention to the acknowledged status of a *hermeneus* found in a Colossian inscription, probably to be dated to the beginning of the second century CE.[32] In that inscription, the dedication is to a certain Markos, "chief interpreter and translator of the Colossians" (Κολοσσηνῶν ἀρχερμηνεῖ καὶ ἐξηγητῆι). Cadwallader suggests these terms refer to an official, bureaucratic role or roles that involved both oral translation skills as well as written, but also called on Markos' skills in mediation and negotiation. He also rightly points out that the use of ἀρχερμενεύς implies a body of interpreters of which Markos was a/the chief, and "a body (board, office or such like) requires an infrastructure, location and demand". Both terms used in this inscription suggest a recognized, official body of people who acted in a wide variety of contexts as translators and therefore as interpreters of texts and speech. Given Colossae's location – its exposure to both east and west – the need for such groups is not surprising.

---

29 Ramsay, *St Paul the Traveller and Roman Citizen* (Grand Rapids, Mich.: Kregel, 2001 [1894–95]), 115.

30 J. A. O. Larsen, 'Book Review', *CP* 54 (1959) 65.

31 Brixhe, "Interactions", 261.

32 A. H. Cadwallader, "A New Inscription, a Correction and a Confirmed Sighting from Colossae", *EA* 40 (2007) 109–118.

Accent and Local Pronunciation

Pronunciation and accent are obviously very noticeable in all speech. In the Lycus Valley, when Greek was the selected language in a particular context, it was spoken with accents and pronunciations that might well have betrayed the speaker's first language. Usage nearly always wins out over grammatical and other language "rules" – one only needs to notice the Americanization of much of English speech today; or notice the use of "he and I" after a preposition even among the most sophisticated of English speakers!

Ramsay comments on "how badly the Greek language was pronounced even where it was used" and that especially in rustic Phrygia and Lykaonia as late as the fourth century where and when Greek was little known or used.[33] The letter to the Colossians was written in Greek. But could the reader understand it? And could the audience understand the reader? Did some need a translator? Did the show-offs correct the pronunciation of the reader or help him out with a difficult word? How did the writer's Greek sound to the Colossians? Would they have recognized his linguistic background?

Note the comment of Strabo, when speaking with the Carians in mind,

When all who pronounced words thickly were being called barbarians onomatopoetically, it appeared that the pronunciations of all alien races were likewise thick, I mean of those that were not Greek. Those therefore they called barbarians, in the special sense of the term, at first derisively, meaning that they pronounced words thickly or harshly; and then we misused the word as a general ethnic term, thus making a logical distinction between the Greeks and all other races. The fact is, however, that through our long acquaintance and intercourse with the barbarians this effect was at last seen to be the result, not of a thick pronunciation or any natural defect in the vocal organs, *but of the peculiarities of their several languages* (κατὰ τὰς τῶν διαλέκτων ἰδιότητας) ... (*Geogr.* 14.2.28; italics mine).

Ovid was exiled in the first decades of the Common Era. In his opinion, Greek and Latin had been so barbarized there as to make them sound like foreign languages. It is yet another example of language mixing. Ovid worried that his Latin had become mingled with "the language of the Pontus" (*Tristia* 3.14.43–52). He complains that "the barbarian tongue knows not a Latin voice, and Greek is mastered by the sound of Getic" (*nesciaque est uocis quod barbara lingua Latinae, Graecaque quod Getico uicta loquela sono est,* 5.2.67–68). Though the region was "a mixture of Greeks and Getae", the latter were dominant (5.7.11–12); "a few retain traces of the Greek tongue, but even this is rendered barbarous by a Getic twang (*in paucis remanent Graecae uestigia linguae, haec quoque iam Getico barbara facta sono*). There is not a single man among these people who perchance might express in Latin any common words whatsoever" (5.7.51–56).

---

33 Ramsay, *St Paul the Traveller*, 98–99.

Ovid is certainly not alone in lamenting the impact of local languages on Greek or on Latin. Dionysius of Halicarnassus shared the sentiment:

By living among barbarians many others have soon forgotten [ἀπέμαθον] all their Greek heritage, so that they neither speak the Greek language nor observe Greek customs ... Those Achaeans who are settled near the Euxine Sea prove my point; for, though originally Eleans, descendants of the most Greek people [ἐκ τοῦ Ἑλληνικοτάτου γενόμενοι], they are now the most savage of all barbarians (*Ant. rom.* 1.89.4).

In other words, people spoke Greek with the inflection, syntax and structure of their own languages. In my own experiences in Papua New Guinea, it was always easier to understand a fellow-Australian speaking a local language than it was an indigenous person.

Illiterates depend on their ears for language learning, and so they possibly develop a sharper sense of language tone, accent, vocabulary, and so on. It is not too difficult, even for an amateur linguist, to detect variations in language speech and to link them with geographical locations. This must have been a very common ability in the ancient world; it is precisely what happens in Matt 26:73 when Peter is identified as a Galilean because his accent (λαλιά) gave him away. Speech accent is remarked upon and noticeable even among those who were very fluent in Greek writing. Philostratos says of Pausanias of Caesarea that he spoke Greek with a "heavy accent, as is the way with Cappadocians, making his consonants collide, shortening the long syllables and lengthening the short ones".[34]

Scholars are now quicker to recognize and to acknowledge that the orthography of inscriptions is a good indicator of pronunciation rather than of orthographical error.[35] So, for example, some speakers when using Greek as a second language might exchange the μ and the β and so say (and write) ἔμδομος for ἔβδομος. Likewise, γαμρός might be used for γαμβρός. For similar phonetic or pronunciation reasons Phrygian Greek-speakers were likely to say πός instead of πρός. The tendency was to use initial κ for χ, so κορός was used for χορός[36] and κεκαρίσμενος was reflected in Phrygian as κεκαρίσμενος. On the other hand, χρῖμα is commonly used for κρῖμα.[37] In addition, Emrys Evans says it was not uncommon in Asia Minor generally for a nasal to be used before non-continu-

---

34 M. Janse, "Aspects of Bilingualism in the History of the Greek Language", in *Bilingualism in Ancient Society* 332–92, on p. 356.

35 D. Taylor, "Bilingualism and Diglossia in Late Antique Syria and Mesopotamia", in *Bilingualism in Ancient Society* 298–331, on p. 308.

36 C. Brixhe, "Épigraphie et grammaire du phrygien: état present et perspectives", in E. Vineis (ed.), *Le lingue indoeuropee di frammantaria attestazione* (Pisa: Società Italiana di Glottologia, 1983) 109–33, on p. 127.

37 See, for an example, W. H. Calder, "Corpus Inscriptionum Neo-Phrygiarum", *JHS* 31 (1911) 161–215, on p. 211.

ous sounds – so ἀνγαθόν, θυγγατρί, Πανπίου.[38] Speakers generally seem to have used or not used nasals such as ν and μ where "orthodox" Greek did or did not. Another common spelling variation that is due to a peculiar phonetic in/ability is the use of θέκνοσι for τέκνοις. It was also not uncommon for prothesis to be found: a vowel is added before a consonant, with the result that Ἐσταρτωνός appears for Στρατωνός. Similarly, ἱστοργή is used for στοργή.[39] In fact, it would seem that Phrygians had difficulty with the Greek "στ" cluster – they tended to drop the "σ" or to use a prothetic vowel. So also στέφανος became τέφανος, ἀνέστησα became ἀνέτησα, εἰ τὸν θεόν was used for εἰς τὸν θεόν and ἰστήλην for στήλην.[40]

It would seem that the local languages of Asia Minor, including those of Phrygia, had trouble with the aspirates or confused them. So φ, θ and χ were commonly confused with π, τ and κ respectively. Spellings such as ἀδελποί, φρεσβύτερος, τυγάτηρ, κάριν, γυναιχί occur frequently. It could be concluded that "the aspirate was, in all probability, foreign to the native Phrygian language".[41] Hierapolis provides a fair number of examples of this;[42] and the forms Ῥοῦπος (*MAMA* VI.43) and ἀδελπός (*MAMA* VI.46) appear also in Colossae. Θ appears to have been an especially difficult sound for Asia Minor native speakers.[43] Common also is the β π confusion which results in the form Σεπαστοῖς being found in Hierapolis (*CIG* III.3906b). Furthermore, the gutterals κ and γ were interchanged so that κεκρίμενος became γεγρείμενος. As this example illustrates, the short vowel ι appears to have been unknown in local Phrygian language and appeared instead in Greek inscriptions as ει (*MAMA* VI.45, 47). Vowel and diphthong sounds tend to be particularly good indicators of the provenance and language background of the speaker and these peculiarities tend to be revealed in inscriptions. So at Colossae, for example, we find διφθεροπύς for διφθεροποιός (*MAMA* VI.44) and ὑός for υἱός (*MAMA* VI.43). Calder gives an example of εὐχήν being inscribed as ὠχήν which "must be the Greek word according to Phrygian pronunciation".[44]

It is becoming increasingly recognized that much can be learned about how Greek was pronounced and how traditional language phonetics influenced the spelling of Greek inscriptions. It is also possible to begin a minor construction of the syntax of Neo-Phrygian, for example, on the basis of the forms found in

38 D. Emrys-Evans, "Notes on the Consonants in the Greek of Asia Minor", *CQ* 12 (1918) 162–70, on p. 165.

39 T. Drew-Bear/F. Demirkök/E. S. Dönmez/M. Türktüzün, *I was born in Anatolia* (Anadolu Kültür – Sanat ve Arkeologi Müzesi, 2007), Inv. 503.

40 Brixhe, "Interactions", 263.

41 Emrys-Evans, 162.

42 Emrys-Evans, 163.

43 Emrys-Evans, 167.

44 Calder, "Corpus Inscriptionum", 193.

Greek-Phrygian inscriptions.[45] This is made a little easier by the fact that Phrygian and Greek were related languages.

Lydian, Carian and Lycian in the Lycus?

What languages are likely to have been spoken in the valley? Because of its location and its history, the long-standing locals were mostly Phrygian speakers, but at various times many of them most likely had strong contact with the Lydian, Carian and Lycian languages. The fact is that there is no inscriptional evidence of those languages in the valley itself. According to Strabo, Lydian had virtually died out of use in Lydia by the turn of the Era – but it was still used in Cibyra in south-west Phrygia where there was a Lydian colony (*Geogr.* 12.4.6). How dependable Strabo is about such matters might be debatable, but until harder evidence is found, we probably have to assume his reliability. It might also be noted that Strabo says that in his own time "Lydians, Carians and Greeks" inhabited the region between Ephesus and Antioch Pisidia (*Geogr.* 14.1.38). Cicero comments that his military auxiliaries while he operated out of Laodicea were made up of "Galatians, Pisidians and Lycians" (*Att.* 6.5). There is valid reason for thinking these groupings are along language lines, even if the terms used are imprecise as language identifiers. And Pausanias, a century after Strabo, says he knows from personal experience of Lydians in Hierocaesarea and Hypaipa who use a *magos* who "sings to some god or other an invocation in a foreign tongue unintelligible to Greeks, reciting the invocation from a book" (5.27.6). Here too it is possible that the language was Lydian since the use of traditional languages in prayer and rituals is quite common.

Lycians from the south west coast of Asia Minor had contact with others by sea trade and travel. Inlanders, such as the Phrygians, wanting to sell their goods overseas, might use Lycian ports as exits. Evidence for Lycian consists of more than 150 inscriptions on stone, some 200 on coins, and a handful on other objects. While a few of the coins may be earlier, the texts on stone all date from the fifth and fourth centuries BCE. All but a few of these are tomb inscriptions with stereotypical wording. An important exception is a lengthy inscription on a *stele* from Xanthus, as well as another inscription at a shrine to Leto with a trilingual inscription in Lycian, Greek and Aramaic. As a spoken language, it appears Lycians tended to add vowels to noun and verb endings (a language characteristic noted among many modern Italians speaking English) and there is evidence of the fricative character of the voiced consonant (β, γ, δ). There is only very little

---

45 See A. Lubotsky, "The Syntax of New Phrygian Inscription No. 88", *Kadmos* 28 (1989) 146–55.

evidence for linguistic influences (loan words, for example) either way between Greek and Lycian.

Carian was spoken in the south west of Asia Minor, in the neighborhood of Ephesus. About 200–250 Carian words have survived in inscriptions. As a language, it was related to Lydian and Mysian. According to Strabo, who heard Carian speakers himself, the Carian language had spread beyond Caria mainly through mercenaries, and like many other languages had introduced Greek loan words into its vocabulary: "it has extremely many Greek words mixed up in it" (*Geogr.* 14.2.28). In turn, Strabo also says, "the barbarous element in their Greek was strong" (τὸ βαρβαρόφωνον ἐπ᾽ ἐκείνων πυκνὸν ἦν). He uses the verb καρίζειν in the sense of "to speak Greek like a Carian".

Phrygian

If there is any evidence at all for a non-Greek language in the Lycus, the best candidate beside Latin is probably Phrygian. There is little doubt that in some regions of Phrygia and for some centuries, that language survived. The continuation of Phrygian personal names as in the case of Μηνόφιλος is evident in the inscription below. Among Christians, we know of at least Apphia, addressed by Paul in *Philemon* 2, Papias and Sagaris among second century CE Christians. Appia, Appa, Dades and Tateis are all common on Phrygian Christian tombs of the third and fourth centuries.[46] Note also Gainas in the time of John Chrysostom. Toponyms[47] and the portrayal of Phrygian deities on coins, especially Cybele Agdistis, Mēn and Sabazios, all indicate a survival of things Phrygian. Clement of Alexandria knows of the Phrygian Sabazios cult in his time (*Protr.* 1.2.16).

The interaction between Greek and Phrygian has been studied closely by Claude Brixhe particularly. The origins of the Phrygians are heavily shrouded, but it would seem they were in Macedonia and Thrace before moving into Asia Minor probably around 1200–1000 BCE. As a language, Phrygian is thought to be closely related to Thracian. In any case, there was strong interrelation between Phrygian and various dialects of Greek for centuries. In that case, it is most likely that many people remained bilingual, speaking both Phrygian and Greek since the latter was quite close to the former.

Palaeo-Phrygian inscriptions are plentiful and quite widespread, while the Neo-Phrygian texts (first to third centuries CE) are much fewer (about 120) with a roughly 50–50 split of bilingual (with Greek) and monolingual inscriptions. In the bilingual inscriptions, nearly all have the Greek first. All the

---

46 Calder, "Studies in Early Christian Epigraphy: II", *JRS* 14 (1924) 85–92.
47 W.G. Arkwright, "Lycian and Phrygian Names", *JHS* 38 (1918) 45–73.

inscriptions are epitaphs and all but a few are curses on anyone contemplating grave-robbing. Brixhe rightly argues that those few inscriptions that are monolingual and not merely curses indicate that Phrygian was also a language used to convey information.[48] The area of distribution is small and uneven. The neo-Phrygian inscriptions are limited in area to Eskisehir/Dorylaion, Kütahya/Kotiaion, Egridir Lake, Laodicea Katakekaumene and Lake Tatta. Brixhe thinks Phrygian speaking communities might have lived in the Middle Hermos basin as late as the Roman era and he notes that neo-Phyrgian has also been found in the vicinity of Pisidian Antioch.[49]

Brixhe is astute enough to realize that the meager inscriptions belie the more likely language situation. There is evidence that Phrygian had an impact on Greek in the region and for that to happen, there needs to have been a significant number and density of Phrygian speakers. Bilingualism endures only if it has constant nourishment from outside. There must have been entire or partial monolingual Phrygian speakers somewhere.[50] Brixhe argues it was possible for groups like women (who stayed indoors and at home most of the time – especially in urban regions), self-sufficient small farmers and farm workers to have known only Phrygian because they had no need to interact with Greek-speakers in trade, the law or public, official business.[51] The evidence indicates that Phrygian survived in written form at least until the third century CE but it appears largely confined to private and religious spheres.[52] The use of the traditional language in a worship context and of the dominant language in other contexts is not uncommon. At Qumran, for example, there is evidence for Hebrew/Aramaic being used in religious texts and contexts, and Greek in many secular transactions. The same can be said to be the case in Palestine generally at the turn of the Era.[53]

I simply include, as illustration, a bilingual inscription (*MAMA* I.413) with the warning in Phrygian and refer to Brixhe and Lubotsky for more qualified comment:

Αὐρ. Μηνόφιλος Οὐενούστου κὲ Μα —
νια Ἀντιόχου ἡ γυνὴ αὐτοῦ Ἀππη καὶ
Οὐεναουίη τέκνοις ἀώροις καὶ
ἑαυτοῖς μνήμης χάριν. ιος
νι σεμουν κνουμανει κακε

---

48 Brixhe, "Interactions", 252.
49 Brixhe, "Interactions" 249, 250.
50 Brixhe, "Interactions", 254–55.
51 Brixhe, "Interactions", 256.
52 Brixhe, "Interactions", 247.
53 M. Silva, "Bilingualism and the Character of Palestinian Greek", *Biblica* 61 (1980) 198–219.

αδδακετ αωρω Ουεναουιας τιγ
γεγαριτμενο ειτου πουρ Ουανα —
κταν κε Ουρανιον ...[54]

Brixhe gives evidence of mutual language infection, and a quick glance at a few
items of the known Phrygian vocabulary will indicate how the dominant language (Greek) infected the local vernacular and how the local vernacular's peculiar phonetics and pronunciation in turn infected the Greek words. For example:

anar, Gk: ἀνήρ
attagos, Gk: τράγος
brater, cognate to Gk: φρατήρ
germe, cognate to Gk: θερμός
meka, Gk: μέγας
zamelon, Gk: χαμηλός

Scythian

Another possible language option in the Lycus was what was called "Scythian".
In Col 3:11, the writer pleads for unity among Christians by claiming: "... there
is no Greek or Jew, circumcised or uncircumcised, barbarian, Scythian, slave or
free, but Christ is all, and is in all". There has been some debate between Martin
and Campbell about this passage, but neither of them interprets the categories
along linguistic lines.[55]

Traditionally, Scythian was read as indicating a generic barbarity. Martin
reads it "from a Scythian viewpoint" and suggests that barbarian equals non-
Scythian (in much the same way as in the phrase "Greeks and barbarians").
Campbell suggests on the basis of the chiastic structure of the passage that
Scythian is to slave as barbarian is to free. I might suggest with a little confidence
that some of these categories are linguistic. After all, being "barbarian" most
often refers to speech more than anything else of a stranger's culture. It could
also mean to speak Greek badly; not just to speak a foreign language (compare
Strabo *Geogr.* 14.2.28). Scythian is sometimes used as a broad term to indicate a
nomadic, non-Greek-speaking or non-Hellenized group. According to Strabo,
it was used to refer to all northerners (*Geogr.* 1.2.27) and as a general term for
many nomadic groups in the region (*Geogr.* 11.8.1-2). The concern of the author

---

54 Brixhe, "Interactions" 256–57.

55 T. Martin, "The Scythian Perspective in Col 3:11", *Nov T* (1995) 249–61, "Scythian
Perspective or Elusive Chiasm: A reply to Douglas A. Campbell", *Nov T* 41 (1999) 256–64;
D. Campbell, "Unravelling Colossians 3:11b", *NTS* 42 (1996) 120–32.

of *Colossians* might well have been for a unity that he saw was threatened by language divisions.

That Scythian survived as a broad language term to cover language groups in the Phrygian area (the terms Indian, Egyptian, Thracian were used similarly for elsewhere) is clear from Chrysostom who occasionally refers to "Greek, barbarian or Scythian" (*Bab.* 2). He also clearly suggests that Scythians did not understand Greek: "Again, he who knew the language that was expressed by the letters (Greek), might have known what was therein contained; but the Scythian, and the Barbarian, and the Indian, and the Egyptian, and all those who were excluded from that language, would have gone away without receiving any instruction" (*stat.* 9.5). The bishop is also said to have used preachers in Scythian language for missionary purposes, suggesting that whatever the term "Scythian" meant, it might even have been a "church" language much like Greek and Syriac and Latin were (Theodoret *Hist. eccl.* 5.30). Chrysostom, who was involved as bishop with the churches of Lydia and Phrygia, thought that glossolalia meant using languages such as Thracian, Scythian, Latin and Persian (*Hom. 1 Cor.* 25.4). Presumably, for him Syriac and Greek did not come into that category which would also suggest that he did not know Scythian.

Like Scythian, the term "Phrygian" appears also to have been used in a broad sense to include those languages that were spoken in a certain region (such as Anatolia) and were not Greek. Demetrius, like others who wanted to revive Attic Greek, exhorts the aspiring writer and orator to avoid neologisms, if possible; otherwise, he suggests, it is best to "follow the analogy of established words, in order to avoid the appearance of introducing Phrygian and Scythian speech into our Greek" (*Elec.* 96). This advice might be akin to a modern French or German speaker who bemoans the increasing use of English (probably in an Americanised version) in those languages and so recommends the avoidance of English words, if possible! If that were the case with Demetrius' concern for "Phrygian and Scythian", then that might well indicate the strength and vitality of those languages.

Since it is used in a letter to Colossians, might "Scythians" in fact refer to Phrygians in this context? Like Scythians, Phrygians were "originally" nomadic and from the north-west, coming into the Lycus Valley from elsewhere but having political and cultural control in the Lycus for a period. A Scythian would then belong to the "in" group; being labeled "barbarian" would put one among the "outsiders". Were there Christians in Colossae and in the Lycus generally who claimed to be "Scythian", meaning they were descendants of the tribes who were the ruling class in the Lycus in the seventh and sixth centuries before the Common Era? If modern mission experiences are anything to go by, language groups are commonly the cause of serious divisions within newly formed Christian communities; in other Christian communities ancestral claims are also seen by some as a claim to status!

Aramaic, Syriac and Persian

Aramaic is also quite likely to have been known and used by some in the Lycus. At some stage in its history, especially when under Persian and eastern control, Phrygia would have been familiar with the sounds of Aramaic almost as much as it was later familiar with Greek. We know that around 210 BCE, some two thousand Jews were relocated from Syria by Antiochus III into Phrygia (Josephus *Ant.* 12.148–53), and they were reasonably numerous and assimilated into their local communities as the inscriptional evidence in Hierapolis and Laodicea suggests. The dominant languages would have been Aramaic and Greek. Aramaic inscriptions have been found as far west as Sardis. Given their proximity and reasonable accessibility to Syria and to Jerusalem, it is quite likely that Aramaic or some form of Syriac was spoken among these Jewish communities for quite a period. The eastern gate of Laodicea was known as the Syrian gate, and that suggests close relations with that region. The second century Christian bishop of Hierapolis, Papias seems to have kept links with the east and was aware of oral traditions from there.

Syriac was one of the "church" languages used in Phrygia in later centuries. The fifth century *Life of Hypatius* speaks of missionaries working in Syriac in Phrygia. As late as the sixth century, John of Ephesus and Jacob of Edessa (540) used Syriac in both Phrygia and Lydia. Frank Trombley suggests that one reason for the difficulties Syrian missionaries had in Phrygia was their lack of knowledge of the vernacular, and by implication, the lack of Greek and/or Syriac language knowledge among the locals.[56]

Finally, the presence and influence of Persian is also quite possible given the history of that power's presence in the region. In the second to third century of the Common Era, Bardesanes wrote of "the descendants of Persians who lived out of Persia" as being still numerous in Egypt, Phrygia, and Galatia, and maintaining their traditional customs there:

And again, I told you, in speaking of the Persians and the Magi, that it is not in the zone of Persia only that they have taken for wives their daughters and their sisters, but that in every country to which they have gone they have followed the law of their fathers, and have preserved the mystic arts contained in that teaching which they delivered to them.[57]

I have elsewhere noted the Persian influence on, and interest in, the Artemis cult in Ephesus that survived possibly into the Common Era.[58] In addition, evidence

---

56 F. Trombley, "Paganism in the Greek World at the End of Antiquity: The Case of Rural Anatolia and Greece", *HTR* 78 (1985) 327–52.

57 H. J. W. Drijvers (ed.), *The Book of the Laws of Countries: Dialogue of Fate of Bardaisan of Edessa* New Jersey: Gorgias Press, 2006), 45–46.

58 R. Strelan, *Paul, Artemis and Jews in Ephesus* (Berlin/New York: de Gruyter, 1996), 41–42.

for the tenacity of Persian names in the recorded nomenclature of Asia Minor is provided by Nicholas Sekunda.[59]

Conclusion and Summary

The surviving evidence suggests strongly that Greek was the dominant language of the Lycus. And maybe that reflects the reality, especially in the towns and among the educated elite. Some form of Greek was almost certainly the language of mutual comprehension for peoples whose mother tongue was not Greek. There is some evidence that the Greek spoken in the region was noticeably marked by vocabulary, accent, pronunciation, grammatical forms that reflected the influence of another language – so much so that one can rightly speak of a "Phrygian Greek". In fact, Brixhe is prepared to call it a dialect.[60] The peculiarities of their own first language betrayed them especially when they spoke Greek (but less so in their written expression). Latin might have been understood by some, but probably not spoken fluently by many apart from those who were settled there in reward for service to Rome. Aramaic-Syriac over some periods of time probably was spoken and understood by some Jews and Christians. It would have been maintained by their links with the Christians from the east – with Syrian and Judean Christians and Jews.

Some of the traditional languages in the region survived, and for the majority in the Lycus Valley Greek was a second language. Phrygian clearly survived well into the Common Era. Lydian, Carian and Lycian most likely survived as late as the end of the first century CE in very small pockets and/or in the heads of the elderly at least. All language groups probably had dialect characteristics as well.

In any Christian community of the Lycus Valley in the first century, these language groups might well have been represented. Since language ability is often a source of pride and since it is also sometimes a marker of personal and group identity, there is a good chance that it was also a cause of division, if not conflict, within these small Christian groups. Greek was the language that held them together, especially in their worship activities, but it is highly likely that many worshipped privately or in smaller groups using their own native language.

---

59 N. Sekunda, "Achaemenid Settlement in Caria, Lycia and Greater Phrygia", in H. Sancisi-Weerdenburg/A. Kuhrt (ed.), *Achaemenid History VI: Asia Minor and Egypt: Old Cultures in a New Empire* (Leiden: Nederlands Instituut voor het Nabije Oosten, 1991) 83–143.

60 Brixhe, "Interactions", 266.

Bibliography

Adams, J. N./Simon Swain, "Introduction" in J. N. Adams/M. Janse/S. Swain (ed.), *Bilingualism in Ancient Society: Language Contact and the Written Word* (Oxford: Oxford University Press, 2002) 1–22.

Arkwright, W. G., "Lycian and Phrygian Names", *JHS* 38 (1918) 45–73.

Bodel, J., "Dealing With the Dead: Undertakers, Executioners, and Potter's Fields in Ancient Rome", in E. Marshall/V. Hope, (ed.), *Death and Disease in the Ancient City* London/New York: Routledge, 2000) 128–51.

Brixhe, C., "Épigraphie et grammaire du phrygien: état present et perspectives", in E. Vineis (ed.), *Le lingue indoeuropee di frammantaria attestazione* (Pisa: Società Italiana di Glottologia, 1983) 109–33.

– "Interactions between Greek and Phrygian under the Roman Empire", in J. N. Adams/M. Janse/S. Swain (ed.), *Bilingualism in Ancient Society: Language Contact and the Written Word* (Oxford: Oxford University Press, 2002) 246–66.

Cadwallader, A. H., "A New Inscription, a Correction and a Confirmed Sighting from Colossae", *EA* 40 (2007) 109–18.

Calder, W. H., "Corpus Inscriptionum Neo-Phrygiarum", *JHS* 31 (1911) 161–215.

– "Studies in Early Christian Epigraphy: II", *JRS* 14 (1924) 85–92.

Campbell, D., "Unravelling Colossians 3:11b", *NTS* 42 (1996) 120–32.

Caragounis, C., *The Development of Greek and the New Testament: Morphology, syntax, phonology, and textual transmission* (Tübingen: Mohr-Siebeck, 2004).

Curchin, L., "Literacy in the Roman Provinces: Qualitative and Quantitative Data from Central Spain", *AJP* 116 (1995) 461–476.

Deissmann, G. A., *Light from the Ancient East Or the New Testament Illustrated by Recently Discovered Texts of the Graeco-Roman World* (Grand Rapids, Mich.: Kregel 2003 [1908]).

Drew-Bear, T./C. Thomas/M. Yoeldoesteran, *Phrygian Votive Steles* (Turkey: Museum of Anatolian Civilizations, 1999).

Drew-Bear, T./Feza Demirkök/E. S. Dönmez/M. Türktüzün, *I was born in Anatolia* (Anadolu Kültür – Sanat ve Arkeologi Müzesi, 2007).

Drijvers, H. J. W., (ed.), *The Book of the Laws of Countries: Dialogue of Fate of Bardaisan of Edessa* (New Jersey: Gorgias Press, 2006).

Durand, J., "Mortality Estimates from Roman Tombstone Inscriptions", *AJS* 65 (1960) 365–73.

Emrys-Evans, D., "Notes on the Consonants in the Greek of Asia Minor", *CQ* 12 (1918) 162–70.

Friesen, S., "Prospects for a Demography of the Pauline Mission: Corinth among the Churches," in S. J. Friesen/D. Schowalter (ed.), *Urban Religion and Roman Corinth: Interdisciplinary Approaches* Cambridge, Mass.: Harvard University Press, 2005), 351–70.

Harland, P., *Associations, Synagogues, and Congregations: Claiming a Place in Ancient Mediterranean Society* (Minneapolis: Fortress Press, 2003).

Holl, K., "Das Fortleben der Volkssprachen in Kleinasien in nachchristlicher Zeit", *Hermes* 43 (1908) 240–54.

van der Horst, P., "Jewish Funerary Inscriptions—Most Are in Greek", *BARev* 18 (1992) 46–57.

Janse, M., "Aspects of Bilingualism in the History of the Greek Language", in J. N. Adams/M. Janse/S. Swain (ed.), *Bilingualism in Ancient Society: Language Contact and the Written Word* (Oxford: Oxford University Press, 2002) 332–92.

Jones, A. H. M., *The Later Roman Empire* (Oxford: Basil Blackwell 1964).

Kaimio, J., *The Romans and the Greek Language* (Helsinki: Societas Scientiarum Fennica, 1979).

Kyle, D., *Spectacles of Death in Ancient Rome* (London: Routledge, 2001).

Lubotsky, A., "The Syntax of New Phrygian Inscription No. 88", *Kadmos* 28 (1989) 146–55.

MacMullen, R., "Provincial Languages in the Roman Empire", *The American Journal of Philology* 87 (1966) 1–17.

Martin, T., "The Scythian Perspective in Col 3:11", *Nov T* (1995) 249–61,

– "Scythian Perspective or Elusive Chiasm: A reply to Douglas A. Campbell", *Nov T* 41 (1999) 256–64.

Mitchell, S., "Iconium and Ninica: Two Double Communities in Roman Asia Minor", *Historia: Zeitschrift für Alte Geschichte* 28 (1979) 409–38.

Moule, C. F. D., *An Idiom Book of New Testament Greek* (Cambridge: Cambridge University Press, 1963).

Price, S., *Rituals and Power: The Roman imperial cult in Asia Minor* (New York: Cambridge University Press, 1984).

Ramsay, W. M., "Sepulchral customs in Ancient Phrygia", *JHS* 5 (1884) 241–63.

– *St Paul the Traveller and Roman Citizen* (Grand Rapids, Mich.: Kregel, 2001 [894–95]).

– *Historical Commentary on Galatians* (Grand Rapids, Mich.: Kregel, 1997 [1899]).

– *The Letters to the Seven Churches of Asia and Their Place in the Plan of The Apocalypse* (Grand Rapids, Mich.: Kregel, 2003 [1904]).

– *Asianic Elements in Greek Civilisation 1915–1916* (London: Murray, 1927).

Sekunda, N. V., "Achaemenid Settlement in Caria, Lycia and Greater Phrygia", in H. Sancisi-Weerdenburg/A. Kuhrt (ed.), *Achaemenid History VI: Asia Minor and Egypt: Old Cultures in a New Empire* (Leiden: Nederlands Instituut voor het Nabije Oosten, 1991) 83–143.

Silva, M., "Bilingualism and the Character of Palestinian Greek", *Biblica* 61 (1980) 198–219.

Strelan, R., *Paul, Artemis and Jews in Ephesus* (Berlin/New York: de Gruyter, 1996).

Taylor, D., "Bilingualism and Diglossia in Late Antique Syria and Mesopotamia", in J. N. Adams/M. Janse/S. Swain (ed.), *Bilingualism in Ancient Society: Language Contact and the Written Word* (Oxford: Oxford University Press, 2002) 298–331.

Tekoğlu, Ş. R., "Corpus Project for Inscriptions in the Pamphylian Dialect, and the Sidetian and Pisidian Languages in the Antalya and Side Museums: 2005", *Anmed* 4 (2006) 75–81.

Trombley, F., "Paganism in the Greek World at the End of Antiquity: The Case of Rural Anatolia and Greece", *HTR* 78 (1985) 327–52.

Chapter 4

Woollen Textiles:
An International Trade Good in
the Lycus Valley in Antiquity[1]

Hatice Erdemir

Through most of ancient time animal materials have provided man's clothing, especially in the northern latitudes where wind–protection and warmth were of paramount importance. Among other natural resources and materials (such as marble and limestone quarries,[2] local clay ceramics[3] and water reservoirs[4]) sheep husbandry and its related sectors created time-honoured processes of production which helped the cities of the Lycus Valley to prosper. Of these industries, woollen textiles, requiring the most labour-intensive production, were rapidly intro-

---

1 I am indebted to Veterinary Doctor Yavuz Palaz who provided me with the background information and readings on sheep, sheep raising, wool and related subjects throughout the preparation of this paper. I am grateful to Alan Cadwallader, Michael Trainor, Rosemary Canavan and Julie Hooke for their encouragement in initiating and discussing the issues raised in this paper. Some ideas herein were first raised in "Sheep Raising and Sector Industries in and around Hierapolis in Antiquity" ("Antikçağ'da Denizli ve Çevresinde Koyun Yetiştiriciliği ve Yan Sektörleri"), in A. Özçelik *et al* (ed.), *Uluslararası Denizli ve Çevresi Tarih ve Kültür Sempozyumu Bildiriler* (2 vol.; Denizli: Pamukkale University, 2007) 1.23–30.

2 For the marble quarries in the Lycus Valley see B. Söğüt, "Salbakos Mountain and its Ruins in the Ancient Period" ("Antik Dönemde Salbakos Dağı ve Kalıntıları"), in Özçelik, *Uluslararası*, 2.15–24.

3 Mellaart suggests that there were trade relations between different parts of Anatolia and different parts of Europe as early as Late Bronze Ages. Especially, particular forms of faience productions of Beycesultan and other bone products and other objects (pottery, decorated bone and antlerwork, spears with socketed shafts) were transported from Anatolia to Europe even in the Late Bronze Ages (1550–1200 BCE). According to Mellaart, the Danube route (which passed through Europe and ran up to the Adriatic) had already been monopolized by Anatolian traders in the Late Bronze Age. J. Mellaart, "Anatolian Trade with Europe and Anatolian Geography and culture Provinces in the Late Bronze Age", *AS* 18 (1968) 187–202, especially pp. 194–195.

4 For the water supply and drainage system of Laodicea see, C. Şimşek/M. Büyükkolancı, "Laodikeia Antik Kenti Su Kaynakları ve Dağıtım Sistemi", Suna-İnan Kıraç Akdeniz Medeniyetleri Araştırma Enstitüsü, *Adalya* IX (2006) 86–88; for public baths in the Lycus Valley, see M. Büyükkolancı, "Laodicea and Hierapolis: The Last Periods of two Cities by the Light of Their Baths Excavations" ("Laodikeia and Hierapolis Hamamlarının Kazı Sonuçlarına Göre İki Kentin Son Dönemleri"), in Özçelik, *Uluslararası*, 2.51–56.

duced to different parts of the world of antiquity rapidly becoming a requisite international commodity. Various types and styles of this product were prominent in international markets. Woollen textiles were probably preferred not only because they represented the wealth and status of people and lead the fashion of the period but they also met the functional requirement of keeping people warm and healthy.

The aim of this study is to investigate the importance of woollen textiles as one of the prime sources of revenue for the Lycus Valley within the global markets of Antiquity. Questions of interest include how woollen textiles were traded within world markets, who (whether men, women or children) were involved in different parts of production and trading from the beginning to the end of the cycle in local and international trade, what ancillary benefits the people of the Lycus Valley gained from this merchandise in addition to its direct economical and material prosperity, whether there were kindred cultural, ideal, social and religious interchanges resulting from this particular trade connection.

Introduction

The beginning of agriculture and animal husbandry may go back as far as the Neolithic Age.[5] Humankind's move into civilised life was largely built on the benefit that derived from taming free-moving animals.[6] In order to provide for

---

5 Excavations in Çayönü (in Diyarbakır in the eastern part of Asia Minor) have shown that sheep, goats, pigs and cattle were already domesticated in the area in the seventh millennium BCE and woollen fabrics were used at least from this period. Bones of sheep and goats have been uncovered in archaeological excavations at Konya, Çatalhöyük and Burdur-Hacılar in Anatolia dating to 5800–5700 BCE. It is not yet settled whether these were domesticated. Discoveries of identifiable textile materials from the sixth millennium BCE in Asia Minor do demonstrate that skilled wool weaving was already established, but the raw materials may have come initially from hunting or trade, with domestication and breeding coming later: see J. Mellaart, *Earliest Civilisation of the Near East* (London: Thames and Hudson, 1965), 78, 82, 84–5, 104–06; P. Dolukhanov, *Eski Ortadoğu'da Çevre ve Etnik Yapı*, translated by Suavi Aydın (Ankara: İmge Kitabevi, 1998), 436–37. Perkins and Redman have both argued that evidence of the domestication of cattle is found among Neolithic settlements at Çatalhöyük: see D. Perkins, "Fauna of Çatal Hüyük: evidence for early cattle Domestication in Anatolia", *AAAS* (NS) 164 (1969) 177–79; C. L. Redman, *The Rise of Civilisation (From Early Farmers to Urban Society in the Ancient Near East)* (San Francisco: Freeman, 1978); compare M. Özdoğan, "Çayönü (Günümüz Uygarlığı'nın Temelleri)", in *Metro Gastro* (İstanbul: Metro Kültür Yayınları, Mayıs-Haziran 2008), 55. Some Hittite clay tablets from the mid-second millennium BCE indicate well-fed sheep, summer pastures and winter pastures for grazing animals. Another tablet witnesses an agreement between Ugarit and Hittite leaders wherein the former agree to pay as tribute to the Hittites a number of blue-purple and red-purple woollen fabrics or general textile goods: see S. Alp, *Hitit Çağı'nda Anadolu* (Ankara: TÜBİTAK, 2000), 73–81, 90–92.

6 Lee accents that there is a strong relationship between stable food resources, sedentary life and the growing population of the first known humans: R. B. Lee, "Lactation, Ovulation,

the basic needs of people, sheep were one of the earliest animals to be domesticated.[7] The feeding, growing, breeding and grazing of sheep are easier than for cattle. Nevertheless, successful sheep husbandry depends on certain geographical, climatic and environmental conditions. Initially, cool climes and well-watered pastures are required for raising animals.[8]

It is known that from the Neolithic Age, sheep were raised in different parts of Anatolia. In the Lycus Valley where the region has suitable plateaus and pasturages, sheep were raised. They met important needs of people in this area and in other parts of the ancient world. Both archaeological studies and literary testimonia demonstrate that the area equivalent to the modern region of Denizli has been suitable for raising sheep from antiquity to the present day. However before analysing the area's woollen textile industry in antiquity, it will be helpful to consider briefly the historical and physical geography of the region at that period.

Historical and Physical Geography

The most important cities and towns of the Lycus Valley in antiquity were situated on the banks of the Lycus (modern name: Çürüksu) and its immediate vicinity.[9] The Lycus Valley ran through the intersection of Caria, Phrygia and Lydia. The river created a famous valley and flowed by the mountain of Salbakos (Babadağ) in the west. The highest mountain, Cadmus (Honaz) is situated at the south of the valley. Tectonic activity in the area gives it a heavily undulating to-

Infanticide, and Woman's Work: a study of hunter gatherer population regulation", in M. N. Cohen/R. S. Malpass/G. E. Hutchinson, (ed.), *Biosocial Mechanisms of Population Regulation* (New Haven/London: Yale University Press, 1980) 321–48.

7 Dolukhanav concludes, on the basis of the interpretation of excavations by Turnbull, Reed and Perkins, that sheep became domesticated as a herd animal some 11000 years before modern times, probably subsequent to the domestication of the dog. The boorish ancestor of *Ovis aries* (domesticated sheep) was *Ovis ammon*. This breed lived between the Zagros Mountains and North Iran and the hilly parts of Turkmenistan. See Dolukhanav, *Eski Ortadoğu'da Çevre*, 249. For the origins of the domestication of sheep see B. C. Yalçın, "Koyun Yetiştiriciliği", in C. N. Aytuğ/E. Alaçam/Ü. Özkoç/B. C. Yalçın/H. Gökçen/H. Türker, *Koyun-Keçi Hastalıkları ve Yetiştiriciliği* (İstanbul: 1990), 378–86. In Herodotus, the herdsman of the Persian king Cambyses, named Mithridates, lived and pastured his oxen in the foothills of the mountain area to the north of Ecbatana towards the Black Sea (Herodotus *Hist.* 1.110).

8 See Dolukhanov, *Eski Ortadoğu'da Çevre*, 249, pl. 4.23.

9 C. Şimşek, "Antik Dönemde Babadağ Çevresi", in Y. Özpınar *et al* (ed.), *I. Babadağ Sempozyumu* (Tarihte ve Günümüzde Babadağ; 1–3 Aralık 1999) *Bildiri Metinleri* (Denizli: Pamukkale Üniversitesi, 1999) 316–62, on pp. 321–22; Şimşek, "Attouda Nekropolü", in A. Öztürk *et al* (ed.), *The First International History, Archaeology and Art History Symposium* (Söke: 2001) 229–45, on p. 229.

pography. The peak of the mountain, the hills and uneven plains have abundant forests, water reserves, pasturage and wide plateaus. There are naturally formed passes that provide access between mountains, plateaus and settlements.[10] Human remains have been found in this area, dating from the Chalcolithic Age (5500–3300 BCE). Cultural artefacts belonging to the Bronze Age (3000–1200 BCE) have also been discovered.[11] The area was subject to a succession of great powers in Asia Minor: the Hittite (1750–1300 BCE), Phrygian (750–545 BCE), Lydian (700–545 BCE), the Persian (546–333 BCE), the Hellenistic (330–30 BCE), the Pergamene (241–130 BCE) and the Romans (129 BCE–395 CE).[12]

Colossae (Honaz) and Peltai (Civril)[13] are thought to be the cities in the region with the oldest origins. At various stages in subsequent periods were created Laodicea (Goncalı-Eskihisar),[14] Hierapolis (Pamukkale), Tripolis (Yenicekent-Buldan), Attouda (Hisarkoy), Tragozapolis (Boludüzü-Bekirlerköyü), Hydriale (Sigma Kasabası) and Karura (Tekkeköy). All these cities were especially important in the Hellenistic and Roman periods.[15] They were joined to Roman

---

10 For details, see S. Göney, *Büyük Menderes Bölgesi* (İstanbul: İstanbul Üniversitesi Edebiyat Fakültesi Matbaası, 1975), 49–50, 231–45, 342; B. Darkot/M. Tuncel, *Ege Bölgesi Coğrafyası* (İstanbul: İstanbul Üniversitesi Edebiyat Fakültesi Matbaası, 1988), 56–8; Şimşek, "Antik", 321–22; "Attouda", 229; Söğüt, "Salbakos Mountain", 15–24; F. D'Andria, "Hierapolis (Pamukkale) Past and Present" ("Hierapolis (Pamukkale) Dün ve Bugün"), in Özçelik, *Uluslararası*, 2.32–37.

11 Y. Kılıç, "Prehistoric Settlements of Denizli Region and Road System Between the Settlements" ("Denizli Yöresinin Prehistoric Yerleşimleri ve Yol Sistemi"), in Özçelik, *Uluslararası*, 2.12–22; for Bronze Age ceramic remains at Colossae see J. Mellaart, "Preliminary Report on a Survey of Pre-Classical Remains in Southern Turkey", *AS* 4 (1954) 175–240, on pp. 230–31, and the chapter by Bahadır and Konakçi in this collection.

12 S. Lloyd/J. Mellaart, *Beycesultan I* (London: BIAA, 1972); Şimşek, "Antik", 321–22, "Attouda", 229–31; T. Gökçe, *XVI ve XVII. Yüzyıllarda Lâzikiyye (Denizli) Kazâsı* (Ankara: TÜBİTAK, 2000), 24; T. Yiğit, "Denizli and Its Environs During the Second Millenium BC" ("M. Ö. II. Binyılda Denizli ve Çevresi"), in Özçelik, *Uluslararası* 2.7–11.

13 Herodotos wrote that the Persian King Xerxes passed through Colossae during his campaign against Athens in 480 BCE: Herodotos *Hist.* 7.30; Xenophon noted that the Persian king, Cyrus, stayed seven days in Colossae in 401 BCE, and added that the king performed an animal sacrifice and arranged games and competitions in Kelainai and then Peltai for the region.

14 Strabo distinguishes this city as "Laodicea near Lycus" from other cities called Laodicea: Strabo *Geogr.* 12.8.16. Laodicea near Lycus had been an older foundation. It was rebuilt as Laodicea in the period of the Seleucid king, Antiochos II: see F. A. Akça, *Denizli Tarihi* (Denizli: 1945), 4; A. H. M. Jones, *Cities of the Eastern Roman Provinces* (New York: Oxford University Press, 1998), 42.

15 Strabo writes "… the part of Phrygia that lies towards Pisidia, and the parts round Amorium and Eumeneia and Synnada, and then Apameia Cibotus, as it is called and Laodicea, which two are the largest of the Phrygian cities. And in the neighborhood of these are situated towns, and … Aphrodisias, Colossae, Themisonium, Sanaus, Metropolis, and Apollonias". Strabo *Geogr.* 12.8.13.

rule upon the testamentary disposition of Attalos III, King of Pergamon. The Romans administered these cities according to their own provincial administration — the declared province of Asia.[16]

Sheep Raising in Antiquity

The domestication of animals began in Anatolia in the Neolithic Age; sheep were part of this process. Colossae and its surrounding area provided the physical geography, fauna and flora that were an especially suitable environment for raising sheep. At least in the Hellenistic and Roman periods there are records that show the cities of the Lycus Valley having an important primary industry of sheep husbandry along with its associated sectors. One of these cities, Laodicea, became a judicial, administrative and commercial centre due to its location on the travel routes of the Lycus Valley.[17]

Strabo noted that black sheep were raised in Laodicea and its vicinity, producing a wool that had a superior quality, unique to the region:

Laodicea though formerly small, grew large in our time … However, it was the fertility of its territory and the prosperity of certain of its citizens that made it great…The country round Laodicea produces sheep that are excellent, not only for the softness of their wool, in which they surpass even the Milesian wool, but also for its raven-black colour, so that Laodikeians derive splendid revenue from it, as do also the neighbouring Colosseni from the colour that bears the same name.[18]

The implication that sheep, whether black or white, were raised throughout the area, including Colossae[19] and presumably Hierapolis, indicates that these three

---

16 For details of Roman provincial designation in the region with extensive bibliography, see H. Palaz Erdemir, "The Administration of Roman Asia (from the first Century BC to the Third Century AD and a Comparison with Osmanlı Government)", unpublished PhD thesis, Department of Classics and Ancient History, University of Wales Swansea, 1998.

17 Laodicea was one of the *conventi* of Asia: see Jones, *Cities*, 61, 64, 73; W. Ramsay, *The Historical Geography of Asia Minor*, (Royal Geographical Society, Supplementary Papers, vol. 4) (Amsterdam: Adolph M. Hakkert, 1962 [1890]), 120, 431; Palaz Erdemir, "Administration", 131–148, for the list of *conventus* centres including Laodicea, see table 4, on pp. 319–20. For detailed information about the functions of these *conventi*, see M. A. Kaya, "Roma Eyaleti Asia'nın Aşağı Büyük Menderes Havzası Mahkeme Bölgeleri", in Öztürk, *First International History* 1–8.

18 Strabo *Geogr.* 12.8.16. Herodotus had noted different sheep species in Arabia (*Hist.* 3.113). For detailed contemporary analysis of sheep species, see Yalçın, "Koyun", 387–422.

19 Lewis and Meyer consider that the wool produced in Colossae was dyed purple or red: N. Lewis/R. Meyer, *Roman Civilisation The Empire (Selected Readings)* (2 vol.; New York: Columbia University Press, 1990), 2.82.

cities probably entered strong partnerships in regard to sheep husbandry and related sector industries.

It is not possible to determine with any scientific accuracy those species of domesticated sheep in this region in antiquity. Those who have made detailed veterinarian studies, indicate that the black sheep that are still raised in the area somehow derive from an earlier species of raven-black sheep which had been crossbred with other types of sheep to create a hybrid; it is thus a breed that has a measure of continuity from the past through to modern times.[20] However, determining the species of ancient sheep would require a detail zooarcheological study, since the physical appearance of today's animals only yields a certain amount of information.[21]

Similarly, there is also no clear information about how animals were raised in the region in antiquity. It may be suggested that sheep were nurtured in sheepfolds in winter and lead out to graze on pastures in spring and summer as at present. One tombstone of a shepherd from Aphrodisias (a neighbouring city to the south) shows that shepherds were almost always mobile, moving their flocks around pastures in the region.[22] This spring and summer activity of sheep agistment in Hellenistic times appears to have been modelled on earlier practice.

---

20 No study has yet determined the particular heredity and species of the sheep in and around the valley. To compare the difficulty of determining with any scientific accuracy those species of domesticated sheep in and around Mediterranean in ancient period in general see, T. D. Bunch/C. Wu/Y.-P. Zhang/S. Wang, "Phylogenetic Analysis of Snow Sheep *(Ovis nivicola)* and Closely Related Taxa", *Journal of Heredity* 97 (2005) 21–30; E. S. Higgs/M. R. Jarman, "The origins of agriculture: a Reconsideration", *Antiquity* 43 (1969) 31–41; C. Broodbank/T. F. Strasser, "Migrant farmers and the Neolithic colonization of Crete", *Antiquity* 65 (1991) 233–245; J. Zilhão, "The spread of agro-pastoral economies across Mediterranean Europe: A View from the Far West", *JMA* 6 (1993) 5–63; J. Blondel/J. Aronson, *Biology and Wildlife of the Mediterranean Region* (Oxford: Oxford University Press, 1999); J-D. Vigne/ H. Buitenhuis/S. Davis, "The first steps in animal domestication into the east of the Euphrates: Cypres and Central Anatolia" (original in French) *Paléorient.* 25/2 (1999) 49–62; L. Martin/ N. Russell/D. Carruthers, "Animal remains from the central Anatolian Neolithic", in F. Gérard/L. Thissen (ed.), *The Neolithic of Central Anatolia* (İstanbul, Turkey: Ege Yayınları; 2002) 193–206; J-D. Vigne/J. Peters/D. Helmer, "New archaeozoological approaches to trace the first steps of animal domestication", in J-D. Vigne/J. Peters/D. Helmer, (ed.), *The First Steps of Animal Domestication.* (Oxford: Oxbow Books, 2005) 1–16; J. Peters/A. von den Driesch/ D. Helmer, "The upper Euphrates-Tigris Basin, cradle of agro-pastoralism?", in Vigne, *First Steps,* 96–124; Melinda A. Zeder, "Domestication and early agriculture in the Mediterranean Basin: Origins, diffusion, and impact", *PNAS* 105 (2008) 11597–11604.

21 See G. Kron, "Archaeozoology and the Productivity of Roman Livestock Farming", *MBAH* 2 (2002) 53–73.

22 J. Reynolds, *Aphrodisias and Rome,* (*JRS Monographs*, No. 1; London: Society for the Promotion of Roman Studies, 1982), 86. For this inscription see T. R. S. Broughton, "Roman Asia Minor", in Tenney Frank, *An Economic Survey of Ancient Rome IV* (Baltimore: The Johns Hopkins University, 1938) 499–916, on pp. 819–21, L. Robert, "Inscriptions d'Aphrodisias", *AC* 36 (1966) 377–423.

Accordingly, we can expect that shepherds connected with Laodicea, Hierapolis and Colossae would not have remained in the tight circle of the city environs but have sought out suitable pastures across the broader area. Where the physical geography allowed passage, shepherds would have made use of the access to graze their flocks. Aphrodisias, Trapezopolis, Attouda, Tripolis, Hydriale and Carura were all likely to have been preferred places and would have witnessed the movement of shepherds through their lands.[23] Stone-built shelters scattered through these parts supports the notion that this general region sustained a strong sheep industry.

Apart from the efforts needed for the pasturing of animals — protection against the elements and marauding beasts — there were the ongoing issues of disease and disease control, not just for the sheep but for humans in relation to the animals. Hydatid disease which affects different parts of the human bodies and rabies were both common diseases in antiquity and can be traced directly to sheep and dogs respectively. The Lycus Valley would not have been hermetically sealed off from the effects of these animal-borne infections.[24]

There are some archaeological clues to sheep raising in the region in antiquity. One striking example was found in Herakleia Salbake: a stone relief to a special localised god, Zeus Ktesis (Ktesios) Patrios. This local manifestation of Zeus has the god depicted as grazing his flock.[25] Another relief (now displayed at the Denizli Müze at Hierapolis) on a small altar to Zeus Ktesis Patrios, seems to confirm that he was the god of sheep and shepherds: the god is depicted on the front of the square stone altar in a distinctive, carved woollen garb (see Figure 1a) and accompanied, on the left face of the stone, by a bounding dog (see Figure 1b).[26] A further tombstone relief portrays Zeus Ktesis Patrios in woollen garb with an eagle in his right hand and a crook in his left (see Figure 2).[27]

Communities in the region also worshipped Hekate in connection with her agricultural fecundity, as also Hermes.[28] Some of the scenes from the mythological stories about such worship are carved as friezes around the Hierapolis Plutonion and Theatre. On the Hierapolis theatre friezes, Thalia is portrayed

---

23 Celal Şimşek outlines the cultural and economic relations among these cities: "Antik", 321–22.

24 See J. Hooke, "Health and Medicine in the Lycus Valley" ("Çürüksu Vadisi'nde Sağlık ve Tıp"), in A.D. Erdemir/Ö. Öncel/Y. Küçükdağ/B. Okka/S. Erer *et al* (ed.), *10th National Congress on the Turkish History of Medicine Proceedings Book, 20–24 May 2008* (Konya: Selçuk University Press, 2008), 1.458–72.

25 S.H. Özdemir, "Eskiçağ'da Denizli ve Kalıntılar", Celal Bayar University Department of History, unpublished honours thesis, (Manisa: 2007). See also MAMA V.175.

26 Özdemir "Eskiçağ'da Denizli". See also *MAMA* VI.87, J. Robert/L. Robert, *La Carie*, II. *Le plateau de Tabai et ses environs* (Paris: de Boccard, 1954), 42. The distinctive Zeus thunderbolt is carved on the right face of the stone: Özdemir, "Eskiçağ'da Denizli".

27 See Özdemir, "Eskiçağ'da Denizli".

28 Hesiod *Theog.* (410–50) tells of the agricultural connections of both.

Fig. 1a Altar to Zeus Ktesis Patrios

Fig. 1b Side of same altar to Zeus

Fig. 2 Funerary relief with Zeus Ktesis Patrios.

with shepherd crook in her hand as found in comedy and pastoral poems.[29] These instances, among many, show how interconnected were religion and the raising of animals.

Related to the agricultural life of Asia, Q. Cicero (who was the governor of Cilicia) in 51–50 BCE mentioned a respected grazing tax company. Cicero trusted this company and acting as a guarantor, he asked P. Silius (then governor of Bithynia), to persuade the people to pay their grazing taxes to this grazing-tax company.[30] Similarly, the custom law of Ephesus originally prepared during the Attalid Kingdom mentions a tax called the *scriptura*. As with other issues of the customs law of Ephesus, the *scriptura* was adapted to local circumstances by the Roman administration and it is likely that this regulation was also related

29 N. Çubuk, "The Cults of Hades and Apollon in Lycus Basin", (Lykos Vadisinde Hades ve Apollon Kültleri), in Özçelik, *Uluslararası*, 2.86–97, especially p. 91.

30 Cicero, *Att.* 5.16, 2; *Fam.* 13.65; 3.8.4 and 13.61.

to the cities of the Lycus Valley. The coastal port stations along the coast of Asia Minor were particularly highlighted in the law, both as to the operations of the ports and as to the collection of dues. However, cities that were affected by the *scripturae* were not confined to ports. All goods that were imported to inland areas or exported from the province of Asia through this region fell within the reach of this law.

It is considered that the *scriptura* was mainly a pasture or grazing tax but there is a lack of precision and clarity about the law. There is no clear explanation about how, from whom and how much *scripturae* would be gathered from people but it does present important information about the usage of pasture that highlights the importance of these lands in Asia Minor in antiquity.[31] Yet a *Senatus Consultum de Aphrodisiensibus* passed in October 39 BCE indicates that there was a pasture due in and around Aphrodisias and the people of Plarasa and Aphrodisias were exempted from this tax.[32] The people who collected this tax were called *scripturarii*.[33]

Economic relations with Laodicea and its neighbouring cities were not restricted to pasture. In Strabo's general comments on the region he noted that "… the Laodiceans derive splendid revenue from it [soft and black sheep wool], as do also the neighbouring Colosseni from the colour which bears the same name."[34] However the traders of Colossae, like Hierapolis, probably raised white-wool sheep also given that highly skilled wool dyers are attested in these two cities. Conversely, they also were likely to have used black wool produced at Laodicea to weave purely black or mixed colour textiles.[35]

31 Reynolds, *Aphrodisias*, 86. For detailed information on the customs regulations of Ephesus see H. Palaz Erdemir, "Anadolu'da Kuralları Tesbit Edilen İlk Gümrük Yasası", *Birinci Uluslararası Aşağı Büyük Menderes Havzası Tarih, Arkeoloji ve Sanat Tarihi Sempozyumu*, (Söke: 2001) 9–18, Palaz Erdemir/Ramazan Gökbunar, "Efes Gümrük Yazıtında Gümrük Vergileri" ("Customs Duties in the Ephesos Custom Inscription"), *Gazi Üniversitesi Iktisadi ve Idari Bilimler Fakültesi Dergisi*, 9 (2007) 227–34; For *scriptura*, see Jones, *Cities*, 164; A. Lintott, *Imperium Romanum: Politics and Administration* (London: Routledge, 1993), 83; Palaz Erdemir, "The Administration", 53. For the exceptional exemptions of free cities of Asia see H. Palaz Erdemir, "Roma'nın Küçük Asya'da İdari Bir Meselesi: Bağımsız Şehirler" ("The "Free cities", a Question of Roman Administration in Asia Minor", *Adalya* 7 (2004) 171–84.

32 The word "'Αννενομίωτος" in the original text was interpreted by Reynolds as τὸ νόμιον or νόμιον τέλος, meaning "pasture dues". See Reynolds, *Aphrodisias*, 59, 62, 86.

33 Lintott, *Imperium Romanum*, 83.

34 Strabo *Geogr.* 12.8.16 (Loeb edition). H. L. Jones in the Loeb edition notes that the "Colossian" wool was dyed purple or madder-red (compare Pliny *Nat.* 25.9.67, 21.9.27). Pliny names a purple colour flower in a different passage, as "Colossian" (see Pliny *Nat.* 21.5). The archaeological excavation of Laodicea for the 2005 season lead by Celal Simşek, found a large fifth century (CE) dyer's workshop: see http://www.pau.edu.tr/laodikeia/2005_Kuzey_atolye.htm.

35 For detailed analysis about wool exchange between these cities, see I. Viaggiatori, *Hierapolis Di Frigia, 1957–* (Lecce: Universita di Lecce, 1987), 88. A well-developed technical processing of textile and design was attested in the area in ancient times: see E. Yavi/ N. Yazıcıoğlu Yavi, *Türkiye'nin Parlayan Yıldızı Denizli* (Denizli: Denizli Valiliği, Neşa Ofset,

There is a drawn-out complex process from raising sheep to the end-product of a weaver's loom and this probably followed familiar long-established practice in antiquity. After the exhausting period of raising sheep, seasonal shearing begins which is then processed through various types of operation until a woollen fabric or rug is manufactured.

While Strabo mentions the natural wealth of the area extending from Hierapolis to Laodicea, he expressly notes that "the water of Hierapolis is suitable for dyeing wool". He explains that the cleaning and dying of wool requires a certain quality of water.[36] This water combined with the madder plant (or alizarin) was critical in the dyeing process and enabled the fauna and flora of the region to contribute a variety of colours to the wool. Strabo even held that wool dyed with the madder plant produced a colour better than the usual reds and purples. All this indicates the contribution that the local water supply and the madder plant made to the development of Hierapolis.[37]

Roman and Byzantine Hierapolis owes a considerable part of its importance to the wool industry. There is some epigraphical evidence for the existence of craft unions and their activities that relate to wool production in the area. Virtually all wool produced in regions administered by cities was controlled by various craft unions. One inscription reads,

ἡ σεμνοτάτη ἐργασία τῶν ἐριοπλυτῶν Τιβ(έριον) Κλ(αύδιον) Ζωτικὸ(ν) Βοὰ τὸν πρῶτον στρατηγὸ(ν) καὶ φιλότειμον ἀγωνοθέτην καὶ γραμ(μ)ατέα ναῶν τῶν ἐν Ἀσίᾳ καὶ πρεσβευτὴν ἔνδοξου καὶ ἀρχιερέα εὐεργέτην τῆς πατρίδος, προνοησάντων τῆς ἀναστάσεως τῶν ... (IHierapJ 40).[38]

Here the "most august guild of wool washers" honours Tiberius Claudius Zotikos Boa, a person who held significant magistracies in the city. This inscription in its context suggests the presence of other guilds — a purple-dyers guild also

1998), 30. The spring clip used in weaving has to have a certain standard of fineness, length, thickness, evenness, density, ondulation, elasticity, endurance, cleanliness, madder, colour and softness: see C. N. Aytuğ/E. Alaçam/Ü. Özkoç/B. C. Yalçın/H. Gökçen/H. Türker, *Koyun-Keçi Hastalıkları ve Yetiştiriciliği*, (İstanbul: Teknografik Matbaası, 1990), 440–449.

36 The warmth and natural chemical compounds of the river Lycus (modern Çürüksu) helps to fasten the colours of textiles and contributes to the quality of the fabric: Yavi/Yazıcıoğlu Yavi, 35, 41.

37 Strabo, *Geogr.* 13.4.14.

38 W. M. Ramsay, *The Cities and Bishoprics of Phrygia* I–II, (Oxford: Clarendon Press, 1895), 118, no. 26; C. Humann/C. Cichorius/W. Judeich/F. Winter, *Altertümer von Hierapolis* (Berlin: Jahrbuch des kaiserlich deutschen Archäologischen Instituts, 1898), no: 40; G. Laberre and M.Th. LeDinahet, "Les metiers du textile en Asie Mineure de l'époque hellé à l'epoque imperiale", in *Aspects de l'artisanat du textile dans le monde méditerranéen (Égypte, Grèce, Monde Romain), Collection de l'Institut d'Archéologie et d'Histoire de l'Antiquité* (2 vol.; Lyon: Université Lumière Lyon, 1996) 2.49–115, especially p. 104, no. 64. See also Jones, *Cities*, 73; Viaggiatori, 88.

Fig. 3 Inscription of the dyers' guild at the Hierapolis necropolis.

honoured the same civic leader (*IHierapJ* 41).[39] We also know of a wool dyers guild. All such guilds probably had many connections between them grounded in wool products and the lofty importance gained from association with or membership of such bodies.[40]

This unique group regulated its life as an association. As far as can be deduced, Jews were involved in the dyeing of wool in Hierapolis in antiquity.[41] There are some clues that indicate that a number of Jewish people were especially active within the purple dyers association, the *purpurarii/porphyrobaphoi*. In Hierapolis, they were able to source the purple dye not from the murex shell

---

39 See W. Ameling, *Inscriptiones Judaicae Orientis II: Kleinasien* (Tübingen: Mohr Siebeck, 2004), 417–18; P. A. Harland, *Dynamics of Identity in the World of the Early Christians* (London: Continuum, 2009), 132 n32.

40 For the operations and functions of guild associations, see O. M. van Nijf, *The Civic World of Professional Associations in the Roman East* (Amsterdam: J. C. Gieben, 1997); M. I. Finley, *The Ancient Economy* (London: University of California Press, 1999), 138–41.

41 For the Jewish community in the area see Cicero *Flac.* 26–68; Ramsay, *Cities and Bishoprics, passim; Asianic Elements in Greek Civilization* (London: John Murray, 1927); A. R. R. Sheppard, "Jews, Christians and Heretics in Acmonia and Eumeneia (RECAM Notes and Studies no. 6)", *AS* 29 (1979) 169–180; F. F. Bruce, "Jews and Christians in the Lycus Valley", *BS* 141 (1984) 3–15; M. Wilson, "Rich Yet Lukewarm: Early Christianity in the Lycus Valley" ("Lycus Vadisinde Erken Hıristiyanlık"), in Özçelik, *Uluslararası* 2.68–72; for Jews involved in wool-dyeing see Jones, *Cities*, 73; Yavi/Yazıcıoğlu Yavi, 38. For detailed analysis related to the *Purpurarii* in the Lycus Valley, see E. Ertekin, "Textile Production and Textile Corporations of Hierapolis and Laodikeia in the Roman Period" ("Roma Çağında Hierapolis ve Laodikeia'da Tekstil ve Tekstil Sektöründeki Meslek Örgütleri (*Ergasia*'lar)") in Özçelik, *Uluslararası* 1.31–41.

but from a cheaper extract, the madder plant.[42] This association was especially valued within the Jewish community, who defined themselves as a "group of citizens" (κατοικία or "public" (λαός).[43]

Furthermore, the customs regulation at Ephesus, as mentioned earlier, also governed the importation of the shells for purple dye. This suggests that both types of dyeing (whether murex shell or madder root) may have been practiced — at least in Ephesus and probably further inland even to the Lycus Valley.[44] According to the custom law of Ephesus, "the collector of fresh purple fish from the sea had to pay a twentieth part of the catch as tax".[45]

An honorary inscription dated to the time of Commodus reveals four different textile based organisations in Laodicea as in Hierapolis. Embroiders, fullers, wool beaters and manufacturers of winter clothing all appear to be related to the same emporium.[46] There is another inscription indicating the existence of wool beaters and manufacturers of winter clothing. It is important for the information it implies about the different kinds of craft organizations related to the different stages of wool-processing and the cloth making industry in the Lycus Valley.

Even though sheep husbandry and related sector industries were located in the three main cities of the Lycus Valley (Colossae, Laodicea and Hierapolis),

---

42 Viaggiatori, 88, 91, 116; R. S. West, *Life in Ancient Rome* (London: The Reader's Digest Association Limited, 1996), 48–9; for the madder plant, see T. Baykara, "Kökboya", *IÜCED* 7 (1964) 221–26. Pliny notes that sea-weed (*phycos thalassion*) in addition to being a remedy for gout, was used in dying fabric purple. There are three kinds of it; probably this type was used in Crete for dyeing cloth (Pliny *Nat.* 26.66). It has yet to be confirmed whether this type was used in Hierapolis. When Pythermus, a Phocaean envoy in the name of Aeolia and Ionia, went to seek help against Cyrus "in order to draw as large an audience as possible, he dressed himself in purple clothes and came forward to make a long speech asking for Spartan aid" since purple coloured dress indicated wealth and power. (Herodotos *Hist.* 1.152). For purple dyers in Asia in general see H. Malay, "Batı Anadolu'nun Antikçağ'daki Ekonomik Durumu", www.localarchives.org/assets/37929155–E43A-431E-AE2A-E88ADDE3E12C.pdf- 16.0.2009, *at 14.15, 58.* In antiquity, textile goods were precious as well as sacred and were offered as gifts to different recipients. There was a scarlet robe among the gifts of Persian king Cambyses sent to the king of Ethiopia (Herodotos *Hist.* 2.20). Among a huge pile of objects Croesus burnt for Delphian Apollo were tunics and other richly coloured garments: Herodotos *Hist* 1.50. Textiles were also used as swaddling-cloth, grave-cloth: Herodotos *Hist.* 1.111, 113; 181, 195, 198, 202–203.

43 Jones, *Cities,* 74, especially fn 74; Yavi/Yazıcıoğlu Yavi, 38; Ameling, 435. Shops belonging to some of the Jewish settlers are attested in Laodicea and Hierapolis: Ramsay, *Tarsus (Aziz Pavlos'un Kenti)* translated by L. Zoroğlu (Ankara: TTK, 2000), 96ff; Harland, *Dynamics of Identity,* 128–34.

44 *SEG* 39.1180; H. W. Pleket, "Models and Inscriptions: Export of Textiles in the Roman Empire", *EA* 30 (1998) 117–28, on p. 123.

45 See H. Engelmann/D. Knibbe, "Zollgesetz der Provinz Asia (Eine neue Inschrift aus Ephesos)", *EA* 14 (1989) 1–206; see nos. 1–7.

46 Ramsay, *Cities and Bishoprics* 74, no. 8; Laberre-LeDinahet, "Les metiers", 49–115, especially on p. 98, no. 55.

Laodicea was the centre of the wool industry in the region.[47] All wool products manufactured in the area, regardless of whether it came from Laodicea or not, were known as 'Laodicean'. This is an important implication derived from the price edict of Diocletian.[48] In the edict, there is a list of textile goods names distinguished by the name "Laodicean", namely, the "Laodicean hooded cloak", the "unmarked Laodicean dalmatic", "Laodicean purple-bordered tunic", the "Laodicean hooded cape" the "Laodicean light cloak." There is no reference to Hierapolis or Colossae. This may bolster our claim that any textiles from the Lycus Valley (even from Asia) were likely to be known internationally as "Laodicean". "Laodicean" may have become a designated style not necessarily a reference to the area from which the material or cut came. Even so, this still reveals that the area was highly influential with certain styles in its woollen products.

Weaving and textile production gained further importance as a marker of status and wealth through refinements and changes in fashion in Rome. Weaving not only provided the basic materials for dress making, but also the fabric for decorative materials in houses, palaces, sanctuaries and churches.[49] Clothing and woven cloth were often among the luxury goods of Roman society. The Customs Law of 62 CE at Ephesus declared a 10 % tax on the manufactured local

---

47 Finley notes that, besides Laodicea in Asia Minor, there were other places in the Roman world which produced woollen fabrics and rugs. Patavium (Padua), for example, in northern Italy became very wealthy because of its wool industry in antiquity: Finley, 137, 193. Strabo mentions another city called Turdetania in Iberia which also produced raven-black textiles (which were produced from cattle) which were exported to Italy in the Roman period: see Strabo *Geogr.* 3.2.6.

48 Jones, *Cities*, 74, especially fn 74. For weaving in Laodicea, see H. Malay, "Antik Devirde Denizli Yöresinde Ekonomik Durum", Türk Kültür Tarihinde Denizli Sempozyumu, (27–30 Eylül 1988), *Bildiriler* (Denizli 1989) 296–98. In order to ease the economic crisis, Diocletian had decided to standardise the prices of different goods, in 301 CE. The edict encompassed, *inter alia*, food products, leather, textiles, cosmetics: for Diocletian's price edict list see E. L. Graser, "The Edict of Diocletian on Maximum Prices", in T. Frank (ed.), *An Economic Survey of Ancient Rome V: Rome and Italy of the Empire* (Baltimore: Johns Hopkins Press, 1940) 310–421; S. Laufer, *Diokletians Preisedikt* (Berlin: de Gruyter, 1971), *sv*; R. H. Barrows, *The Romans* (Middlesex: Pelican Book, 1962), 171–72; J. M. Reynolds, "The Aphrodisias copy of Diocletian's Edict on Maximum Prices", *ZPE* 33 (1979) 46; Palaz Erdemir, "Sheep Raising", 23–30; Joyce Reynolds, "Diocletian's Edict on maximum prices: the chapter on wool", ZPE 42 (1981) 283–84. See also Ertekin, "Textile Production", 31–41.

49 Anthony Macro recognises that textiles among various products, though produced in limited quantities, though subject to local demand and though their carriage was slow, risky and expensive, was nevertheless exported by land and sea to far distant places. As a result of the woollen textile trade in and beyond the Lycus Valley, other Asian cities, such as Ephesus, Smyrna and Apameia also derived a share of wealth associated with the movement of these goods: A. D. Macro, "The Cities of Asia Minor Under Roman Imperium", *ANRW*, II, Hildegard Temporini (ed.), (Berlin/New York: Walter de Gruyter, 1980) 658–97, on pp. 684–85. Finley notes that St Paul's home city, Tarsus, was famous for its fine quality, cotton textile cloth which was expensive even for local citizens: Finley, 136–37, 193.

products that passed through the port, regardless of where they came from.[50] Textile products from Laodicea and Hierapolis (especially woollen ones) were classified as luxury consumables and attracted tax. However some exemption from this tax was granted since Roman citizens were required to wear different-coloured woollen or serge togas in public life. Though Rome was able to obtain woollen togas from other (and closer) centres, the name "Laodicean" began to be subscribed to the garments.[51]

Wool was not the only textile merchandise produced in the area. Cotton textile weaving was also developed. Garments made in various styles, colours and designs were exported from the Lycus Valley to Rome, Italy and Europe in antiquity and expanded the range of fine fashion. In the necropolis of Hierapolis, one marble sarcophagus inscription, dated to the second century CE, notes that the owner is a certain Menandrianos and mentions a "cotton textile corporation".[52]

Commercial Travel

Textiles, amongst a range of locally produced goods, were transported by local or Roman merchants to external markets. In imperial times, as in modern times, businessmen and commercial purveyors had great opportunity to travel overseas and observe different peoples and cultures. Again from the Hierapolis necropolis comes a famous funerary inscription that remembers the first century merchant T. Flavius Zeuxis. He had been through the Peloponnese (in the southern part of Greece) 72 times en route to Italy.[53] From the same section of the necropolis comes another funerary inscription set with a relief of a sailing ship. The third century sarcophagus of the brothers Aelianus and Acydinus probably is designed to represent their overseas trade as merchants.[54]

Manufacturers in the Lycus Valley became rich not only by producing textile goods in themselves but they also gained considerable wealth from their maritime mercantile connections forged with overseas countries. One funerary inscription belonging to a businessman *Laudacenarius* found in Lyon indicates

---

50 S. Mitchell, *Anatolia (Land, Men and Gods in Asia Minor)* (2 vol.; Oxford: Clarendon Press, 1993), 1.257; G. Kantor, *Ancestral Laws Under The Roman Rule: The Case of Lycia*, (submitted for confirmation of Ph.D Oxford 2006), 22, especially fn. 73, *users.ox.ac.uk/~ball1674/ lycian_text.rtf* -; H. W. Pleket, "Note on a Customs-Law from Caunus", *Mnemosyne* 11 (1958) 128–35; B. Levick, "The Roman Economy: Trade in Asia Minor and the Niche Market", *Greece and Rome* 51 (2004) 180–98.

51 Yavi/Yazıcıoğlu Yavi, 38, 44.

52 Özdemir, "Eskiçağ'da Denizli", 201.

53 *IGR* IV.841, *SIG*³ 1229.

54 H. W. Pleket, "Greek Epigraphy and Comparative Ancient History: Two Case Studies", *EA* 12 (1988) 25–38; Özdemir, "Eskiçağ'da Denizli", 203.

that the textile goods of Laodicea and the Lycus Valley generally were destined not only for Italy, but beyond, to Gaul and other parts of Europe.[55]

Although Laodicea was not the only important source for wool production, its position at a junction of major trade routes enhanced its commercial potential. One main highway connected Laodicea with the large cities of Ephesus, Pergamum and Smyrna, that were centres of trade and culture in western Asia Minor. From these centres sprang major road and sea networks to Europe. The same avenue for travel unfolded to the east, proclaimed at Laodicea by the name given to one of its gates: the "Syrian Gate". A major road also linked Laodicea to southern cities and ports.[56] The transit charge, the *portorium* mentioned in the custom law of Ephesus was another fiduciary due that implies the intensity of overseas trade relations and the significance of taxation on this activity for the Asian cities. Piecemeal decrees or rules touching on transit dues were promulgated at different periods during the Roman Republic. Although only the coastal cities of Asia were mentioned as port stations and not all the goods liable to the taxation were mentioned, the custom Law of Ephesus is one of the sources of comprehensive regulations about *portorium*. Ephesus and Smyrna (also mentioned in the law) were two main ports for the inland cities generally as for the cities of Lycus Valley in particular.[57]

An honorary limestone pedestal inscription for the chief translator of Colossae found in Colossae strengthens the idea that international trade was vast. Cadwallader states that "this inscription points to the importance of interpretation in the affairs of the city at a mundane, oral, mediating level". This required translators or translator associations (as this was a *chief* translator for Colossae) for presentation and marketing of goods and mediation between sellers and buyers or among their agents.[58]

Women in the textile industries

While woollen textile goods were commercially traded mainly by men in antiquity, the spinning and weaving of the products were the provinces of women. Wool-working was considered a sacred duty and women's commitment to spin-

---

55 J. Rougé, "Un negotiator Laudecenarius à Lyon", *ZPE* 27 (1977) 263–69; Pleket, "Greek Epigraphy", 34 and "Models and Inscriptions: Export of Textiles in the Roman Empire", *EA* 30 (1998) 126, n14. For detailed information on the relationship of elites and commerce in the Roman East, see Pleket, "Urban Elites and the Economy in the Greek Cities of the Roman Empire", *MBAH* 3 (1984) 3–36.

56 The significance of this road was manifest in 301 BCE during the battle in Ipsus between Lysimarchos, king of Thrace and King Seleucos: Ramsay, *Historical Geography*, 35.

57 A number of coastal cities were mentioned in the custom law of Ephesus. For details see, Engelmann/Knibbe, "Zolgesetz".

58 A. H. Cadwallader "A New Inscription [=Two New Inscriptions], a Correction and a Confirmed Sighting from Colossae", *EA* 40 (2007) 109–18, especially pp. 113–14.

ning and weaving was deemed to secure their family's destiny.[59] An application of a spell for men's impotence in Anatolia in the Hittite period (in 2nd millennium BCE) shows clearly the gender division of work. In the Hittite text, a magician explained how she would cure a man from impotency: "At the beginning I leave the man outside the door and give into his hand a mirror and a spindle to hold [representing womanly practice]. Then I let him go through the door and I take the spindle from him and I give him a bow [representing manly habit]."[60] King David's curse on Joab in the Old Testament which says "let the distaff never depart from his sons" (meaning a curse that they may be effeminate)[61] adds weight to the understanding that the Hittite spell shows the gender-separation of tasks in the ancient period.

Other texts also emphasize the same associations for weaving. In Homer's *Iliad*, Hector exclaims to his wife, "...Go home now, and attend to your own work, the loom and the spindle, and see that the maidservants get on with theirs. War is men's business ...".[62] In the *Odyssey*, Telemachus interrupted his mother "... So go to your quarters now and attend to your own work, the loom and the spindle, and see that the servants get on with theirs. The bow is the men's concern, and mine above all; for I am master of this house."[63] Similarly Herodotus refers to Paris and Helen wandering in Sidon and recalls a section of the poem called the *Deeds of Diomed* which runs,

"There were the bright robes woven by the women of Sidon, |
Whom the hero Paris, splendid as a god to look on."[64]

He recognises that weaving was a woman's work in ancient times. Mythology supports the same idea. Athena was known as the goddess who invested women with weaving ability and protected them in this realm. Ovid, for example, tells the story of Athena and Arachne to show how weaving could bring an intense rivalry even between mortal and immortal females.[65]

---

59 In ancient times, certain types and colours of clothing were sacred. The priests in Egypt were the only ones permitted to wear certain linen clothing (Herodotos *Hist.* 2.37). "The dress of the Babylonians consists of a linen tunic reaching to the feet with a woollen one over it and a short white cloak on top." (Herodotos *Hist.* 1.195).

60 See A.M. Dinçol, "Hititler, Geç Hititler", *Anadolu Uygarlıkları* I (1982) 93–94; G. Erginöz, *Hititlerde Anatomi ve Tıp*, (İstanbul: İstanbul University Press, 1999), 162 especially at n. 38.

61 For the curse on Joab by King David see 2 Sam 3:29; see also Plutarch *Mor.* 72e.

62 Homer *Il.* 6.490–95.

63 Homer *Od.* 21.350–55.

64 Herodotos *Hist.* 2.116. Herodotos also explains that "the Egyptians, in their manner and customs seem to have reversed the ordinary practices of mankind. For instance, women attend market and are employed in trade, while men stay at home and do the weaving." Herodotos *Hist* 2.35.

65 Ovid *Metam.* 6.53–58.

Funerary reliefs of women carry the symbols of weaving carved into stone. A large number of examples from antiquity related to this subject have been found in different parts of Anatolia. From these reliefs from Central Phrygia and Upper Tembris Valley between first and third centuries CE certain symbols seem to have been standard on epitaphs for women. Exemplary women were represented with spindle or wool basket (some baskets were depicted as full of wool, some empty) on different gravestones.[66]

Though not from Asia Minor, there are striking examples of funerary relief carvings of women at Palmyra Museum in Syria. Women who were involved in weaving in their lifetime are immortalized on fine quality limestone reliefs. Palmyrene women are represented as having been busy with spinning and knitting yarn through their lives. In fact, most of the women have been embossed with yarn in their embrace on the funerary reliefs. One middle aged lady is depicted with two spindles in her left hand and showing her right hand empty towards the audience. This represents the mortality of life, though no word is written on it. The relief expresses, "I wove for my lifetime but I go to the hereafter, my hands empty".[67] There is naturally some danger in relying on funerary reliefs to indicate what the actual life of the deceased was. Many of the reliefs present conventional portrayals of life, especially women's life. These, as well as the inscriptions and literary references about women, frequently present an ideal about women, their behaviour and their gendered work practices. For example, noble women had probably long directed the distaff and loom to their slaves, in spite of how they were presented on reliefs. There is also the issue of the literary texts, written by men, prescribing certain behaviours for women.[68]

As in Palmyra, so in the Lycus Valley and across the world of antiquity, women, especially ordinary or servant or slave women were the ones who, throughout their lives, were preoccupied with spinning wool and knitting yarn. Clearly then, the woollen industry was reliant upon women for its productivity and, conversely, women were never separate from socio-economic life. Such artefactual material from the Lycus Valley is more rare, but is available. An example of a woman's funerary relief similar to those found in the Tembris Valley occurs at Hierapolis. It contains the distinctive female symbols of a basket full of wool and a mirror.[69] More evidence is likely to be found when new researches and archaeological excavations are initiated in the area.

Laodicea, Hierapolis and Colossae were cities that cultivated strong relationships through its industries of wool, weaving and textile design. These and re-

---

66 See *MAMA* IX.198, 208, 274, 304, 320, 388, 426, 449, 516.

67 See H.P. Erdemir, "Akademik Gezi Gözlem-Palmyra (Tedmür)", *Arkeoloji ve Sanat Yayınları*, (2009) forthcoming.

68 See Robert Sallares, *The Ecology of the Ancient Greek World* (Ithaca, NY: Cornell University Press, 1991), 83.

69 Özdemir, "Eskiçağ'da Denizli", 202.

lated industries provided a clear direction in the formation of different craft unions. The Roman interest in fashion, dress and associated finery as indications of status provided a ready market opening for shoes, bags, couplings made from leather and other materials. Although more evidence needs to be found, sheep rearing cities of the Lycus Valley were also busy with leatherwork and its trade. One example has been found in Colossae. An epitaph dated to the late 2nd or 3rd century CE on a limestone bomos found on the northern side of the Colossae necropolis honoured Dion the leatherworker.[70] Another piece of evidence about the leatherwork industry was the bust erected by a leading shoemaker to honour a well known person of the city of Caesarea (Yeşilova).[71] This underscores the reputation of the union of shoe-producers in the social and economic life of society. The existence of such a craft union also illustrates how raw leather material for shoes was crucial to the city itself whether produced locally or imported from neighboring cities.[72] It is not easy to explain which sector of trade good (textile, leatherworks or other sub-sectors of sheep products) was considered important in each of the cities of the area. There might be a leading city or cities yet also rivalry between the local cities or the exchange of assistance in the process of production and trade.

The breeding of sheep early on in human civilization was clearly in response to human need. Laodicea, Hierapolis and Colossae, cities that are described as key sheep raising cities of Phrygia, derived revenue from related animal products such as mutton,[73] milk,[74] gut[75] and horn as well as wool and weaving sec-

---

70 *MAMA* VI.44; see Cadwallader, "Two New Inscriptions", 115–17.

71 Caesarea was named as Moagetids in the Hellenistic period.

72 Jones, *Cities*, 74. "There were some manufactures deliberately designed for export, such as the shoes and summer mantles, made we do not know where, which an Athenian brought to Cyrene once a year in such small supply that Bishop Synesius was impatient lest he miss the opportunity to buy." Finley, 136. The Ionians used sheep and goat skin as paper in the ancient period and this vellum became widespread throughout antiquity. (Herod *Hist* 5.58). For the shoemakers in Asia in general see, H. Malay, "Batı Anadolu'nun Antikçağ'daki Ekonomik Durumu", *supra*.

73 The most famous doctor of the Roman period, Galen, explained how mutton and other kinds of meat were used for curing different illnesses. The most striking part of Galen's explanations is that which specifies animals according to their growing areas. Animals raised on high plateaus and woods were held to be more nutritious than those farmed on plains. For Galen, the improved nutritional value and taste was attributable to the opportunity for the animals to be fed with different kinds of flora. It is thought that sheep raised in Hierapolis and its vicinity had access to rich resources of fodder and therefore their meat, on this understanding, would have been more nutritious and tasty: see P. N. Singer, *Galen* (Selected Works) (World's Classics; Oxford: Oxford University Press, 1997), 313–316.

74 Milk was used to feed babies and children as well as being used in cooking and the production of cheese in antiquity. Galen explains how sheep, goat, cow, pig and mule milk was used, in addition to cheese production, as a remedy for curing the sick: Singer, *Galen*, 318–324.

75 It is considered that animal and sheep intestines were converted into contraceptive devices like condoms or even for the provision of fibre for surgical procedures. Small pieces

tors. In addition, lanolin, an expensive by-product of sheep wool, was a key ingredient in cosmetics and cream used by rich and noble women. Lanolin is not easy to extract and requires a significant scale of operation in wool production, hence requiring the resources and size of cities such as Laodicea, Hierapolis, and Colossae.[76]

Conclusion

This study has revealed how economically important and extensive was the industry of sheep raising in the key cities of the Lycus Valley. The seasonal constraints of pasturing the animals, combined with the significant Roman demand for value-added sheep products, made some textile goods deemed to be luxury items exempt from customs levies, even though *scripturae* were extensively collected in the Roman period.

Animal husbandry was a key contributor to the commercial, economic, social and cultural infra-structure of a city. This spontaneous economic development in the Lycus Valley created more precious farming products "light in bulk, high in value" compared to crops. It generated an enormous range of occupations and associated craft organizations that arranged and protected the rights of their members. Hence craft unions, such as wool washers, wool beaters, wool dyers, weavers, tailors, dress makers, leather-workers, and the like would have predominated and been significant indicators of the economic vitality of the Lycus Valley.[77]

It is clear that such economic dependence on sheep extended to other cities at the boundaries of the valley, cities such as Trapezopolis, Tripolis, Attouda and Aphrodisias, whose wealth in no small measure can be attributed to this economic sector. The leatherwork trade was also significant as part of this sector but compared to textile production was less important to cities like Laodicea, Hierapolis and Colossae. According to Strabo, the goods produced in the region were of a better quality than in Miletos and this suggests that some competition and rivalry may have existed between at least some of the cities as well.

As a general rule, black sheep were mainly grown in colder climates. Only in Laodicea (and may be Hierapolis and Colossae) a special case appears, contradicting the general rule. From this perspective, it is surprising that while white sheep were grown in cities closer to the coast, raven-black sheep were grown only in the Lycus Valley from the ancient period onwards.

---

of animal intestines were found in Ephesus, in the bedrooms of the Terrace Houses ("Yamaç Evler") suggestive of contraceptive use.

76 West, 31,50. For the use of sheep and associated by-products see Barrows, *The Romans*, 15.

77 See Broughton, "Roman Asia Minor", 844.

Ancient cities around the Lycus Valley, in the east of Maeander Valley, within Phrygia and Caria, situated between Mediterranean and territorial climates, benefited from the breadth of climatic conditions. In the Roman period, the main highway running west-east connecting Ephesus, Tralles and its neighbouring cities in the province of Asia for administrative purposes in the province of Asia, was well-maintained and inevitably well-used for the passage of trade goods. The highway not only provided increased ease of access to export markets but facilitated stronger relations with other cities around the Lycus Valley. While western shore of Aegean Sea (namely Hellas) had been dominant in Mediterranean and world trade, the Roman occupation of Asia Minor and further east increased the importance of the eastern Mediterranean ports. This change inevitably contributed to the further development of the cities such Laodicea, Hierapolis, and Colossae. Particularly during the imperial period of Rome, the international trade between Rome and its provinces developed largely due to the security and stability of empire. In general, local merchants and traders became active in Mediterranean as well as Roman businessmen in the first century of Roman empire.[78] The cities of the Lycus Valley enjoyed economic prosperity in spite of the severe damage they suffered from time to time because of earthquakes. Their prosperity was based on their principal industry – the manufacture and preparation of woollen fabrics, which were carried to the Aegean coast and exported to various parts of the ancient world.[79] This overseas trade was the key factor for Asian cities growth in the production and transportation of goods not only within Asia and the East but also through the western edge of Europe.

In sum, the economic development of the Lycus Valley was founded on the raising of animals and its associated by-products and sector industries, and depended to a significant extent upon the geography of the area, the adjustment to the new world and administration, the changing trade routes, overseas supply and demand and the entrepreneurial aptitude of the people of the region. Here, the Zeuxis inscription has to be recalled where it was emphasised that he had the initiative and courage to make so many journeys and that his local Hierapolitan society would attach significant honour to his exemplary entrepreneurship.

This may also throw light on the unwavering relationship of people with the local natural sources and the relations of the cities of the Lycus Valley within the production and international trade capacity.

---

78 M. P. Charlesworth, *Trade Routes and Commerce of Roman Empire*, (Hildesheim: Olms, 1961), 96. See also Levick, "The Roman Economy", 180–198.

79 Bruce, 3–15. For transport by sea see L. Casson, *Ships and Seamanship in the Ancient World*, (Princeton, NJ: Princeton University Press, 1971).

Bibliography

Akça, F. A., *Denizli Tarihi* (Denizli: 1945).

Alp, S., *Hitit Çağı'nda Anadolu* (Ankara: TÜBİTAK, 2000).

Ameling, W., *Inscriptiones Judaicae Orientis II: Kleinasien* (Tübingen: Mohr Siebeck, 2004).

D'Andria, F., "Hierapolis (Pamukkale) Past and Present" ("Hierapolis (Pamukkale) Dün ve Bugün"), in A. Özçelik *et al* (ed.), *Uluslararası Denizli ve Çevresi Tarih ve Kültür Sempozyumu Bildiriler* (2 vol.; Denizli: Pamukkale University, 2007) 2.32–37.

Aytuğ, C. N./E. Alaçam/Ü. Özkoç/B. C. Yalçın/H. Gökçen/H. Türker, *Koyun-Keçi Hastalıkları ve Yetiştiriciliği* (İstanbul: Teknografik Matbaası, 1990).

Barrows, R. H., *The Romans* (Middlesex: Pelican Book, 1962).

Baykara, T., "Kökboya", *İÜCED* 7 (1964) 221–26.

Blondel, J./J. Aronson, *Biology and Wildlife of the Mediterranean Region* (Oxford: Oxford University Press, 1999).

Broodbank, C./T. F. Strasser, "Migrant farmers and the Neolithic colonization of Crete", *Antiquity* 65 (1991) 233–245.

Broughton, T. R. S., "Roman Asia Minor", in T. Frank (ed.), *An Economic Survey of Ancient Rome IV* (Baltimore: The Johns Hopkins University, 1938) 499–916.

Bruce, F. F., "Jews and Christians in the Lycus Valley", *BS* 141 (1984) 3–15.

Bunch, T. D./C. Wu/Y.-P. Zhang/S. Wang, "Phylogenetic Analysis of Snow Sheep (*Ovis nivicola*) and Closely Related Taxa", *Journal of Heredity* 97 (2005) 21–30.

Büyükkolancı, M., "Laodicea and Hierapolis: The Last Periods of two Cities by the Light of Their Baths Excavations" ("Laodikeia and Hierapolis Hamamlarının Kazı Sonuçlarına Göre İki Kentin Son Dönemleri") in A. Özçelik *et al* (ed.), *Uluslararası Denizli ve Çevresi Tarih ve Kültür Sempozyumu Bildiriler* (2 vol.; Denizli: Pamukkale University, 2007) 2.51–56.

Cadwallader, A. H. "A New Inscription [=Two New Inscriptions], a Correction and a Confirmed Sighting from Colossae", *EA* 40 (2007) 109–118.

Casson, L., *Ships and Seamanship in the Ancient World* (Princeton, NJ: Princeton University Press, 1971).

Charlesworth, M. P., *Trade Routes and Commerce of Roman Empire* (Hildesheim: Olms, 1961).

Çubuk, N., "The Cults of Hades and Apollon in Lycus Basin", (Lykos Vadisinde Hades ve Apollon Kültleri), in A. Özçelik *et al* (ed.), *Uluslararası Denizli ve Çevresi Tarih ve Kültür Sempozyumu Bildiriler* (2 vol.; Denizli: Pamukkale University, 2007) 2.86–97.

Darkot, B./M. Tuncel, *Ege Bölgesi Coğrafyası* (İstanbul: İstanbul Üniversitesi Edebiyat Fakültesi Matbaası, 1988).

Dinçol, A. M., "Hititler, Geç Hititler", *Anadolu Uygarlıkları* I (1982) 93–94.

Dolukhanov, P., *Eski Ortadoğu'da Çevre ve Etnik Yapı* (translated by Suavi Aydın; Ankara: İmge Kitabevi, 1998).

Engelmann H./D. Knibbe, "Zollgesetz der Provinz Asia (Eine neue Inschrift aus Ephesos)", *EA* 14 (1989) 1–206.

Erdemir, H., "The Administration of Roman Asia (from the first Century BC to the Third Century AD and a Comparison with Osmanlı Government)", unpublished PhD thesis, Department of Classics and Ancient History, University of Wales Swansea, 1998.

- "Anadolu'da Kuralları Tesbit Edilen İlk Gümrük Yasası", *Birinci Uluslararası Aşağı Büyük Menderes Havzası Tarih, Arkeoloji ve Sanat Tarihi Sempozyumu* (Söke: 2001) 9–18.

- "Sheep Raising and Sector Industries in and around Hierapolis in Antiquity" ("Antikçağ'da Denizli ve Çevresinde Koyun Yetiştiriciliği ve Yan Sektörleri"), in A. Özçelik *et al* (ed.), *Uluslararası Denizli ve Çevresi Tarih ve Kültür Sempozyumu Bildiriler* (2 vol.; Denizli: Pamukkale University, 2007) 1.23–30.

- "Roma'nın Küçük Asya'da İdari Bir Meselesi: Bağımsız Şehirler" ("The "Free cities", a Question of Roman Administration in Asia Minor"), *Adalya* 7 (2004) 171–84.

- "Akademik Gezi Gözlem-Palmyra (Tedmür)", *Arkeoloji ve Sanat Yayınları* (2009).

Erdemir, H. Palaz/R. Gökbunar, "Efes Gümrük Yazıtında Gümrük Vergileri", ("Customs Duties in the Ephesos Custom Inscription"), *Gazi Üniversitesi İktisadi ve İdari Bilimler Fakültesi Dergisi*, 9 (2007) 227–34.

Erginöz, G., *Hititlerde Anatomi ve Tıp* (İstanbul: İstanbul University Press, 1999).

Ertekin, E., "Textile Production and Textile Corporations of Hierapolis and Laodikeia in the Roman Period" ("Roma Çağında Hierapolis ve Laodikeia'da Tekstil ve Tekstil Sektöründeki Meslek Örgütleri (*Ergasia'lar*)") in A. Özçelik *et al* (ed.), *Uluslararası Denizli ve Çevresi Tarih ve Kültür Sempozyumu Bildiriler* (2 vol.; Denizli: Pamukkale University, 2007) 1.31–41.

Finley, M. I., *The Ancient Economy* (London: University of California Press, 1999).

Gökçe, T., *XVI ve XVII. Yüzyıllarda Lâzikiyye (Denizli) Kazâsı* (Ankara: TÜBİTAK, 2000).

Göney, S., *Büyük Menderes Bölgesi* (İstanbul: İstanbul Üniversitesi Edebiyat Fakültesi Matbaası, 1975).

Graser, E. L., "The Edict of Diocletian on Maximum Prices", in T. Frank (ed.), *An Economic Survey of Ancient Rome V: Rome and Italy of the Empire* (Baltimore: Johns Hopkins Press, 1940) 310–421.

Harland, P. A., *Dynamics of Identity in the World of the Early Christians* (London: Continuum, 2009).

Higgs, E. S./M. R. Jarman, "The Origins of Agriculture: a Reconsideration", *Antiquity* 43 (1969) 31–41.

Hooke, J., "Health and Medicine in the Lycus Valley" ("Çürüksu Vadisi'nde Sağlık ve Tıp"), in A. D. Erdemir/Ö. Öncel/Y. Küçükdağ/B. Okka/S. Erer *et al* (ed.), *10th National Congress on the Turkish History of Medicine Proceedings Book*, *20–24 May 2008* (2 vol., Konya: Selçuk University Press, 2008) 1.458–72.

Humann, C./C. Cichorius/W. Judeich/F. Winter, *Altertümer von Hierapolis* (Berlin: Jahrbuch des kaiserlich deutschen Archäologischen Instituts, 1898).

Jones, A. H. M., *Cities of the Eastern Roman Provinces* (New York: Oxford University Press, 1998).

Kaya, M. A., "Roma Eyaleti Asia'nın Aşağı Büyük Menderes Havzası Mahkeme Bölgeleri" in A. Öztürk *et al* (ed.), *The First International History, Archaeology and Art History Symposium* (Söke: 2001) 1–8.

Kılıç, Y., "Prehistoric Settlements of Denizli Region and Road System Between the Settlements" ("Denizli Yöresinin Prehistoric Yerleşimleri ve Yol Sistemi") in A. Özçelik *et al* (Eds), *Uluslararası Denizli ve Çevresi Tarih ve Kültür Sempozyumu Bildiriler* (2 vol.; Denizli: Pamukkale University, 2007) 2.12–22.

Kron, G., "Archaeozoology and the Productivity of Roman Livestock Farming", *MBAH* 2 (2002) 53–73.

Laberre, G./M.Th. LeDinahet, "Les metiers du textile en Asie Mineure de l'époque hellé à l'epoque imperiale", in *Aspects de l'artisanat du textile dans le monde méditerranéen (Égypte, Grèce, Monde Romain), Collection de l'Institut d'Archéologie et d'Histoire de l'Antiquité* (2 vol.; Lyon: Université Lumière Lyon, 1996) 2.49–115.

Laufer, S., *Diokletians Preisedikt* (Berlin: de Gruyter, 1971).

Lee, R.B., "Lactation, Ovulation, Infanticide, and Woman's Work: a study of hunter gatherer population regulation", in M.N. Cohen/R.S. Malpass/G.E. Hutchinson (ed.), *Biosocial Mechanisms of Population Regulation* (New Haven/London: Yale University Press, 1980) 321–48.

Levick, B., "The Roman Economy: Trade in Asia Minor and the Niche Market", *Greece and Rome* 51 (2004) 180–98.

Lewis, N./R. Meyer, *Roman Civilisation The Empire (Selected Readings)* (New York: Columbia University Press, 1990).

Lintott, A., *Imperium Romanum: Politics and Administration* (London: Routledge, 1993).

Lloyd, S./J. Mellaart, *Beycesultan I* (London: BIAA, 1972).

Macro, A.D., "The Cities of Asia Minor Under Roman Imperium", *ANRW*, II, edited by Hildegard Temporini (Berlin-New York: Walter de Gruyter & Co., 1980) 658–97.

Malay, H., "Antik Devirde Denizli Yöresinde Ekonomik Durum", Türk Kültür Tarihinde Denizli Sempozyumu, (27–30 Eylül 1988), *Bildiriler* (Denizli 1989) 296–98.

– "Batı Anadolu'nun Antikçağ'daki Ekonomik Durumu", www.localarchives.org/assets/37929155-E43A-431E-AE2A-E88ADDE3E12C.pdf- 16.0.2009.

Martin, L./N. Russell/D. Carruthers, "Animal remains from the central Anatolian Neolithic", in F. Gérard/L. Thissen (ed.), *The Neolithic of Central Anatolia* (İstanbul, Turkey: Ege Yayınları; 2002) 193–206.

Mellaart, J., "Preliminary Report on a Survey of Pre-Classical Remains in Southern Turkey", *AS* 4 (1954): 175–240.

– *Earliest Civilisation of the Near East* (London: Thames and Hudson, 1965).

– "Anatolian Trade with Europe and Anatolian Geography and culture Provinces in the Late Bronze Age", *AS* 18 (1968) 187–202.

Mitchell, S., *Anatolia (Land, Men and Gods in Asia Minor)* (2 vol.; Oxford: Clarendon Press, 1993.

van Nijf, O.M., *The Civic World of Professional Associations in the Roman East* (Amsterdam: J.C. Gieben, 1997).

Özdemir, S.H., "Eskiçağ'da Denizli ve Kalıntılar", Celal Bayar University Department of History, unpublished honours thesis, Manisa 2007.

Özdoğan, M., "Çayönü (Günümüz Uygarlığı'nın Temelleri)", in *Metro Gastro* (İstanbul: Metro Kültür Yayınları, Mayıs- Haziran 2008), 55.

Perkins, D., "Fauna of Çatal Hüyük: evidence for early cattle Domestication in Anatolia", *AAAS* (NS) 164 (1969) 177–79.

Peters, J./A. von den Driesch/D. Helmer, "The upper Euphrates-Tigris Basin, cradle of agro-pastoralism?" in J-D. Vigne/J. Peters/D. Helmer, (ed.), *The First Steps of Animal Domestication.* (Oxford: Oxbow Books; 2005) 96–124.

Pleket, H.W., "Note on a Customs-Law from Caunus", *Mnemosyne* 11 (1958) 128–35.

– "Urban Elites and the Economy in the Greek Cities of the Roman Empire", *MBAH* 3 (1984): 3–36.

- "Greek Epigraphy and Comparative Ancient History: Two Case Studies", *EA* 12 (1988) 25–38.
- "Models and Inscriptions: Export of Textiles in the Roman Empire", *EA* 30 (1998) 117–28.

Ramsay, W. M., *The Historical Geography of Asia Minor* (Royal Geographical Society, Supplementary Papers, vol. 4; Amsterdam: Adolph M. Hakkert, 1962 [1890]).
- *The Cities and Bishoprics of Phrygia* I–II (Oxford: Clarendon Press, 1895).
- *Asianic Elements in Greek Civilization* (London: John Murray, 1927).
- *Tarsus (Aziz Pavlos'un Kenti)* translated by L. Zoroğlu (Ankara: TTK, 2000).

Redman, C. L., *The Rise of Civilisation (From Early Farmers to Urban Society in the Ancient Near East)* (San Francisco: Freeman, 1978).

Reynolds, J., "The Aphrodisias copy of Diocletian's Edict on Maximum Prices", *ZPE* 33 (1979) 46.
- *Aphrodisias and Rome*, (*JRS Monographs*, No. 1; London: Society for the Promotion of Roman Studies, 1982).

Robert, L. "Inscriptions d'Aphrodisias", *AC* 36 (1966) 377–423.

Robert, J./L. Robert, *La* Carie, II. Le plateau de Tabai *et ses environs* (Paris: de Boccard, 1954).

Sallares, R., *The Ecology of the Ancient Greek World* (Ithaca, NY: Cornell University Press, 1991).

Sheppard, A. R. R., "Jews, Christians and Heretics in Acmonia and Eumeneia (RECAM Notes and Studies no. 6)", *AS* 29 (1979) 169–180.

Şimşek, C., "Antik Dönemde Babadağ Çevresi", in Y. Özpınar *et al* (ed.), *I. Babadağ Sempozyumu* (Tarihte ve Günümüzde Babadağ), 1–3 Aralık 1999, *Bildiri Metinleri* (Denizli: Pamukkale Üniversitesi, 1999) 316–62.
- "Attouda Nekropolü", in A. Öztürk *et al* (ed.), *The First International History, Archaeology and Art History Symposium* (Söke: 2001) 229–45.

Şimşek, C./M. Büyükkolancı, "Laodikeia Antik Kenti Su Kaynakları ve Dağıtım Sistemi", Suna-İnan Kıraç Akdeniz Medeniyetleri Araştırma Enstitüsü, *Adalya* IX (2006) 86–88.

Singer, P. N., *Galen* (Selected Works), (World's Classics) Oxford: Oxford University Press, 1997.

Söğüt, B., "Salbakos Mountain and its Ruins in the Ancient Period" ("Antik Dönemde Salbakos Dağı ve Kalıntıları") in A. Özçelik *et al* (ed.), *Uluslararası Denizli ve Çevresi Tarih ve Kültür Sempozyumu Bildiriler* (2 vol.; Denizli: Pamukkale University, 2007) 2.15–24.

Viaggiatori, I., *Hierapolis Di Frigia, 1957–* (Lecce: Universita di Lecce, 1987).

Vigne, J-D./H. Buitenhuis/S. Davis, "The first steps in animal domestication into the east of the Euphrates: Cypres and Central Anatolia" (original in French) *Paléorient.* 25/2 (1999) 49–62.

Vigne, J-D./J. Peters/D. Helmer, "New archaeozoological approaches to trace the first steps of animal domestication", in J-D. Vigne/J. Peters/D. Helmer, (ed.), *The First Steps of Animal Domestication* (Oxford: Oxbow Books, 2005) 1–16.

Wilson, M., "Rich Yet Lukewarm: Early Christianity in the Lycus Valley" ("Lycus Vadisinde Erken Hıristiyanlık"), in A. Özçelik *et al* (ed.), *Uluslararası Denizli ve Çevresi Tarih ve Kültür Sempozyumu Bildiriler* (2 vol.; Denizli: Pamukkale University, 2007) 2.68–72.

West, R. S., *Life in Ancient Rome* (London: The Reader's Digest Association Limited, 1996).

Yalçın, B. C., "Koyun Yetiştiriciliği" in C. N. Aytuğ/E. Alaçam/Ü. Özkoç/B. C. Yalçın/ H. Gökçen/H. Türker, *Koyun-Keçi Hastalıkları ve Yetiştiriciliği* (İstanbul: 1990) 378–86.

Yavi, E./N. Yazıcıoğlu Yavi, *Türkiye'nin Parlayan Yıldızı Denizli* (Denizli: Denizli Valiliği, Neşa Ofset, 1998).

Yiğit, T., "Denizli and Its Environs During the Second Millenium BC" ("M. Ö. II. Binyılda Denizli ve Çevresi"), in A. Özçelik *et al* (ed.), *Uluslararası Denizli ve Çevresi Tarih ve Kültür Sempozyumu Bildiriler* (2 vol.; Denizli: Pamukkale University, 2007) 2.7–11.

Zeder, M. A., "Domestication and early agriculture in the Mediterranean Basin: Origins, diffusion, and impact", *PNAS* 105 (2008) 11597–11604.

Zilhão, J., "The spread of agro-pastoral economies across Mediterranean Europe: A View from the Far West", *JMA* 6 (1993) 5–63.

Chapter 5

Epigraphic Evidence for the Social Impact of Roman Government in Laodicea and Hierapolis

Rosalinde A. Kearsley

Laodicea and Hierapolis were close neighbours of Colossae. Moreover, excavations have been carried out at each of the sites and much archaeological and epigraphic material has been published.[1] Because of the proximity of the three cities within the Maeander basin and the evidence for intra-regional roads traversing the Lycus and Maeander valleys,[2] Laodicea and Hierapolis are likely to have had much in common with Colossae and are likely to provide a useful cultural framework within which future discoveries at Colossae may be considered.[3]

Under Roman government, use of the valleys of the Maeander river system increased markedly. The roads, some of which most likely pre-existed Roman rule, were improved during the imperial period in line with their usefulness for Rome's military and administrative purposes. The road built between 129–26 BCE by the first Roman governor of Asia, Manius Aquillius, travelled across the area in a

---

1 See, for example, C. Şimşek, *Laodikeia (Laodikeia ad Lycum)* (Istanbul: Ege Yayınları, 2007); T. Ritti, (translated by P. Arthur), *An Epigraphic Guide to Hierapolis (Pamukkale)* (Istanbul: Ege Yayınları, 2006); D. De Bernardi Ferrero (ed.), *Saggi in Onore di Paolo Verzone, Hierapolis Scavi e Ricerche* IV (Rome: G. Bretschneider, 2002); F. D'Andria, "The Evolution of Hierapolis of Phrygia", in D. Parrish (ed.), *Urbanism in Western Asia Minor* ((*JRS* Suppl 45; Portsmouth, RI: 2001) 94–115; F. D'Andria/F. Silvestrelli (ed.), *Ricerche archeologiche Turche nella Valle del Lykos* (Lecce: Congedo Editore, 2000); T. Corsten, *Die Inschriften von Laodikeia am Lykos* I (*IK* vol. 49) (Bonn: Habelt, 1997); W. H. Buckler/W. M. Calder, *MAMA* VI [Manchester: Manchester University Press, 1939]; *cf.* S. Mitchell, "Italian and Turkish archaeological work in the Lycus valley around Laodicea and Hierapolis", *JRA* 14 (2001) 632–34.

2 Ritti, *Epigraphic Guide to Hierapolis*, 188–92. Colossae lies approximately 15 kilometres east of Laodicea (Buckler/Calder, *MAMA* VI, xi).

3 The culturally-diverse nature of the whole region is clear: compare S. E. Johnson, "Laodicea and Its Neighbors", *BA* 13 (1950) 1–18, on pp. 5–8, 14; Corsten, *Die Inschriften von Laodikeia*, 192–93 no. 111, 198–99 no. 116; P. Ö. Aytaçlar/E. Akıncı, "A List of Female Names from Laodicea", *EA* 39 (2006) 113–16; E. Miranda, "La communità giudaica di Hierapolis di Frigia", *EA* 31 (1999) 109–56; Ritti, *Epigraphic Guide to Hierapolis*, 55–56 no. 5; C. P. Jones/R. R. R. Smith, "Two Inscribed Monuments of Aphrodisias", *AA* (1994) 455–72, on p. 459.

roughly north-south orientation. It led via Cibyra to the southern seaport of Side. Northwards it crossed Lydia and terminated at Pergamum. Aquillius' road intersected a road traversing Anatolia with an East-West orientation near Laodicea. It followed the Lycus River, a major tributary of the Maeander towards the west, then continued along the valley of the Maeander River itself towards the Aegean ports of Miletus and Ephesus. In an eastward direction, this road linked Asia Minor with the kingdoms in Syria and beyond.[4]

For strategic and practical reasons related to its easy accessibility by road, Laodicea was a centre of Roman government where the judicial assizes were held periodically.[5] The evidence for visits to both Laodicea and Hierapolis by Roman emperors and Roman officials, similarly, attests to the importance of both places.[6] These roads were also much used for commerce during the imperial period and the neighbouring cities benefited greatly. The fertility of the Maeander basin was exploited by Laodicea, Hierapolis, and Colossae. They prospered as intra-regional connections strengthened.[7] Better access to both the Aegean and south coast port-cities also offered the possibility of trade further afield. The numerous professional associations which feature in the epigraphic record of both Laodicea and Hierapolis reflect this economic activity.[8] The inscriptions also reveal that Laodicea and Hierapolis were centres in which Romans and their dependents established their businesses and their homes.[9] Thus, in both the political and economic areas of life, Roman government resulted in many changes to the lives of inhabitants under its control.

---

4 D.H. French, "The Roman Road-system of Asia Minor", *ANRW* II, 7.2, 698–729, on p. 704; S. Mitchell, "The Administration of Roman Asia from 133 BC to AD 250", in W. Eck (ed.), *Lokale Autonomie und römische Ordnungsmacht in den kaiserzeitlichen Provinzen vom 1. bis 3. Jahrhundert* (Munich: Oldenbourg 1999) 17–46, on pp. 17–21.

5 Mitchell, "The Administration of Roman Asia", 22–23.

6 Emperors: Corsten, *Die Inschriften von Laodikeia*, 50–51 no. 14, p. 170; *AE* (2003) 588–89 no. 1696; Ritti, *Epigraphic Guide to Hierapolis*, 165–67 no. 38. Officials: Corsten, *Die Inschriften von Laodikeia*, 89–90 no. 43; Ritti, *Epigraphic Guide to Hierapolis*, 142–44 no. 31.

7 T. Ritti, "Miliari di Hierapolis di Frigia", in D. De Bernardi Ferrero (ed.), *Saggi in Onore di Paolo Verzone, Hierapolis Scavi e Richerche* IV (Rome: Bretschneider, 2002) 87–107, on p. 90.

8 Ritti, *Epigraphic Guide to Hierapolis*, 196. See also G. Labarre and M.-T. Le Dinahet, "Les métiers du textile en Asie Mineure de l'époque hellénistique à l'époque impériale", *Aspects de l'artisanat du textile dans le monde méditerranéen: Egypte, Grèce, monde romain* (2 vol.; Lyon: Université Lumière, 1996) 2.49–115, on pp. 55–56; H.W. Pleket, "Models and Inscriptions: Export of Textiles in the Roman Empire", *EA* 30 (1998) 117–28, on pp. 122–27; Corsten, *Die Inschriften von Laodikeia*, 102–4 no. 50.

9 Corsten, *Die Inschriften von Laodikeia*, 99–101 no. 48; 158–63 no. 82, 199–200 no. 117; W. Judeich, *Altertümer von Hierapolis* (Berlin: Jahrbuch des kaiserlich deutschen Archäologischen Instituts, 1898), 81–83 no. 32; Ritti, *Epigraphic Guide to Hierapolis,* 90–91 no. 15, and p. 196.

The construction of major monuments was a product of this burgeoning civic life. There was a marked social impact on the inhabitants of the cities also, as the following discussion of three inscriptions from Laodicea will help to illustrate. The first two of these show how freedmen members of the imperial household, primarily agents of Roman administration in the area, adopted social, religious and linguistic features of their local context. The third concerns a Greek elite family and reveals how a wealthy woman participated in public life.

These two topics have been selected for discussion because each represents a distinctive characteristic of the cities in western Asia Minor during early imperial times. Members of the *familia Caesaris* begin appearing in the epigraphic record in the late first century BCE and they continue to do so during the succeeding centuries. Such individuals are frequently attested in the cities, sometimes as agents of the Roman ruler and sometimes as civic benefactors. Understanding the nature of their involvement in society, then, is important in the reconstruction of life in the Greek communities where they resided.

The increased prominence of elite women in public life is also linked to Rome's earliest imperial government according to epigraphic evidence. Wealthy Greek families, including the wives and daughters as well as the males, responded positively to the political and social opportunities offered by the patronage of the Augustan imperial family and by the activities associated with the development of imperial cults. Female members of the successive imperial families provided models for imitation by women in a range of ways. Their prominence also contributed to the Greek cities' acceptance of wealthy women's participation in public life.

The city gate donated by Claudius Tryphon

Two categories of Roman slaves and freedmen can be identified in Laodicea as they can in cities throughout the empire: those who belonged to individuals, typically known as private slaves or freedmen, and those who were members of the *familia Caesaris*. It is the latter group which is of particular interest here because, in contrast to the senatorial and equestrian officials of the Roman government, members of the imperial household might remain in their provincial posts for many years.[10]

Membership of the imperial household appears to have given some of these men a significant local standing, regardless of their actual rank in Roman society. They were accepted as respected citizens in the Greek cities. Public inscriptions where the names of imperial freedmen are found suggest that they

---

10 P. R. C. Weaver, *Familia Caesaris. A Social Study of the Emperor's Freedmen and Slaves* (Cambridge: Cambridge University Press, 1972) 279–80.

Fig. 1 Fragments of the inscribed city gate donated by Claudius Tryphon at Laodicea

sometimes had substantial means which they might use for the good of their Greek fellow citizens.[11]

At Laodicea, the activity of one wealthy imperial freedman is documented in these inscriptions from the, now totally destroyed, eastern gateway of the city:[12]

[Imp(eratori) [[Domitiano]] Caesa[ri Aug(usto) [[Germ(anico)]]] dedicante Sex(to) [Iulio Frontino] pro[c]o[(n)s(ule)]

[Διὶ Μεγίστωι Σωτῆρι καὶ Αὐτοκράτορι [[Δομιτιανῶι]] Καίσαρι Σεβαστῶι Γερμανικῶι], ἀρχιερεῖ μεγιστωι, δημαρχικῆς ἐξο[υσίας τὸ δ', ὑπάτωι τὸ ιβ΄, πατρὶ πατρί]δος [Τειβέριος Κλαύδιος Σεβαστοῦ ἀπελεύθερος Τρύφων] τοὺς πύργους καὶ τὸ τρίπυλον σὺν [- -] Ο. Ι [- - - - - - - -] Ιωι [ἀ]ν[έθηκεν].

11 R. A. Kearsley, *Greeks and Romans in Imperial Asia. Mixed Language Inscriptions and Linguistic Evidence for Cultural Interaction until the end of AD III* (IK vol. 59) (Bonn: Habelt 2001) 124–25 no. 151, 134–35 no. 160, 138–39 no. 163.

12 Corsten, *Die Inschriften von Laodikeia*, 67–68 no. 24 (a).

For Imperator Domitian Caesar Augustus Germanicus, Sextus Iulius Frontinus the proconsul made the dedication.

For Zeus Megistos Soter, and for Imperator Domitian Caesar Augustus Germanicus, pontifex maximus, in the fourth year of tribunician power, consul for the twelfth time, father of his nativeland.

Tiberius Claudius Tryphon, freedman of the emperor, donated the towers and the triple gateway with ...

On the other side of the gateway the text was engraved in Greek only:[13]

Διὶ Μεγίστωι Σωτῆρι καὶ Αὐτοκράτορι ⟦Δομιτιανῶι⟧ Καίσαρι Σεβαστῶ[ι Γερμανικῶι, ἀρχιερεῖ μεγιστωι, δημαρχικῆς ἐξουσίας τὸ δ', ὑπάτω]ι τ[ὸ ιβ'], πατρὶ πατρίδος Τειβέριος Κλαύδιος Σεβαστοῦ ἀπελεύθερος Τρύφων τοὺς πύργ[ους καὶ τὸ τρίπυλον ἀνέθηκεν, Σέξτος Ἰούλιος Φροντῖνος ἀνθύπατος τὸ σύμπ]αν ἔ[ργ]ον καθιέ[ρ]ω[σεν].

For Zeus Megistos Soter, and for Imperator Domitian Caesar Augustus Germanicus, pontifex maximus, in the fourth year of tribunician power, consul for the twelfth time, father of his nativeland.

Tiberius Claudius Tryphon, freedman of the emperor, donated the towers and the triple gateway, the proconsul Sextus Iulius Frontinus dedicated the whole construction.[14]

The inscriptions' reference to the towers and triple passageways indicates Laodicea's gate closely resembled in appearance that, still largely preserved, at the northern entrance to Hierapolis.[15] Both gateways were dedicated by the same Roman proconsul, Sextus Iulius Frontinus, and in the same year, 84/85.

The Hierapolis gateway, like that at Laodicea, was inscribed with bilingual inscriptions in Latin and Greek.[16] The inscriptions are identical in content on both the north and south sides of the gateway and they record the provision of the structure from imperial funding by Domitian and the dedicating of it by Sextus Frontinus *(Figs. 2, 3)*.[17]

The Hierapolis text reads:[18]

[Imp(eratore) Domitiano] Caesare Aug(usto) Germ[an]ico, pont(ifice) max(imo), trib (unicia) potes(tate) IIII, co(n)sule XII, p(atre) p(atriae), portam et tu[rres et novam] viam faciendas curavit Sex(tus) Iul[i]us Fron[tinus] proco[(n)s(ul) - - -]

---

13 Corsten, *Die Inschriften von Laodikeia*, 68 no. 24 (b).

14 Corsten, *Die Inschriften von Laodikeia*, 71 discusses lexical factors affecting the translation.

15 Corsten, *Die Inschriften von Laodikeia*, 69–70.

16 Corsten, *Die Inschriften von Laodikeia*, 69.

17 It was not uncommon in Asia Minor generally for Roman government to use Greek as well as Latin in official contexts. The mirroring of the text was a standard feature of official bilingual inscriptions. The Greek version was usually inscribed below the Latin in smaller letters. For the lettering at Laodicea, see Şimşek, *Laodikeia*, 101, Fig. 44a; at Hierapolis: Ritti, *Epigraphic Guide to Hierapolis*, 73–75, Fig. 27. In private inscriptions, there was more variation in the relative positions of the languages and the size of lettering: Kearsley, *Greeks and Romans in Imperial Asia*, 149–50.

18 Most recently, Ritti, *Epigraphic Guide to Hierapolis*, 73–74 no. 10.

Fig. 2 The northern gateway at Hierapolis

Fig. 3 Detail of the northern gateway at Hierapolis
showing the Frontinus' inscription

[Αὐτοκράτορι [[Δομιτιανῷ]] Καίσαρι Σεβασ]τῷ Γερμανικῷ, ἀρχιερεῖ με[γισ]τῷ, δημαρ
[χικ]ῆς ἐ[ξουσία]ς τὸ δ᾽, ὑπά[τῳ τὸ ιβ᾽, πα]τρὶ πατρίδος, τὴν πύλην καὶ τοὺς πύργους
καὶ τὴν καιν[ὴν ὁδὸν ἐποίη]σεν Σέξτος [᾽Ι]ούλιος Φρον[τῖνος ἀνθύπατος - - -]

For Imperator Domitian Caesar Augustus Germanicus, pontifex maximus, in the
sixth year of tribunician power, imperator for the fourteenth time, consul for the
twelfth time, father of his nativeland, Sextus Iulius Frontinus the proconsul saw to the
building of the gate and towers and new road ...

The importance of the highway probably led to the offer of imperial help for rebuilding the cities of the Maeander basin after they suffered from a severe earthquake in 60 (Tacitus *Ann.* 14.27.1).[19] Roman interest in the road system within
the area is demonstrated at Hierapolis by the reference in the dedicatory inscriptions of the gateway to the construction of a new road. A milestone bearing
Frontinus' name was found near the road leading towards the north from Hierapolis.[20] The Maeander highway was a vital part of life in Laodicea as well. The
east city gate was known in antiquity as the Syrian gate.[21]

It is not surprising, therefore, that imperial aid for reconstruction was available to the people of Laodicea as it was to the Hierapolitans. The citizens of
Laodicea, however, chose to rely on their own resources (Tacitus *Ann.* 14.27.1).
This fact is the reason for some distinctive features of the Laodicean inscriptions, despite the strong architectural similarity and the shared historical circumstances concerning construction of the city gate at Hierapolis.

At Laodicea the inscriptions on the two sides of the gateway did not mirror
each other. On one side there was a bilingual pair of inscriptions. On the other
side, there was only one inscription and it was in Greek.[22] The fact that the gate
bore three different inscriptions, even though the same basic information was
conveyed, suggests serious consideration was given to the formulations. Such
forethought is most likely attributable to the donor.

The donor is mentioned in two of the three inscriptions as Tiberius Claudius
Tryphon, an imperial freedman. His name appears in both of the Greek inscriptions but not in the Latin one. In the bilingual pair of inscriptions the proconsul appears in the Latin text but not in the more extensive Greek version. On the
other side of the gate, in the text which stood alone, the proconsul's name appears only at the end. Frontinus is acknowledged as the one who dedicated the
gate but Claudius Tryphon, as the donor whose funds paid for the gate's con-

---

19 For later sources referring to earthquake damage at Colossae and Hierapolis also, see
Corsten, *Die Inschriften von Laodikeia*, 70.

20 Ritti, *Epigraphic Guide to Hierapolis*, 189.

21 Philostratos, *Vitae Sophistarum* 1.25, p. 543 (discussed in Corsten, *Die Inschriften von
Laodikeia*, 70).

22 None of the blocks forming the gate were found *in situ* and it is not possible to know
which version of the inscriptions was on the internal facade and which on the external.

struction, is more clearly in view.[23] The point being made to the reader is that the gate was given to the city by a private individual rather than imperial benefaction. The involvement of the Roman government was limited to the proconsul's dedication of the gate when it was opened for public use. The ordinator, most probably Tryphon himself, has deliberately constructed the relative length and positions of the inscriptions on the gate, as well as the alternation of languages to convey this important message.[24]

The difference in length and content between the Latin and the Greek inscriptions merits further examination. In the Latin text, the emperor and the proconsul, alone, are briefly named, no doubt in appropriate acknowledgement of the overall authority of the imperial government. In the Greek text there is a fuller version of the emperor's titulature. One might have expected it to be the other way around since Latin was the language of Rome. However, Claudius Tryphon's personal status within the city arose from his membership of the imperial household. By displaying the emperor's titles in all their detail, Tryphon impresses on the Laodiceans the importance of his patron.

A further noteworthy feature of these inscriptions is that the Greek inscriptions yield the first place to *Zeus Megistos Soter*, a deity of prime importance within Laodicea.[25] The emperor's name is in second place only. The acknowledgement of Zeus' importance in this way amounts to an expression of identification with his fellow citizens by Claudius Tryphon.[26] Tryphon must have had the people of Laodicea in mind as his readers when he drew up the Greek text and gave it to the stone mason for carving.[27] His intention seems to have been to appeal to the local political and social milieu.[28]

---

23 See Corsten, *Die Inschriften von Laodikeia*, 48–49, no. 13 for another imperial freedman who donated a building at Laodicea; compare Kearsley, *Greeks and Romans in Imperial Asia*, 154.

24 On language usage in public inscriptions, see Kearsley, *Greeks and Romans in Imperial Asia*, 151–53, 155.

25 L. Robert, "Inscriptions" in J. des Gagniers et al., *Laodicée du Lycos: le Nymphée, Campagnes 1961–1963* (Quebec: L'Université Laval, 1969), 7.

26 Corsten, *Die Inschriften von Laodikeia*, 70 refers to Tryphon as a citizen. Certainly, there is evidence of imperial freedmen being citizens elsewhere: O. Kern, *Die Inschriften von Magnesia am Maeander* (Berlin: de Gruyter, 1900), 101–2 no. 113; Kearsley, *Greeks and Romans in Imperial Asia*, 70–71 no. 97, and page 156.

27 Compare the formulation of the bilingual inscription on the arched gateway of Mithridates and Mazaeus at Ephesus (Kearsley, *Greeks and Romans in Imperial Asia*, 124–25 no. 151) where it is only in the Greek section that the *Demos* of Ephesus is mentioned alongside the imperial patrons of the freedmen.

28 In the bilingual epitaph for Marcus Sestius Polemo at Laodicea: Corsten, *Die Inschriften von Laodikeia*, 99–101 no. 48; similarly, the relevance of the local context is acknowledged by the use of Greek for the acclamation of the deceased by the *conventus* of Roman residents as well as for that by the *Demos*.

The acquisition of a large arched gateway not only appropriately represented the Roman government among the Greek inhabitants of Asia Minor, it added to the impressive character of the city. Claudius Tryphon's generosity would certainly have been rewarded by civic honours and increased local respect.[29] With this in mind, it is important to note that he includes the status designation, Σεβαστοῦ ἀπελεύθερος, after his name. A modern perspective may make it difficult to acknowledge the social benefit flowing from Tryphon's openness in this respect. However, since members of the imperial household, whether still in slavery or manumitted, do the same thing in other cities it is clear that social advantage did accrue from it.[30] Tryphon, nevertheless, like other imperial freedmen making large civic donations, omits any reference to his actual occupation within the *familia*.[31] Presumably, then, his membership of the imperial household and the imperial authority which arose from that was more important as a status indicator. Members of the imperial household were accorded high status and might be honoured with or without reference to the nature of their employment.[32]

The relationship of respect and appreciation between an imperial freedman who was benefactor and donor with his city is well illustrated by the monument erected for Gaius Iulius Zoilus at Aphrodisias in the late first century BCE. The iconography of its relief frieze is detailed in its allegorical allusions to Zoilus' beneficial impact on the life of the city.[33]

---

29 Compare the civic honours and privileges granted to two other imperial freedmen: Kern, *Die Inschriften von Magnesia am Maeander*, 101–2 no. 113; *MAMA* VI.183 (Apameia).

30 See Kearsley, *Greeks and Romans in Imperial Asia*, 92–94 no. 122; J. Reynolds, *Aphrodisias and Rome* (London: Society for the Promotion of Roman Studies, 1982), 161–3 nos 36–38; *cf.* R.A. Kearsley, "Bilingual Inscriptions at Ephesos: The Statue Bases from the Harbour Gymnasium", in H. Friesinger/F. Krinzinger (ed.), *100 Jahre Österreichische Forschungen in Ephesos. Akten des Symposions Wien 1995*, (Österreichische Akademie der Wissenschaften, Philosophisch-historische Klasse, Denkschriften vol. 260; Vienna: Österreichische Akademie der Wissenschaften, 1999) 147–55, on pp. 149–50.

31 Kearsley, *Greeks and Romans in Imperial Asia*, 124–25 no. 151, 134–35 no. 160.

32 Compare P.R.C. Weaver, "Social Mobility in the Early Roman Empire: The Evidence of the Imperial Freedmen and Slaves", *Past and Present* 37 (1967) 3–20, on pp. 3–6. Weaver, *Familia Caesaris*, 1–8 provides a valuable overview of the varying statuses within the *familia Caesaris*. From this it is likely that high rank, such as that of procurator, should be understood here.

33 R.R.R. Smith, *The Monument of C. Iulius Zoilos* (Mainz: von Zabern, 1993), 38–42, 60–62, pl. 33.

The Epitaph of Aurelius Heliodorus

The epitaph of Aurelius Heliodorus, another imperial freedman at Laodicea, forms a contrast to the public inscriptions of the city gate:[34]

Fig. 4 Epitaph of Aurelius Heliodorus[35]

Αὐρ(ήλιος) Ἡλιόδωρος Σεβαστῶν ἀπελεύθερος
ἐπεσκεύασεν τὸ ἡρῷον ἑαυτῷ καὶ τῇ θυ-
γατρὶ αὐτοῦ Αὐρηλίᾳ Ἡλιοδώρᾳ τῇ καὶ Πολυχρονίᾳ
4 καὶ τῇ γυναικὶ αὐτοῦ Αὐρηλίᾳ Φλαβίᾳ καὶ τοῖς οἰκείοις αυ'-
τοῦ ἀπελευθέροις· ἥτις Ἡλιοδώρα ἡ καὶ Πολυχρονία
ἀνέθηκεν τῇ Ἰάδι φυλῇ τῶν βουλευτῶν στεφα-
νωτικοῦ ὀνόματι X̄,α ἐπὶ τῷ στεφανοῦσθαι αὐ-
8 τὴν πρὸς ἔτος τῇ πρὸ α' καλανδῶν Νοεμβρίων,
μη(νὸς) γ' ιη'· μηδενὸς ἑτέρου ἔχοντος ἐξουσίαν
κηδευθῆναι ἐν τῷ ἡρῴῳ ἢ ὑπεναντίον
τι ποιήσας τῶν προγεγραμμένων εἰσοί-
12 σει εἰς τὸ ἐράριν δήμου Ῥωμαίων X̄ ,βφ'.
τούτου ἀντίγραφον ἀπετέθη εἰς τὸ ἀρχεῖ-
ον· ἐγένετο ἐν Λαοδικείᾳ ἱερεῖ Τρύφωνι.

---

34 Corsten, *Die Inschriften von Laodikeia*, 168–71 no. 85.
35 Photograph by William Calder which became the plate (pl. 5) supporting *MAMA* VI.18, used by permission of Manchester University Press.

Aurelius Heliodorus, freedman of the emperors, had the tomb repaired for himself and his daughter, Aurelia Heliodora, also called Polychronia, and for his wife Aurelia Flavia, and for his own freedslaves. This Heliodora, also called Polychronia, donated to the tribe Ias of the members of the council 1,000 denarii with the designation for a crown in order that (the sarcophagus) be crowned every year on the day before the Kalends of November, the 18th day of the third month.[36] No one else has the right to be buried in the heroon or he, if he does anything against what is written above, will pay 2,500 denarii to the treasury of the Roman people. Of this a copy has been placed in the archive. It took place in Laodikeia when Tryphon was the priest.

The tomb, to which this epitaph was once attached, was for the burial of Aurelius Heliodorus himself, his daughter and his wife, both of whom are specified by name, and for his freedslaves. The numerous burials for which the epitaph allows indicates the tomb must have been of considerable size. The term used for it in the epitaph, *heroon*, may indeed refer to a substantial structure.[37] Unfortunately, the tomb's actual form is unknown because the stone bearing the inscription had been disassociated from it by the time it was discovered.[38] Heliodorus specifies that he repaired the tomb.[39] He would surely not have included this fact if the tomb belonged to him previously. His gratuitous statement, in the epigraphic context where words are always measured, provokes curiosity about the origin of the tomb.

Perhaps it did not belong to Heliodorus but to someone else. There is evidence for individuals finding a place in someone else's tomb by concession from the owner.[40] Or perhaps it had belonged to someone else and had only recently come into the possession of Heliodorus. According to the imprecation and the mention of the registry-office towards the end of the epitaph, Heliodorus is asserting exclusive and legal ownership of the tomb.[41]

---

36 Although not specifically mentioned, it was surely the sarcophagus which was to be crowned; compare Judeich, *Altertümer von Hierapolis*, 98–99 nos 75–76; Ritti, *Epigraphic Guide to Hierapolis*, 65.

37 Compare Corsten, *Die Inschriften von Laodikeia*, 178–80 no. 95; Labarre/Le Dinahet, "Les métiers du textile", 102 no. 61 (Hierapolis); R. Merkelbach/J. Nollé, *Die Inschriften von Ephesos* VI (*IK* vol. 16; Bonn: Habelt, 1980), no. 2121 *l*. 1; J. Kubinska, *Les monuments funéraires dans les inscriptions grecques de l'Asie Mineure* (Warsaw: PWN, 1968) 31 notes the rare use of a diminutive form: ἡρῷδιον (*TAM* I.73).

38 The inscription is preserved on a rectangular marble plaque with raised edge. It was found in secondary context (*MAMA* VI.18).

39 See Corsten, *Die Inschriften von Laodikeia*, 169 for a discussion of the vocabulary of construction, purchase and repair of burial places.

40 Ritti, *Epigraphic Guide to Hierapolis*, 56–59 no. 5, 139–41 no. 30, 152–53 no. 35.

41 Compare Jones and Smith, "Two Inscribed Monuments of Aphrodisias", 468–70.

The epitaph does not say that the tomb was an ancestral one or that he bought it,[42] however. This leaves open the possibility that it came into his possession as a gift.[43] Perhaps it was from someone unrelated,[44] or perhaps Heliodorus gained the tomb through a favourable family-, or marriage-connection.[45] In either case, mention of the repair of the tomb indicates it was of importance, not just to him but also to any passerby. Perhaps the tomb stood in a prominent place and had fallen into a state of disrepair. Heliodorus' reference to his renovation of the tomb would then be a relevant way of drawing attention to the change in ownership of it. It is conceivable that Heliodorus and his wife, Romans in a Greek city, lacked land on which to construct a burial place.

The nomenclature of Heliodorus' daughter differs from that of her parents. She has both a Roman and a Greek name. Corsten, looking primarily at the meaning of 'Polychronia', proposes that she was a long-awaited natural baby of the couple.[46] But, since the by-name formulation as well as the name is Greek rather than Roman, Polychronia may more probably have been a local woman who had been adopted by a childless Heliodorus and his wife.[47] It seems to me to be of significance in attempting to reconstruct the relationships within this family that Polychronia's name precedes her mother's in the epitaph. A child is not commonly privileged in this manner and it is something which speaks of her special significance within the family. In other words, taking into consideration the order of names in the epitaph together with Heliodora's by-name, the circumstances by which Heliodorus acquired the tomb may have been due to a favourable alliance sealed by the adoption. A Laodicean woman born into a wealthy, landed family might have brought the tomb with her when transferring from her parents' household to that of the freedman.[48] An inscription from

---

42 For tombs where purchase is acknowledged, see L. Robert, *La Carie* II (Paris: Boccard, 1954) 188–89 no. 92B, 194–95 nos 107–11 (Herakleia Salbake). Tombs designated as ancestral ones bear the word προγονικός: Ritti, *Epigraphic Guide to Hierapolis*, 66 no. 8; *cf.* Kubinska, *Les monuments funéraires*, 151–53.

43 Compare Jones and Smith, "Two Inscribed Monuments of Aphrodisias", 466–68.

44 Judeich, *Altertümer von Hierapolis*, 176 no. 348; Kearsley, *Greeks and Romans in Imperial Asia*, 81 no. 110 (Prymnessos).

45 Compare *MAMA* VI.42 (Colossae); Merkelbach/Nollé, *Die Inschriften von Ephesos*, no. 2121.

46 Corsten, *Die Inschriften von Laodikeia*, 169.

47 Compare Jones/Smith, "Two Inscribed Monuments of Aphrodisias", 471 on the prevalence of fosterage at Aphrodisias and elsewhere. Corsten, *Die Inschriften von Laodikeia*, 169 suggests that the tomb might have belonged to the family of Heliodorus' wife.

48 Compare R. A. Kearsley, "A Bilingual Epitaph from Ephesos for the Son of a *tabularius* in the *familia Caesaris*", in P. Scherrer, H. Taeuber and H. Thür (ed.), *Steine und Wege – Festschrift für Dieter Knibbe* (Österreichisches Archäologisches Institut Sonderschriften, vol. 32) (Vienna: Österreichisches Archäologisches Institut, 1999), 77–90 on p. 86.

Aphrodisias demonstrates how a woman who had been adopted nevertheless retained within the new family importance which was hers by virtue of birth.[49]

It is surely not irrelevant in this context to take note that it was Polychronia who initiated the crowning of the tomb.[50] The negotiations with the council and particularly the identification of what was probably the oldest tribe in Laodicea, similarly, suggest that Polychronia was a member of an elite family.[51] Her local standing is reflected in both the ability to supply the financial resources for the foundation and in the city's compliance with her intent.[52] The depositing of a copy of the epitaph in the city archive guarantees the official nature of the transaction.

The council's willingness to undertake an annual commemoration at his tomb also suggests that a respectful relationship existed between Heliodorus, himself wealthy according to the fact that he possessed freed slaves of his own, and the inhabitants of the city. The language of the epitaph is Greek rather than Latin, a significant choice which must, at least, reflect the majority of anticipated readers. There are some linguistic details within the monolingual Greek text which reveal the composer's familiarity with Latin,[53] hence the family's language choice may also speak for identification with their local community, rather than with Rome, being of primary importance. However this remains uncertain given our ignorance of the tomb in its original state.[54]

Both Roman and Greek practices are represented elsewhere in the epitaph. The dating of the crowning, a ceremony common to the region,[55] by both the Laodicean and the Roman calendars is one example.[56] Another is found in the

---

49 *MAMA* VIII.492b, *ll.* 1–8.

50 For crowning ceremonies donated by relatives see *MAMA* VI.42 with A.H. Cadwallader, "Revisiting Calder on Colossae", *AS* 56 (2006) 103–11 on p. 107 (Colossae); Labarre/Le Dinahet, "Les métiers du textile", 101–2 no. 60 (Hierapolis).

51 The name Ias is associated with the mythology of Laodicea's foundation: Robert, *Laodicée du Lycos*, 328–31.

52 Compare G.M. Rogers, *The Sacred Identity of Ephesos* (London: Routledge, 1991) 24–30; G.M. Rogers, "Demosthenes of Oenoanda and Models of Euergetism", *JRS* 81 (1991) 91–100, on pp. 93–96 for the manner in which negotiations between benefactor and city underpinned the establishment of foundations.

53 For example, the omission of the definite article before the participle in *l.* 10 and use of the dative for the eponymous priesthood (representing the Latin ablative) rather than the genitive with ἐπί in *l.* 14 (Robert, *Laodicée du Lycos*, 326); compare J.N. Adams, *Bilingualism and the Latin Language* (Cambridge: Cambridge University Press, 2003), 76–84 on translations of clichés and formulae as evidence for the existence of bilingualism.

54 A fully Latin version of the epitaph may have existed originally and not been preserved. Separate inscriptions, each in a different language, were provided for a single tomb at Assos: see Kearsley, *Greeks and Romans in Imperial Asia*, 50 no. 71.

55 Robert, *Laodicée du Lycos*, 326, 328.

56 The epitaph of Publius Aelius Glykon at Hierapolis (Ritti, *Epigraphic Guide to Hierapolis*, 127–129 no. 26) contains dual dating for the crowning according to the Roman Kalends and the Jewish festival of Pentecost. It underlines that acculturation in the region was not limited to Greeks and Romans but was multi-faceted.

manner Heliodorus has replicated the frequent regional custom of imposing a fine on anyone appropriating or mistreating the tomb.[57] In association with this, nevertheless, any money collected as a fine was to be deposited in the Roman *fiscus* rather one of the local treasuries used by other.[58]

These pointers to a bilingual linguistic context for the epitaph prompt curiosity about who wrote it. If, as is possible, it was the freedman himself who planned how he would like to be commemorated, then the epitaph provides interesting insights into his own level of acceptance of local customs and language. If, alternatively, Polychronia not only instituted the foundation but also wrote the epitaph after her father had died, then it becomes a useful piece of evidence for an imperial freedman's cultural and linguistic influence in a domestic context.[59]

The epigraphic evidence for the two imperial freedman discussed above displays a range of the social, political, religious, material, linguistic, and intellectual characteristics which reflect cultural exchange.[60] When the chronology of Heliodorus' epitaph and the gate inscriptions is taken into account, it demonstrates that this process of what is broadly labelled acculturation was a sustained aspect of Graeco-Roman society in Laodicea.[61]

The honour for Antonia

According to the epitaph for Heliodorus and his family, Polychronia negotiated with the Laodicean *Boule* concerning her tomb's crowning. A more recently discovered document from Laodicea also reveals an elite woman playing a role in civic life, this time by the bearing of public offices. The stone bearing the inscrip-

---

57 *IGR* IV.871; *MAMA* VI.43 (Colossae); Ritti, *Epigraphic Guide to Hierapolis*, 61.

58 Compare *MAMA* VI.42, 43 (Colossae); J.J. Harland, "Acculturation and Identity in the Diaspora: A Jewish Family and "Pagan" Guilds at Hierapolis", *JJS* 57 (2006) 222–44, on pp. 224, 226; Corsten, *Die Inschriften von Laodikeia*, 189–90 no. 108, 191–92 no. 110. For use of the *fiscus* and the varying size of fines at Colossae and elsewhere, see Cadwallader, "Revisiting Calder on Colossae", 108.

59 On the complexities of identifying authorship of inscriptions and the variables that the possibility of multiple authorship can introduce, see Adams, *Bilingualism*, 84–93.

60 Compare J.M.G. Barclay, *Jews in the Mediterranean Diaspora* (Berkeley/Edinburgh: University of California Press/T & TClark, 1996), 92–98. The typology and discussion of M. Leiwo, "From Contact to Mixture: Bilingual Inscriptions from Italy", in *Bilingualism in Ancient Society* 168–95, on pp. 172–77 are also helpful for identifying and classifying various types of language mixture.

61 Heliodorus' epitaph is to be dated no earlier than the second half of the second century since Σεβαστῶν (*l*. 1) is more likely to refer to either Marcus and Verus or to Marcus and Commodus than to successive, unnamed, emperors given the Aurelian *nomen* of Heliodorus. It may belong as late as early III CE if the testamentary foundation was actually instituted by Polychronia sometime after her father's death: Corsten, *Die Inschriften von Laodikeia*, 168–69.

tion is broken on all sides but enough survives to make clear, in the first instance, that this was an honor erected for a woman named Antonia:[62]

- - - - -

[Ἀν]τωνίαν· Λ· Ἀγ[τωνίου]
[Ζή]νωνος μεγ[ίστου ἀρχ]–
[ιερ]έως μὲν τῆς [Ἀσίας, ἱερ]–
4 [έως] δὲ τῆς Πόλε[ως   ]
[γυ]μνασιάρχο[υ   ? γυναῖ]–
[κα] ἀρίστην, νε[ωκόρον καὶ]
[ἀρ]χιέρειαν τῆ[ς Ἀσίας καὶ]
8 [ἱέ]ρειαν τῆ[ς   ]
[   ]. γυμν[ασιαρχ–   ]

- - - - -

… For Antonia, daughter of L(ucius) Antonius Zeno, greatest highpriest of Asia, priest of the Polis, … gymnasiarch …, the best woman, neokoros and highpriestess of Asia and priestess of …, gymnasiarch …

Antonia's name and her patronymic indicate she was a member of the most famous family in Laodicea's history. Many generations of the Antonii are known commencing in the Triumviral period when a Laodicean called Polemo received the Roman *nomen* Antonius. Polemo was also favoured by Marcus Antonius with a kingdom in northern Asia Minor. This was confirmed to him by Octavian/Augustus when he became sole leader of Rome not many years afterwards. The Antonia of the above inscription, as the daughter of Lucius Antonius Zeno, was probably the great-grand-daughter of King Antonius Polemo. She flourished during the second half of the first century CE.[63]

Later generations of Antonia's family are documented well into the second century CE but, even by her own lifetime, the family's royal standing had been transformed under Roman government into an elite civic status.[64] Antonia upheld the reputation of her family according to the tradition of Graeco-Roman elites everywhere by undertaking a number of public offices.[65] Furthermore,

---

62 Corsten, *Die Inschriften von Laodikeia*, 109–12 no. 53 with plate (previously unpublished). Whether or not it is a *post-mortem* funerary honour remains unknown.

63 Robert, *Laodicée du Lycos*, 306–9; A.M. Burnett *et al.*, *Roman Provincial Coinage* vol I, pt 1 (London: British Museum Press, 1992) 475–76; Corsten, *Die Inschriften von Laodikeia*, 109–11. The inscription is dated by the lettering and according to the reconstruction of the family *stemma*.

64 Compare R.A. Kearsley, "Women and Public Life in Imperial Asia Minor: Hellenistic Tradition and Augustan Ideology", *Ancient West and East* 4 (2005) 98–121, on pp. 103, 118.

65 Compare R. van Bremen, *The Limits of Participation* (Amsterdam: G.C. Gieben, 1996) 96–100.

this inscription, the sole evidence for Antonia's life, may indicate she actually excelled among her Laodicean peers in her achievements. Lines 5–6 of the inscription, as restored, bear the words γυναῖκα ἀρίστην, "best woman".

As well as being used to denote a personal characteristic, the adjective ἀριστη belongs to the class of superlatives which, as *termini technici*, appear in the graded honours awarded by cities to their benefactors, both female and male.[66] The phrase γυνὴ ἀρίστη in this inscription, then, may well have that sense and record a civic acclamation in recognition of Antonia's public achievements.[67] A comparative example for such an acclamation is found at Aphrodisias in the person of Tata, the daughter of Diodoros. This woman was praised by the *Boule*, *Demos*, and *Gerousia* with the foremost honours (ταῖς πρώταις τειμαῖς). She was also honoured as 'Mother of the City' and her extensive civic participation is set out in detail to demonstrate the context in which she won this acclaim.[68]

A statue of Antonia would have accompanied this inscription. An example of the type of honorific statue commonly erected for prominent females in the early imperial period is provided by the well-preserved one of the Pergean benefactress, Plancia Magna.[69] This is now on display in the Antalya Museum and the honorific decree prompting the erection of the statue is engraved on its base.[70] Plancia Magna undertook the highest magistracy and several important traditional priesthoods. She also, like Antonia, served as high-priestess in the imperial cult. She was *archiereia* of the civic imperial cult at Perge. The Pergaeans responded to her generosity by honouring her as 'daughter of the city' because of her exceptional service in public office and for her generosity in funding monumental structures within the city.[71]

Certainly, it would not be unexpected if Antonia was acclaimed in this way as belonging to the top rank of Laodicean women. Her family background alone, given its royal ancestry, would justify it. In addition, she may also have served as

---

66 Compare *MAMA* VIII.471 *ll*. 1–2; 474; 477–78, 480; 503; 515 (Aphrodisias); A. Chaniotis, "New Inscriptions from Aphrodisias (1995–2001)", *AJA* 108 (2004) 377–416, on pp. 389–90 no. 60; Robert, *La Carie* II, 110 no. 13 (Tabai), 163–64 no. 40, *ll*. 15–16; 177 no. 70 (Heraklea Salbace).

67 Compare, for example, Judeich, *Altertümer von Hierapolis*, 84 no. 36; 88 no. 43b (restored); *MAMA* VIII.461–62, 464, 471 *ll*.4–5 (Aphrodisias); compare van Bremen, *Limits of Participation*, 165–70; Kearsley, "Women and Public Life", 107–113.

68 *MAMA* VIII.492b (Iulio-Claudian period); van Bremen, *Limits of Participation*, 312.

69 The statue belongs to the type known as the Large Herculanean Woman (M. Pehlivaner *et al.*, *Sculptures of the Museum in Antalya* I [Antalya: Antalya Museum Publications, 1996], pl. 43 comm.). See J. Trimble, "Replicating the Body Politic: the Herculaneum Women Statues", *JRA* 13 (2000) 41–68, especially 41–42.

70 The statue and base are illustrated in Pehlivaner, *Sculptures*, pl. 43.

71 S. Şahin, *Die Inschriften von Perge* I (*IK*, vol. 54) (Bonn: Habelt, 1999), 107–45 nos 86–109; van Bremen, *Limits of Participation*, 104–7, 123–24, 344.

gymnasiarch and the priestess of the city, following the example of her father.[72] But it is the fact that Antonia had served twice in a sanctuary of the imperial cult at the provincial level which must have constituted the most remarkable feature of her public career.[73]

In attaining of the provincial high-priesthood Antonia joins a select group of elite women, both before and after her lifetime, who are also known to have achieved the office.[74] This inscription has unique significance, however, because it extends the range of public offices currently documented for women in the Graeco-Roman cities of Asia Minor at this stage of our knowledge.[75] Antonia is the only female so far known to have filled the office of imperial *neokoros* at the provincial level.[76]

It has been suggested that Antonia's provincial high-priesthood might have been shared with her father.[77] This would not downgrade her achievement if it was the case. However, while it is true that her father held the provincial high-priesthood at some stage, there is no indication in the text that he shared office with his daughter.[78] The same is true of Antonia's neokorate. In this case, in fact, her father is not accorded that post at all.

It is possible, but it remains unclear from the text, that Antonia occupied both the provincial imperial high-priesthood and the neokorate concurrently. Such ambiguity is found in many honorific inscriptions which detail public careers, whether of a male or a female. Occasionally, clarity is provided by phrases such

---

72 Corsten, *Die Inschriften von Laodikeia*, 111–12.

73 Her terms of office cannot have been in Laodicea as the city was not *neokoros* before the time of Commodus: Corsten, *Die Inschriften von Laodikeia*, 214. Laodicea's neighbour, Hierapolis, is an unlikely location also. It became *neokoros* at the beginning of the third century: Ritti, *Epigraphic Guide to Hierapolis*, 29. It is only in Pergamum, Smyrna, and Ephesus that provincial sanctuaries were in existence during the second half of the first century CE (S. J. Friesen, *Twice Neokoros. Ephesus, Asia and the Cult of the Imperial Family* [Leiden: Brill, 1993], 7–28, 49).

74 See, for examples, R. A. Kearsley, "Asiarchs, *Archiereis*, and the *Archiereiai* of Asia", *GRBS* 27 (1986) 183–92; *ibid.* "A Leading Family of Cibyra and Some Asiarchs of the First Century", *AS* 38 (1988) 43–51.

75 In the Late Hellenistic period, Epie of Thasos was *neokoros* of a local cult of Athena repeatedly (van Bremen, *Limits of Participation*, 26–27; compare *SEG* 18.343, *ll.* 43–54). The praise accorded her for this and for the fact that, when no-one else could be found to undertake the position, she was prepared to do so underlines its importance. The office must have been held in very high regard within the imperial cult also. In Ephesus, during the Flavian period, no lesser figure than Tib. Claudius Aristion, a former *archiereus* of Asia, occupied it: see Friesen, *Twice Neokoros*, 46–47 (Chronological Chart).

76 Corsten, *Die Inschriften von Laodikeia*, 111 proposes instead that the neokorate was part of an unnamed civic cult.

77 So Corsten, *Die Inschriften von Laodikeia*, 111.

78 A discussion of the range of terminology indicating the sharing of office may be found in Kearsley, "Women and Public Life", 113–15.

as κατὰ τὸ αὐτό or by a participial construction.[79] These are exceptions rather than the rule however.

The testimony of Antonia's career in public life is part of a larger body of related evidence for the role of elite women during the Late Hellenistic and early Imperial periods.[80] Beginning in the first century CE, inscriptions record that there were female office-bearers in a number of cities. The honours they received reveal that this was not only socially acceptable at the time, it was welcomed by the inhabitants of the Graeco-Roman cities.[81] The question of why this practice flourished in Asia Minor under Roman government, to a far greater extent than elsewhere, can be investigated by adopting a socio-historical perspective on the phenomenon. The public lives of such women actually represent an aspect of the process of acculturation between the Graeco-Roman cities and imperial Rome.[82] When the phenomenon of elite women in public office is situated within the life of these cities from the period of the Iulio-Claudian dynasty onwards, it shows that the debate about whether females in Asia Minor could be office-bearers or not should not revolve around expectations of gender roles, as it often does.[83]

Similarly, analysis of the epigraphic testimony for imperial freedmen as prominent citizens and civic leaders in the Greek cities must not be restricted to only one aspect of their lives, such as their rank in Roman society. To do so hinders a true appreciation of the role played by men such as Tiberius Claudius Tryphon in Asia Minor. He, like other imperial freedmen elsewhere, undertook a public role in the Graeco-Roman cities which was well above his legal rank. Expenditure of significant funds enabled them to gain acceptance and respect within local communities. The culture of civic euergetism provided opportunities to exploit their membership of the imperial household.

---

79 Compare R. A. Kearsley, "M. Ulpius Eurycles of Aezani: Panhellene, Asiarch and Archiereus of Asia", *Antichthon* 21 (1987) 49–56, on pp. 53–54 and n32.

80 Kearsley, "Women and Public Life", 98–99. For cities in the region of Laodicea and Hierapolis, see the convenient collection of references in van Bremen, *Limits of Participation*, 310–14 (Aphrodisias; Herakleia Salbake); 323 no. 1, 338 (Laodicea); 323–24 (Magnesia on the Maeander); 332–33 (Tralles); 338 (Hierapolis).

81 Kearsley, "Women and Public Life", 103, 116–17.

82 Kearsley, "Women and Public Life", 117–18. J. H. M. Strubbe's discussion ("Bürger, Nicht-Bürger und Polis-ideologie", in K. Demoen (ed.), *The Greek City from Antiquity to Present* [Louvain: Peeters, 2001] 27–39, on pp. 38–39) links early Augustan features with the Late Hellenistic period. In so doing he overlooks the social and political changes in the Greek cities of Asia Minor under Roman imperial government.

83 The refusal by some modern scholars to accept the literal meaning of such inscriptions detrimentally affects the way the history of Asia Minor is reconstructed on a broader scale. See discussions in Kearsley, "Asiarchs, *Archiereis*, and the *Archiereiai* of Asia", 183–92; "Asiarchs, *Archiereis* and *Archiereiai* of Asia: New Evidence from Amorium in Phrygia", *EA* 16 (1990) 69–80 with van Bremen, *Limits of Participation*, 121 and Kearsley, "Women and Public Life", 115–16 and n85.

In summary, despite their obvious differences, members of the emperor's household and elite, office-bearing, Greek women both contributed to the richness and diversity of social and political life within the cities of Asia Minor. It is epigraphic evidence alone which discloses this aspect of the communities' lives during the early imperial period for historical investigation.

The proliferation of communities with civic organisation throughout the much-traversed Maeander basin during the Hellenistic and Imperial periods is well documented. These are the source of a wealth of information about their own histories as well as the history of the broader region which was so important for communications within and across Asia Minor.[84]

The Lycus valley where Colossae lies was an important part of this same pattern of prosperity and growth, as the wealth of epigraphic and archaeological information now available from Laodicea and Hierapolis demonstrates. This fact is the basis for the expectation of an equally rewarding supply of inscriptional evidence from Colossae once excavation is undertaken in the city and its territory is subjected to extensive archaeological survey. Colossae is a major resource which remains largely uninvestigated. We may expect it will make an important contribution to our understanding of the social, economic, and political history of the region in future years.[85]

Bibliography

Adams, J. N., *Bilingualism and the Latin Language* (Cambridge: Cambridge University Press, 2003).

D'Andria, F., "The Evolution of Hierapolis of Phrygia", in D. Parrish (ed.), *Urbanism in Western Asia Minor* (*JRS* Suppl 45; Portsmouth, Rhode Island, 2001) 94–115.

D'Andria, F./F. Silvestrelli (ed.), *Ricerche archeologiche Turche nella Valle del Lykos* (Lecce: Congedo Editore, 2000).

Aytaçlar, P. Ö./E. Akıncı, "A List of Female Names from Laodicea", *EA* 39 (2006) 113–16.

Barclay, J. M. G., *Jews in the Mediterranean Diaspora* (Berkeley/Edinburgh: University of California Press/T & T Clark, 1996).

Baysal, H. H., "Le antiche città della Valle del Lykos", in F. D'Andria/F. Silvestrelli (ed.), *Ricerche archeologiche Turche nella Valle del Lykos* (Lecce: Congedo Editore, 2000) 19–49.

van Bremen, R., *The Limits of Participation* (Amsterdam: G. C. Gieben, 1996).

---

84 R. T. Marchese, *The Lower Maeander Flood Plain. A Regional Settlement Study (British Archaeological Reports International Series* 292[i]) (Oxford: BAR, 1986), 155–95. See also H. Hüseyin Baysal, "Le antiche città della Valle del Lykos", in *Ricerche archeologiche Turche nella Valle del Lykos,* 19–49.

85 In the meantime, Cadwallader, "Revisiting Calder on Colossae", 103–11 demonstrates the value of archival research in maximising the value of earlier work at the site.

Burnett, A. M., et al., Roman Provincial Coinage vol I, pt 1 (London: British Museum Press, 1992).

Cadwallader, A. H., "Revisiting Calder on Colossae", AS 56 (2006) 103–11.

Chaniotis, A., "New Inscriptions from Aphrodisias (1995–2001)", AJA 108 (2004) 377–416.

Corsten, T., Die Inschriften von Laodikeia am Lykos I (IK vol. 49; Bonn: Habelt, 1997).

Ferrero, D. de B., (ed.), Saggi in Onore di Paolo Verzone, Hierapolis Scavi e Ricerche IV (Rome: Giorgio Bretschneider, 2002).

Friesen, S. F., Twice Neokoros. Ephesus, Asia and the Cult of the Imperial Family (Leiden: Brill, 1993).

French, D. H., "The Roman Road-system of Asia Minor", ANRW II, 7.2, 698–729.

Harland, J. J., "Acculturation and Identity in the Diaspora: A Jewish Family and "Pagan" Guilds at Hierapolis", JJS 57 (2006) 222–44.

Johnson, S. E., "Laodicea and Its Neighbors", BA 13 (1950) 1–18.

Jones, C. P. and R. R. R. Smith, "Two Inscribed Monuments of Aphrodisias", AA (1994) 455–72.

Judeich, W., Altertümer von Hierapolis (Berlin: Jahrbuch des kaiserlich deutschen Archäologischen Instituts, 1898).

Kearsley, R. A., "Asiarchs, Archiereis, and the Archiereiai of Asia", GRBS 27 (1986) 183–92.

– "M. Ulpius Eurycles of Aezani: Panhellene, Asiarch and Archiereus of Asia", Antichthon 21 (1987) 49–56.

– "A Leading Family of Cibyra and Some Asiarchs of the First Century", AS 38 (1988) 43–51.

– "Asiarchs, Archiereis and Archiereiai of Asia: New Evidence from Amorium in Phrygia", EA 16 (1990) 69–80.

– "Bilingual Inscriptions at Ephesos: The Statue Bases from the Harbour Gymnasium", in H. Friesinger/F. Krinzinger (ed.), 100 Jahre Österreichische Forschungen in Ephesos. Akten des Symposions Wien 1995, (Österreichische Akademie der Wissenschaften, Philosophisch-historische Klasse, Denkschriften. vol. 260; Vienna: Österreichische Akademie der Wissenschaften, 1999) 147–55.

– "A Bilingual Epitaph from Ephesos for the Son of a tabularius in the familia Caesaris", in P. Scherrer/H. Taeuber/H. Thür (ed.), Steine und Wege – Festschrift für Dieter Knibbe (Österreichisches Archäologisches Institut Sonderschriften, vol. 32; Vienna: Österreichisches Archäologisches Institut, 1999) 77–90.

– Greeks and Romans in Imperial Asia. Mixed Language Inscriptions and Linguistic Evidence for Cultural Interaction until the end of AD III (IK vol. 59; Bonn: Habelt, 2001).

– "Women and Public Life in Imperial Asia Minor: Hellenistic Tradition and Augustan Ideology", Ancient West & East 4 (2005) 98–121.

Kern, O., Die Inschriften von Magnesia am Maeander (Berlin: de Gruyter, 1900).

Kubinska, J., Les monuments funéraires dans les inscriptions grecques de l'Asie Mineure (Warsaw: PWN, 1968).

Labarre, G., and M.-T. Le Dinahet, "Les métiers du textile en Asie Mineure de l'époque hellénistique à l'époque impériale", Aspects de l'artisanat du textile dans le monde méditerranéen: Egypte, Grèce, monde romain (2 vol.; Lyon: Université Lumière, 1996) 2.49–115.

Leiwo, M., "From Contact to Mixture: Bilingual Inscriptions from Italy", in J. N. Adams/M. Janse/S. Swain (ed.), *Bilingualism in Ancient Society: Language Contact and the Written Word* (Oxford: Oxford University Press, 2002) 168–95.

Marchese, R. T., *The Lower Maeander Flood Plain. A Regional Settlement Study* (British Archaeological Reports International Series 292[i]); Oxford: BAR, 1986).

Merkelbach, R./J. Nollé, *Die Inschriften von Ephesos* VI (*IK* vol. 16; Bonn: Habelt, 1980).

Miranda, E., "La communità giudaica di Hierapolis di Frigia", *EA* 31 (1999) 109–56.

Mitchell, S., "The Administration of Roman Asia from 133 BC to AD 250", in W. Eck (ed.), *Lokale Autonomie und römische Ordnungsmacht in den kaiserzeitlichen Provinzen vom 1. bis 3. Jahrhundert* (Munich: Oldenbourg 1999) 17–46.

– "Italian and Turkish archaeological work in the Lycus valley around Laodicea and Hierapolis", *JRA* 14 (2001) 632–34.

Pehlivaner, M., *et al.*, *Sculptures of the Museum in Antalya* I (Antalya: Antalya Museum Publications, 1996).

Pleket, H. W., "Models and Inscriptions: Export of Textiles in the Roman Empire", *EA* 30 (1998) 117–28.

Reynolds, J., *Aphrodisias and Rome* (London: Society for the Promotion of Roman Studies, 1982).

Ritti, T., "Miliari di Hierapolis di Frigia", in D. De Bernardi Ferrero (ed.), *Saggi in Onore di Paolo Verzone, Hierapolis Scavi e Richerche* IV (Rome: Bretschneider, 2002) 87–107.

– (transl. P. Arthur), *An Epigraphic Guide to Hierapolis (Pamukkale)* (Istanbul: Ege Yayınları, 2006).

Robert, L. "Inscriptions" in J. des Gagniers *et al.*, *Laodicée du Lycos: le Nymphée, Campagnes 1961–1963* (Quebec: L'Université Laval, 1969) 247–389.

Robert, J./L. Robert, *La Carie* II (Paris: Boccard, 1954).

Rogers, G. M., *The Sacred Identity of Ephesos* (London: Routledge, 1991).

– "Demosthenes of Oenoanda and Models of Euergetism", *JRS* 81 (1991) 91–100.

Şahin, S. *Die Inschriften von Perge* I (*IK*, vol. 54; Bonn: Habelt, 1999).

Şimşek, C., *Laodikeia (Laodikeia ad Lycum)* (Istanbul: Ege Yayınları, 2007).

Smith, R. R. R., *The Monument of C. Iulius Zoilos* (Mainz: von Zabern, 1993).

Strubbe, J. H. M., "Bürger, Nicht-Bürger und Polis-ideologie", in K. Demoen (ed.), *The Greek City from Antiquity to Present* (Louvain: Peeters, 2001) 27–39.

Trimble, J., "Replicating the Body Politic: the Herculaneum Women Statues", *JRA* 13 (2000) 41–68.

Weaver, P. R. C., "Social Mobility in the Early Roman Empire: The Evidence of the Imperial Freedmen and Slaves", *Past and Present* 37 (1967) 3–20.

– *Familia Caesaris. A Social Study of the Emperor's Freedmen and Slaves* (Cambridge: Cambridge University Press, 1972).

Chapter 6

Refuting an Axiom of Scholarship on Colossae: fresh insights from new and old inscriptions

Alan H. Cadwallader

Down-sizing Colossae: The Development of an Axiom

One does not have to read very much on Colossae to discover that, as far as scholarship is concerned, Colossae was in a parlous state by the end of the first century CE. In fact, the sheer absence of any substantial monograph on the ancient city is indicative of the assessment of the site. The closest one comes to anything substantial about Colossae is in the introduction to commentaries on the New Testament letter to the Colossians and in the earlier works of archaeology, such as the writings of William Mitchell Ramsay, Émile Le Camus and William Calder.

Almost from the moment of the re-entry of European travellers onto the actual landscape of south-west Turkey, the assessment of the city became increasingly bleak, even though, initially they weren't too sure where the place actually was. In fact, Colossae's absence from cartographical precision, unlike Ephesus or Smyrna, contributed to a less than scientific, even sanguine attitude. When *a* site finally was visited and broached as "ancient Colossae", European disappointment was palpable – whether applied to Honaz or the ancient mound three kilometres to the village's north. Occasionally, imaginative, though ultimately impotent, desire was directed to the sizeable medieval fortress that still loomed from the side of arcane Mount Cadmus above Honaz.[1]

The disappointment and indicting ignorance wrung a return to the very sources relied upon to find the place – the occasional notices in classical histories and geographies and the isolated references in patristic writings.[2] In the absence of significant material remains, these references began to be read with a jaundiced eye such as to yield results that wedded with the paucity of evidence displayed at the site. Given the similar paucity of literary references, writing about

---

1 P. de Tournefort, *Relation d'un Voyage du Levant* (2 vol.; Paris: L'imprimerie Royale, 1717), 1.319; R. Pococke, *Description of the East and some other Countries* (2 vol.; London: W. Bowyer, 1745), 78–79.

2 Note the recognition by Colonel W. M. Leake, *Journal of a Tour in Asia Minor with comparative remarks on the ancient and modern geography of that country* (London: John Murray, 1824), xxi.

Colossae became a creative repetition of the same scant material compounded by little critical assessment. An earthquake began to gain a special prominence and by fusion with the reprise of disappointments with the site became the effective determinant of the rendition of the evidence. It is perhaps not surprising that an axiomatic interpretation developed, one which required that Colossae be viewed through the wrong end of the telescope.

The terminology of the European discourse that was laid down for Colossae was "town" even "village" rather than "city"; it was minor and had become (by the first century) insignificant in comparison to a former greatness. Destruction and/or decline marked its life and ultimately displacement and replacement by Chonai. Its esteem was only salvaged by the lifeline of a New Testament letter carrying its name and by a repetitious grouping, though with an emaciating comparison, with Hierapolis and Laodicea. This limited lexicon has determined the perception of Colossae into the twenty-first century.

The Scholarly Establishment of the Axiom of Destruction

Early anecdotal comments from European travellers were uniformly disparaging. In 1740, the Anglican archdeacon and later bishop, Richard Pococke visited a site which, because "it is a plain spot on which there are no ruins" was perfunctorily adjudged as not qualifying as Colossae, being at best an "unfinished fortress".[3] The authoritative estimations of churchmen continued, with John Hartley observing in 1833, "Colossae has become doubly desolate … its ruins are scarcely visible,"[4] and Edwin Davis summing up in 1870 "Colossae could never have been a place of much importance."[5] The predominance of the combination of classicist and theologian in these writers bred a sometimes conflicted response. On the one hand, the eagerness for the discovery of visible ruins and associated artifacts is as clear as the dismay at the absence of such returns from what was supposed to witness to ancient magnitude. The dearth of monumental evidence became mirrored, in the hands of European writers, with an inconsequential textual notice both in ancient authors and modern interpretation. On the other hand, there was a scramble to explain theologically the address of a New Testament letter to a place blatantly insignificant given the poverty of its textual and material remains.

More scientific reputations were already heavily shaped by the accepted patterns of assessment of Colossae. The French explorer, Alexandre Laborde either

---

3 Pococke, *Description*, 78, 79. The perceived fortress is not to be confused with the castle on Mt Cadmus which impressed him far more.

4 J. Hartley, *Researches in Greece and the Levant* (London: Seeley, 1833), 11.

5 E.J. Davis, *Anatolica: or a Visit to Some of the Ancient Ruined Cities of Caria, Phrygia, Lycia and Pisidia* (London: Grant, 1874), 116.

because of his assessment of Colossae at the time of his visit (1826) or because
he was miffed at the honours of "discovery" being heaped upon the English-
men, Frances Arundell (1826) and William Hamilton (1836),[6] could not hide
his disdain: "the exultation of Colossae rests on practically nothing: there are
foundation stones without sequence, fragments of no magnitude, the remains
of a theatre of miserable dimensions, an acropolis with no imposing flair ..."[7]
His countryman, Ernst Renan was even more scornful and perhaps allowed the
previous rhetoric to incite him to heights of blatant inaccuracy: "The ruins of
Colossae are of a very second-rate town ... the tombstones are bizarre, without
inscription ... Colossae never recovered [after the earthquake in Nero's time]; she
disappeared from the company of the churches ... She has no imperial coins."[8]

Two writers ultimately became foundational and formative of an almost un-
animous chorus of dismissal of the significance of Colossae, though they cannot be blamed for the genesis of the negative appraisal.[9] They were doyens of
their disciplines: Joseph Barber Lightfoot the biblical commentator and early
church historian, and the surface archaeologist and epigrapher, William Mitchell Ramsay. Their reputations served to bolster their opinions which, almost unchallenged, provided both template and argumentation for subsequent scholarship.

Lightfoot drew a direct correlation between nineteenth century remains and
first century importance: "Its comparative insignificance is still attested by its
ruins, which are few and meagre...without doubt Colossae was the least important church to which any epistle of St Paul is addressed"[10] The Cambridge don
applied almost every scrap of information about Colossae to its demise. Thus the
conflict in the spelling of the name of the city in manuscripts of classical, biblical and Byzantine texts – Colossae versus Colassae – was put down to "its comparative obscurity and its early extinction".[11] He claimed that coins ceased to be
struck at Colossae during the time of the Emperor Gordian.[12] The absence of
any inscription from the site providing the name seemed to add to the overall

6 F. V. J. Arundell, *Discoveries in Asia Minor* (2 vol.; London: R.Bentley, 1834), W. J. Hamilton, *Researches in Asia Minor, Pontus and Armenia* (2 vol.; London: J. Murray, 1842).

7 L. de Laborde, *Voyage de l'Asie Mineure* (2 vol.; Paris: Firmin Didot, 1861 [1838]), 102. On
Laborde's chagrin, see S. Mitchell and M. Waelkens, *Pisidian Antioch: The Site and its Monuments* (London: Duckworth, 1998), 22–23.

8 E. Renan, *Histoire des origines du Christianisme* (6 vol.; Paris: Michel Lévy Frères,
1863–79), 3.357, *L'Antechrist* (Paris: Michel Lévy, 1873), 99 and note.

9 See, for example, J. Williams, *Two essays on the geography of ancient Asia: intended
partly to illustrate the campaigns of Alexander, and the Anabasis of Xenophon* (London: John
Murray, 1829), 85, who, in some ways, lays out the lines that the later arguments would follow.

10 J. B. Lightfoot, *Saint Paul's Epistles to the Colossians and Philemon* (London: Macmillan,
9th Ed, 1890 [1875]), 16.

11 *Ibid.*

12 *Ibid.* 17.

perception.[13] Thus, the πόλισμα term applied to Colossae by Strabo[14] was translated as "small town".[15] The translation, having bowed to the vacuum of material support, now returned to provide evidence. Similarly, Pliny's listing of towns of Phrygia[16] became graded so that Colossae was confined to "decayed and third-rate towns."[17] The dominant assessment that the view from the West signalled importance[18] surfaced in his observation that Ptolemy fails to mention Colossae.[19] This applied also to the Roman notice of Laodicea's rise from the devastation of an earthquake in 60 CE;[20] in the absence of any such notice mentioning Colossae, it was assumed, firstly (with a little resort to Eusebius of Caesarea and Ororios)[21] that Colossae had been similarly or more extremely devastated and, secondly, in the absence of any residual wealth or prestige, Colossae had never recovered. The problem for Lightfoot was that, in holding to the authorship of the New Testament Letter to the Colossians as being by Paul the Apostle, some effort was required to explain the lack of reference to such a "devastating" natural disaster in the text. Colossae was seen as overshadowed in perpetuity by Laodicea and even Hierapolis, both historically and (via Revelation 3:14–22) theologically.[22] She remained "an unimportant place"[23] unworthy of (Roman, western) notice. On the other hand, Lightfoot expressed a leaning towards accepting Eusebius as reliable thus placing the earthquake later than the Pauline letter written, he deemed, in 63CE.[24] Therefore either because sufficient time had passed from Tacitus' earthquake in 60 CE (and used to confirm the late date assigned to the letter)[25] or because, following Eusebius' date of 64 CE it had not yet happened, the letter is preserved in its Pauline authorship and the "town" is preserved as

---

13 *Ibid.* 13–14 and n1. Lightfoot rightly was suspicious of Boeckh's reconstruction (*CIG* § 3956) of a fragmentary inscription recorded (probably inaccurately) by Arundell. The reconstruction seized on the letters HNΩN and separated them from the rest of the copy in order to reconstruct ὁ δῆμος ὁ Κολοσσ]ηνῶν a reflection more of a desire to pinpoint Colossae using the then common method of inscriptional testimony than rigorous epigraphical discipline. See A. H. Cadwallader, "A New Inscription [=Two New Inscriptions], A Correction and a Confirmed Sighting from Colossae" *EA* 40 (2007) 109–18, on pp. 114–15.

14 Strabo *Geogr.* 12.8.13.

15 Lightfoot, 16.

16 Pliny *Nat.* 5.32.41.

17 Lightfoot, 16 n1.

18 See H. Sancisi-Weerdenburg "The Fifth Oriental Man and Hellenocentrism", in H. Sancisi-Weerdenburg/A. Kuhrt (ed.), *Achaemenid History II: The Greek Sources* (Leiden: Nederlands Instituut Voor Het Nabija Oosten, 1987) 117–31.

19 Lightfoot, 16.

20 Tacitus *Ann.* 14.27 *cf Sib. Or.* 4.107.

21 Eusebius *Chron.* § 210, Ororios 7.7.12.

22 Lightfoot, 16, 41.

23 Lightfoot, 32.

24 Lightfoot, 37.

25 Lightfoot, 40.

unimportant in the region and in the empire. The hold of this interpretation becomes so strong for Lightfoot that his unfolding of ecclesiastical history concentrates on Laodicea and Hierapolis. "Colossae" he declares, "was from the very first a cipher."[26] Thus, for him, nothing in church history is connected with its name. Bishops bearing the name of Colossae are implied to be no more than eponymous (and ineffectual).[27] A brief acknowledgement of "Chonae" is mentioned only as the successor to the city which, he conjectured, was finally sealed in the tomb by "its ancient enemy, the earthquake" in 262 CE.[28] Theological commitments had become inextricably entwined in historical analysis.

A sometime student of Lightfoot, William Mitchell Ramsay, provided a modulation on the developing axiom with a more systematic examination of and addition to the existing evidence,[29] though consistency was not always his hallmark. The end result – the insignificance and demise of Colossae – was substantially the same and the more pervasive because of constant repetitions of the main lines across many of Ramsay's publications. For Ramsay however, the key moment was not the ubiquitous earthquake; he held that "violent change in the landscape is in all cases a doubtful hypothesis".[30] He much preferred a gradual historical degeneration. The construction of the hellenistic city of Laodikeia and the resultant impact on the regional infrastructure was the engine of change. This ushered in the dwindling of Colossae's influence and prosperity: "The change of road system, and the foundation of Laodicea, proved its ruin".[31] Hierapolis, because of its famous white cliff landmark and equally famous aggregate of inscriptional and monumental remains, was not adversely affected. Colossae was again the poor member of a regional conglomerate, and, again, the Book of Revelation reference "must be taken as representative of the Churches of the whole Lycus valley".[32] The classical texts therefore were reassessed. Pliny (*Nat.* 5.32.41) now offered no more than an historical retrospect of Colossae's greatness and Strabo's view of Colossae as a πόλισμα (*Geog* 12.8.13) – understood

---

26 Lightfoot, 68.

27 Lightfoot, 68.

28 Lightfoot, 68 and n3. Curiously, Markus Barth opts for a later earthquake, in 692 CE; see M. Barth/H. Blanke, *The Letter to Philemon: a new translation with notes and commentary* (Grand Rapids, Mich.: Eerdmans, 2000), 261.

29 See his own statement of his work: *The Bearing of Recent Discovery on the Trustworthiness of the New Testament* (London: Hodder and Stoughton, 1915), 35.

30 W. M. Ramsay, "Antiquities of Southern Phrygia and the Border Lands I", *AJA* 3 (1887) 344–68, on p. 358.

31 W. M. Ramsay, *The Cities and Bishoprics of Phrygia* (2 vol.; Oxford: Clarendon Press, 1895, 1897), 209. Yet, elsewhere Ramsay could claim that Colossae remained "on the most important route of commerce and intercourse": W. M. Ramsay, "Colossae", in J. Hastings, *et al* (ed.), *A Dictionary of the Bible* (4 vol.; Edinburgh: T&TClark, 1898) 1.454.

32 Ramsay, "Colossae", 1.454; similarly, *The Letters to the Seven Churches. And their place in the plan of the Apocalypse* (London: Hodder and Stoughton, 1904), 180.

as "small town" – was to be endorsed.[33] Ptolemy was regarded as far less useful than later authorities such as Hierocles.[34] Coinage came into play even more.
Lightfoot may have recognised the existence of homonoia coins elsewhere[35] – the
coins expressing strong ties of interest and commerce formally made between
cities. Ramsay now added that the absence of any such coins displaying Colossae
was telling. Colossae, he claimed, "was too humble"[36] for such an alliance to be
struck. In any case, Colossae's coins were very few and of no merit.[37] The impact
of an earthquake did not seem to hit the Letter to the Colossians – it was now to
be dated to 61 CE.[38] Any inscriptions dating after the first century were nothing more than a vain attempt by the city to claw after its long-receded position.
Ramsay deduced from one inscription (*IGR* IV.870) that Colossae had no gymnasium.[39] According to the second century Greek travel writer, Pausanias, this
would disqualify Colossae from the distinction of being a πόλις,[40] in fact if not
in law. Even so, Colossae for Ramsay held on somewhat longer than Lightfoot allowed and its final demise had a different cause. Colossae became subject to the
arab incursions of the seventh and eight centuries. "Colossae as a defenceless city
in the level plain sank into decay in the Byzantine wars."[41] Even though a huge
church of St Michael survived in proximity to the city, Ramsay held that a migration of people to a better-protected new city, called Chonai, occurred, and
he used the shift in episcopal titles in the *Notitiae* (or lists of Episcopal sees)
to provide the date: 692–787 CE.[42] The story of the archangel St Michael, upon
which he had initially pinned so many hopes for topographical and historical
information,[43] then became a textual confirmation of Colossae's departure from
popular consciousness. The text only mentioned Chonai, "so utterly was the
name Colossae lost..."[44]

---

33 Ramsay, *Cities and Bishoprics*, 209–10.

34 W. M. Ramsay, "The Cities and Bishoprics of Phrygia", *JHS* 4 (1883) 371.

35 Lightfoot, 31.

36 Ramsay, *Seven Churches*, 422.

37 Ramsay, *Cities and Bishoprics*, 212, 238.

38 Ramsay, *St Paul the Traveller and the Roman Citizen* (London: Hodder and Stoughton, 11th Ed., 1895) 349.

39 Ramsay, *Cities and Bishoprics*, 212.

40 Pausanias 10.4.1.

41 W. M. Ramsay, *The Historical Geography of Asia Minor* (London: J. Murray, 1890), 135.

42 Ramsay, "Antiquities", 359.

43 Ramsay, "The Cities and Bishoprics of Phrygia II", *JHS* 8 (1887) 461–519, on pp. 473. Mina Martens considers Ramsay to have given insufficient attention, however: "L'archange Michel et l'héritage eschatologique pré-chrétien: Essai de contribution à la connaissance des mentalités populaires avant 600: de la croyance au culte", in A. Abel/A. Destrée, *Mélanges Armand Abel* (3 vol.; Leiden: Brill, 1974) 3.141–59, on p. 148.

44 W. M. Ramsay, *The Church in the Roman Empire* (London: Hodder and Stoughton, 1903), 479; similarly *Cities and Bishoprics*, 213–14.

These two writers took two different approaches, one cataclysmic and geological, the other evolutionary and human. Both contributed the substance for the axiom that read, in reductionist summation, a declining Colossae had been destroyed by an earthquake in the 60s of the Common Era and whatever in the city survived, sooner (third century) or later (seventh or eighth century) moved to a new centre called Chonai.[45] One can feel the influence of nineteenth century British paternalism in their efforts that followed to explain why the Apostle Paul would bother to write to such an insignificant, run-down settlement,[46] especially given that in both estimations, Laodicea was, from its Seleucid foundation, the more important.

Reiteration as an Element in Establishing an Axiom

Both Lightfoot and Ramsay have been recycled continually since their works were published. Little critical appraisal has been offered; rather their ideas have either been creatively improvised or, in the rare event of the addition of some new evidence or information to the investigation, have formed the frame guiding the analysis of the material. Classical and Biblical dictionary articles provided syntheses of these two writers, from the old Paulys to the new.[47] Ramsay provided the main lead for Sherman Johnson, George Bean and Hüseyin Baysal even as Markus Barth distilled Lightfoot.[48]

The lack of surviving monuments continued to be a factor in the assessment of Colossae's importance. Bo Reicke, the Scandinavian biblical scholar, in a piece

---

45 Chonai was not the only possibility. Earlier, Williams had, on the presumption of the destruction of Colossae, moved the inhabitants to Tripolis: Williams, *Two essays*, 85, 87.

46   Lightfoot, 16, followed by, *inter alia*, A. Barry, *Ellicott's New Testament Commentary: Colossians* (London: Cassell, c. 1880) 4, A. L. Williams, *The Epistles to the Colossians and to Philemon* (Cambridge Greek Testament; Cambridge: Cambridge University Press, 1907) xi.

47 W. Ruge, "Kolossai", in G. Wissowa (ed.), *Paulys Real-Encyclopädie der Classichen Altertumswissenschaft* (Stuttgart: J. B. Metzlersche, 1921) Vol. 11.1, 1119 (earthquake), T. Drew-Bear, "Kolossai", in H. Cancil/H. Schneider (ed.), *Der Neue Pauly* (Leiden/Boston: Brill, 2007) online (no earthquake); compare the biblical interpreters: W. Ewing/J. E. H. Thomson, *The Temple Dictionary of the Bible* (London: J. M. Dent, 1910) 102–3, M. J. Mellink, "Colossae", in G. A. Buttrick *et al* (ed.), *The Interpreter's Dictionary of the Bible* (4 vol.; NY: Abingdon, 1962) 1.658 (no earthquake), C. E. Arnold, "Colossae", in D. N. Freedman *et al* (ed.), *The Anchor Bible Dictionary* (6 vol.; New York: Doubleday, 1992) 1.1089–90 (earthquake).

48 S. E. Johnson, "Laodicea and its Neighbours", *BA* 13 (1950) 1–18, "Early Christianity in Asia Minor", *JBL* 77 (1958) 1–17; G. Bean, *Turkey Beyond the Maeander* (London: John Murray, 1980) 222–23; H. H. Baysal, "Le antiche Citta' della Valle del Lykos", in F. d'Andria/F. Silvestrelli (ed.) *Ricerche Archeologiche Turche nella Valle del Lykos* (Lecce: Congedo Editore, 2000) 19–49, on pp. 24–25; M. Barth/H. Blanke, *The Letter to Philemon: a new translation with notes and commentary* (Grand Rapids, Mich.: Eerdmans, 2000) 124, 128, 261, *Colossians* (AB; New York: Doubleday, ¹1994) 9–10.

claiming to provide the historical setting of Colossae, wrote, "The impressive ruins of Laodicea and Hierapolis illustrate their importance during the first post-christian centuries, a fact to which Colossae does not offer any counterpart ... All available historical documents produced after the year 61 contain no concrete remarks on the city of Colossae."[49] Eduard Lohse said the same: "Colossae ... was overshadowed by its neighbouring city and completely lost its importance. Probably it fell victim to an earthquake and was not rebuilt ... The name of Colossae, however, disappeared from history."[50]

However, for Reicke this "fact" was critical for it became an argument in the defence of the authenticity of Paul's authorship of the letter to the Colossians – a regrettable demonstration of history being tailored to fit a theological position.[51] He stands in a line of scholarly adjustment of the dating of Colossians which has successively been moved earlier as the date of the earthquake was shifted from 64 CE (following Eusebius and Orosius) to, now, 60 CE (following Tacitus).[52] Paul therefore wrote, "before news of the earthquake at an unknown date in that year had reached Rome."[53] Wherever the date is placed, such scholarship cannot conceive of St Paul – their undoubted author of the Letter to the Colossians – referring to the earthquake that (now) undoubtedly destroyed their city.[54] Conversely, the letter as written before the catastrophe, left the destruction unchallenged. The earthquake has been used in the argument

---

49 B. Reicke, "The Historical Setting of Colossians", *Review and Expositor* 70 (1973) 429–38, on p. 430.

50 E. Lohse, *Colossians and Philemon* (Hermeneia) translated by W. R. Poehlmann/R. J. Karris (Philadelphia: Fortress Press, 1971) 9.

51 Reicke, "Historical Setting", 432.

52 Earlier commentators privileged the church historian, Eusebius, for the date over the pagan writer, Tacitus: T. Milner, *History of the Seven Churches of Asia ... with notices of the Churches of Tralles, Magnesia, Colossa, Hierapolis, Lyons and Vienna designed to show fulfilment of Scripture Prophecy* (London: Holdsworth and Ball, 1832) 357; T. K. Abbott, *The Epistles to the Ephesians and to the Colossians* (ICC; Edinburgh: T & TClark, 1909) xxxi. The Eusebian date has been supported recently by Ben Witherington as a separate earthquake from one which hit Laodicea in 60–61 CE. This however would seem to require that Laodicea be hit twice in three to four years: see his *The Letters to Philemon, the Colossians, and the Ephesians: a Socio-Rhetorical Commentary on the Captivity Epistles* (Grand Rapids, Mich.: Eerdmans, 2007) 19, 34.

53 C. J. Hemer, *The Book of Acts in the Setting of Hellenistic History* (Winona Lakes, IN: Eisenbrauns, 1990) 275.

54 See A. Lindemann, "The Epistle to the Colossians", in E. Fahlbusch/G. W. Bromiley (ed.), *The Encyclopedia of Christianity* (5 vol.; Grand Rapids, Mich.: Eerdmans, 1999) 1.614–15, on p. 615. One writer, has suggested there *are* veiled allusions to the devastating earthquake (which therefore pushes the dating of the letter back to 64 CE!): L. J. Kreitzer, "Living in the Lycus Valley: Earthquake Imagery in Colossians, Philemon and Ephesians", in J. Roskovec/J. Mrázek/P. Pokorný (ed.), *Testimony and Interpretation: early Christology in its Judeo-Hellenistic Milieu* (London/New York: T & TClark, 2004) 81–94.

for pseudepigraphy of the letter as well, taking the "cipher" of Lightfoot to a level he never intended by arguing that the Laodiceans were the intended recipients.[55]

A chorus of other commentators sings from the same song-sheet: Petr Pokorný, Margaret McDonald, Peter O'Brien, and Robert McL. Wilson to name a few among many.[56] One paleo-seismologist (Piccardi) ties the Byzantine story of the miracle of St. Michael of Chonai, where the archangel miraculously impacts the mountainous landscape to rescue an esteemed healing sanctuary from malignant floodwaters, to this first century cataclysm. The axiom has become the factual geological basis for a story that in its earliest complete text comes 900 years later, ironically a story that tells of survival! Another writer shifts the "Roman city by the name of Chonai" to the "second century" so that a replacement for the "laid waste and abandoned" city could be quickly found, a fact, he claims, "attested to by the numismatic evidence."[57]

Perhaps the last word demonstrating the stranglehold of the axiom (and its distortions of the evidence) should be left to Tom Wright: "I am frustrated to stand on the large mound where a first century earthquake buried the town of Colossae in Western Turkey."[58] It seems that the mound has now become a first century funerary tumulus – a large one at that!

The Non-Believers

There have been a few counters to the axiom. These are remarkable both for the independence of their approach as for the failure of their alternate views to gain currency. As early as 1838, William Fleming, whilst admitting the impact of an earthquake "about two years after St Paul sent his Epistle", claimed the city was rebuilt "and became a flourishing place".[59] Its name became "Chonae" and

---

55 A. Lindemann, "Die Gemeinde von 'Kolossä': Erwägungen zum 'Sitz im Leben' eines pseudopaulinischen Briefes", *WuD* 16 (1981) 111–34. This has been repeated recently by W. T. Wilson, *The hope of glory: education and exhortation in the Epistle to the Colossians* (Leiden: Brill, 1997) 82–83.

56 P. Pokorný, *Colossians: A Commentary* (translated by S. S. Schatzmann) (Peabody, Mass.: Hendrickson, 1991) 19; M. Y. MacDonald, *Colossians and Ephesians* (Sacra Pagina; Minneapolis: Liturgical Press, 2008) 9 (tentatively); P. O'Brien, *Colossians and Philemon* (WBC; Waco, TX: Word, 1982) xxvi–xxvii; R. McL. Wilson, *A Critical and Exegetical Commentary on Colossians and Philemon* (ICC; Edinburgh: T & TClark, 2005) 4, 18, 19, 34.

57 V. A. Pizzuto, *A Cosmic Leap of Faith: an authorial, structural and theological Investigation of the Cosmic Christology in Col 1:15–20* (Leuven: Peeters, 2006) 82, mis-citing for support, R. E. Brown, *An Introduction to the New Testament* (New York: Doubleday, 1997) 616 and n39. Brown, nevertheless, writes of Colossae as "in ruins from an earthquake".

58 N. T. Wright, *Judas and the Gospel of Jesus: Have we missed the Truth about Christianity?* (London: SPCK, 2006) 1.

59 Fleming, *Gazetteer*, 365 – rebuilt but not so flourishing according to Milner, *Seven Churches*, 357.

survives as "the present village of Conus". One can see here the power of visible material remains[60] and of a lack of clarity about the location of Colossae to influence interpretation.[61] Non-compliant interpretations after Lightfoot and Ramsay were also influenced by materiality and the classical testimonia, but the results were quite different.

The biblical commentator James Dunn allowed that Colossae's significance was much reduced in comparison to Laodicea and Hierapolis by the early years of the Roman Empire, but thought that Lightfoot and Ramsay's translation of Strabo's πόλισμα as "small town", to describe Colossae, was misleading. Cities like Ecbatana and Athens were so described. Even though Athens was a less influential city by the first century CE, it still numbered about 30,000 people according to modern historical demographers.[62] Dunn further notes Strabo's probable grouping of Colossae with Aphrodisias, no light-weight centre of population and culture.[63] Indeed, the *de facto* conversion of πόλισμα into a diminutive of πόλις misrepresents the likely nuance of the word. Thomas Nielsen's thorough study of πόλις and πόλισμα from Xenophon to other Greek writers brought him to conclude "There is ... no marked difference between the use of *polis* and that of *polisma* ... though *polisma* may be specifically appropriate in a non-Greek context." At times it refers to "the urban centre of a *polis*."[64] Accordingly, Dunn is right to caution us that much of the notion of Colossae's decline hangs on a particular interpretation of only two texts: Strabo and the elder Pliny.[65]

In Byzantine studies, Glenn Peers has seriously questioned a separation between Colossae and Chonai and the geopolitical displacement of the former by the latter. Unlike biblical commentators and biblical archaeologists, he is far more prepared to give credence to Byzantine writers who write of their own time, like Nicetas Choniates or Constantine Porphyrogenitus. For him, the word Chonai is just the sort of etymologically produced name-change that would occur when a site has become identified as a powerful religious or political centre.[66]

---

60 By contrast, the vast extent of Laodicea's ruins "at the present day" were taken as the indication of "the ancient importance of Laodicea": T. Lewin, *The Life and Epistles of St Paul* (London: Francis and John Rivington, 1851), 206.

61 W. Fleming, *A Gazetteer of the Old and New Testaments to which is added ...* (Edinburgh: Edinburgh Printing and Publishing Co, 1838), 365.

62 R. Stark, *The Rise of Christianity: A Sociologist Reconsiders History* (Princeton, NJ: Princeton University Press, 1996), 132 (drawing on the work of T. Chandler, G. Fox, R. M. Grant and J. C. Russell).

63 The observation has even greater import given the evidence of the homonoia coin (below).

64 T. H. Nielsen, "Xenophon's Use of the Word *Polis* in the *Anabasis*" in P. Flensted-Jensen (ed.), *Further Studies in the Ancient Greek Polis* (Stuttgart: Franz Steiner, 2000), 133–39 on p. 138.

65 J. D. G. Dunn, *The Epistles to the Colossians and to Philemon* (NIGTC; Grand Rapids, Mich.: Eerdmans, 1996), 20.

66 G. Peers, *Subtle Bodies, Representing Angels in Byzantium* (Berkeley: University of California Press, 2001), 163.

This is particularly evident in the way Colossae is described in a list of main cities in the Byzantine province or "theme" of Thrakesion. The major work of Constantine Porphyrogenitus "On the Themes" routinely runs through the cities of Thrakesion until he comes to the twelfth city, the city listed between Hierapolis and Laodicea. Suddenly an extended description is given:

Κολοσσαὶ αἱ νῦν λεγόμεναι Χῶναι, οὗ ἔστι ναὸς διαβόητος τοῦ ἀρχαγγέλου Μιχαήλ

Colossae the place now called Chonai, where there is a famous shrine of the archangel Michael.[67]

For Peers, the name reflects a shift of identity and identification not a migration. Unquestionably for him, Colossae-become-Chonai remained noticeably intact. On the basis of coins and inscriptions, Angela Standhartinger is in agreement, though she still opts for a "diminished settlement" reading.[68]

The historian of Roman Asia Minor, David Magie had no particular axiom to grind when he turned to Colossae. Of particular significance was an inscription known to Lightfoot but was only used by him, incorrectly, to prove that Sarapis was part of the religious make-up of Colossae.[69] Of greater import in the inscription was the list of magistracies held by a particular leading citizen.[70] Ramsay felt he needed to marginalise the significance of the long honorific inscription by the peculiar claim that the listed conglomeration of titles in one person indicated an impoverished leadership pool. Moreover because the usual person who controlled the supply of oil was, in his opinion, the *gymnasiarch* not the *elaiones* as in this inscription, he made the incredible deduction that Colossae had no gymnasium. As a final dismissal he obfuscated the date.[71] Magie however placed the honorific list alongside comparable examples to deduce that "Colossae was an important place in the imperial period…[showing] the usual officials."[72]

---

67 *Them.* 3.24 (edition: A. Pertusi, *De thematibus Introductione, testo critico, commento* (Città del Vaticano, Biblioteca apostolica vaticana, 1952), 68.32–40) (my translation).

68 A. Standhartinger, *Studien zur Entstehungsgeschichte und Intention des Kolosserbriefs* (Leiden: Brill, 1999), 10–16. In fact, she comes close to Lightfoot's "cipher" when she reads the "selection of a small town somewhere in the hinterland of Asia Minor [as] manifestly [demonstrating] the spread of the gospel throughout the world": "Colossians and the Pauline School", *NTS* 50 (2004) 572–93, on p. 586.

69 Lightfoot, 13. Lightfoot was following Le Bas-Waddington's edition (1693b). The reconstruction remained in *IGR* IV.870. It was Louis Robert who removed Sarapis on the basis of a reconstruction better informed by related inscriptions: see his "Inscriptions", in J. des Gagniers *et al*, *Laodicée du Lycos: le Nymphée, Campagnes 1961–1963* (Quebec: L'Université Laval, 1969) 247–389, on pp. 269, 277–78.

70 The inscription was damaged, leaving the honorand unknown.

71 Ramsay, *Cities and Bishoprics*, 212.

72 D. Magie, *Roman Rule in Asia Minor* (Princeton, NJ: Princeton University Press, 1950), 986. This was sufficient material weight for F. F. Bruce to part company from the axiom as well: see his *The Epistles to the Colossians, to Philemon and to the Ephesians* (NICNT; Grand Rapids, Mich.: Eerdmans, 1984), 5.

A Summary of the Elements forging the Axiom

From this brief overview judiciously sharpened by a small company of counter-vailing voices, we can recognise that the development of the axiom about the demise of Colossae has been shaped by:

- too great a reliance upon and over-reading of a very narrow store of literary texts
- a repeated European disappointment at the absence of monumental remains
- a failure to trace critically the trajectory of the history of the immediate area, in particular, a prejudgment of a separation of Colossae and Chonai in time, space, and civic continuity
- a consistent tendency either to speculate or to make deductions from silence
- a reliance on notice by Rome thereby reinscribing imperial ideology: namely, significance is determined by the gaze of the central power.
- an uncritical rehearsal of the grouping of three cities spawned by the letter to the Colossians (4:13 *cf* 15, 16) so that a myopia develops in historical deductions; other geopolitical connections, such as with Apameia, Tripolis, Smyrna, Balbura and Aphrodisias, are marginalised or ignored, in spite of the existence of evidence for these relationships.
- a desire to tie the date of the letter to the Colossians to the date of the earthquake as a defence of authentic Pauline authorship.
- a constant regurgitation of the argument over 150 years.

The consequence of the development of the axiom has been a decline of historical judgement.

The Determination of Evidence according to this Axiom

Once the perspective takes on a form of an axiom, any evidence which comes its way is almost bound to be assessed on the basis of the axiom rather than on its own merits. One pronounced example of this has been in the handling of the so-called autonomous coins. The only use that these coins have had for scholarship on the letter to the Colossians has been the removal of doubt over the spelling – there had been a Byzantine practice of spelling the place Colassae. Lightfoot, as we have seen, tied this idiosyncrasy to Colossae's demise. Ramsay thought the same on the basis of what he judged to be few coins.[73] Yet he refused to make a similar judgment of the city of Lystra, which had rarely yielded coins.[74] 158 coins

---

73 Lightfoot, 16; Ramsay, *Cities and Bishoprics*, 238.

74 Ramsay, *The Cities of St Paul: Their Influence on His Life and Thought* (London: Hodder and Stoughton, 1907) 411.

from Colossae, on the current count,[75] though small, is nevertheless significant, especially since the dates of the coins naming Colossae span four hundred years, through to the closure of civic and koinon coinage by the end of Gallienus' reign.[76]

Ramsay's attitude to Lystra (which initially had languished like Ramsay's Colossae) had been "set aside by the irony of fate as knowledge progresses", by which he meant a new discovery.[77] The spade's turn on his argument from silence for his judgment on Colossae came in 1983 when D.J. MacDonald published pictures and a report of a homonoia coin of Colossae.[78] Significantly, the alliance lies with Aphrodisias through the pass to the south-west; it does not confirm the Eusebian and biblical-derived hypothesis of a Lycus Valley triangle, at least for the city if not for fledgling christian congregations.

Though Ramsay cannot be expected to know von Aulock's 153 coins, he can be expected to have known the coin of the sun-god Helios riding a quadriga, from the reign of Commodus *(Fig. 1)*.[79]

---

75 153 coins in the comprehensive compilation of Hans von Aulock, *Münzen und Städte Phrygiens* (2 vol.; Tübingen: Ernst Wasmuth Verlag, 1980, 1987), 2.83–94; one coin on display at the Manisa Museum (I am grateful to Rosemary Canavan for alerting me to this); two new coins given by Bahadır Duman and Erim Konakçi in this volume; the homonoia coin following; and one unpublished (and unverified?) Hellenistic coin displaying the radiate head of Apollo and the legend ΚΟΛΟΣ-ΣΗΝΩΝ on the obverse, and a kithara of three strings on the reverse. This was found at www.asiaminorcoins.com/gallery/displayimage. php?album=177&pos=0 (last accessed February 2010), and is recorded as sold by auction in Germany in 2007. Von Aulock (2.89) rejected a possible coin of Augustus from Colossae published in 1885 (by M. d'Auguste in the *Révue Belge de Numismatique et de Sigillographie* page 58) and identified by von Aulock as identical to one previously listed incorrectly by Mionnet (see below). One coin (of Caligula) accepted by von Aulock has been subsequently questioned as to authenticity: see A. Burnett/M. Amandry/P. Ripollès, *Roman Provincial Coinage: Supplement 1* (London: British Museum Press, 1998), 35 § 2891. Dieter Salzmann has re-classified a coin type of Hadrian's reign from a Helios quadriga to that of Artemis Ephesiaca: "Artemis stat Helios. Zu einer Bronzemünze aus Kolossai", *Annotazioni Numismatiche* 38 (2000) 877–78.

76 A few cities of Asia Minor continued minting city-identified coins under the emperors Aurelion and Tacitus. Provincial coinage finally ceased throughout the empire under Diocletian (around 296 or 297 CE): see C.J. Howgego/V. Heuchert/A.M. Burnett, *Coinage and Identity in the Roman Provinces* (Oxford: Oxford University Press, 2008), 33.

77 Ramsay, *Cities of St Paul*, 412.

78 D.J. Macdonald, "The Homonoia of Colossae and Aphrodisias", *Jahrbuch für Numismatik und Geldgeschichte* 33 (1983) 25–27.

79 The coin is listed in and was included as a striking example of a coin from Colossae by E. le Camus, "Colosses", in F. Vigouroux (ed.), *Dictionnaire de la Bible* (5 vol.; Paris: Letouzey et Ané, 1899) 2.860–64, on p. 860 (pictured). The coin had been listed and described in a succession of early numismatic collections. Joseph Pellerin listed one in his *Recueil de Médailles de Rois* (Paris: H.L. Guerin and L.F. Delatour, 1762), followed by J.H. van Eckhel, *Doctrina numorum veterum* ... (8 vol.; Vindobonae: J. Camesina, 1792–98), 3.147. T.E. Mionnet's vast collection, *Description de Médailles Antiques Grecques et Romaines* ... (6 vol.; Paris:

324. — Monnaie de Colosses de Phrygie.
ΔΗΜΟΣ | ΚΟΛ...; Tête du *Démos* de Colosses, lauré, à droite.
— ℞. ΚΟ | ΛΟΣ || ΣΗ | ΝΩΝ. Quadrige de face.

Fig. 1 An early reproduction of the famous Colossian quadriga coin

But this apparently fell under his "scant and uninteresting" judgment.[80] The art historian Claude Vermeule however, deemed the coin "one of the most startling compositions of all Greek numismatics."[81] One can only explain Ramsay's failure to appreciate its artistry by a judgment shaped by other considerations – perhaps not the least being the lack of coins becoming available on the local antiquities market, and, of those presented, "none worth buying".[82]

Coins have also proven a problem for other interpreters. New Testament commentators from Lightfoot to Wilson have repeated inadequate and sometimes flagrantly mistaken appreciations of the coins of Colossae. One recent commentator, Wilson, following Pokorný following Schweizer, claims there are no coins prior to Antoninus Pius.[83] The statement is simply wrong. The editors of Roman Provincial Coinage note the numismatic evidence from the time of Hadrian, though that of Caligula is discounted.[84] However, coins reflecting Colossae's hellenistic period from the second century BCE are known. Lightfoot's effort to

Bibliothèque du Roi, 1809), 4.268 included an example, with a similar instance in the Supplement, (volume 7, 1835), 541 which he listed (wrongly) under the emperor Augustus. The British Museum acquired an example of this coin in 1882 (Registration Number 071.4, Catalogue Number 155.5). My gratitude for permission to examine this coin is extended to Dr Andrew Meadows, Curator of Coins at the British Museum.

80 Ramsay, *Cities and Bishoprics*, 209.

81 C.C. Vermeule, *Roman Imperial Art in Greece and Asia Minor* (Cambridge, Mass.: L Belknap Press, 1968), 164. For a description of the development of this distinctive iconography, see Vermeule, "Greek and Roman Gems", *Boston Museum Bulletin* 64 (1966) 18–35, on p. 30.

82 Davis, *Anatolica*, 121.

83 Wilson, *Colossians and Philemon*, 4 n7.

84 Burnett, *RPC Suppl I*, 35 § 2891 and note the accuracy of Ruge, "Kolossai", 1119 (in 1921).

use the supposed Gordian-coin as an indication of the terminal decline of Colossae is not only wrong in fact (there are coins from the time of Gallien), but is also misleading in interpretation. A massive monetary crisis in the empire during the time of Gallien lead to a huge reorganisation of the money supply after 276 CE so that many so-called autonomous mints either went out of existence or lost any ability to indicate their fictive autonomy.

Mention has already been made of the key-word in the Strabo text: πόλισμα. It is noteworthy that prior to the European re-discovery of Colossae and the consequent disappointment it caused, the word was *not* used to demean Colossae's significance or size. Michael Le Quien, whose faulty, albeit massive work on the ecclesiastical patriarchates was published in 1740, simply used Strabo to say that Colossae was one of the cities of Phrygia. His use of *urbs* as a translation equivalent for the Greek πόλισμα shows that no nicety of distinction between πόλις and πόλισμα had come to his notice.[85] The momentum appears to have been a nineteenth century one, when exploration seemingly failed to uncover the surface evidence of a proud ancient city.

Christian commentators have given church historians the greatest weight: Eusebius, writing over two centuries later than the axiomatic event and Orosius, over a century after that. They state that Colossae was destroyed along with Laodicea and Hierapolis in the devastating earthquake that occurred during the time of Nero. Eusebius and Orosius' accuracy about the earthquake has not generally been questioned even though their date differs from that of Tacitus (64 *cf* 60/61 CE). Yet Orosius has been assessed as little more than an imitator of Eusebius and completely unreliable for anything before 378 CE. The text of Eusebius' *Chronicle* has suffered the same indictment.[86] The text of Eusebius' *Chronicle* is itself unstable, given the propensity of scribes and translators such as Jerome to interpolate and modify the wording.[87] Eusebius has been noted repeatedly as shaping his history from a number of theological agendas. Colin Hemer, for example, explains the difference in dates between Tacitus and Eusebius as the latter wanting to use the earthquake as a judgment on the pagan world because of Nero's persecution of christians,[88] an interesting secularisation of the judgment on Colossae (through blending with Laodicea) applied by nineteenth century European visitors. But trite theological amalgams are a frail foundation for critical history.

85 M. Le Quien, *Oriens Christianus in quatuor Patriarchatus digestus; quo exhibentur Ecclesiae, Patriarchae, caeterique Praesules totius Orientis ... Opus posthumum* (3 vol.; Paris: Ex Typographia Regia, 1740), 1.813–14.

86 A.C. Johnson, "The Archon Philocrates", *CP* 10 (1915) 457.

87 See, for example, B. Croke, "The Originality of Eusebius' *Chronicle*", *AJP* 103 (1982) 195–200.

88 Hemer, *Acts*, 274 n60.

The unquestioned collation of Colossae, Hierapolis and Laodicea must be scrutinised. The collation derives from the Epistle to the Colossians (4:13). The sudden appearance of the same triad in Eusebius, not to mention its repetition by Orosius, should have warranted caution. The inscriptional and numismatic evidence that links Colossae with Smyrna,[89] Balbura,[90] Aphrodisias and Tripolis[91] has never received the like paradigmatic imitation, nor has adequate attention been given to Rome's administrative (?) pairing of Hierapolis and Laodikeia.[92] Because the three cities were mentioned as having christian communities with some links in the apostolic period, this has fostered a myopia that reads a Second Testament mention of christian community as evidence for the city/ies.

An increasingly rigid pre-judgment has coloured the interpretation of evidence, marginalised other testimony and, as a result, has reinforced the axiomatic premise with which this exercise began. Two key background influences noted in other literary analyses of the nineteenth century apply here. The constant aside in the writing about Colossae is the absence of anything monumentally interesting at Colossae. Monumentalism was a key value for aspiring imperial nations in Europe. They unashamedly copied Greece and Rome in architecture, money, behaviours, all the while promoting their christian baptism as a testament to their rightful inheritance of the greatness of Rome as well as their moral improvement on its life. Colossae simply gave nothing to these aspirations – no monuments, no money, no agreeable people. It had become as a dark continent bereft of civilisation.

Evidence for Refuting the Axiom

So far the refutation of the axiom has
i)   recognised a long-term binding trend in scholarly interpretation
ii)   noted the failure independently to check references of previous scholars or to criticise jaundiced assessments of isolated pieces of evidence or
iii) exposed the removal of some evidence from consideration.

There is also some direct evidence that Colossae was not destroyed in the 60s and that any shadow cast by Laodicea from the 260s BCE was not so dark or long-lasting as to send the proud city into an unremitting, snivelling vertical decline.

---

89 *IK* 23.440.
90 *CIG* 4380*k³*.
91 *MAMA* VI.40.
92 See M. Christol/T. Drew-Bear, "Un senateur de Xanthos", *Journal des Savants* (1991) 195–226, especially on p. 213.

The evidence is drawn from a re-examination of some archaeological, numismatic and textual materials that have long been known and also from the discovery of new items in the last 15 years or so.

Re-Examined Evidence

Numismatic evidence

The homonoia coin mentioned already reflects the action of a city confident of its own influence and status and which is attractive to another city on a similar basis. There may be competition with its stronger and more recognised neighbour, Laodicea, perhaps coinciding with Laodicea's pretensions to be metropolis of both Phrygia and Caria, reflected on one of Laodicea's coins.

The discovery of a Byzantine coin on the höyük of Colossae is one of the very few coins for which a direct provenance with Colossae can be traced. Early European antiquarians were more interested in rarity and value than provenance and so we have almost no information on where the coins from Colossae were discovered. It may be that Byzantine coins have, in the past, been a regular find at Colossae. We simply do not know, and, for Byzantine coins, there are no legends that name the city. Such a practise had effectively gone from the time of Gallienus. What confirms a pronounced Byzantine presence on the site, within which the coin becomes unexceptional, is Duman and Konakçi's surface survey of ceramic fragments on the höyük that established a significant long-term Byzantine presence.[93]

The continuation of the "fiskus"

A regular feature of epitaphs from Asia Minor is the presence of a fine or fines for damage or interference with the tomb of the deceased. Colossae is no exception. With the discovery of a previously unpublished fragment of an inscription from the 1933 Notebook of the archaeologist, William Calder,[94] there are now four recorded epitaphs, all second century, requiring a fine to be paid to the *fiskus*, rather than to the *tameion* or some constituted voluntary association.[95] The *fiskus* was the Roman treasury. The presence of the *fiskus* indicates that Colossae

---

93 E. Konakçi/B. Duman, "Arkeolojik ve Yazılı Kanıtlar Isığında Kolossai", in *International Symposium on the History and Culture of Denizli and its Surroundings* (2 vol.; Denizli: Pamukkale University, 2007) 2.57–67. See also their essay in this collection.

94 See my "Revisiting Calder on Colossae", *AS* 56 (2006) 103–11, on p. 108.

95 A distinction between these entities is clear from *IK* 52.285, *MAMA* IV.276A compare *IEph* VII².3827.

was a recognised *polis* in the Roman empire. Such a *polis* had the right and duty to have a Roman treasury in its official architectural and bureaucratic organization rather than carry the status-lowering indignity of ferrying its requisite taxes through the *fiskus* of another,[96] neighbouring city for transfer to central imperial coffers. And it may have drawn upon Roman interdiction for at least some of its regulations regarding funerary administration. In any case, it is clear that in the second century at least not only did Colossae have a thriving funeral industry, it was also recognised by Rome, at least insofar as taxation and fines were concerned, as a πόλις. Three centuries later, in 530 CE, Hierocles' *Synekdemos* (a collection of imperial administrative regions and their member cities) still listed Colossae as a πόλις.[97]

The pan-Hellenic tour of Hadrian in 129 CE

J. G. C. Anderson discovered an inscribed pedestal in 1897 "in a field near the ruins" as he less than helpfully located it.[98] It is an honorific pedestal for the emperor Hadrian, erected by a tribune of his praetorian guard, Loukios Macedo, that is, Loukios Statius Macedo.[99] The Emperor Hadrian's second Asia Minor tour in 129 CE followed the conferring of the title of (Zeus) Olympios on Hadrian by the city of Athens.[100] The recognition attracted dedicatory statues in the Athenian Olympeion sponsored by colonies and cities from across the empire.[101] It was the most fitting honour they could engineer in response to the enormous benefaction the emperor delivered in finally bringing to completion the awesome temple of Zeus.

A tour of the east followed and cities clambered to display their Hellenic credentials and mimetic honouring of the Olympian emperor. Over three dozen cities across five provinces are attested as having acknowledged the emperor as "Olympios" in statue, coin and inscription.[102] In part or whole, this was the

---

96 The emperor Hadrian stepped in to settle a dispute between Thyatira and Stratonika. The latter had, prior to being declared a polis, paid tribute to Rome via the *fiskus* of Thyatira. Hadrian ruled that once a city, it was to pay its imperial taxes direct: see Ramsay, *Cities and Bishoprics*, 330n1.

97 E. Honigmann, *Le Synekdèmos d'Hiéroklès et l'Opsucule Géographique de Georges de Chypre* (Brussels: Institute of Philology, 1930), § 666.1 (p. 24).

98 J. G. C. Anderson, "A Summer in Phrygia II", *JHS* 18 (1898) 81–128, on p. 90, § 25. It is now usually cited as *IGR* IV.869.

99 This was conclusively argued by H-G. Pflaum, *Les Carrières Procuratoriennes Équestres sous le Haut-Empire romain* (2 vol.; Paris: P. Geuthner, 1960) 1§ 109 (pp. 262–64).

100 Plutarch *Pericles* 8.2, 39.2.

101 A. S. Benjamin, "The Altars of Hadrian in Athens and Hadrian's Panhellenic Program", *Hesperia* 32 (1963) 57–86, on p. 58.

102 See Magie, 1478–79 nn27, 28.

necessary preparation for receiving the imperial entourage. While David Magie doubts whether every sycophantic city was graced by the emperor's visit,[103] there are good reasons for thinking that Colossae was so honoured.[104] For Anthony Birley, the most logical route, in terms of the necessaries for a large entourage and one of the most symbolic for the occasion, was the Royal Road. He thinks that sometime in June 129 CE Hadrian or at least some of his entourage was stationed at Colossae.[105] Colossae is known for its honouring of Zeus.[106] This would increase Colossae's claims for a visit. Only a city of significance could have attracted the imperial attention.

Theodoret of Cyrrhus and two pilgrimage sites

Theodoret of Cyrrhus (393–458 CE) in his New Testament commentaries mentions a shrine to St. Michael and the house of Philemon surviving to "the present day".[107] It doesn't matter whether this was the actual house or not (though if it was it seriously questions the impact of the 60/61 CE earthquake for those who claim that Philemon and Colossians were both written prior to the supposed destruction). Rather in the fourth century to early fifth century at least two sites *at Colossae* were places of christian devotion and pilgrimage.

Further evidence from the second to the fifth centuries CE.

Space prevents any detailed examination of other evidence. Suffice to point out that the Dokimeion marble garland sarcophagi that were in vogue from Asia Minor to Rome from about 140–180 CE has a witness from Colossae – a testimony to wealth, status and a presumed audience of appreciation.[108] The evidence of a

---

103 *Ibid.* 618.

104 This appears to have been first noted by W. Weber, *Untersuchungen zur Geschichte des Kaisers Hadrianus* (Leipzig: B.G. Teubner, 1907), 223. The reconstruction of the Hadrianic tour as taking in Colossae was expanded by Pflaum (*loc. cit.*) and followed by H. Halfmann, *Itinera principum: Geschichte und Typologie der Kaiserreisen im Römischen Reich* (Stuttgart: Steiner, 1986), 206.

105 A. Birley, *Hadrian, the Restless Emperor* (London/New York: Routledge, 1997), 222. A different date (14th August) is given by Buckler and Calder (*MAMA* VI.18, p.10). A different route is given by Magie who has Hadrian going south from Laodikeia (620).

106 One of Colossae's earliest coins testifies to Zeus: von Aulock, 2.83 §§ 443–446.

107 *PG* 82.871–72A.

108 *MAMA* VI.51 p.18. A third section of the sarcophagus had been recognised in the depot of Denizli Müze by the then assistant director, Bay Ali Cayley. It has now been restored to the other pieces and is on display in the Museum grounds. It has been published in D'Andria/ Silvestrelli, *Valle del Lykos*, 134, fig. 27.

full range of offices and an extended prosopography from coins running from the time of Hadrian through to the Gallienus financial crisis is also much in need of closer examination.[109] The evidence testifies to a fully functioning city in the second and third centuries. The re-use for inscriptions of at least two pieces of stone on the site of Colossae is also evidence of an on-going, resilient and somewhat pragmatic approach to social and political life at the city.[110] With the discovery of a reference to ten churches at Colossae/Chonai by the Reverend Dr John Luke in 1668, a late antique (possibly fifth century) inscription recorded by Calder in 1933 which puns on the name of Theodore gains added significance.[111] Here is a further religious centre (a church of St Theodore) in the fifth century. Colossae, on this evidence, hardly seems in decline.

New Evidence

Two new pieces of evidence are of particular importance. Both inscriptions belong to the late first, possibly early second, century. The first is a pedestal in local limestone; the second is a columnar bomos in fine white marble.

The honorific pedestal to the chief-interpreter/translator of Colossae (Fig. 2)

The reconstruction and translation of the text of the metre high pedestal give:

Μάρκωι Μάρκου Κολοσσηνῶν ἀρχερμηνεῖ καὶ ἐξηγητῆι

[… dedicated this] to Markos son of Markos, chief interpreter and translator for the Colossians.

A detailed analysis of the inscription cannot be given here.[112] It attests the importance of interpretation in the affairs of the city at a mundane, oral, mediating level, probably focussed on the activities of the commercial and civic agoras.[113] The presence of a "chief" interpreter implies a body of interpreters. Such a board

---

109 A helpful beginning is provided by G. Lang, *Klassische Antike Stätten Anatoliens* (2 vol.; Norderstedt: Books on Demand, 2003), 1.597–99.

110 *MAMA* VI.38 with *MAMA* VI.42; see also the next note.

111 *MAMA* VI.49. See further my "The Reverend Dr. John Luke and the Churches of Chonai", *GRBS* 48 (2008) 319–38.

112 See my "A New Inscription", 112–18.

113 Rosalinde Kearsley has observed that, at Ephesos, the greatest incidence of bilingualism (that is of the use of Greek and Latin in the same inscription) occurs in the commercial and civic agoras: *Greeks and Romans in Imperial Asia* (IK 59; Bonn: Rudolf Habelt, 2001), 155.

Fig. 2 An honorific inscription for Markos,
Colossae's head translator and interpreter

requires an infrastructure, location and demand. Colossae's strategic location in the flow of the royal road,[114] with the interchange of ethnic groups (compare Ep Col 3:11), agricultural produce, and, as seen in the Hadrianic and "fiskus" inscriptions, the city's continuing involvement in matters of imperial policy all inform this snippet of evidence.

The repair of the baths at Colossae (*Figs. 3–5*)

The 1.2m high white marble bomos was found in March 2005 at the rear of a remote small farm house in the mountain range behind Honaz, the closest town to the ancient site of Colossae. The stone had been removed from the general site of Colossae two decades previously by agricultural workers and it bears the marks of damage occasioned by the difficulties of transfer.

---

114 Compare C. Foss, *Ephesus after Antiquity: A Late Antique, Byzantine and Turkish City* (Cambridge: Cambridge University Press, 1979), 195.

Fig. 3 An honorific bomos for Korumbos, repairer of Colossae's baths

Again, I express my gratitude to Professor Ender Varinlioğlu for his kind permission to publish this inscription. A full transcription and analysis comes elsewhere.[115]

The stone is of considerable significance; only a few elements can be mentioned here.

The bomos focuses its honour on Korumbos, described as a patriot. He has engineered the repair of the baths at Colossae from his own expense. The immediate cause that called forth the repair is not named. The reconstructed text running on the front and back rings of the circular upper element and profiled molding reads:

---

115 "Honouring the Repairer of the Baths: a new inscription from Kolossai", *Antichthon* 46 (2012) forthcoming. An assessment of the inscription for early Christianity will be found in S. Llewellyn *et al* (ed.), *New Documents Illustrating Early Christianity Vol 10*, forthcoming. See also my "Greeks in Kolossai: centre and periphery in the letter to the Kolossians and its context", in D. Sim/J. McLaren (ed.), *Attitudes to Gentiles in Judaism and Christianity* (London: Continuum) forthcoming.

Fig. 4a, b Detail from the honorific bomos for Korumbos

ἀγαθῆι τύ[χηι | Κορύμβωι φιλοπά[τριδι | ... εἰς ἐπισκευὴν βαλαν[εῖου 15–17 missing letters] καὶ εἰς ἐπιρουείαν | ... αὐτάρ?]κειαν τοῦ δήμου [16–18 letters]ν τῷ βωμῷ ἐξ ἰδίων | ἀναλωμάτων | ✗ʹAN

For good fortune. For Korumbos the patriot ... for the repair of the baths ... and for the water channel ... the self-sufficiency (?)[116] of the demos ... (contributed) for the bomos from their own expenses, 1050 denarii.

---

116 This reconstruction is offered with considerable doubt. Depending on where the lines of text began on the molding (the stone is severely damaged at the left hand side) the reconstruction could equally be καὶ εὐέρκειαν following on from εἰς ἐπιρουείαν in the previous line (which is secure for the end of this line). See the *editio princeps*.

The baths at Colossae have a long history that, with this honorific inscription, appear to extend from before the fourth century BCE[117] into the second century CE and probably beyond. By the first century in Asia Minor, baths and gymnasia had begun to coalesce into one entity.[118]

There are on the shaft a further thirty lines of names listing the donors, each with a genealogy – some as many as five generations. Sixty-six names survive on the stone in full or part. The list is a snapshot of the genealogical archive that was probably kept at a gymnasium – a sort of civic register of citizens. Here then is a very large onomastic profile of the leaders of Colossian society mostly of the first century CE, and, in a couple of instances, retreating into the preceding century.

On the stylistic grounds of letter formation and the Greek genealogical schema used, the inscription can be dated from late first century to early second century, that is, squarely in the period when the axiom dictates that Colossae was destroyed, or was in terminal decline as little more than a small town cowering in Laodicea's shadow. This becomes a highly significant piece in the destruction of the axiom of destruction. If the damage to the baths, which is the focus of reparative benefaction, can be tied to the upheaval caused by the earthquake of 60/64 CE, then Laodicea is not the only city in the Lycus Valley that can boast of a leading citizen warding off the need for Roman largesse.[119] It simply demonstrates that Roman notice is not the determinant of wealth and prestige. The fecundity of Colossae seems further to be indicated by the hunting hound and fruit-bearing leaf carved in relief at the lower right of the shaft *(Fig. 5)*.

Colossae's ancient renown as a place of abundance is thus clearly presented as the spring from which comes the ability to provide for the repair of the baths. The amount contributed as the subscription for the honour bestowed on Korumbos (1,050 denarii) indicates a modest spread of prosperity amongst a significant group of men of the city, whom, with some confidence, we can claim as citizens.

If the baths were damaged by the earthquake of 60 or 64 CE, then within a relatively short time Colossae's treasured public facility was repaired and the benefactor honoured – both requiring significant outlays of resources. Whilst earthquakes in Asia Minor did sometimes drive a city's surviving population to another area, more often repairs and rebuilding were the determined response of the locals. From the weight of evidence deriving from inscriptions of the late first century and second centuries, it is clear that Colossae's fierce pride and abundant resources saw it maintain considerable prestige of presence and influence well beyond the first century.

---

117 See Diodorus Siculus 14.80.8, Polyaenus 7.16.

118 See F. Yegül, *Baths and Bathing in Classical Antiquity* (New York: Architectural History Foundation, 1992), 23–24.

119 Tacitus *Ann.* 14.27.1.

Fig. 5 The incised reliefs on the Korumbos bomos

Conclusion

Each piece of evidence is small but precious for a picture of Colossae. Cumulatively, they show clearly the danger of reliance upon the axiom regarding Colossae as destroyed or decayed, an axiom masquerading as history. In matters of substance the axiom has proceeded as an argument from silence, the more problematic because it has been built in tandem with the equally rehearsed lament that Colossae has never been excavated. As more attention is being paid to the site, many of the summary judgements that issued from the giants of the nineteenth century and which have channelled the lines of interpretation thus far, are beginning to collapse.

Colossae would have suffered the vagaries of existence common to all Greco-Roman cities in Asia Minor but it was dwarfed into insignificance neither by some first century earthquake nor by the star of Laodicea, a star that fell long before the same fate overtook Colossae-Chonai.

Bibliography

Abbott, T. K., *The Epistles to the Ephesians and to the Colossians* (ICC; Edinburgh: T & T Clark, 1909).

Anderson, J. C. G., "A Summer in Phrygia II", *JHS* 18 (1898) 81–128.

Arnold, C. E., "Colossae", in D. N. Freedman *et al* (ed.), *The Anchor Bible Dictionary* (6 vol.; New York: Doubleday, 1992) 1.1089–90.

Arundell, F. V. J., *Discoveries in Asia Minor* (2 vol.; London: R.Bentley, 1834).

Barry, A., *Ellicott's New Testament Commentary: Colossians* (London: Cassell, c. 1880).

Barth, M./H. Blanke, *Colossians* (AB; New York: Doubleday, [1]1994).
- *The Letter to Philemon: a new translation with notes and commentary* (Grand Rapids, Mich.: Eerdmans, 2000).
Baysal, H. H., "Le antiche Citta' della Valle del Lykos", in F. d'Andria/F. Silvestrelli (ed.), *Ricerche Archeologiche Turche nella Valle del Lykos* (Lecce: Congedo Editore, 2000) 19–49.
Bean, G., *Turkey Beyond the Maeander* (London: John Murray, 1980).
Benjamin, A. S., "The Altars of Hadrian in Athens and Hadrian's Panhellenic Program", *Hesperia* 32 (1963) 57–86.
Birley, A., *Hadrian, the Restless Emperor* (London/New York: Routledge, 1997).
Brown, R. E., *An Introduction to the New Testament* (New York: Doubleday, 1997).
Bruce, F. F., *The Epistles to the Colossians, to Philemon and to the Ephesians* (NICNT; Grand Rapids, Mich.: Eerdmans, 1984).
Burnett, A./M. Amandry/P. Ripollès, *Roman Provincial Coinage: Supplement 1* (London: British Museum Press, 1998).
Cadwallader, A. H., "Revisiting Calder on Colossae", *AS* 56 (2006) 103–11.
- "A New Inscription [=Two New Inscriptions], A Correction and a Confirmed Sighting from Colossae", *EA* 40 (2007) 109–18.
- "The Reverend Dr. John Luke and the Churches of Chonai", *GRBS* 48 (2008) 319–38.
- "Honouring the Repairer of the Baths: a new inscription from Kolossai", *Antichthon* 46 (2012) forthcoming.
- "Greeks in Kolosai: centre and periphery in the letter to the Kolossians and its context" in D. Sim/J. McLaren (ed.), *Attitudes to Gentiles in Judaism and Christianity* (London: Continuum), forthcoming.
le Camus, E., "Colosses", in F. Vigouroux (ed.), *Dictionnaire de la Bible* (5 vol.; Paris: Letouzey et Ané, 1899) 2.860–64.
Christol, M./T. Drew-Bear, "Un senateur de Xanthos", *Journal des Savants* (1991) 195–226.
Croke, B., "The Originality of Eusebius' Chronicle", *AJP* 103 (1982) 195–200.
Davis, E. J., *Anatolica: or a Visit to Some of the Ancient Ruined Cities of Caria, Phrygia, Lycia and Pisidia* (London: Grant, 1874).
Drew-Bear, T., "Kolossai", in H. Cancil/H. Schneider (ed.), *Der Neue Pauly* (Leiden/Boston: Brill, 2007) online.
Dunn, J. D. G., *The Epistles to the Colossians and to Philemon* (NIGTC; Grand Rapids, Mich: Eerdmans, 1996).
van Eckhel, J. H., *Doctrini numorum veterum* ... (8 vol. Vindobonae: J. Camesina, 1792–98).
Ewing, W./J. E. H. Thomson, *The Temple Dictionary of the Bible* (London: J. M. Dent, 1910).
Fleming, W., *A Gazetteer of the Old and New Testaments to which is added* ... (Edinburgh: Edinburgh Printing and Publishing Co, 1838).
Foss, C., *Ephesus after Antiquity: A Late Antique, Byzantine and Turkish City* (Cambridge: Cambridge University Press, 1979).
des Gagniers, J. et al, *Laodicée du Lycos: le Nymphée, Campagnes 1961-1963* (Quebec: L'Université Laval, 1969).
Halfmann, H., *Itinera principum: Geschichte und Typologie der Kaiserreisen im Römischen Reich* (Stuttgart: Steiner, 1986).

Hamilton, W. M., *Researches in Asia Minor, Pontus and Armenia* (2 vol.; London: J. Murray, 1842).

Hartley, J., *Researches in Greece and the Levant* (London: Seeley, 1833).

Hemer, C. J., *The Book of Acts in the Setting of Hellenistic History* (Winona Lakes, IN: Eisenbrauns, 1990).

Honigmann, E., *Le Synekdèmos d'Hiéroklès et l'Opsucule Géographique de Georges de Chypre* (Brussels: Institute of Philology, 1930).

Howgego, C. J./V. Heuchert/A. M. Burnett, *Coinage and Identity in the Roman Provinces* (Oxford: Oxford University Press, 2008).

Johnson, S. E., "Laodicea and its Neighbours", *BA* 13 (1950) 1–18.

– "Early Christianity in Asia Minor", *JBL* 77 (1958) 1–17.

Kearsley, R. A., *Greeks and Romans in Imperial Asia* (Inschriften griechischer Städte aus Kleinasien 59; Bonn: Rudolf Habelt, 2001).

Konakçi, E./B. Duman, "Arkeolojik ve Yazılı Kanıtlar Isığında Kolossai" in *International Symposium on the History and Culture of Denizli and its Surroundings* (2 vol.; Denizli: Pamukkale University, 2007) 2.57–67.

Kreitzer, L. J., "Living in the Lycus Valley: Earthquake Imagery in Colossians, Philemon and Ephesians", in J. Roskovec/J. Mrázek/P. Pokorný (ed.), *Testimony and Interpretation: early Christology in its Judeo-Hellenistic Milieu* (London/New York: T & T Clark, 2004) 81–94.

de Laborde, L., *Voyage de l'Asie Mineure* (2 vol.; Paris: Firmin Didot, 1861 [1838]).

Lang, G., *Klassische Antike Stätten Anatoliens* (2 vol.; Norderstedt: Books on Demand, 2003).

Le Quien, M., *Oriens Christianus in quatuor Patriarchatus digestus; quo exhibentur Ecclesiae, Patriarchae, caeterique Praesules totius Orientis … Opus posthumum* (3 vol.; Paris: Ex Typographia Regia, 1740).

Leake, W. M. *Journal of a Tour in Asia Minor with comparative remarks on the ancient and modern geography of that country* (London: John Murray, 1824).

Lewin, T., *The Life and Epistles of St Paul* (London: Francis and John Rivington, 1851).

Lightfoot, J., *Saint Paul's Epistles to the Colossians and Philemon* (London: Macmillan, 9th Ed, 1890 [1875]).

Lindemann, A., "Die Gemeinde von 'Kolossä': Erwägungen zum 'Sitz im Leben' eines pseudopaulinischen Briefes", *WuD* 16 (1981) 111–34.

– "The Epistle to the Colossians", in E. Fahlbusch/G. W. Bromiley (ed.), *The Encyclopedia of Christianity* (5 vol.; Grand Rapids, Mich.: Eerdmans, 1999) 1.614–15.

Lohse, E., *Colossians and Philemon* (Hermeneia) (translated by W. R. Poehlmann/ R. J. Karris) (Philadelphia: Fortress Press, 1971).

Macdonald, D. J., "The Homonoia of Colossae and Aphrodisias", *Jahrbuch für Numismatik und Geldgeschichte* 33 (1983) 25–27.

MacDonald, M. Y., *Colossians and Ephesians* (Sacra Pagina; Minneapolis: Liturgical Press, 2008).

Magie, D., *Roman Rule in Asia Minor* (2 vol.; Princeton, NJ: Princeton University Press, 1950).

Martens, M., "L'archange Michel et l'héritage eschatologique pré-chrétien: Essai de contribution à la connaissance des mentalités populaires avant 600: de la croyance au culte" in A. Abel/A. Destrée (ed.), *Mélanges Armand Abel* (3 vol.; Leiden: Brill, 1974) 3.141–59.

Mellink, M. J., "Colossae", in G. A. Buttrick, *et al* (ed.), *The Interpreter's Dictionary of the Bible* (4 vol.; New York: Abingdon, 1962) 1.658.

Milner, T., *History of the Seven Churches of Asia ... with notices of the Churches of Tralles, Magnesia, Colossa, Hierapolis, Lyons and Vienna designed to show fulfilment of Scripture Prophecy* (London: Holdsworth and Ball, 1832).

Mionnet, T. E., *Description de Médailles Antiques Grecques et Romaines ...* (Paris: Bibliothèque du Roi, 1809).

Mitchell, S./M. Waelkens, *Pisidian Antioch: The Site and its Monuments* (London: Duckworth, 1998).

Nielsen, T. H., "Xenophon's Use of the Word Polis in the Anabasis", in P. Flensted-Jensen (ed.), *Further Studies in the Ancient Greek Polis* (Stuttgart: Franz Steiner, 2000) 133–39.

O'Brien, P., *Colossians and Philemon* (WBC; Waco, TX: Word, 1982).

Peers, G., *Subtle Bodies, Representing Angels in Byzantium* (Berkeley: University of California Press, 2001).

Pellerin, J., *Recueil de Médailles de Rois* (Paris: H. L. Guerin and L. F. Delatour, 1762).

Pertusi, A., *De thematibus Introductione, testo critico, commento* (Città del Vaticano: Biblioteca apostolica vaticana, 1952).

Pflaum, H-G., *Les Carrières Procuratoriennes Équestres sous le Haut-Empire romain* (Paris: P. Geuthner, 1960).

Piccardi, L., "The AD 60 Denizli Basin earthquake and the apparition of Archangel Miachael at Colossae (Aegean Turkey)" in L. Piccari/W. B. Masse (ed.), *Myth and Geology* (London: Geological Society, 207) 95–115.

Pizzuto, V. A., *A Cosmic Leap of Faith: an authorial, structural and theological Investigation of the Cosmic Christology in Col 1:15–20* (Leuven: Peeters, 2006).

Pococke, R., *Description of the East and some other Countries* (2 vol.; London: W. Bowyer, 1745).

Pokorný, P., *Colossians: A Commentary* (translated by S. S. Schatzmann) (Peabody, Mass.: Hendrickson, 1991).

Ramsay, W. M., "Antiquities of Southern Phrygia and the Border Lands I", *AJA* 3 (1887) 344–68.

– "The Cities and Bishoprics of Phrygia II", *JHS* 8 (1887) 461–519.

– *The Historical Geography of Asia Minor* (London: John Murray, 1890).

– *St Paul the Traveller and the Roman Citizen* (London: Hodder and Stoughton, [11]1895).

– *The Cities and Bishoprics of Phrygia* (2 vol.; Oxford: Clarendon Press, 1895, 1897).

– "Colossae", in J. Hastings, *et al* (ed.), *A Dictionary of the Bible* (4 vol.; Edinburgh: T & T Clark, 1898) 1.454.

– *The Church in the Roman Empire* (London: Hodder and Stoughton, 1903).

– *The Letters to the Seven Churches. And their place in the plan of the Apocalypse* (London: Hodder and Stoughton, 1904).

– *The Cities of St Paul: Their Influence on His Life and Thought* (London: Hodder and Stoughton, 1907).

– *The Bearing of Recent Discovery on the Trustworthiness of the New Testament* (London: Hodder and Stoughton, 1915).

Reicke, B., "The Historical Setting of Colossians", *Review and Expositor* 70 (1973) 429–38.

Renan, E., *Histoire des origines du Christianisme* (6 vol.; Paris: Michel Lévy Frères, 1863–79).

Robert, L., "Inscriptions", in J. des Gagniers/P. Devambez/L. Kahl/R. Ginouves, *Laodicée du Lycos: Le Nymphée. Campagnes 1961-63* (Quebec: L'Université Laval, 1969) 247-389.

Ruge, W., "Kolossai", in G. Wissowa (ed.), *Paulys Real-Encyclopädie der Classichen Altertumswissenschaft* (Stuttgart: J. B. Metzlersche, 1921) 11.1.1119.

Salzmann, D., "Artemis stat Helios. Zu einer Bronzemünze aus Kolossai", *Annotazioni Numismatiche* 38 (2000) 877-78.

Sancisi-Weerdenburg, H., "The Fifth Oriental Man and Hellenocentrism", in H. Sancisi-Weerdenburg/A. Kuhrt (ed.), *Achaemenid History II: The Greek Sources* (Leiden: Nederlands Instituut Voor Het Nabija Oosten, 1987) 117-31.

Standhartinger, A., *Studien zur Entstehungsgeschichte und Intention des Kolosserbriefs* (Leiden: Brill, 1999).

– "Colossians and the Pauline School", *NTS* 50 (2004) 572-93.

Stark, R., *The Rise of Christianity: A Sociologist Reconsiders History* (Princeton, NJ: Princeton University Press, 1996).

de Tournefort, P., *Relation d'un Voyage du Levant* (2 vol.; Paris: L'imprimerie Royale, 1717).

Vermeule, C. C., "Greek and Roman Gems", *Boston Museum Bulletin* 64 (1966) 18-35.

– *Roman Imperial Art in Greece and Asia Minor* (Cambridge, Mass.: L Belknap Press, 1968).

Weber, W., *Untersuchungen zur Geschichte des Kaisers Hadrianus* (Leipzig: B. G. Teubner, 1907).

Williams, A. L., *The Epistles to the Colossians and to Philemon* (Cambridge Greek Testament; Cambridge: Cambridge University Press, 1907).

Williams, J., *Two essays on the geography of ancient Asia: intended partly to illustrate the campaigns of Alexander, and the Anabasis of Xenophon* (London: John Murray, 1829).

Wilson, R. McL., *A Critical and Exegetical Commentary on Colossians and Philemon* (ICC; Edinburgh: T & T Clark, 2005).

Wilson, W. T., *The hope of glory: education and exhortation in the Epistle to the Colossians* (Leiden: Brill, 1997).

Witherington, B., *The Letters to Philemon, the Colossians, and the Ephesians: a Socio-Rhetorical Commentary on the Captivity Epistles* (Grand Rapids, Mich.: Eerdmans, 2007).

Wright, N. T., *Judas and the Gospel of Jesus: Have we missed the Truth about Christianity?* (London: SPCK, 2006).

Yegül, F., *Baths and Bathing in Classical Antiquity* (New York: Architectural History Foundation, 1992).

Chapter 7

Christians in the Lycus Valley: the view from Ephesus and from Western Asia Minor

Paul Trebilco

Introduction

As far as we know, during the first century CE there were three significant early Christian communities in the Lycus Valley – at Colossae, Laodicea and Hierapolis, with the latter two being 18 and 24 kilometres respectively from Colossae.[1]

Our information about the Christian community in Colossae is of course quite limited. Our only direct evidence is the letter to the Colossians, for which Paul, in my view was responsible, and which is perhaps to be dated between 57 and 60.[2] We can reconstruct some elements of the Christian community at Colossae from the text of Colossians.

Our additional "evidence" for Christianity in Colossae is all circumstantial – why is it *not* one of the seven churches addressed in Revelation, and why does Ignatius *not* write to the church in Colossae, when he does write to other churches in Western Asia Minor? Does this indicate something about the theological position of the Christian community in Colossae at these particular times? Or is the silence because the Christian community was destroyed along

---

1 See C.E. Arnold, "Colossae", in *ABD* 1.1089–90 on p. 1089. Colossae was 18 kilometres SE of Laodicea and 24 kilometres SSE of Hierapolis.

2 I find Dunn's view most convincing; see J.D.G. Dunn, *The Epistles to the Colossians and to Philemon. A Commentary on the Greek Text* (Grand Rapids, Mich.: Eerdmans, 1996), 35–41. He thinks (page 38) "the most plausible solution is probably that the letter was written at about the same time as Philemon but actually composed by someone other than Paul himself. ... if Timothy did indeed write for Paul at Paul's behest, but also with Paul's approval of what was in the event written ... then we have to call the letter 'Pauline' in the full sense of the word". Hence, although I will continue to write about what Paul says in Colossians, strictly speaking I regard it as what Timothy wrote, but with Paul's imprimatur. By contrast, many argue that Colossians was written by a disciple of Paul sometime after Paul's death; see for example, J.L. Sumney, *Colossians: A Commentary* (Louisville: Westminster John Knox Press, 2008), 1–9, who suggests a date of 62–64, and P. Pokorný, *Colossians: A Commentary* (Peabody: Hendrickson, 1991), 10–19 who argues for approximately 70 CE or later.

with the city in the earthquake which hit the region in 61/62 CE,[3] with the Christian community never recovering? However, as we will note later, the claim that Colossae was abandoned at this time is improbable.

Our evidence for the other Christian communities in the Lycus Valley is even more fragmentary. With regard to Laodicea, apart from the brief note in Colossians 2:1 and 4:13, 16, our only evidence is Revelation 3:14–22 written to the Church there, and Hierapolis is mentioned only in Colossians 4:13. So the *specific* evidence we have for early Christianity in the Lycus Valley is strictly limited.

So here I want to take a wider approach. We know much, much more about early Christianity in Ephesus – from a whole range of documents which arguably give evidence for Ephesus – 1 Corinthians, Acts, the Pastoral Epistles, the Johannine Letters, Revelation and Ignatius' *To the Ephesians*. Accordingly, I will look at what our evidence for Ephesus might tell us about Christianity in the Lycus Valley.

Beyond this, we have wider evidence for Christianity in the second century in Western Asia Minor in general. How might *this* wider picture shed light on the Lycus Valley? If the Lycus Valley was similar to other parts of Western Asia Minor – Ephesus, but further afield too – then what might the Christian communities in the Lycus Valley have been like?

Perhaps we could think of the situation in these terms: imagine that an archaeological dig in Colossae will discover a text entitled "The history of Christianity in Colossae and the Lycus Valley from 50 into the second century", a wonderful document written by a hitherto unknown Christian in the mid-second century. What might that document say, given what we know of Christianity in Ephesus, and in Western Asia Minor? But first, I will briefly discuss some background issues.

Founding the Church at Colossae

We know that Paul did not found the Church at Colossae, for in Colossians 2:1 he writes: "For I want you to know how much I am struggling for you, and for those in Laodicea, and for all who have not seen me face to face." Rather, Epaphras probably founded the church, as is implied by Colossians 1:7–9 where we read: "This you learned from Epaphras, our beloved fellow servant. He is a faithful minister of Christ on your behalf, and he has made known to us your love in the Spirit. For this reason, since the day we heard it, we have not ceased praying for you ..." Further information is given by Colossians 4:12–13: "Epaphras, *who*

---

3 For the earthquake see Tacitus *Ann.* 14.27; D. Magie, *Roman Rule in Asia Minor to the end of the third century after Christ* (2 vol.; Princeton: Princeton University Press, 1950), 2.1421.

is one of you, a servant of Christ Jesus, greets you. He is always wrestling in his prayers on your behalf, so that you may stand mature and fully assured in everything that God wills. For I testify for him that he has worked hard for you and for those in Laodicea and in Hierapolis." Epaphras is "one of you" (ὁ ἐξ ὑμῶν); he has also *"made known to us* (ὁ καὶ δηλώσας ἡμῖν) your love in the Spirit" (Col 1:8). He is most likely the founder of the church. Perhaps he had been in Ephesus, where he heard the Gospel, and then returned home to Colossae, taking the Gospel with him.[4]

Clearly Epaphras is in what we might call "the Pauline circle".[5] In Colossians 1:7 Paul calls him "our beloved fellow servant (Ἐπαφρᾶ τοῦ ἀγαπητοῦ συνδούλου ἡμῶν)", which suggests a close relationship with Paul, and that he is a Pauline co-worker whom Paul holds in high regard.[6] It is not as if he had been in Ephesus for a couple of days, and then heard the Gospel and went back home to Colossae. Rather, he is "our beloved fellow servant" and so clearly someone who is part of Paul's group of co-workers.[7]

In addition, in Colossians 4:13 Paul says that Epaphras "has worked hard for you and for those in Laodicea and in Hierapolis". He is clearly with Paul as Paul writes Colossians (Col 4:12) and has "worked hard" in prayer (see Col 4:13) for the three Lycus Valley churches; it seems most likely that all three churches have sent Epaphras to support Paul whilst he is in prison (Col 4:10). That they have sent Epaphras to Paul suggests that there is a close bond between these three churches and Paul – that is, they are in the Pauline circle of churches. The strong connection that exists between these three churches, especially between Colossae and Laodicea (Col 4:15; 2:1) is also significant; Epaphras has some responsibility for all three cities.[8]

Finally, the very fact that Paul writes Colossians at all suggests that Paul sees a close relationship between himself and the church there. Thus Epaphras was part of Paul's wider missionary circle, and Colossae, Hierapolis and Laodicea mentioned in Colossians 2:1 and 4:13, 15–16 were part of the Pauline "sphere". This is reinforced by Colossians 1:8 which speaks of the love of the Colossians for Paul.

---

4 See R. McL. Wilson, *A critical and exegetical commentary on Colossians and Philemon* (London: T & TClark International, 2005), 6–7; J. Becker/U. Luz, *Die Briefe an die Galater, Epheser und Kolosser* (Göttingen: Vandenhoeck & Ruprecht, 1998), 184.

5 Although since Epaphras is only mentioned in Col 1:7; 4:12–13 and Phlm 23, it seems that his work as a Pauline co-worker was highly localised in the Lycus Valley.

6 Wilson, *Colossians*, 6.

7 Philemon was probably also a leader in Colossae (Phlm 2), as was Nympha (Col 4:15).

8 See Wilson, *Colossians*, 3, 6.

The view from Ephesus

The most likely time when the church at Colossae was founded is when Paul was based in Ephesus.[9] This is clear from Acts 18:19–20:38. Luke can write in Acts 19:9–10 about Paul arguing daily in the hall of Tyrannus; he goes on "This continued for two years, so that all the residents of Asia, both Jews and Greeks, heard the word of the Lord". Clearly this is something of an exaggeration, but the period of mission implied in this passage is the most likely period for the founding of the Churches in the Lycus Valley.

So this is the period when Paul was active in Western Asia Minor – and when someone like Epaphras would have become part of Paul's group of co-workers. Paul's mission in Ephesus was probably from late 52 or early 53 to early to mid 55 CE. He writes a little about his ministry in Ephesus in 1 Corinthians, and Acts tells us about this time. What does this evidence tell us? What can we say about early Christianity in the Lycus Valley, given the Pauline mission in Ephesus?

But let me first make a general point about mobility. Romans 16 indicates how mobile the early Christians were. Here Paul, writing in Corinth, sends greetings to 28 people in Rome. He had not visited Rome, yet he can greet this number of people. It is likely that he had met some of them during *his* travels, when they lived elsewhere, but he had also met some of them during *their* travels. This is a snapshot of the mobility of the earliest Christians.

Further, as Bauckham writes, "mobility and communication in the first-century Roman world were exceptionally high. Unprecedentedly good roads and unprecedentedly safe travel by both land and sea made the Mediterranean world of this time more closely interconnected than any large area of the ancient world had ever been."[10] All sorts of people travelled, from the wealthy to ordinary people going to healing shrines or festivals. Slaves also travelled with their masters, although if they were travelling alone they were presumed to be runaways, unless they could prove otherwise.

The mobility of at least some of the early Christians led to their interconnectedness. Of course there were divisions and disputes within the early Christian communities; different ideas were circulating. But the evidence for conflict and disagreement suggests, not enclaves of isolated churches, but teachers and leaders promoting different things in different places and an intense interest in conflicts happening elsewhere. This speaks of strong interconnectedness. Another example of interconnectedness is that in 1 Corinthians 16:19 Paul

---

9 See J. Gnilka, *Der Kolosserbrief* (Freiburg: Herder, 1980), 3.

10 R. Bauckham, "For Whom Were Gospels Written?", in R. Bauckham (ed.), *The Gospels for All Christians. Rethinking the Gospel Audiences* (Grand Rapids, Mich.: Eerdmans, 1998) 9–48, on p. 32; see also M.B. Thompson, "The Holy Internet: Communication Between Churches in the First Christian Generation" in *The Gospels for All Christians* 49–70. In general see L. Casson, *Travel in the Ancient World* (London: Allen & Unwin, 1974).

gives greetings not only from the Christians in Ephesus (where he is living as he writes) but also from "the churches of Asia". He is clearly in contact with other churches in Asia then, and can pass on greetings. This is a cameo of interconnectedness and communication.[11]

So we can suggest that early Christianity was not a collection of relatively isolated, introverted communities, but rather a network of communities in close communication with each other; one dimension of their social identity was a strong, lively and informed sense of participation in a wider movement. We see a network of geographically dispersed communities with close and constant communication amongst themselves.

This clearly applies to Christians in the Lycus Valley. Colossae, the least significant of the three cities in the first century, was about 190 kilometres east of Ephesus. The prosperity of the cities of the Lycus Valley was greatly indebted to their location. Laodicea "controlled the junction of two important roads: the main road from Ephesus via Apameia to the Euphrates River in the east, and the north-south route from Pergamon via Sardis, Philadelphia, Kibyra and Xanthos to the Mediterranean."[12] Colossae was a little further east from Laodicea on the major east-west trade route. The Lycus Valley was on the main highway.

So at a number of points I will be speaking of the mobility of some of the early Christians, and of the transfer of ideas and movements from one place to another. Given this mobility, some influence in the Lycus Valley of the vibrant Christian communities in Ephesus,[13] and elsewhere in Western Asia Minor in general seems reasonable. Movements that influenced other places may also have been found in the Lycus Valley.

Collaborative ministry

What then does our knowledge of Ephesus contribute to our understanding of Christianity in the Lycus Valley? Paul's ministry in Ephesus was collaborative. Paul wrote 1 Corinthians from Ephesus (1 Cor 16:8), which means that 1 Corinthians gives us evidence for people who are, or who have been, with Paul in the city. We learn then that those involved in ministry in Ephesus included Aquila

---

11 See J.B. Lightfoot, *Saint Paul's Epistles to the Colossians and to Philemon* (London: Macmillan & Co, ⁵1880), 30–31.

12 E.J. Schnabel, *Early Christian Mission* (2 vol.; Downers Grove: IVP, 2004), 1237.

13 The *homonoia* (or "concord") coins struck between Ephesus and Laodicea, and Ephesus and Hierapolis (see Lightfoot, *Colossians*, 31), indicate that these cities had entered into a formal "concord", and so suggest some positive interactions between the inhabitants of these cities. This positive contact between Ephesus and the Lycus Valley is an additional reason for arguing that there may have been some impact on the Christian communities in the latter area from the Christians in Ephesus.

and Prisca (1 Cor 16:19 shows they have a house church in Ephesus) and Timothy (1 Cor 4:17), who each probably worked with Paul for much of the time he was in Ephesus, as well as Sosthenes ("the brother", mentioned in 1 Cor 1:1), Apollos (1 Cor 16:12, which shows that Apollos has been in Ephesus),[14] and Titus (2 Cor 8:6, which suggests that after 1 Corinthians had been written, Titus probably visited Corinth, probably from Ephesus, since this was where Paul was and Titus visited Corinth at Paul's request).

This adds weight to the picture given in Acts that "all the residents of Asia heard the word of the Lord, both Jews and Greeks" (Acts 19:10).[15] We should envisage a group working from Ephesus – and going to other places. This means it makes perfect sense that Epaphras was involved in founding the church in Colossae at this time. One can easily imagine the "Pauline mission" in Ephesus sending co-workers off to places like the Lycus Valley. Did Epaphras found the church in Colossae alone? I would suggest not. Given that ministry in the Pauline corpus is collaborative ministry, and the extent of such collaborative work in Ephesus, it seems likely that Epaphras founded the Colossian church with someone else. Only Epaphras is mentioned in Colossians in such glowing terms because he is the only founder currently with Paul as he writes (Col 4:12). The collaborative nature of Paul's mission work would certainly suggest that there was more than one person who took the Gospel "inland" to the Lycus Valley.

This evidence also suggests that Paul would not have abandoned the church in Colossae after its foundation by the Pauline mission. Paul had an active group of workers in Ephesus, and we can suggest that others from the group would have visited the Lycus Valley soon, especially given the mobility of the early Christians. That Paul, or a leader in the Pauline tradition, wrote Colossians is all of a piece with this too. Collaborative founding of the church leads on to shared pastoral responsibility.

---

14 See P.R. Trebilco, *The Early Christians in Ephesus from Paul to Ignatius* (Tübingen: Mohr Siebeck, 2004), 67–70. That he was not in Ephesus at the time Paul writes 1 Corinthians is shown by the lack of greeting from Apollos in 1 Cor 16:20. That Paul was not at loggerheads with Apollos is shown by 1 Cor 3:9 and 16:12 where he calls Apollos συνεργός and ἀδελφός respectively.

15 As I noted above, this verse is clearly using hyperbole. See also Acts 19:26: "You also see and hear that not only in Ephesus but in almost the whole of Asia this Paul has persuaded and drawn away a considerable number of people by saying that gods made with hands are not gods."

Opposition

In 1 Corinthians 15:32 Paul speaks about fighting "with wild animals at Ephesus". Paul is clearly speaking metaphorically, and the reference is most likely to opponents.[16] That Paul implies in 1 Corinthians 15:30 that his physical life is in danger from these people probably means the danger came from non-Christian (rather than from Christian) opponents,[17] although we cannot say whether they were Jewish or Gentile; indeed, perhaps they were both.

The Acts account also speaks of opposition – from Jews and from Gentiles – especially from the silversmiths. Indeed a regular feature of early Christianity in Asia Minor was that these communities encountered substantial opposition.[18] We can suggest that controversy, suffering and opposition would be a regular and on-going feature of the life of the Christian communities in the Lycus Valley.

Potential Diversity

Acts shows that there are a number of signs of potential diversity in the community in Ephesus – an unknown group of Jewish Christian "brothers and sisters" who wrote to fellow disciples in Achaia about Apollos (Acts 18:27); the Ephesian 12 (Acts 19:1–7) who were probably "disciples" of John the Baptist prior to their conversion by Paul; Jews converted to the new faith by preaching in the synagogue (Acts 19:8–9); Gentiles converted by preaching in the Hall of Tyrannus (Acts 19:9); Christians who had a background in magic (19:19), or who had been worshippers of Artemis (since conversions had an impact on the sale of artefacts connected to her cult – Acts 19:27).[19] Among the Christians in Ephesus there may well have also been Gentiles who had been "God-fearers" and so who had some form of attachment to the synagogue prior to their conversion.

Here we see potential strands of diversity – people who would have brought into the Christian community different strands of thinking, which they derived from their diverse backgrounds. Such people may have formed house churches

---

16 These adversaries are probably also spoken of in 1 Cor 16:8–9 – "But I will stay in Ephesus until Pentecost, for a wide door for effective work has opened to me, and there are many adversaries." See further Trebilco, *Early Christians in Ephesus*, 58–67.

17 But note the plot against Paul by the Hellenist Christians mentioned in Acts 9:29.

18 It is noteworthy that there is no real indication of opposition from outsiders in Colossians, although Colossians 1:11 may hint at some difficulties. Colossians 4:5–6, which concerns relationships with outsiders, does not speak of persecution or hardship from this source.

19 For detailed discussion see Trebilco, *Early Christians in Ephesus*, 110–170. Here I am drawing on Acts as a historical source; see Trebilco, *Early Christians in Ephesus*, 104–107 for arguments that Luke has some reliable sources for his Ephesian material and so this material in Acts can be used in our historical reconstruction.

which retained their own continuing and distinctive identity, which would have fostered the continuance of difference.

How might this help us understand Colossae and Colossians? It underlines the point that the *Christian* community was diverse. If the situation in Ephesus is anything to go by, there was certainly no uniformity of background amongst the earliest Christians. In addition, the on-going life of Christians could well have been quite different, with some, for example, continuing their links with a Jewish community, and others continuing to be involved in trade guilds or associations. These on-going "foregrounds" for the earliest Christians are also important. Therefore if we see evidence for different ideas or "philosophies" emerging among those combated in Colossians,[20] then we do not *have* to look to an influence *outside* the Christian community for a source for these views. The diverse backgrounds of early Christians, and the varieties of their ongoing contexts, provide sufficient explanation for diverse views amongst Christians themselves, although of course we can never rule out the potential impact of outside views, or of worldviews or philosophies coming directly from an outside context.

Jews and Gentiles

We may instinctively think that Paul, as the apostle to the Gentiles (Rom 11:13; Gal 2:8), would have primarily converted Gentiles. However, there are suggestions in Acts that Paul also converted Jews in his work in Ephesus (eg Acts 19:9; see also Acts 18:27), even if Jews were a minority amongst his converts.

We do not know whether there was a substantial Jewish population in Colossae.[21] But if there were Jews in Colossae, it seems very likely that a person like Epaphras connected with the Pauline mission would seek to convert them, and hence that the Jewish elements in the "Colossian teaching" (sabbaths and probably food laws, see Col 2:16, 21), would have found a ready reception amongst Jewish Christians, as well as among Gentile Christians in the Christian community in Colossae. The reference in Colossians 2:13 to "the uncircumcision of your flesh (τῇ ἀκροβυστίᾳ τῆς σαρκὸς ὑμῶν)" suggests the community was predominantly Gentile, but Wilson notes that "it would seem unwise to deny the possibility that there was also a Jewish element" in the Christian community.[22]

---

20 There is of course extensive discussion about the "Colossian heresy"; for discussions see for example C. E. Arnold, *The Colossian Syncretism. The Interface between Christianity and Folk Belief at Colossae* (Tübingen: Mohr Siebeck, 1995); J. D. G. Dunn, "The Colossian Philosophy: A Confident Jewish Apologia", *Biblica* 76 (1995) 153–181.

21 On the substantial Jewish community in Hierapolis see P. A. Harland, "Acculturation and Identity in the Diaspora: A Jewish Family and 'Pagan' Guilds at Hierapolis", *JJS* 57 (2006) 222–244.

22 Wilson, *Colossians*, 6 n10.

False teachers and divisions in the following years

In Acts 20:29–30, as part of Paul's speech to the Ephesian elders in Miletus, Luke has Paul saying: "I know that after I have gone, savage wolves will come in among you, not sparing the flock. Some even from your own group will come distorting the truth in order to entice the disciples to follow them."

This passage has been the cause of much debate. The following points are relevant here. Firstly, the "savage wolves" are Christian teachers from another community. They are presented as having a considerable impact on the Christian community – they will rampage and destroy. Nothing is said of their theological position.

Secondly, it is said that some Ephesian elders themselves will pervert the Gospel and draw others away after them. This suggests the break-away elders will attempt to establish new and rival communities.[23] The emphasis in Acts is not on the nature of the teaching but rather on its seriousness, since it is said to involve a corruption of the Gospel and division in the Christian community.

Thirdly, although Acts 20:29–30 is given in what is generally Lucan language, I would suggest that at this point in the Miletus speech, Luke may be drawing on Pauline tradition, perhaps local Ephesian tradition.[24] But would Luke have retained this traditional material, or in fact written anything at all on the matter, if *nothing* like this had actually happened? Since Luke regularly portrays the early Christian communities as united, and this is the only point in Acts when he mentions Christian teachers who are regarded as false,[25] it seems likely that he included the note in 20:29–30 because false teachers became a problem after Paul's time. Further, Johnson points out that the prophecies in Luke-Acts are fulfilled,[26] and Peterson shows how significant this motif of fulfilment is in Luke-Acts.[27] This suggests that we are to think of prophecies like Acts 20:29–30 as being fulfilled, but after the events described at the end of Acts. That after Paul's time and prior to Luke writing Acts (perhaps about 80 CE),[28] there

---

23 See Trebilco, *Early Christians in Ephesus*, 191.

24 See Trebilco, *Early Christians in Ephesus*, 191–3. Parallels in Paul's letters to what is said in Acts 20:29–30 indicate that Luke could be drawing on tradition at this point.

25 But lack of harmony is mentioned, for example, in Acts 6:1–2; 15:36–39; 21:20–21.

26 L. T. Johnson, *The Acts of the Apostles* (Collegeville, Minn.: The Liturgical Press, 1992), 8 writes: "Paul's final words in Acts, 'this word of salvation has been sent to the Gentiles, and they will listen' (28:28), is meant to be understood as a prophecy that is – like all prophecies in Luke-Acts – brought to fulfillment."

27 See D. Peterson, "The Motif of Fulfilment and the Purpose of Luke-Acts", in B. Winter/A. D. Clarke (ed.), *The Book of Acts in Its Ancient Literary Settings* (Grand Rapids, Mich.: Eerdmans, 1993) 83–104.

28 C. K. Barrett, *A Critical and Exegetical Commentary on the Acts of the Apostles* (2 vol.; Edinburgh: T & TClark, 1994, 1998) 2.xlii–xliii suggests a date in the late 80s or early 90s for

was trouble among the early Christians in Ephesus from both insiders and out-siders, including leaders attempting to set up new and rival communities, seems very likely.

Fourthly, the speech is quite general – Luke intends it to be an address to early Christian leaders. Whilst he has clearly localised it in Ephesus, we can suggest that its fulfilment was not limited to Ephesus.[29]

Hence, we can suggest that after Paul's time false teachers from within and from without were a problem – not only in Ephesus, but perhaps in other Pauline communities as well. This suggests that in the Lycus Valley Christian communi-ties, there may well have been conflicts, disputes and divisions.

The Pastorals

So far in "the view from Ephesus" I have concentrated on 1 Corinthians and Acts. But the Pastorals are also very interesting at this point. I would suggest that they are written around 80, and by someone who saw themselves as in the Pauline tra-dition. A strong argument can be mounted that 1 and 2 Timothy are addressed to Ephesus; clearly they testify to the on-going significance of the Pauline tradi-tion in the area. But they also show the rise of "false teachers" – those who claim that the resurrection is past (2 Tim 2:18) and who advocate asceticism and some Jewish practices. The Miletus speech is fulfilled here.[30]

But do the Pastorals help us in looking beyond Ephesus? Not directly, since 1 and 2 Timothy are addressed to the Pauline community in Ephesus, Titus to the Pauline community in Crete. But if the sorts of things revealed by these texts can happen in one Pauline community in Western Asia Minor, perhaps they can also happen in others too. At the very least, "the view from Ephesus" shows us some of the things that may have happened in the Lycus Valley. So by the 80's the Christian communities in the Lycus Valley may have been influenced by false teachers – with an over-realised eschatology and ascetic tendencies. More poten-tial diversity emerges therefore.

Acts; see also J. A. Fitzmyer, *The Acts of the Apostles* (New York: Doubleday, 1998), 51–55 who suggests 80–85; C. K. Barrett, "The Historicity of Acts", *JTS* ns 50 (1999) 515–34. F. F. Bruce's comment (*The Book of the Acts* (Grand Rapids, Mich.: Eerdmans, 1988), 392) concerning v25 is relevant here: "Luke would not have reported [these words] and repeated them so em-phatically if he had known that, in the event, they were falsified."

29 See Trebilco, *Early Christians in Ephesus*, 194 for a discussion of this point.

30 Of course it could be fulfilled in other ways too. On the matters mentioned in this para-graph, see Trebilco, *Early Christians in Ephesus*, 197–236.

The arrival of the Johannine group?

"The view from Ephesus" gives us a further suggestion of what might have happened in the Christian communities of the Lycus Valley, subsequent to the writing of Colossians. This involves the arrival of Johannine Christianity.

It seems to me to be very likely that John's Gospel was written from Ephesus.[31] Our earliest evidence from a range of sources links John's Gospel with Ephesus. Polycrates (bishop of Ephesus in the last decade of the second century) and Irenaeus both link John's Gospel with the city. It seems likely that Polycarp was the basis for the tradition of the link with Ephesus found in Irenaeus, which strengthens the credibility of that tradition. We can also argue that Polycarp of Smyrna knew John, which suggests that John lived nearby; again this is compatible with Ephesus as John's home. The *Acts of John*, written around 150 CE, provides further evidence for the location of the Gospel in Ephesus. With some confidence then, we can locate John's Gospel in Ephesus.

The author of John's Gospel (whom I would suggest was John the Elder)[32] also demonstrates reliable knowledge of Galilee and Jerusalem.[33] Thus, it seems likely that John lived in Palestine for quite some time and later travelled to Ephesus. One suggestion here is that he moved to Ephesus around the time of the Jewish War (66–70 CE), perhaps with a group of other Christians. Although we have no direct evidence for the arrival of such a group in Ephesus, it remains a reasonable suggestion.[34] Polycrates also gives evidence that Philip, who had left Jerusalem after the persecution of Stephen and had gone to Caesarea (Acts 8:40, where he was still living sometime later, see Acts 21:8–10) emigrated at some point to Hierapolis with his daughters.[35] "John" may well have similarly emigrated to

---

31 See Trebilco, *Early Christians in Ephesus*, 241–263; C. E. Hill, *The Johannine Corpus in the Early Church* (Oxford: Oxford University Press, 2004), 471–2.

32 In my view, John the Elder wrote John's Gospel and 1–3 John, while a different John (whom I will call John the Seer) wrote Revelation; see Trebilco, *Early Christians*, 246–267, 293.

33 On the accurate knowledge in John's Gospel of Galilee and Jerusalem as it was before 70 CE, see R. E. Brown, *The Gospel According to John. Introduction, Translation, and Notes* (2 vol.; Garden City: Doubleday, 1966), 1.xlii–xliii.

34 See in general T. A. Robinson, *The Bauer Thesis Examined. The Geography of Heresy in the Early Christian Church* (Lewiston/Queenston: Edwin Mellen Press, 1988), 98; N. A. Dahl, *Studies in Ephesians. Introductory Questions, Text- & Edition-Critical Issues, Interpretation of Texts and Themes* (Tübingen: Mohr Siebeck, 2000), 457. In *Ant.* 20.256, Josephus, speaking of the Procuratorship of Gessius Florus (64–66 CE), writes: "The ill-fated Jews [of the province of Judaea], unable to endure the devastation by brigands that went on were one and all forced to abandon their own country and flee, for they thought that it would be better to settle among gentiles, no matter where." See also Josephus, *J. W.* 7.410–19. It seems likely that some of these refugees went to Asia Minor, and Ephesus in particular. Compare M. Günther, *Die Frühgeschichte des Christentums in Ephesus* (Frankfurt am Main: Peter Lang, 1995), 121, 211.

35 See Eusebius, *Hist. Eccl.* 3.31.3; 5.24.2.

Western Asia Minor, specifically Ephesus, at this time and subsequently written the Fourth Gospel there. 1–3 John are written in the same location as the Gospel, and so are also to be connected to Ephesus and give evidence for a "Johannine movement" in and around the city, perhaps around 100 CE.

Would the Johannine group, once established in Ephesus around 70 CE, have had influence in other areas of Western Asia Minor? Would the Johannine movement have "spread out" and planted "daughter churches" in Western Asia Minor, or would they have had some impact on or involvement in other established groups in Western Asia Minor? Would their impact have extended, over time, to the Lycus Valley?

There are two points that argue for the wider impact of Johannine Christianity (as represented by John's Gospel and 1–3 John). Firstly, our general point about networking and mobility in earliest Christianity argues for this; Johannine Christians would travel. Secondly, the evidence for travel by emissaries of the groups spoken of in 2–3 John, provided by the following passages, also argues for this:

Many deceivers have gone out into the world, those who do not confess that Jesus Christ has come in the flesh; any such person is the deceiver and the antichrist! Be on your guard ... Do not receive into the house or welcome anyone who comes to you and does not bring this teaching; for to welcome is to participate in the evil deeds of such a person. (2 John 7–8, 10–11).

The author disagrees with these deceivers, but it is clear from the context that they are itinerants, and from the Johannine circle.

I was overjoyed when some of the friends arrived and testified to your faithfulness to the truth, namely how you walk in the truth. ... Beloved, you do faithfully whatever you do for the friends, even though they are strangers to you; they have testified to your love before the church. You will do well to send them on in a manner worthy of God; for they began their journey for the sake of Christ, accepting no support from non-believers. Therefore we ought to support such people, ... (3 John 3, 5–8).

Diotrephes, who likes to put himself first, does not acknowledge our authority. So if I come, I will call attention to what he is doing in spreading false charges against us. And not content with those charges, he refuses to welcome the friends, and even prevents those who want to do so and expels them from the church (3 John 9–10).

I have much to write to you, but I would rather not write with pen and ink; instead I hope to see you soon, and we will talk together face to face (3 John 13–14).

Here are many indications of mobility – travel undertaken not only by the Johannine members, but also by their opponents. This suggests that Johannine Christianity could well have travelled to the Lycus Valley.

Revelation – Ephesus, the Nicolaitans and Laodicea

The Book of Revelation, written around 95–96 CE, adds to our picture of "the view from Ephesus". That John the Seer addresses "the church in Ephesus" first (Rev 2:1–7) reinforces the particular significance of Ephesian Christians in Western Asia Minor and increases the likelihood that Ephesian Christians would be influential in the Lycus Valley.

John speaks of the Nicolaitans, who are or have been present in Ephesus (Rev 2:6), Pergamum (Rev 2:14–15) and Thyatira (Rev 2:20–23).[36] They are a group with itinerant leaders who taught that it was acceptable for Christians to eat food which had been offered to idols and to be involved in some way in pagan worship (Rev 2:14, 20). Although the matter is debated, they are probably best seen as a group that is similar to the "strong" at Corinth, and their origins may lie in a misunderstanding or development of Pauline teaching.[37] Although John the Seer does not mention the Nicolaitans in his letter to the church in Laodicea (Rev 3:14–22) and he does not write to Colossae or Hierapolis, it is certainly possible that over time, the Nicolaitans had a presence in the Lycus Valley. They add another potential dimension to the diversity of these Christian communities.

John also writes to the "church in Laodicea" (Rev 3:14–22), and this adds some valuable insight into one of the churches in the Lycus Valley which we can discuss briefly here. Revelation 3:15–16 contains the well-known reference to the Laodicean Christians being "Neither cold nor hot … so, because you are lukewarm, and neither cold nor hot, I am about to spit you out of my mouth". The allusion is to the local water supply; the water of Laodicea is neither hot like the medicinal waters of Hierapolis, nor cold like the pure water of Colossae. The image is thus one of effectiveness. According to John the Seer, the Laodicean Christians are lukewarm like their own water supply, and so are good for nothing. The congregation is thus taken to task for the barrenness of its works.[38]

In Revelation 3:17–18 we read: "For you say, 'I am rich, I have prospered, and I need nothing.' You do not realize that you are wretched, pitiable, poor, blind, and naked. Therefore I counsel you to buy from me gold refined by fire so that you may be rich; and white robes to clothe you and to keep the shame of your nakedness from being seen; and salve to anoint your eyes so that you may see." The community cannot be literally rich and poor simultaneously; it seems most likely that they are in fact literally wealthy, and that the risen Christ berates them

---

36 Most scholars would equate the Nicolaitans, the teaching of Balaam and the teaching of Jezebel.

37 For discussion see Trebilco, *Early Christians in Ephesus*, 307–335.

38 See S.S. Smalley, *The Revelation to John. A Commentary on the Greek Text of the Apocalypse* (Downers Grove: IVP, 2005), 98.

for being materially rich but spiritually poor, blind and naked,[39] and advises them to become spiritually rich. Thus, the Christian community in Laodicea is saying "I am rich", and in fact they are quite wealthy. Local factors are probably significant here, since Laodicea became prosperous during the last part of the first century BCE, and although it suffered from earthquakes during the time of Tiberius and Nero, it became a major city by the second century CE. The wealth of the city is indicated by the fact that, although it was destroyed by the earthquake in 61/62 CE, it refused imperial financial assistance for what was a considerable rebuilding programme.[40] Beale argues that the Christians of the city had become wealthy because they had been willing to cooperate with the worship of the trade guilds and the economic institutions of their culture. This sort of spiritual compromise for economic gain meant that their witness was ineffective, which explains why Christ is introduced as the "faithful and true witness" at the beginning of the letter to Laodicea in Revelation 3:14.[41] This seems the most likely explanation of the source of the Laodiceans' wealth, and of the fact that John the Seer is strongly opposed to them being wealthy. Unfortunately we do not have socio-economic data for the Christians in Colossae and Hierapolis at this time, and so are unable to make any comparison with Laodicea.

Pauline, Johannine and Nicolaitan Christians in the Lycus Valley?

We have noted that Pauline Christianity was present in the Lycus Valley and that Johannine Christianity could well have travelled there in due course. And how might the Nicolaitans fit in, if they were present too?

With regard to Pauline and Johannine strands, the question is, how would these two movements have related to one another? How would the Pauline strand, dating from Epaphras and the 50s, relate to this newly arrived Johannine strand? Again, the "view from Ephesus" is helpful.

There are two broad options. Firstly, the two strands could have *merged* together in particular cities. There are a variety of possibilities within this option. Perhaps a Pauline community could have been visited by a Johannine group, and become Johannine. Or a Pauline community could have genuinely adopted some

---

39 See D. E. Aune, *Revelation 1–5* (Dallas: Word Books, 1997), 259.

40 See Tacitus, *Ann.* 14.27; C. J. Hemer, *The Letters to the Seven Churches of Asia in their Local Setting* (Sheffield: JSOT Press, 1986), 180–2, 191–201; Aune, *Revelation 1–5*, 249.

41 G. K. Beale, *The Book of Revelation. A Commentary on the Greek Text* (Grand Rapids, Mich.: Eerdmans, 1999), 304–5. A. Yarbro Collins, *Crisis and Catharsis: The Power of the Apocalypse* (Philadelphia: Westminster Press, 1984), 133, also notes with regard to John's condemnation of wealth here: "The underlying reason seems to be that it was possible to get and to maintain wealth only by accommodating to the polytheistic culture."

Johannine elements into their Pauline group, with the result being that the community reflected traditions from both strands. These different possibilities can all be seen basically as the "Merger Theory", or the "Take over Theory". The two strands merge into one.

But secondly, it is possible for the two strands to remain separate. So two separate strands could have co-existed – one Pauline, the other Johannine, and so two separate groups of house churches in say Colossae. They might have had cordial relations, but retained their specificity, and individual group identity. This is what I think happened at Ephesus (see further below). Would it have happened in much smaller centres? Or would the tendency for them to get together and support one another in a smaller centre have been very strong, provided the group did not grow too big. But I suggest the continued existence of separate strands at least for a time is the most likely view.

Given the geography of the Lycus Valley, one variant on this can be considered, which also takes the possible presence of the Nicolaitans into account. It is entirely possible that each of the three cities came to reflect *different* strands of early Christianity. Colossae could have been and remained "Pauline"; Hierapolis could have become "Johannine" (we know that Papias of Hierapolis knew John's Gospel) and Laodicea could have become – at least for a time – Nicolaitan. We can suggest that there would have been good relations between the Pauline and the Johannine groups – and very strained relations with the Nicolaitans.

But let me present the situation in Ephesus.[42] I cannot argue in detail here for why the Pauline strand and the Johannine strand would remain separate. But let me give one argument for why I think this is most likely to have happened.

Take one example. There are significant differences between the Pastoral Epistles and the Johannine Letters with regard to leadership structures and the locus of authority.[43] In the Pastorals we have the development of appointed leadership positions,[44] and the beginnings of institutionalisation. The locus of authority is in the Pauline tradition, but this is mediated by recognised and authorised teachers.

By contrast, the author of 1 John can write this letter without mentioning any leaders and indeed stresses that the community does not need a teacher. In 1 John 2:27 we read: "As for you, the anointing that you received from him

---

42 The likelihood that John the Elder and others with him travelled from elsewhere to Ephesus, and so had some sense of group cohesion prior to arriving in Ephesus, reinforces the probability that this community remained as a distinct group there.

43 For detailed discussion of this issue in the Pastorals and the Johannine Letters, see Trebilco, *Early Christians in Ephesus*, 446–490, 503–6.

44 Although note that, as in the earlier Pauline letters, there seems to be more than one leader of a group in view, with a *group* of elder-overseers being envisaged as leaders; see for example, 1 Tim 5:17. The singulars in 1 Tim 3:1 and Titus 1:7 (*cf* 1:5) are to be thought of as generic, and not as indicating a single leader for a sizable community.

abides in you and so you do not need anyone to teach you. But as his anointing teaches you about all things and is true and is not a lie, and just as it has taught you, abide in him." Further the locus of authority is the whole community, and it is the community as a whole which functions as the tradition-bearer. This is shown in what the author writes about witness (1 Jn 4:14, 16), about the anointing (1 Jn 2:20, 27) and about what was "from the beginning" (1 Jn 1:1; 2:7, 13–14, 24; 3:11). The community as a whole is the witness, receives the anointing which enables them to "know", and the community as a whole has known or heard what was "from the beginning". The predominant sense of the locus of authority that we gain from 1 John is of the collective authority of the community, with the individual authority of the author of 1 John being very much a subsidiary factor.[45] There are significant differences then between the Pastorals and 1 John. Further, on this topic it seems clear that we are not seeing simply the views of the author, but the actual situation prevailing among the readers. This indicates that these sets of documents are written to different and distinct communities.

We can suggest then that if a Pauline group and a Johannine group existed in a city in the Lycus Valley, they would have remained as separate communities. Further, a Nicolaitan group would also be separate, since it seems to be a distinct movement with its own teaching and disciples (Rev 2:14–15, 20, 22–23).

The later picture –
the view from Western Asia Minor to the Lycus Valley

Having looked at the situation in the Lycus Valley from Ephesus, and discussed the book of Revelation, I now want to look at the wider picture in Western Asia Minor – what light might this wider picture shed on Christianity in the Lycus Valley? Does the sort of evidence we have from Western Asia Minor confirm the view from Ephesus? I am suggesting a sort of dual approach then – from the specific evidence provided by Ephesus, and the more over-arching evidence from Western Asia Minor.

---

45 While the act of writing itself assumes some form of authority, see Trebilco, *Early Christians in Ephesus*, 476–7 for the case that the author does not stand above the community but rather places himself within it and sees himself first and foremost as part of the group that includes the readers. In 2 and 3 John "the elder" asserts some form of authority, but this seems to be personal authority based on witness and being a tradition-bearer rather than the authority of office or of appointment. 3 John 9 indicates that individual authority was a contentious issue.

Pauline influence

What can we say about Pauline Christianity in the wider area? The highly influential Walter Bauer thought Pauline influence vanished from Western Asia
Minor in the decades after Paul.[46] However, it seems clear that we have the following chain of on-going influence from Pauline thought and from traditions
associated with him in the area.[47] As we know, in the early 50s, Paul established
communities in Western Asia Minor and the Gospel spread from Ephesus during his time there, since it was such a communication centre. As part of the Pauline corpus we have 1 and 2 Timothy, which were written to Ephesus.[48] As we
have noted, these letters, written perhaps around 80, are clearly within the Pauline tradition and testify to the on-going importance of that tradition at this
date.[49] Bauer does not give sufficient credence to this evidence, since he thinks
the Pastorals were written after 140 CE.[50]

It seems likely that the writing of Acts, probably in the 80s CE,[51] would have
increased the profile of Paul. Surely one of the places to which the book of Acts
would quickly have been sent, and where it would have been avidly read, was
Western Asia Minor, which featured so prominently in the story.[52] That Poly-

---

46 See W. Bauer, *Orthodoxy and Heresy in Earliest Christianity* (Philadelphia: Fortress,
1971), 83–4. For a more detailed discussion of what is argued here, see P. R. Trebilco, "Christian Communities in Western Asia Minor into the Early Second Century: Ignatius and
Others as Witnesses Against Bauer", *JETS* 49 (2006) 17–44, some of which is drawn on in this
section.

47 M. C. de Boer, "Comment: Which Paul?" in, W. S. Babcock (ed.), *Paul and the Legacies of Paul* (Dallas: Southern Methodist University Press, 1990) 45–54 raises a key issue,
when he notes (page 48) the need to distinguish "between an appeal to the person or name of
Paul – a *Paulusbild* – and the appropriation of his theological legacy as we know this legacy
from his letters – what we may label the 'epistolary Paul.'" Here my concern is with the on-
going appeal to Paul and "the influence of certain theological traditions associated with Paul's
name" (page 52), rather than with the actual appropriation of the theology of the historical
Paul.

48 See 1 Tim 1:3; 2 Tim 1:18; 4:12.

49 See Trebilco, *Early Christians in Ephesus*, 197–205.

50 Bauer thought the Pastorals had not been written by 140 CE, when Marcion made his
collection of Paul's letters; see Bauer, *Orthodoxy*, 222–7. Against this, see for example F. W.
Norris, "Asia Minor before Ignatius: Walter Bauer Reconsidered", in E. A. Livingstone (ed.),
Studia Evangelica VII (Berlin: Akademie-Verlag, 1982) 365–77, on pp. 370–1. There are also
strong arguments that Polycarp used the Pastorals much earlier than this; see P. Hartog,
*Polycarp and the New Testament. The Occasion, Rhetoric, Theme, and Unity of the Epistle
to the Philippians and its Allusions to New Testament Literature* (Tübingen: Mohr Siebeck,
2002), 178–9.

51 See footnote 28 above; I note that the date of Acts continues to be debated.

52 Recall the discussion above about mobility and interconnectedness in early Christianity.

carp probably knew Acts reinforces this.[53] It would quickly have supplemented the image of Paul among its readers.[54]

Ignatius shows that knowledge of Paul was alive in Ephesus when he wrote. In Ignatius *Eph.* 12.2 we read: "You are a passageway for those slain for God; you are fellow initiates with Paul, the holy one who received a testimony and proved worthy of all fortune. When I attained to God, may I be found in his footsteps, this one who mentions you in every epistle in Christ Jesus."[55] Bauer thinks this is "in no way based upon Paul's apostolic activity but rather on the fact that the road to martyrdom, which Paul also travelled, leads past this city".[56] But that Ignatius can praise the Ephesians as "fellow initiates with Paul (Παύλου συμμύσται)" and is clearly aware that Paul mentions the Ephesians in his letters,[57] strongly suggests that the Ephesians Ignatius had talked with had spoken of this as an important matter to them (and clearly he had spoken with a number of Ephesians),[58] and Ignatius knows that the reference to Paul will be well received amongst his Ephesian readers. It is evidence then for the vitality of traditions about Paul amongst some of Ignatius' Ephesian readers.[59]

---

53 See Polycarp *Phil.* 1.2 and Acts 2:24, which share the phrase "having loosed the pains λύσας τὰς ὠδῖνας" of death or Hades, an adaptive allusion to Ps 18:4–6. Hartog (*Polycarp*, 185) writes: "It seems unlikely that both Acts and Polycarp would have made the same allusive translation independently." See also Barrett, *Acts*, 1.36–7; B. D. Ehrman, editor and translator, *The Apostolic Fathers* (Cambridge: Harvard University Press, 2 vols, 2003), p335; Hartog (*Polycarp*, 195) notes that Polycarp may be "an important first witness to Acts". M. W. Holmes ("Polycarp's *Letter to the Philippians* and the Writings that later formed the New Testament" in A. Gregory/C. Tuckett (ed.), *The Reception of the New Testament in the Apostolic Fathers* (Oxford: Oxford University Press, 2005) 187–227, on p. 201) notes "the use of Acts in *Philippians* cannot be demonstrated; at the same time, knowledge of Acts on the part of Polycarp cannot be excluded." On other early witnesses to Acts see Barrett, *Acts*, 1.35–48. On whether Ignatius knew Acts see W. R. Schoedel, *Ignatius of Antioch* (Philadelphia: Fortress, 1985), 228.

54 Bauer overlooks the importance of Acts here; he writes (*Orthodoxy*, 85): "Only the canonization of the book of Acts and of the Pauline letters, including the Pastorals, once again provided clear insight into the real situation with respect to Paul." He refers to Irenaeus *Adv. Haer.* 3.3.4 and the Acts of Paul at this point, and so clearly thinks of canonization (and hence the impact of Acts) as occurring late in the second century.

55 Ignatius also mentions Paul in *Rom.* 4.3: "I am not enjoining you as Peter and Paul did. They were apostles, I am condemned; they were free, until now I have been a slave."

56 Bauer, *Orthodoxy*, 83.

57 There has been much debate about the phrase "who mentions you in every epistle in Christ Jesus", since the Ephesians are only mentioned in 1 Cor 15:32 and 16:8 (and 1 Tim 1:3; 2 Tim 1:18; 4:12). Lindemann writes (A. Lindemann, "Paul in the Writings of the Apostolic Fathers," in *Paul and the Legacies of Paul*, 25–45, here page 36): "Ignatius is simply trying to link the Apostle Paul and the Church of Ephesus as intimately as possible."

58 See Ignatius *Eph.* 1.3–2.1; he had met Onesimus, Crocus, Burrhus, Euplus, and Fronto.

59 See H. Koester, "Ephesos in Early Christian Literature", in H. Koester (ed.), *Ephesos: Metropolis of Asia. An Interdisciplinary Approach to Its Archaeology, Religion, and Culture* (Valley Forge, Pennsylvania: Trinity Press International, 1995) 119–40, on pp. 133, 140.

Polycarp, bishop of Smyrna, whose letter to the Philippians can be dated with confidence to around 110–115 CE,[60] refers to Paul three times, including writing of "the wisdom of the blessed and glorious Paul", which Polycarp says "neither I nor anyone like me is able to replicate" (Polycarp *Phil.* 3.2).[61] It is clear that Polycarp admired and valued Paul, and regarded him as an authority.[62] Polycarp also knows a number of Paul's letters — Romans 1 Corinthians, Galatians, Ephesians, Philippians and 1 Timothy, with use of 2 Corinthians and 2 Timothy being probable.[63] But Pauline influence is not limited to particular allusions, since Polycarp is indebted to Paul for elements in his thought.[64] As Lindemann writes, "There is certainly no basis for the notion that Paul was forgotten or unimportant in the (wing of the) church in which 'Clement,' Ignatius, and Polycarp did their work."[65] We have a strong case then for Pauline influence continuing in Smyrna at this time.[66]

None of this is to deny that the Pauline tradition was a contested one, and that there were different interpretations of "Paul". This is clear, particularly with regard to the *Acts of Paul and Thecla*, Marcion and those Gnostics who saw Paul as their spiritual father.[67] However, these texts and authors are generally later than

---

60 See Hartog, *Polycarp*, 169 dates the letter to "c. A. D. 115"; this is dependent on the unity of the Epistle, for which he argues convincingly on pages 148–69. Hill, *The Johannine Corpus*, 416 dates it around 110 CE.

61 See also Polycarp *Phil.* 9.1 ("Therefore I urge all of you to obey the word of righteousness and to practice all endurance, which you also observed with you own eyes not only in the most fortunate Ignatius, Zosimus, and Rufus, but also in others who lived among you, and in Paul himself and the other apostles"); 11.2–3 ("Or do we not realize that 'the saints will judge the world?' For so Paul teaches. But I have neither perceived nor heard that you have any such thing in your midst, among whom the most fortunate Paul labored and who are found in the beginning of his epistle. For he exalted in you among all his churches …").

62 See Hartog, *Polycarp*, 202–3, 221.

63 See Hartog, *Polycarp* 177–9, 195, 228–31. For example, Gal 6:7 in Polycarp *Phil.* 5.1; Rom 14:10–12 is used in Polycarp *Phil.* 6.2; 1 Cor 6:2 is referred to in Polycarp *Phil.* 11.2. Use of 2 Thess is possible. This issue is complicated by the fact that Polycarp seems to have usually quoted from memory; see Hartog, *Polycarp*, 172. For a somewhat different assessment see Holmes, "Polycarp's Letter", 201–227. On determining when literary borrowing from the NT has occurred, see the very important discussion in Hill, *Johannine Corpus*, 67–71, 425–7.

64 See further Lindemann, "Paul", 43–44 on Pauline influence in Polycarp's letter; K. Berding, "John or Paul? Who was Polycarp's Mentor?" *TB* 59 (2008) 135–143.

65 Lindemann, "Paul", 45; compare C. J. Roetzel, "Paul in the Second Century," in J. D. G. Dunn (ed.), *The Cambridge Companion to St Paul* (Cambridge: Cambridge University Press, 2003) 227–41, on pp. 227–8.

66 See further Hartog, *Polycarp*, 194. Bauer again does not take sufficient note of this evidence. See Bauer, *Orthodoxy*, 212–228.

67 This is a very large area of discussion in itself, with considerable disagreement amongst scholars. See for example, E. H. Pagels, *The Gnostic Paul: Gnostic Exegesis of the Pauline Letters* (Philadelphia: Fortress, 1975); *Paul and the Legacies of Paul*; Roetzel, "Paul in the Second Century", 227–41; H. Räisänen, "Marcion" in A. Marjanen/P. Luomanen (ed.), *A Companion to Second-Century Christian 'Heretics'* (Leiden: Brill, 2005) 100–124; I. Dunderberg, "The School

the Pastorals, Acts, Ignatius and Polycarp (although books like the *Acts of Paul and Thecla* may well contain earlier traditions). But there is no doubt that there were different images of Paul "in the air", even during Paul's lifetime, with the variety of images and interpretations growing as time went on.

But my key point here is that it seems most likely that there was *on-going influence from Pauline thought and from traditions associated with him* in Western Asia Minor from Paul's day to the time of Polycarp and beyond.[68] This is certainly more likely than Bauer's view that Paul was completely forgotten. This does not mean that some of Paul's communities did not encounter difficulties – Acts 20:30 speaks of this and we have noted that the fact that Luke includes it shows that it was true in his time. But encountering difficulties with regard to false teachers is one thing; completely losing all memory of Paul is another. We certainly have good evidence that suggests that traditions associated with Paul were a strong and significant component of Christian tradition well into the second century in Western Asia Minor.

Johannine influence in Western Asia Minor[69]

What of Johannine influence in Western Asia Minor? We have already noted some points here in arguing for the arrival of Johannine Christianity. Additional points indicate the extent of Johannine influence in Western Asia Minor.

As already indicated, it seems likely that John, the author of the Gospel, arrived in Ephesus around the time of the Jewish War of 66–70 CE, and there are very strong grounds for Ephesus as the place where John's Gospel was written,

---

of Valentinus" in *A Companion to Second-Century Christian 'Heretics'* 64–99; J. N. Bremmer (ed.), *The Apocryphal Acts of Paul and Thecla* (Kampen: Kok Pharos, 1996).

68 For a discussion of the silence of John the Seer in Revelation about Paul see Trebilco, *Early Christians in Ephesus*, 621–5. On the lack of mention of Paul in Papias' writing, as given in Eusebius, see Lightfoot, *Colossians*, 50–54.

69 On Bauer's view (*Orthodoxy*, 206–8) that John's Gospel was first used by the heretics, see Hill, *Johannine Corpus*, 2–3, 13–15. Hill (*Johannine Corpus*) convincingly opposes what he takes to be the consensus view that "the reception of this Gospel by heterodox groups is said to have been swift and enthusiastic, while among the orthodox it endured a long and mighty struggle for acceptance, until about the time of Irenaeus." (p. 2) He calls this "orthodox Johannophobia" – the hesitation by orthodox writers to use the fourth Gospel because of gnostic use (p. 3). He shows that there was no silence among the writers of the mainstream Church with regard to the Fourth Gospel, which was known and used by many authors; see passim; the chart on page 450 is a helpful summary; see also C. E. Hill, "The Fourth Gospel in the Second Century: The Myth of Orthodox Johannophobia", in J. Lierman (ed.), *Challenging Perspectives on the Gospel of John*, (Tübingen: Mohr Siebeck, 2006) 135–169; C. E. Hill, "'The Orthodox Gospel'. The Reception of John in the Great Church prior to Irenaeus", in T. Rasimus (ed.), *The Legacy of John: Second Century Reception of the Fourth Gospel* (Leiden: Brill, 2010) 233–300.

probably in the 80s.[70] Slightly later 1–3 John were written to a community in and around Ephesus, and bear witness to the on-going impact of Johannine thought in the area.[71]

The oldest clear allusion to 1 John is by Polycarp of Smyrna in his Epistle to the Philippians,[72] probably to be dated around 115–120 CE.[73] Although Polycarp does not directly quote John's Gospel,[74] the broader Johannine tradition, as shown in 1 John, is clearly known in Smyrna at this time.[75] Hill has argued strongly that Ignatius knew the Fourth Gospel.[76] This relates more strongly to the situation in Antioch, but it is also relevant to Western Asia Minor.

Papias of Hierapolis, who wrote between 120–135, gives the first six disciples in an order which reflects John's Gospel, and additional strong arguments can also be offered that he knew the Fourth Gospel.[77] Not only this, but Bauckham has argued convincingly that "Papias valued the Gospel of John very highly – more highly than the other Gospels he knew."[78]

---

70 For a discussion of the likely date of John's Gospel see G.N. Stanton, *The Gospels and Jesus* (Oxford: Oxford University Press, ²2002), 120.

71 See Trebilco, *Early Christians in Ephesus*, 263–90. As noted above, Revelation is not written by the same person as the Gospel, but it is linked theologically to the Gospel and shows the on-going impact of the broader Johannine movement in Western Asia Minor; on the relationship between Revelation and John's Gospel see P. Prigent, *Commentary on the Apocalypse of St John* (Tübingen: Mohr Siebeck, 2001), 36–50. However, here by "Johannine influence" or the "Johannine movement" I mean the Gospel of John and 1–3 John, excluding Revelation.

72 G. Strecker, *The Johannine Letters. A Commentary on 1, 2, and 3 John* (Minneapolis: Fortress, 1996), xxix; see also H. Paulsen and W. Bauer, *Die Briefe des Ignatius von Antiochia und der Brief des Polykarp von Smyrna* (Tübingen: J.C.B. Mohr (Paul Siebeck), 2ⁿᵈ Ed., 1985), 120. It is generally agreed that Polycarp *Phil.* 7:1–2, alludes to 1 John 4:2–3 and 2 John 7. See discussion of other possible parallels in R.E. Brown, *The Epistles of John* (Garden City: Doubleday, 1982), 6–9; Strecker, *Johannine Letters*, xxix.

73 See Hartog, *Polycarp*, 157–8, 169, 238.

74 See Hill, *Johannine Corpus*, 416–20; Hartog, *Polycarp*, 188.

75 There are good grounds for accepting the authenticity of the claim made by Irenaeus that Polycarp knew John "the disciple of the Lord" (probably John the elder); see Irenaeus *Adv. Haer.* 3.3.4; Eusebius *Hist. eccl.* 5.20.6; 5.24.16; Hartog, *Polycarp*, 37–41; M. Hengel, *The Johannine Question* (London: SCM Press, 1989), 102–8; R. Bauckham, "Papias and Polycrates on the Origin of the Fourth Gospel", *JTS* n.s. 44 (1993) 24–69.

76 See Hill, *Johannine Corpus*, 421–43; he cites others who are of this opinion. See for example Ignatius *Magn.* 7.1 and John 5:19; 8:28 and Ignatius *Phld.* 7.1 and John 3:6, 8; 8:14. For a discussion of Foster's view (P. Foster, "The Epistles of Ignatius of Antioch and the Writings that later formed the New Testament", in *The Reception of the New Testament in the Apostolic Fathers*, 183–4), see Hill, "'Orthodox Gospel'".

77 See Hill, *Johannine Corpus*, 385–396. See Eusebius, quoting Papias in *Hist. eccl.* 3.39.4; compare John 1:40, 21:2. See also the additional argument given in Hill, *Johannine Corpus*, 386–94 regarding Eusebius *Hist. eccl.* 3.24.5–13, for which he thinks the source is Papias; compare Bauer, *Orthodoxy*, 187.

78 R. Bauckham, *Jesus and the Eyewitnesses. The Gospels as Eyewitness Testimony* (Grand Rapids, Mich.: Eerdmans, 2006), 423.

There is also evidence for the knowledge of John's Gospel in the *Epistula Apostolorum*.[79] Hill argues strongly for its provenance in Asia Minor.[80] It was probably written sometime in the 140s in Asia Minor, perhaps Smyrna, although it could also be dated just before 120.[81]

We do know that the Gospel of John was used outside Asia from the middle of the second century,[82] but its use in Asia is highly noteworthy. Hengel comments:

This special significance of the Johannine Corpus (including the Apocalypse) for theology in Asia Minor becomes especially visible in the paschal dispute and the Montanist movement: the typology of the passover lamb and the chronology of the passion in the Fourth Gospel support the Quartodeciman custom of the paschal feast as practised in Asia Minor; the new prophetic movement starting from Montanus and his prophetesses could hardly have come into being without the link between the Gospel and the Apocalypse; ... In the Montanist prophecy the Paraclete promised in the Farewell Discourses spoke to believers, and according to Maximilla the heavenly Jerusalem of Apocalypse 21 was to descend in Pepuza. However, J. J. Gunther is surely misleading in stating that 'the creation of a Johannine Asian myth started with Montanism'. This new prophetic movement, beginning about 157 (?), already presupposed it.[83]

Thus, we see there is considerable evidence for the impact of John's Gospel in Western Asia Minor from the beginning of the second century. This evidence not only supports an Ephesian provenance for the Gospel, but is also compatible with the suggestion that there were Christians who favoured John's Gospel (or at the very least used it along with other texts) in various locations in Western Asia Minor. Again, none of this is to deny that, as with the Pauline tradition, the Johannine tradition was a contested one. This is clear in the use made of John's Gospel by Gnostic writers, and by Noetus of Smyrna and others;[84] but it is important to recall that these Gnostic and other texts and authors are generally later than those we have discussed above.[85]

---

79 See Hill, *Johannine Corpus*, 366–74; see also C. E. Hill, "The *Epistula Apostolorum*: An Asian Tract from the Time of Polycarp", JECS 7 (1999) 1–53; see for example *Ep. Apost.* 5.1–3 and John 2:1–11 and Hill, *Johannine Corpus*, 367–9.

80 Hill, "*Epistula Apostolorum*", 1–53; see also A. Stewart-Sykes, "The Asian Context of the New Prophecy and of *Epistula Apostolorum*," VC 51 (1997): 416–438.

81 See Hill, *Johannine Corpus*, 367. Hengel (*Johannine Question*, 12–14) also argues strongly that Justin Martyr knows and uses the Fourth Gospel; compare R. A. Culpepper, *John, the Son of Zebedee* (Columbia: University of South Carolina Press, 1994), 112–14.

82 See Culpepper, *John*, 123.

83 Hengel, *Johannine Question*, 5.

84 See E. H. Pagels, *The Johannine Gospel in Gnostic Exegesis: Heracleon's Commentary on John* (Nashville: Abingdon Press, 1973); and especially Hill, *Johannine Corpus*, 205–293.

85 Hill ("'Orthodox Gospel'", 71) writes: "From a time very early in the second century it is clear that materials which appear uniquely or almost uniquely in the Fourth Gospel were in use among the mainstream or 'apostolic' churches, those associated with Ignatius and his addressees, and elders of the generation preceding Papias."

We can thus trace a chain of Johannine tradition in Western Asia Minor from the probable arrival of John in Ephesus around 70 CE, to the Johannine community evident in 1–3 John, and then the continuing influence of Johannine tradition on Polycarp, Papias, the author of the *Epistula Apostolorum*, the Montanist Movement and the Quartodecimans. This evidence does not *require* that there were "Johannine groups" in Western Asia Minor at this time and earlier – but it is certainly compatible with this suggestion. But we certainly can speak of ongoing influence of the Johannine tradition.

This on-going chain of *both* Pauline and Johannine tradition in Western Asia Minor is very significant. It suggests that from the 50s in the case of Pauline tradition, and probably from the 70s in the case of Johannine tradition, through to the 120s and probably later,[86] we can argue for the on-going "presence" and importance of both Johannine and Pauline tradition in Western Asia Minor. As far as we can tell, both are "on-going" traditions. Now as we have noted, there were strong "counter-voices" – the opponents combated in the Pastorals, the secessionists mentioned in 1 and 2 John, the Nicolaitans,[87] the docetists and Judaizers combated by Ignatius, later Gnostics and so on; traditions were contested and we have evidence for strong disagreement. But alongside this we can also suggest that the presence of Pauline and Johannine tradition is early, strong and as far as we can tell, more or less continuous from the time of the Pauline mission and the arrival of a Johannine group into the second century.

This reinforces my suggestion based on "the view from Ephesus" that in the Lycus Valley, at some point from the late first century onwards, there were both Pauline and Johannine communities. There may well have been Nicolaitan or other groups too, although our evidence here is strictly limited. Of course at some point *one* community may come to value *both* Paul and John – Polycarp is clearly an example of this. But perhaps at first and for some time, communities would favour one tradition or the other, and only later would they use both.

---

86 This is simply the point to which we have limited our enquiry, and is not to suggest a sudden decline at this point. Particularly for the Johannine tradition, the evidence continues strongly after this point. On the situation for the rest of the second century see Babcock, *Paul* and Hill, *Johannine Corpus*.

87 It has been suggested that the Nicolaitans were Paulinists, and that Revelation is antagonistic to this strand of Pauline tradition; for a discussion of this view and arguments that the Nicolaitans are related to the "strong" in Corinth, see Trebilco, *Early Christians in Ephesus*, 331–5.

The silence of John the Seer and of Ignatius

I need now to address an issue of silence, which could undermine my sugges-tion of the on-going impact of both Pauline and Johannine traditions in the Lycus Valley. Around 105–110 CE, Ignatius writes to a range of places – Ephe-sus, Magnesia on the Meander, Tralles, Rome, Philadelphia and Smyrna – and to Polycarp. But why does Ignatius *not* write to at least one of the communities in the Lycus Valley? Is not my suggestion of on-going Pauline and Johannine in-fluence in Western Asia Minor, including the Lycus Valley, challenged, even un-dermined, by this silence?

In response to this silence, Walter Bauer thought that the churches to which John the Seer in Revelation and/or Ignatius did *not* write were "heretical"; for Bauer, John the Seer and Ignatius avoided these communities because they knew they could gain no support there. Hence, Bauer builds up a list of "heretical" communities simply by noting known Christian communities to which John or Ignatius did *not* send letters.

An obvious example here was Colossae – addressed by neither John the Seer in Revelation, nor Ignatius. Similarly, the Christian community in Hierapolis (Col 4:13), was addressed by neither John nor Ignatius. To explain this Bauer suggests: "John selected the most prominent communities from those in his area *which met the prerequisite of seeming to afford him the possibility of exerting a real influence.*"[88] Thus, Bauer infers that John the Seer did not write to some commu-nities – such as Colossae and Hierapolis – because they did not agree with him theologically, and so are to be seen as heretical. Bauer notes that Ignatius does not write to these communities either. He writes: "The community of Hierapolis (Col 4.13) and that of Colossae are bypassed in icy silence by both John [the Seer in Revelation] and Ignatius."[89] They would not be Pauline or Johannine commu-nities at least.

What do we make of this argument? In the first century Colossae was over-shadowed by Hierapolis (24 kilometres away) and particularly Laodicea (18 ki-lometres away), which was the most prominent city in the Lycus Valley by the Roman imperial period.[90] As we have noted, Colossae was probably hit by an earthquake in 61/62 CE,[91] but we do not know how quickly it recovered. Stand-hartinger writes: "The claim that it [Colossae] was abandoned in 61/62 CE in

---

88 Bauer, *Orthodoxy*, 78 (emphasis added).

89 Bauer, *Orthodoxy*, 80. Bauer (*Orthodoxy*, 80) thought Ignatius travelled through Hiera-polis, and close by Colossae; this is possible, but not certain. For what we do know of his route see Schoedel, *Ignatius*, 11.

90 See Wilson, *Colossians*, 3–6; Strabo *Geogr.* 12.8.16.

91 Tacitus (*Ann.* 14.27.1) notes that Laodicea was destroyed; Colossae is not mentioned; see Magie, *Roman Rule*, 564, 1421 n73; Arnold, in *ABD* 1.1089.

the wake of an earthquake, though often made, is improbable as far as we can know from the archaeological remains like coins and known inscriptions."[92] Thus, a Christian community probably was meeting in Colossae when John wrote Revelation, although we cannot be absolutely certain of this. But it is precarious to argue that John and Ignatius both *chose* not to address the Christian community in Colossae because they knew it was "heretical" and so not in agreement with them. It is just as possible that the Christian community was very small in the city between 95 and 110 because of the slow recovery from the earthquake.

What of Hierapolis? We learn of the Christian group in the city from Colossians 4:13 and it is likely that Philip and some of his daughters settled in Hierapolis sometime around 70 CE.[93] Papias, who wrote "An Exposition of Dominical Sayings" between 120–135 CE, was bishop of Hierapolis.[94] This is the only detail we know relating to the first half of the second century.[95] To say that John and Ignatius avoided writing to the Christian community in Hierapolis because of its theological position is possible, but given our very fragmentary knowledge, seems unwise.

Scholars have had very different views about why John the Seer chose his particular seven churches in Revelation.[96] It is possible that they were all on a postal

---

92 A. Standhartinger, "Colossians and the Pauline School", *NTS* 50 (2004) 572–93, on p. 586. Magie (*Roman Rule*, 986, n22) also writes "Colossae was an important place in the imperial period, for an inscription of this time and coins issued in the second and third centuries after Christ show the usual officials." See also P. T. O'Brien, *Colossians, Philemon* (WBC; Texas: Word Books, 1982), xxvi–xxvii; M. Barth/H. Blanke, *Colossians. A New Translation with Introduction and Commentary* (New York: Doubleday, 1994), 9–10 who note that coins minted about 150 CE attest that Colossae was in existence at that time, but we do not know anything more about the late first century. Unfortunately there are no Christian inscriptions from this area from the second century, which might aid us here; see S. Mitchell, *Anatolia. Land, Men and Gods in Asia Minor* (2 vol.; Oxford: Clarendon Press, 1993), 2.37–43. For the later history, see Lightfoot, *Colossians*, 45–72.

93 See F. F. Bruce, "Hierapolis" in *ABD* 3, 195; Eusebius, *Hist. eccl.* 3.31.2–5; 3.39.9; 5.24.2; see also F. F. Bruce, "Jews and Christians in the Lycus Valley", *BS* 141 (1984) 3–15, on p. 10; L. J. Kreitzer, "The Plutonium of Hierapolis and the Descent of Christ into the 'Lowermost Parts of the Earth' (Ephesians 4,9)", *Biblica* 79 (1998) 381–93.

94 See the discussion of dating in Hill, *Johannine Corpus*, 383–84; he suggests Papias wrote "probably in the 120s or possibly as late as the early 130s." Compare W. R. Schoedel, "Papias," in *ANRW II.27.1*, 1992, 235–70, on pp. 236–7 who opts for a date around 110. On Papias in general see Schoedel, "Papias", 235–70.

95 For evidence relating to the second half of the second century and later from Hierapolis, Colossae and Laodicea, see Bruce, "Jews and Christians in the Lycus Valley", 11–13.

96 On the symbolism of the number seven, see A. Yarbro Collins, "Numerical Symbolism in Jewish and Early Christian Apocalyptic Literature," in *ANRW*, II.21.2, 1984, 1221–1287, on pp. 1275–9; Aune, *Revelation 1–5*, 29. Whilst the number seven is clearly symbolic, this does not tell us why John chose these particular seven churches. It remains possible that he intended these seven to be representative of a range of spiritual conditions.

route as Ramsay suggested,[97] but positive evidence for this is lacking.[98] Was it simply that, as an itinerant prophet,[99] these seven were the churches with which John had had regular contact? He knows their situation well, and clearly has had pastoral involvement with them in the past (see for example Rev 2:21); there would be a limit to the number of churches with which John could have had such pastoral interaction.[100] Thus, he may not have written to Colossae and Hierapolis simply because he did not know them well — they were not part of his "circuit" as it were. But the fact that we can give a range of possible explanations for John's choice of churches – and hence for why he did not chose some other places – means that we *cannot* infer that the communities he left out were theologically in disagreement with him.

What of the communities addressed by John the Seer but not by Ignatius? Ignatius writes to three of the communities addressed by John – Ephesus, Smyrna and Philadelphia – but does not address four of John's seven churches – Pergamum, Thyatira, Sardis and Laodicea.[101] Bauer asks,

Is it by chance that the communities of Pergamum, Thyatira, Sardis, and Laodicea are missing from Ignatius' audience – communities that [John] the seer vehemently rebukes. ... Is it too much to claim if, on the basis of what Ignatius both says and does not say, and considering the evidence of the Apocalypse, one concludes that in his attempt to stretch the circle of his influence as widely as possible for the sake of his constituency there was nothing Ignatius could hope for from the Christian groups represented at Pergamum, Thyatira, Sardis, and Laodicea, because no points of contact existed for him there – no 'bishop'"was present whom he could press into service, because the heretics had maintained, or had come to exercise, leadership there?[102]

Yet we do not know why Ignatius chose to write to particular communities. Ignatius also acknowledges that there are other churches to which he did not write. In

---

97 W. M. Ramsay, *The Letters to the Seven Churches of Asia and their Place in the Plan of the Apocalypse* (London: Hodder & Stoughton, 1904), 185–96; see also Hemer, *The Letters to the Seven Churches*, 14–15.

98 See Aune, *Revelation 1–5*, 131 writes "Ramsay's hypothesis of a circular post road has no firm basis in archeological fact but is rather an inference based on the location of cities."

99 On John as an itinerant prophet, see D. E. Aune, "The Social Matrix of the Apocalypse of John", *BR* 26 (1981) 16–32, on pp. 26–7; R. Schnackenburg, "Ephesus: Entwicklung einer Gemeinde von Paulus zu Johannes", *BZ* 35 (1991) 41–64, on p. 56.

100 Aune (*Revelation 1–5*, 131) notes that all seven were within 161 kilometres of Ephesus "and might have formed an established circular route for itinerant Christian prophets and teachers, perhaps since Paul's day."

101 Bauer (*Orthodoxy*, 78) writes: "Subsequently, Ignatius apparently followed a similar procedure [to John] and in turn made a selection from among those seven communities."

102 Bauer, *Orthodoxy*, 79–80; see also H. Koester, "GNOMAI DIAPHORA: The Origin and Nature of Diversification in the History of Early Christianity" in H. Koester/J. M. Robinson (ed.), *Trajectories Through Early Christianity* (Philadelphia: Fortress, 1971), 114–157, here page 148.

his letter to Polycarp 8.1 he states: – "Because I have not been able to write to all the churches – since, as the divine will enjoins, I am unexpectedly to set sail from Troas to Neapolis – you are to write to the churches that lie before me [Or: "on this side"] (γράψεις ταῖς ἔμπροσθεν ἐκκλησίαις)".[103] The context suggests there were a number of such churches. Further, Ignatius clearly did not determine the route that he took through Asia Minor – nor do we know exactly what that route was.[104] So it is futile to speculate that he went through a particular place and yet ignored the Christians there. This is entirely an argument from silence, and again there are alternative explanations.[105]

Take Sardis as one example. John writes to Sardis, but Ignatius does not. Does this mean that by 110 Sardis had changed theologically, as Bauer suggests?[106] This is possible, but again it is an argument from silence. Further, since Bauer wrote, Melito's *On the Pascha* has been discovered. This is probably to be dated a little before 164 CE, so later than the rest of the evidence on which I have drawn.[107] The text does not explicitly refer to Christians in Sardis, but clearly it shows that there was a community of Christians in the city in the 160's.[108] Whilst we cannot deduce from this sermon what the situation was in the city 50 years earlier, it is at least clear that in the 160's in Sardis there were readers interested in a text like *On the Pascha*.[109] Further, the discovery of Melito's sermon reminds us of the fragility of the argument from silence – which is what Bauer's argument is at this

---

103 Translation, including that in square brackets, from Ehrman, *Apostolic Fathers*, 1, 319 (italics original); he writes that the phrase "ταῖς ἔμπροσθεν ἐκλησίαις" is "Possibly referring to the churches that lie between Smyrna and Antioch or between Troas and Rome". M. W. Holmes, (*The Apostolic Fathers. Greek Text and English Translations* (Grand Rapids, Mich.: Baker Academic, 3rd Ed., 2007), 271) favours the translation "on this side" – that is between Smyrna and Antioch. See also A. von Harnack, *The Mission and Expansion of Christianity in the First Three Centuries.* (London: Williams and Norgate, 1908), 185 n3 who notes "Ignatius, too, merely gives a selection". 1 Peter also points to the existence of other churches.

104 See Schoedel, *Ignatius*, 11–12.

105 See further Norris, "Asia Minor", 374–5. Bauer is aware of the problem of using the argument from silence, but continues to do so; see *Orthodoxy*, 74–5.

106 See Bauer, *Orthodoxy*, 79–80.

107 On the date, see Hill, *Johannine Corpus*, 294–5; see also S. G. Hall, *Melito of Sardis on Pascha and Fragments. Texts and Translations* (Oxford: Clarendon Press, 1979), xxii.

108 We might have hoped that Melito would give us some details about his readers and their theological stance or an indication of issues they were facing, but Melito gives very few references to his audience in the *Peri Pascha* (*PP*). They are addressed as "beloved" (*PP* 2, 35) and there are references to "us" (*PP* 67), and "our salvation" (*PP* 69); see also *PP* 103.

109 The sermon contains anti-gnostic features; see Hall, *Melito*, xli; F. L Cross/E. A. Livingston (ed.), *The Oxford Dictionary of the Christian Church* (Oxford: Oxford University Press, 3 1997), 1068 notes, "There is an anti-Gnostic insistence on the true humanity of Christ and on the unity of the Old and New Covenants." For a discussion of Melito's own theological position see Hall, *Melito*, xl–xlv.

point. So, the further evidence that has been discovered since Bauer's time certainly does not support his view.[110]

Bauer's argument from silence, which he used extensively, is fragile. We cannot say that there were "heretical" communities in Colossae, Hierapolis and Laodicea, as well as Pergamum, Thyatira and Sardis simply on the basis that John and/or Ignatius did not write to these places.

My key point is then that the lack of a letter to the Christian communities in the Lycus Valley by John the Seer in Revelation (in the case of Colossae and Hierapolis) or by Ignatius (in the case of all three cities) does *not* undermine my suggestion that, in the time after Colossians was written, these three Christian communities witnessed the on-going impact of both Pauline and Johannine influence – and other influences besides.

Conclusions

What does "the view from Ephesus" suggest then about the Christians of Colossae, and the Lycus Valley more generally?

Firstly, my view from Ephesus, and from the situation in Western Asia Minor in general, is somewhat speculative. Factors that apply generally, or in another place, may not necessarily apply in the Lycus Valley. It is difficult to argue from the general to the particular. There is a degree of (hopefully) disciplined imagination here then, but this is, I think, preferable to saying nothing – which *is* the situation when it comes to Colossae after the writing of Colossians.

Secondly, we can suggest a number of points about the earliest days in the Christian community in Colossae and the other Lycus Valley communities. These relate to ministry being collaborative, to opposition from outsiders and potential diversity within the groups, and the presence of false teachers and of division in the years following Paul's death. The arrival of Johannine Christianity in Ephesus is also significant, as is the probable influence of Johannine Christianity in Western Asia Minor. The presence of the Nicolaitans in the area and glimpses of the Christians in Laodicea near the end of the first century have also been noted. We have also suggested that the on-going Pauline community remained distinct from the Johannine community in Ephesus for some time and that this may well have been the case elsewhere too.

---

110 The little we know of Laodicea in the second century indicates it was not heretical. F. F. Bruce, "Laodicea", in *ABD* 4.231, notes the warning to the church in Revelation 3:14–22 and goes on "The warning was apparently effective: the church of Laodicea continued for long to maintain its Christian witness. Between A. D. 161 and 167 a bishop of Laodicea, Sagaris by name, suffered martyrdom. In his time, said Melito, bishop of Sardis, at the beginning of his Easter Festival, there was much debate at Laodicea about the proper day for the celebration of Easter (Eusebius *Hist. eccl.* 4.26.3)."

Thirdly, we have indicated the on-going "presence" and strength of both the Pauline tradition or traditions associated with Paul, and the Johannine tradition in Western Asia Minor through to the 120s and probably later.[111] I am not suggesting that for a long period in the second century we necessarily have separate "Pauline" and "Johannine" communities; clearly as time progresses and as Christian communities gather more of a collection of Christian texts it becomes more likely that one community will value *both* Pauline and Johannine traditions, and other besides. This would be the effect of the process of collecting texts into a proto-canon. Changes of church structure, which led to a city-wide structure for the Christian community must also be taken into account here. We must also take account of other theological tendencies that are present in the area – the Nicolaitans as well as Docetic and Gnostic forms of Christianity and so on, which are clearly influential although our evidence for these groups is unfortunately very limited. But I am suggesting that in the Lycus Valley well into the second century, both Pauline and Johannine influences are very significant and perhaps determinative for the nature of Christianity in this area.

Bibliography

Arnold, C. E., *The Colossian Syncretism. The Interface between Christianity and Folk Belief at Colossae* (Tübingen: Mohr Siebeck, 1995).

– "Colossae", in D. N. Freedman *et al* (ed.), *The Anchor Bible Dictionary* (6 vol.; New York: Doubleday, 1992) 1.1089–90.

Aune, D. E., "The Social Matrix of the Apocalypse of John", BR 26 (1981) 16–32.

– *Revelation 1–5* (Dallas, TX: Word Books, 1997).

Barrett, C. K., *A Critical and Exegetical Commentary on the Acts of the Apostles* (2 vol.; Edinburgh: T & T Clark, 1994, 1998).

– "The Historicity of Acts", JTS ns 50 (1999) 515–34.

Barth, M./H. Blanke, *Colossians. A New Translation with Introduction and Commentary* (New York: Doubleday, 1994).

Bauckham, R., "Papias and Polycrates on the Origin of the Fourth Gospel", JTS n.s. 44 (1993) 24–69.

– "For Whom Were Gospels Written?", in R. Bauckham (ed.), *The Gospels for All Christians. Rethinking the Gospel Audiences* (Grand Rapids, Mich.: Eerdmans, 1998) 9–48.

– *Jesus and the Eyewitnesses. The Gospels as Eyewitness Testimony* (Grand Rapids, Mich.: Eerdmans, 2006).

Bauer, W., *Orthodoxy and Heresy in Earliest Christianity* (Philadelphia: Fortress, 1971).

Beale, G. K., *The Book of Revelation. A Commentary on the Greek Text* (Grand Rapids, Mich.: Eerdmans, 1999).

---

111 Again, note that this is simply the point to which we have limited our enquiry, and is not to suggest a sudden decline at this point.

Becker, J. and U. Luz, *Die Briefe an die Galater, Epheser und Kolosser* (Göttingen: Vandenhoeck & Ruprecht, 1998).

de Boer, M. C., "Comment: Which Paul?", in W. S. Babcock (ed.), *Paul and the Legacies of Paul* (Dallas: Southern Methodist University Press, 1990) 45–54.

Bremmer, J. N. (ed.), *The Apocryphal Acts of Paul and Thecla* (Kampen: Kok Pharos, 1996).

Brown, R. E., *The Gospel According to John. Introduction, Translation, and Notes* (2 vol.; Garden City: Doubleday, 1966).

– *The Epistles of John* (Garden City: Doubleday, 1982).

Bruce, F. F., "Jews and Christians in the Lycus Valley", *BS* 141 (1984) 3–15.

– *The Book of the Acts* (Grand Rapids, Mich.: Eerdmans, 1988).

Casson, L., *Travel in the Ancient World* (London: Allen & Unwin, 1974).

Collins, A. Y., *Crisis and Catharsis: The Power of the Apocalypse* (Philadelphia: Westminster Press, 1984).

– "Numerical Symbolism in Jewish and Early Christian Apocalyptic Literature", in *ANRW*, II.21.2 (1984) 1221–87.

Culpepper, R. A., *John, the Son of Zebedee* (Columbia: University of South Carolina Press, 1994).

Dahl, N. A., *Studies in Ephesians. Introductory Questions, Text- & Edition-Critical Issues, Interpretation of Texts and Themes* (Tübingen: Mohr Siebeck, 2000).

Dunderberg, I., "The School of Valentinus", in A. Marjanen/P. Luomanen (ed.), *A Companion to Second-Century Christian 'Heretics'* (Leiden: Brill, 2005) 64–99.

Dunn, J. D. G., "The Colossian Philosophy: A Confident Jewish Apologia", *Biblica* 76 (1995) 153–181.

– *The Epistles to the Colossians and to Philemon* (NIGTC; Grand Rapids, Mich: Eerdmans, 1996).

Ehrman, B. D., (ed. and trans.), *The Apostolic Fathers* (2 vol.; Cambridge: Harvard University Press, 2003).

Fitzmyer, J. A., *The Acts of the Apostles* (New York: Doubleday, 1998).

Foster, P., "The Epistles of Ignatius of Antioch and the Writings that later formed the New Testament", in A. Gregory/C. Tuckett (ed.), *The Reception of the New Testament in the Apostolic Fathers* (Oxford: Oxford University Press, 2005) 159–86.

Gnilka, J., *Der Kolosserbrief* (Freiburg: Herder, 1980).

Günther, M., *Die Frühgeschichte des Christentums in Ephesus* (Frankfurt am Main: Peter Lang, 1995).

Hall, S. G., *Melito of Sardis on Pascha and Fragments. Texts and Translations* (Oxford: Clarendon Press, 1979).

Harland, P. A., "Acculturation and Identity in the Diaspora: A Jewish Family and 'Pagan' Guilds at Hierapolis", *JJS* 57 (2006) 222–244.

von Harnack, A., *The Mission and Expansion of Christianity in the First Three Centuries* (London: Williams and Norgate, 1908).

Hartog, P., *Polycarp and the New Testament. The Occasion, Rhetoric, Theme, and Unity of the Epistle to the Philippians and its Allusions to New Testament Literature* (Tübingen: Mohr Siebeck, 2002).

Hemer, C. J., *The Letters to the Seven Churches of Asia in their Local Setting* (Sheffield: JSOT Press, 1986).

Hengel, M., *The Johannine Question* (London: SCM Press, 1989).

Hill, C. E., "The Epistula Apostolorum: An Asian Tract from the Time of Polycarp", *JECS* 7 (1999) 1–53.

- *The Johannine Corpus in the Early Church* (Oxford: Oxford University Press, 2004).

- "The Fourth Gospel in the Second Century: The Myth of Orthodox Johanno-phobia", in J. Lierman (ed.), *Challenging Perspectives on the Gospel of John* (Tübingen: Mohr Siebeck, 2006) 135–169.

- "'The Orthodox Gospel'. The Reception of John in the Great Church prior to Irenaeus", in T. Rasimus (ed.), *The Legacy of John: Second Century Reception of the Fourth Gospel* (Leiden: Brill, 2010) 233–300.

Holmes, H. W. "Polycarp's Letter to the Philippians and the Writings that later formed the New Testament", in A. Gregory/C. Tuckett (ed.), *The Reception of the New Testament in the Apostolic Fathers* (Oxford: Oxford University Press, 2005) 187–227.

Holmes, M. W., *The Apostolic Fathers. Greek Text and English Translations* (Grand Rapids, Mich.: Baker Academic, 3rd Ed., 2007).

Johnson, L. T., *The Acts of the Apostles* (Collegeville, Minn.: The Liturgical Press, 1992).

Koester, H., "Ephesos in Early Christian Literature", in H. Koester (ed.), *Ephesos: Metropolis of Asia. An Interdisciplinary Approach to Its Archaeology, Religion, and Culture* (Valley Forge, Pennsylvania: Trinity Press International, 1995) 119–40.

Kreitzer, L. J., "The Plutonium of Hierapolis and the Descent of Christ into the 'Lowermost Parts of the Earth' (Ephesians 4,9)" *Biblica* 79 (1998) 381–93.

Lightfoot, J. B., *Saint Paul's Epistles to the Colossians and to Philemon* (London: Macmillan & Co, ⁵1880).

Magie, D., *Roman Rule in Asia Minor to the end of the third century after Christ* (2 vol.; Princeton: Princeton University Press, 1950).

Mitchell, S., *Anatolia. Land, Men and Gods in Asia Minor (2 vol.;* Oxford: Clarendon Press, 1993).

Norris, F. W., "Asia Minor before Ignatius: Walter Bauer Reconsidered", in E. A. Livingstone (ed.), *Studia Evangelica VII* (Berlin: Akademie-Verlag, 1982) 365–77.

O'Brien, P. T., *Colossians, Philemon* (WBC; Waco, TX: Word Books, 1982).

Pagels, E. H., *The Johannine Gospel in Gnostic Exegesis: Heracleon's Commentary on John* (Nashville: Abingdon Press, 1973).

Paulsen, H. and W. Bauer, *Die Briefe des Ignatius von Antiochia und der Brief des Polykarp von Smyrna* (Tübingen: J. C. B. Mohr (Paul Siebeck), ²1985).

Peterson, D., "The Motif of Fulfilment and the Purpose of Luke-Acts", in B. Winter/A. D. Clarke (ed.), *The Book of Acts in Its Ancient Literary Settings* (Grand Rapids, Mich.: Eerdmans, 1993) 83–104.

Prigent, P., *Commentary on the Apocalypse of St John* (Tübingen: Mohr Siebeck, 2001).

Räisänen, H., "Marcion", in A. Marjanen/P. Luomanen (ed.), *A Companion to Second-Century Christian 'Heretics'* (Leiden: Brill, 2005) 100–24.

Ramsay, W. M., *The Letters to the Seven Churches of Asia and their Place in the Plan of the Apocalypse* (London: Hodder & Stoughton, 1904).

Robinson, T. A., *The Bauer Thesis Examined. The Geography of Heresy in the Early Christian Church* (Lewiston/Queenston: Edwin Mellen Press, 1988).

Roetzel, C. J., "Paul in the Second Century", in J. D. G. Dunn (ed.), *The Cambridge Companion to St Paul* (Cambridge: Cambridge University Press, 2003) 227–41.

Schnabel, E. J., *Early Christian Mission* (2 vol.; Downers Grove: IVP, 2004).

Schnackenburg, R., "Ephesus: Entwicklung einer Gemeinde von Paulus zu Johannes", *BZ* 35 (1991) 41–64.

Schoedel, W. R., *Ignatius of Antioch* (Philadelphia: Fortress, 1985).

– "Papias", in *ANRW II.27.1*, (1992) 235–70.

Smalley, S. S., *The Revelation to John. A Commentary on the Greek Text of the Apocalypse* (Downers Grove: IVP, 2005).

Stanton, G. N., *The Gospels and Jesus* (Oxford: Oxford University Press, ²2002).

Standhartinger, A., "Colossians and the Pauline School", *NTS* 50 (2004) 572–93.

Stewart-Sykes, A., "The Asian Context of the New Prophecy and of *Epistula Apostolorum*", *VC* 51 (1997) 416–438.

Strecker, G., *The Johannine Letters. A Commentary on 1, 2, and 3 John* (Minneapolis: Fortress, 1996).

Sumney, J. L., *Colossians: A Commentary* (Louisville: Westminster John Knox Press, 2008).

Thompson, M. B., "The Holy Internet: Communication Between Churches in the First Christian Generation?", in R. Bauckham (ed.), *The Gospels for All Christians. Rethinking the Gospel Audiences* (Grand Rapids, Mich.: Eerdmans, 1998) 49–70.

Trebilco, P. R., *The Early Christians in Ephesus from Paul to Ignatius* (Tübingen: Mohr Siebeck, 2004).

– "Christian Communities in Western Asia Minor into the Early Second Century: Ignatius and Others as Witnesses Against Bauer", *JETS* 49 (2006) 17–44.

Wilson, R. McL., *A critical and exegetical commentary on Colossians and Philemon* (London: T & T Clark International, 2005).

Chapter 8

Reading Colossians in the Ruins: Roman Imperial Iconography, Moral Transformation, and the Construction of Christian Identity in the Lycus Valley

Harry O. Maier

The letter to the Colossians represents one of the most dramatic transpositions of Paul's theology in the New Testament. Here a future-oriented eschatology becomes fully realized. The apostle who in earlier letters looks forward at the end of the age to resurrection, reconciliation, and the subjection of all things to God through Jesus' imminent second coming (for example, 1 Cor 15:21–28) now celebrates an already enthroned Jesus, to whom and for whom all things are reconciled, with whom believers are even now raised from the dead, enthroned alongside him, high above all rulers and authorities (Col 2:12; 3:1–3). If in the earlier letters the focus is on crucifixion and exaltation (e.g. Phil 2:6–11; Rom 1:3–4), in Colossians, the interest turns to preexistence and incarnation (Col 1:15–20). These shifts in emphasis call for an explanation. Most often they are accounted for by reference to the situation of the letter writer's opponents.[1] Those opponents, exegetes argue, urged the Colossians to forms of religious and ascetical practices which involved devotion to intermediary cosmic powers as a means, along the honorific scheme of Greco-Roman religion, of gaining their beneficence and patronage (thus, for example, Col 2:8–9, 16–23). To oppose this the Colossians author insisted that its audience desist from such practices, reminding them that far from being subject to such powers, they are in fact above them, already raised from the dead with Christ (Col 3:1–3). They are not obliged to submit themselves to these powers because these powers were themselves created by and for Christ (Col 1:15–20). The presence of these differences from earlier letters from Paul, in other words, is to be explained by the author's adaptation of his theology for a polemical rhetorical situation.

---

1 Thus, for example, W.G. Kümmel, *Introduction to the New Testament*, H. Clark Kee (trans.) (Nashville: Abingdon, 1975), 342–45; H. Koester, *Introduction to the New Testament. Volume Two: History and Literature of Christianity* (Philadelphia: Fortress, 1983), 264.

Imperial Iconography and the Transformation
of Pauline Ideas

I propose that attention to imperial iconography and ideology offers a broader context for understanding how it is that Paul's theology can be deployed in this striking polemical manner in Colossians. A reading of Colossians amidst imperial imagery, and amidst the ruins of imperial public monuments such as those dedicated to the worship of the imperial family at Aphrodisias, furnish us an alternative means of apprehending significant transformations of Paul's theological ideals and hopes. Colossians has achieved a social construction of Paul's Gospel by drawing from elements of imperial ideology in a way that must have found particular resonance amongst the inhabitants of an Asia Minor city in the heartland of an enthusiastic cult of the emperor.[2] Colossae was not an imperial foundation or capital as Philippi or Thessalonica, but it was a notable imperial centre nonetheless. It possessed a license to mint imperial coins and there is good evidence it was a stopping point for imperial visits.[3] It had an imperial altar and cult.[4] Moreover, it was less than a day's journey from Aphrodisias, the birthplace of Venus, the divine matriarch of the Julio-Claudian dynasty and hence an important centre for the imperial cult.[5] And there is important numismatic evidence revealing close political ties between the two cities.[6] This is not to deny the importance of polemic in achieving these Colossian innovations of an earlier theology. It is rather to broaden the perspective to give a wider account of these ideas.

---

2 For a review of emperor worship in Asia Minor, and more specifically in the Lycus Valley, see S. R. F. Price, *Rituals and Power: the Roman Cult in Asia Minor* (Cambridge: Cambridge University Press, 1984); C. C. Vermeule, *Roman Imperial Art in Greece and Asia Minor* (Cambridge: Belnap, 1968), 212–28.

3 Although, that evidence falls slightly outside our period to the reign of Hadrian, when Colossae figures prominently: thus, H-G. Pflaum, *Les Carrières Procuratoriennes Éqestres sous le Haut-Empire romain* (2 vol.; Paris: P. Geuthner, 1960), 1.263; A.S. Benjamin, "The Altars of Hadrian in Athens and Hadrian's Panhellenic Program", *Hesperia* 32 (1963) 57–86, on p. 82; H. Halfmann, *Itinera principum: Geschichte und Typologie der Kaiserreisen im Römischen Reich* (Stuttgart: Steiner, 1986), 206; A. Birley, *Hadrian: The Restless Emperor* (London: Routledge, 1997), 222.

4 Thus, Price, *Rituals*, xii, xxv.

5 For discussion of the Sebasteion, its connection with Julio-Claudian dynastic claims and emperor worship, and its general lay-out and architectural features see, R. R. R. Smith, "The Imperial Reliefs from the Sebasteion at Aphrodisias", *JRS* 77 (1987) 88–138; C. B. Rose, *Dynastic Commemoration and Imperial Portraiture in the Julio-Claudian Period* (Cambridge: Cambridge University Press, 1997), 163–69.

6 For numismatic evidence depicting diplomatic ties, D. J. Macdonald "The Homonoia of Colossae and Aphrodisias", *Jahrbuch für Numismatik und Geldgeschichte* 33 (1983) 25–27, P. R. Franke/M. K. Nollé, *Die Homonoia-Münzen Kleinasiens und der thrakischen Rangebiete* (Saarbrücken: Saarbrücken Verlag, 1997).

The presence of imperial themes in Colossians echoes a similar application in earlier letters. Most importantly, the ideals of moral transformation the author holds up for his readers (Col 3:5–11) is at home in imperial ethical ideals, especially in the representation of once unruly peoples brought into subjection to Roman morals.[7] Imperial iconographers, as we will see, represented in dramatic ways the transformation of once unruly and factious peoples into subjects living peaceably under Roman rule. This finds its way into the ethical representation of the once-pagan, now Christian Colossians: if under the patient rule of Caesar once contending and unruly ethnes find themselves tamed and civilized, so under the throne of Christ, as it were, slave and free, Jew and Greek, Scythian and barbarian are reconciled and brought under one saving rule, transformed into unity by the civilizing ethics of Jesus' rule.

If today we need to struggle to recognize the imperial valences of this way of representing the world, for our first-century Colossians listeners, such ideals and representations would have been immediately recognizable from the ubiquitous signs of imperial presence. They were inscribed on coins and erected on buildings and imperial monuments.[8] Most importantly, portraits of imperial rulers associated with and enthroned amongst cosmic powers above conquered peoples was a central means of communicating to local populations that the gods had conspired to establish the Julio-Claudian emperors as lords of the earth. At the Sebasteion at Aphrodisias, as we shall see, this was given dramatic testimony by the careful spatial deployment of imagery so that iconography depicting imperial victory was placed at the top level of a three-story structure, with representations of subject peoples below them on the second tier.[9] Coins repeatedly depict emperors associated with victory; one from Colossae depicts Caligula on

---

7 For the social construction of the ethnic "barbarian" see Susan P. Mattern, *Rome and the Enemy: Imperial Strategy in the Principate* (Berkeley: University of California Press, 1999), 66–80; for the right of Rome to rule and civilize "barbarians," see A. A. T. Ehrhardt, "Imperium und Humanitas. Grundlagen des römischen Imperialismus", *Studium Generale* 14 (1961) 646–64; F. Klingner, "Humanität und Humanitas", in *Römische Geisteswelt. Essays zur lateinischen Literatur* (Stuttgart: Reclam, 1979⁶) 704–46.

8 For a general iconographical orientation to the history and uses of imagery depicting subject peoples in Roman imperial art see, Ann L. Kuttner, *Dynasty and Empire in the Age of Augustus: The Case of the Boscoreale Cups* (Berkeley: University of California Press, 1995), 69–123; R. R. R. Smith, "*Simulacra Gentium*: The *Ethne* from the Sebasteion at Aphrodisias", *JRS* 78 (1988) 50–77 for bibliography and discussion of a history of iconographical representation of subject peoples in Julio-Claudian art. P. Bienkowski, *De simulacris barbararum gentium apud Romanos* (Cracow: Gebethner, 1900) and M. Jatta, *Le rappresentanze figurate delle Provincie Romane* (Rome: Loescher, 1908) remain foundational studies.

9 For the orientation of the Sebasteion as well as the organization of its imagery, see Smith, "Reliefs", 89–93. Citation of images that follow will be given a numerical attribution as follows, in order to bring out the spatial characteristics of this imagery, which, I will show, reinforces an imperial reading of the spatial descriptions in Colossians: I, the top tier; II, the middle tier; III the bottom tier of the monument.

the obverse with Nike on the reserve.[10] Victory, unity, and growth, worldwide peace and reconciliation, and agrarian abundance – all were divinely appointed and in cooperation with the cosmic powers regulating human affairs. The Colossian representation in 1:15–20 of a Jesus above all rule and authority, through whom and for whom all things exist, who brings all into reconciliation is at home in the contact zone of imperial ideology, and one can understand how persuasive and recognizable such ideas would have been once related to the repertoire of Roman imperial imagery carefully and self-consciously deployed everywhere in the Roman Empire.

Everywhere Colossians makes use of imperial themes and commonplaces. Most obvious of course is Colossians' representation in 2:15 of Jesus' crucifixion as a victory parade. But this is only the most evident example. As striking from an imperial perspective is the presentation of Paul who acclaims a Gospel which has come not only to the Colossians but to "the whole world" (1:6), and which brings all into its embrace, including those in Roman imperial imagination at the furthest reaches of civilization, namely the barbarians and Scythians of Col 3:11. Even as Augustus' birth was promoted as a universal Gospel of salvation, so Paul brings the Good News of salvation to every creature under heaven (1:23), advancing a cosmic understanding of the Jesus Event.[11] The language of enthronement the Colossian letter magnifies echoes the imperial language of earlier letters, especially the Philippians Hymn (Phil 2:6–11), but also the Corinthian and Thessalonian portraits of Jesus' coming as an imperial adventus which brings all into subjection under God's rule (1 Cor 15:24–28; 1 Thess 4:14–18). The Philippian Hymn fully at home in its provincial Roman colony acclaims a time to come when everything and everyone on earth and below the earth acclaims Jesus as Lord; 1 Thessalonians similarly reflecting its social location as provincial capital has the dead meeting the Lord as he arrives in imperial state, coming out to meet him even as emperors were met by civic dignitaries enroute to the Thessalonians. The living in the meantime (1 Thess 5:8–11) show their civic good order by keeping hard at work and living in peace as expression of the rule of Christ, clothed with the imperial uniform – the breastplate of faith and the helmet of salvation.

Once we recognize the imperial connections of this language, the Colossian representations of Jesus' rule as similarly imperial become immediately recognizable; Colossians adapts Pauline themes and redeploys them for a new rhetor-

---

10 Thus, H. von Aulock, *Münzen und Städte Phrygiens* (2 vol.; Tübingen: Ernst Wasmuth, 1987), 1.§ 545, 89 plus plate.

11 The Priene Inscription (*OGIS*, 458.30–62); V. Ehrenberg/A. H. M. Jones, *Documents Illustrating the Reigns of Augustus and Tiberius* (Oxford: Clarendon, 1983²), 81–4, no. 98 is representative. In it Greek cities in the province of Asia honour the emperor's achievement in securing worldwide peace by acclaiming Augustus' birthday (23 September) as the start of the New Year since his birth "marked for the world the beginning of good news through his coming."

ical situation. Even as all acclaim Jesus as Lord in Philippians, so Jesus as cosmic Lord is "the head of all rule and authority" (Col 2:10). In the same way the Thessalonian Jesus brings peace to his subjects (1 Thess 5:23; cf 2 Thess 3:16), the Colossians benefit from the peace of Christ ruling in their hearts (3:15). But the Colossian letter dramatizes this further and in a strikingly new way by drawing on the civic metaphor of the body politic with Christ as head not only of the Church, but now the whole universe, bringing all into harmony and unity, growth and prosperity (1:15–20). We are not far in this deployment from Seneca's representation of the Colossian letter's contemporary, the Emperor Nero, whom the court philosopher similarly designates as head of the Empire, whose health as head flows through the rest of the body of his Empire, bringing well-being and wholeness.[12] Jesus', like Nero's, is a cosmic imperial rule that in heaven as on earth brings warring factions into harmony.

The Colossian language to describe this is imperial: it is a reconciliation of once competing elements and powers and authorities, an ἀποκαταλάσσειν (1:20), an emphatic use of a term reserved for political diplomacy and the bringing together of once warring factions in peace.[13] These factions are presumably those warring elements led in victory by the crucified Jesus, brought into being by and for Jesus, for whom the Gospel is also acclaimed, and which with the Colossians are subject to the Lord's rule. As the reference in 1:20 affirms and 2:15 makes clearest, this comes paradoxically through a death rather than a glorious military victory. Jesus the Colossian Nero we might say offers an imperial peace for the Colossians by means other than that the emperor imposes by military force – namely by his death. So it is that even as Nero celebrated – with some irony – his reign by representing himself in harmony with his consort, so the Colossians show forth the good order that comes down from the enthroned head by regulating their household affairs well, in concord and harmony. "Let the peace rule your hearts" the letter instructs the Colossians in laying out its ethical ideals.

We are now ready to see – literally – how all of this is not only imperial sounding but it in fact is imperial looking as well. Let us then turn to a consideration of Colossians amidst the ruins of its imperial culture.

---

12 Thus, Seneca, *Clem.* 1.3.4; 1.5.1; 1.13.4; 2.2.1–2.

13 For the political uses of the term see C. Breytenbach, *Versöhnung. Eine Studies zur paulinischen Soteriologie* (Düsseldorf: Neukirchener, 1989), 68–80; A. Bash, *Ambassadors for Christ: An Exploration of Ambassadorial Language in the New Testament* (Tübingen: Mohr/ Siebeck, 1997), 29–32.

Colossians, the Drama of Transformation, and Imperial Monumental Art

The imperial monuments that Roman authorities and civic elites erected to publish and promote Roman rule deployed a relatively narrow repertoire of images to celebrate and legitimate a rule of peace established through military power and skilful diplomacy.[14] That repertoire was designed to help make immediately recognizable the right of Rome to rule its subjects, and to make the divine legitimation of that rule persuasive. Enthroned emperors dominate Roman imperial iconography. When the Colossian letter represents the ethical ideal of letting the peace of Christ rule its audience's hearts (3:15), there is here not only a presentation that is an ethical exhortation, there is also here an echo of what could be seen on imperial coins, on imperial monuments, in statuary and on imperial reliefs.

Everywhere imperial iconographers sought to communicate similar ideals – that with the Julio-Claudian imperial household a certain eschatological order had been realized. In multiple media, ranging from public monuments to household decoration, iconographers represented the pacification of once hostile and warring peoples. Often they depicted conquered peoples at the feet of emperors, as attested, for example, by the Boscoreale Cups which quote ubiquitous imperial iconography.[15] On one cup, for example, we see Augustus enthroned above suppliant Gallic chieftains with the infants.[16] Throughout the Julio-Claudian period imperial mints portrayed conquered subjects displaying submission to their rulers. This iconography rehearsed similar images spread across the Empire on victory monuments and imperial statues.[17]

The so-called sebasteion at Aphrodisias, for example, personified all the nations and ethnes conquered by Augustus and his successors as a series of female statues placed in a long line along the courtyard of the temple from its west en-

---

14 For an overview of the iconographical repertoire of Rome's theology of victory see, P. Zanker, *The Power of Images in the Age of Augustus*. A. Shapiro (trans.) (Ann Arbor, Mich: University of Michigan Press, 1990), 33–100.

15 For discussion of the imperial imagery and iconographical background of the Boscoreale cups, together with plates, see Kuttner, *Dynasty*. The cups, excavated from a Roman villa at the foot of Mt Vesuvius at the end of the nineteenth century, are an important witness to popular and household uses of imperial iconography in the Julio-Claudian period contemporary with the Letter to the Colossians.

16 Thus, Kuttner, *Dynasty*, plate 4.

17 For an account of the Roman imperial coinage with subject peoples and the personifications of conquered nations see J. Toynbee, *The Hadrianic School: A Chapter in the History of Greek Art* (Cambridge: Cambridge University Press, 1934); for exposition of subject barbarian coin types and their relation to monumental art, see A. Caló Levi, *Barbarians on Roman Imperial Coins and Sculpture* Numismatic Notes and Monographs 123 (New York: The American Numismatic Society, 1952); Kuttner, *Dynasty*, 78–86.

Fig. 1 Armenia's integration into the Empire,
from Tier I of the Aphrodisias Sebasteion

try to its east dais where the emperor was worshiped.[18] These were erected below
statues of emperors cast as divinities or heroes vanquishing female figures who
similarly represented peoples pacified by Roman might and diplomacy. Contemporary with the epistle to the Colossians, the representation at the Sebasteion of
Nero conquering Armenia gives powerful testimony to Roman imperial ideology
of a conquering emperor reaching down to a conquered Armenia to raise her to
her feet and so make of an erstwhile enemy a client of Roman power. Here a triumphant Nero lifts the conquered personified Armenia to her feet as symbol of
Armenia's integration into the Empire *(Fig. 1)*.[19]

Nudity here expresses the patriarchal discourse of a dominant military order wherein the nude female body in a posture of humiliation symbolizes an un-
tamed, unregulated state brought to heel by the clothed, civilizing male power

18 See Smith, "*Simulacra*", for discussion with images.
19 See Smith, "Reliefs", Plates XVI–XVII for further images.

Fig. 2 The Ethnos of the Piroustae,
from Tier II of the Aphrodisias Sebasteion[20]

above it. The nude figure on her knees contrasts sharply with the standing clothed figures arranged on the monument's second storey just below her *(Fig. 2)*.

Again a patriarchal ideology dominates: naked women contrasted with clothed ones symbolize the drama of Roman colonization and civilization, and as such exploit commonplace ideals that the rightly regulated and cultivated woman can be recognized by her dress.[21] The sebasteion attests to that unfolding drama where it represents one of the conquered ethnes as a female showing shoulder lain bare by an improperly arranged peplos, and stray hair not properly coiffed.

---

20 For further images, see Smith, *"Simulacra"*, Plates I–V.

21 For the contrasting dress of the virtuous versus the adulterous woman, see J. L. Sebesta, "Symbolism in the Costume of the Roman Woman", in J. L. Sebesta/L. Bonfante (ed.), *The World of Roman Costume* (Madison, Wisc.: University of Wisconsin Press, 2001), 46–53; B. W. Winter, *Roman Wives, Roman Widows: The Appearance of New Women and the Pauline Communities* (Grand Rapids, Mich.: Eerdmans, 2003), 17–74.

Fig. 3 Ethnos with a bull,
from Tier II of the Aphrodisias Sebasteion

This figure *(Fig. 3)* contrasts sharply with the other correctly dressed women. This is a potent iconographical analogue to the Colossian ideal of "putting off" (ἀπεκδυσάμενοι) vice and the command to "put on" (ἐνδύνασθε) virtue (Col 3:9,12) as symbolic celebration of a movement from a life of unregulated vice toward Christian virtue. Roman imperial imagery at Aphrodisias gave visible support to Rome's claim on the rulership of the world; Colossians' ideals echo its visual codes. So it was that victory monuments that were everywhere scattered across the Empire and of which today only the barest fraction survive, rehearse scenes of once warring peoples brought to submission. But this art did not only celebrate victory and triumph over the vanquished. As the stark contrast between the nation personified as recently vanquished nude and the clothed female figure indicates, imperial iconography also told a story of transformation and it is here that we find another way that the Epistle to the Colossians reflects its imperial background.

As is well known, Roman imperial iconography often combines classical with Hellenistic forms in its representations.[22] This has sometimes been interpreted as evidence of an unpatterned combination of styles more or less juxtaposed against one another without design or purpose. However, the Heidelberg archaeologist and iconologist Tonio Hölscher offers an iconographical model for interpreting this imagery.[23] Rejecting the notion that Roman imperial art represents a mindless quotation of classical and Hellenistic subjects, or a careless pastiche of differing artistic styles, he argues that imperial iconographers carefully drew on classical and Hellenistic styles and quoted subjects and styles to communicate a carefully constructed semiotic code. Rather than representing reality, Roman imperial art sought to communicate types and ideals. The combination of styles – classical poses and ideals represented alongside Hellenistic ones – urged observers to recognize a carefully constructed picture-language through which observers were to see themselves belonging to a social order of transformation and renewal. Classical forms were used to depict the self-control and moderation of Roman rule realizing a worldwide imperium while Hellenistic forms helped to communicate the dynamic unfolding of that rule through the labour and effort of Roman rulers.

What is sometimes called the realized eschatology of Roman imperial art was designed to communicate the advent of an age of moral renewal, represented most forcefully by its development of neo-classicism. As an ideal brought through rigorous practice and exercise typifying the agonistic culture of Roman civilization, the humankind come of age under the supervision of Roman politics and culture was to fashion itself through ethical striving to mirror the self-controlled and sobre repose of the classically portrayed emperor. Hölscher shows that when the iconographical tradition represents battle-ready or conquering emperors in the more dramatic Hellenistic style, the ideal communicated is one of movement and drama – the transformation of the world from immoderation and passion toward regulation and self-mastery.[24] This semiotic system of picture language, Hölscher argues, was a universally shared communication system and was recognized by both elite and non-elite viewers. This iconographical semiotic language was an important means for constructing an imperial worldview, and for helping to fashion social identity in the Roman Empire.

---

22 For discussion of blending of styles in Roman iconography, the uses of neo-classicism, and the meaning of eclectic forms, see Zanker, *Power*, 239–63.

23 T. Hölscher, *The Language of Images in Roman Art*, A. Snodgrass (trans.) (Cambridge: Cambridge University Press, 2004).

24 See especially his discussion of Hellenistic and classical iconographical codes in military iconography, in "Images of War in Greece and Rome: Between Military Practice, Public Memory, and Cultural Symbolism", *JRS* 93 (2003) 1–17.

We can see the uses of iconography to represent social and political transformation on the Gemma Augustea.[25] The Gemma invites the observer to participate in a narrative of imperial transformation.[26] In doing so it offers a potent example of the kind at work in the monumental semiotic code in the Aphrodisias temple complex and the importance of that code for recognizing aspects of Colossians left unexplored or invisible through more traditional lexicographical and historical-critical approaches. Here Augustus depicted in classical style as Jupiter contrasts with the movement and drama unfolding around him. The Gemma's lower register develops the drama of its upper half by depicting Roman victory. John Pollini has made a convincing case for interpreting the Gemma as a depiction of Tiberius' return to Rome in triumph after his victories in Illyricum in 9 CE. Already, however, another victory is anticipated for Tiberius is returning to his chariot where Victory awaits him with reins and whip in hand. That forthcoming campaign is depicted in the lower register where in retaliation for the defeat of Varrus' legions the gem depicts Germans as already vanquished. Future victory and retaliation is already made present by way of artistic representation.

Here is an iconographic display of a victory that is even now but not yet – a world in a process of transformation whose outcome is guaranteed from the outset.

This offers an intriguing iconographical parallel for interpreting the realised eschatology of Colossians that transforms a future enthronement of Jesus into something already present. The relative repose of the members of the upper half of the register contrasts with the emotion of those in the lower half. Together with that contrast we discover a studied verticality. Augustus in the upper half of the gem, in the self-controlled classical pose, is represented in a position that would have immediately identified him with the Sullan Jupiter Capitolinus. Surrounded by the deity Oikoumene crowning him with victory, seated along side Roma to his right, and to the left beside Oceanus and Tellus, with the symbol of a cornucopia – the agrarian abundance of Augustan realized eschatology – Augustus is a study in tranquility, *virtus*, and moderation. From this flows the command to his prince to go forth into battle to subject the peoples personified in the lower half of the gem. By contrast with Augustus' calm repose, here drama and movement dominate. Every item in the lower half represents peoples

---

25 For the image, see Zanker, *Power*, p. 231, figure 182. The Gemma, from the early first century, is a large cameo (19.5 X 22.86 cm.) carved from Arabian Onyx and is an important witness to themes in Augustan imperial art. Divided in two registers, it depicts Augustus and the imperial court, surrounded by deities in its upper half, with a scene of military victory in the lower half.

26 See J. Pollini, "The Gemma Augustea: Ideology, Rhetorical Imagery, and the Construction of a Dynastic Narrative", in P. Holliday (ed.), *Narrative and Event in Ancient Art* (Cambridge: Cambridge University Press, 1994) 258–98, for an excellent account.

in varying degrees of subjection. Those at the extreme end of subjugation the artist represents as the bound and stricken vanquished, with hair disheveled and, in the case of the female figure to the extreme right, clothes unregulated. The auxiliaries depicted here have been identified as the Thracians and Spaniards who will be sent forth into battle to achieve the victory over the Germans the upper register already celebrates.

On a more general level, however, they communicate an ideal far beyond any specific historical referent. Themselves subject peoples, they are in a more advanced state of romanisation than the conquered Germans below them: their hair properly cut, the military uniforms they wear incorporate the ethnic costume of their national identities. The flowing cape of the legionary, in the Hellenistic style, pulling up the military trophy at the center lends drama and movement to the scene – a representation of the transformation from unregulated to civilized peoples the politics Jupiter's regent, Augustus, in the above register achieves. The juxtaposition of the drama of the lower register with the calm and tranquility of the upper one expresses an ideal transformation of the world from immoderation and dissension toward self-control and utopian harmony.

The sebasteion at Aphrodisias represents a similar drama of transformation in the organization of statuary and reliefs. The architects designed the monument to be a dramatic affirmation of Julio-Claudian imperial victory theology and dynastic achievement. On the third and highest story imperial artists offered snapshots as it were, capturing emperors in moments of triumph over vanquished enemies, some of them naked figures personifying subject nations and peoples. On the second story under these scenes of victory depicted above them were female personifications of nations subject to Rome. We have already drawn attention to the contrast between the nude Armenia and the clothed female figures below. As with the imagery of the Gemma Augustea what is remarkable is the contrast between the calm of this register as compared with the dramatic representation of victory and defeat portrayed directly above. But even in the imperial reliefs of the upper stories acclaiming the military and diplomatic achievement of the imperial household, a similar contrast appears. A remarkable example offers a relief of an unidentified emperor or imperial prince crowned by a togate figure perhaps representing the Roman people or senate, with a female figure kneeling below him *(Fig. 4)*.

The artist has sculpted the imperial figure in the classical style; a sobre contenance contrasts with the emotional drama of the mourning conquered woman kneeling at his feet, a drama amplified by her unbound shoulder length hair, and her exposed breast and half-clothed torso. Conceived in a more Hellenistic style, deeply chiseled features contrast with the smoother lines of the imperial figure as well as the trophy held above her, a contrast echoed also in the heavily folded drapery of the properly coiffed togate figure to his left. In another example, a different sculptor has portrayed Augustus combining a frontal classi-

Fig. 4 Imperator with Roman People or Senate,
from Tier I of the Aphrodisias Sebasteion.

cal nude style with Hellenistic dynamism: the emperor's posture is one of movement and drama, echoed by the emotional depiction of personified Land and Sea
at his feet *(Fig. 5)*.

However, the moderation and sobriety of his face matches the classical lines
of his body. Receiving a cornucopia from Earth and a ship's prow from Sea, the
relief in bringing together classical repose with Hellenistic dynamism celebrates
Augustan achievement as the dramatic extension of imperial rule and growth in
prosperity assured through self-control and moderation. Here is a snapshot of a
world in a process of transformation.

Colossians which is most probably contemporary with Nero's reign contains
ideals strikingly at home in Roman imperial moral imagination. Paul in Colossians is someone who strives for the Colossians and the Colossians in turn are
similarly to strive by putting to death what is earthly in them (1:29; 3:5; 4:2). He
puts forward a set of agonistic moral ideals that celebrate the achievement of a
moral transformation. Delivered from the "dominion of darkness and trans-

Fig. 5 Augustus by Land and Sea,
from Tier I of the Aphrodisias Sebasteion.

ferred ... to the kingdom of God's beloved Son" (1:13), the Colossians at once
enjoy and strive to realize the putting off an old life and the realization of a new
one. While some have argued from the citation of Scythians that in fact there
were enslaved Scythians in the Colossian community, once read in the light of
Roman imperial iconographical schemes, as Hölscher has shown, the idea communicated is not a representation of empirical reality, but a code for transformation.[27] The allusion to Scythians and barbarians at 3.11 expresses an ideal movement from lives of immoderation toward ones of sobriety and self-regulation.
Whatever the religious and textual backdrop for conceiving of this ethical meta-
morphosis, representations of moral transformation were a commonplace feature of imperial art and was a significant, even determining force, in helping to
make Colossian ethical ideals persuasive.

---

27 For example, T. Martin, "The Skythian Perspective in Col. 3.11", *NovT* 37 (1995) 249–61.

The Aphrodisias Haustafel

The Colossian moral ideal is most prevalent in the author's application of a Household Code (Col 3:18–4:1). While the sources and Colossian adaptations of the long cultural heritage of household rules has achieved enormous attention in the exegetical literature, iconography as a possible influence on the Colossian Haustafel has received no attention. Again, the Sebasteion at Aphrodisias offers several images of domestic harmony. An illustrative example is the relief depicting Claudius and his wife Agrippina *(Fig. 6)*.

Claudius is again in classical repose, in an idealized nude posture, with his hand extended to his consort. The grasped hand is symbolic of civic concord and Agrippina echoes the concord that extends to the world through the right regulation of the imperial household: she is the properly coiffed and dressed matron. This example from an imperial monument was echoed on coins representing the concord and familial bonds of the imperial household preservative of the

Fig. 6 Claudius and Agrippina,
from Tier I of the Aphrodisias Sebasteion.

Fig. 7 Nero and Agrippina
from Tier I of the Aphrodisias Sebasteion.

Empire's well being. From the Julio-Claudian household concord flows forth to the nations, preserving the divinely established order.

A similar representation found its way onto coins where Nero and his wife Poppaea are presented as co-rulers, or where Nero is represented in civic harmony with his mother, Agrippina *(Fig. 7).*

At Aphrodisias she is presented as harmonious rule beside her son, holding the cornucopia, so that the view is that the imperial household's domestic harmony guarantees and realizes imperial bounty.[28] Similarly, the imperial order celebrated the concord of the royal family by having its mint publish coins depicting the harmonious co-rulership of Nero and his mother.[29] Such images

---

28 Smith, "Reliefs", plate XXIV.

29 Examples include issues linking Nero with his mother as *mater augusti*: e.g., *RIC* 150, 6; 185, nos. 607–11; as well as those representing Nero as son of the deified Claudius: 150, nos. 1–3; 185, nos. 607–12 [obverse legends].

Fig. 8 Germanicus with a Captive,
from Tier I of the Aphrodisias Sebasteion

were designed to show that the good of the Empire flowed from the concord
of its governing dynasty. Suzanne Dixon refers to this imagery as promoting
what she calls "the sentimental ideal of the Roman family."[30] However sentimental, the iconography expresses the locus of moral striving to assure a correctly
governed world. The sebasteion's household code also reveals correct governance
of the world in its representation of slavery. One of its reliefs represents the imperial prince in the nude – again in the classical style – holding an orb in his
left hand (symbol of global domination); at the left his military costume is on
a mount; between his and his uniform is a bound male child whose barbarian
origins are represented by his long shoulder-length hair, his half-clothed torso,
and trousers. Germanicus towers over the child, size, age, and physiognomic features conspiring to make the contrast dramatic and memorable *(Fig. 8)*.

---

30 S. Dixon, "The Sentimental Ideal of the Roman Family", in B. Rawson (ed.), *Marriage,
Divorce, and Children in Ancient Rome* (Oxford: Clarendon, 1991) 99–113, on p. 107.

In all these images, the sebasteion urges its viewers to believe that the peace that rules the imperial world issues forth from a well-regulated Roman household where all, matrons, sons, wives, and slaves are in their right place; in the Colossian letter the peace that rules the church expresses itself most directly in the properly governed Christian household where each as well is in its right place and in its correct relationship. The Colossian Christian Haustafel when read against the backdrop of the Aphrodisias "household code" gains potency and becomes more immediately recognizable, even as it distances itself somewhat from an ideology of domination and violence by its tempering language of love and just treatment (3:19; 4:1).

Paul's Chains and the Reversal of Imperial Ideals

The letter to the Colossians concludes with the exhortation to remember Paul's chains (Col 3:18–4:1). It is here I would like to close these brief reflections. For the agonistic ideals the letter proposes finally returns to Paul's prison cell. The apostle who strives to preach his Gospel to every creature under heaven, who formulated ideals recognizable in the imperial repertoire of imagery we have been rehearsing, is also one who bears on his body the marks of Roman imperial rule. To remember his chains is for the Colossians to remember their imperial location. But if in the imperial repertoire of pacification of the unruly the ideal is to Romanize subjects by integrating them under the aegis of the imperium of the sword, here the apostle discovers pacification by another means. The customary translation of Col 2:15 is that Christ disarmed the principalities and powers and made a public display of them triumphing over them on the cross. However, an alternative equally grammatical translation is that Christ disarmed himself, making a public display of the principalities and powers by his humiliation, and thereby made the cross the originary point of triumphal procession.[31] We can see Paul using imperial language, but inverting it, so that the victim is now conqueror, those who strip the crucified and expose them are exposed, those who would triumph are now triumphed over. Colossians finds itself paradoxically both in and out of Roman imperial modes of believing and acting. Iconography furnishes a backdrop for conceiving Paul's subjection. His exhortation to remember his fetters helps us to see how that subjugation was disrupted even as the author of Colossians used imperial ideology to articulate communal ideals. A reading such as this, amongst the ruins as it were, allows us to recognize the

---

31 For a discussion of grammatical issues and possible translations, see, W. Carr, *Angels and Principalities: The Background, Meaning and Development of the Pauline Phrase* hai archai kai hai exousiai (Cambridge: Cambridge University Press, 1981), 47–86; also, R. Yates, "Col. 2.15: Christ Triumphant", *NTS* 37 (1991) 573–91.

degree to which Colossians echoes with imperial sounding ideas and how the letter comes to life when read against the backdrop of imperial imagery, while revealing to us at the same time the ways in which its audience was invited to remain ill at ease in that context.

Bibliography

von Aulock, H., *Münzen und Städte Phrygiens* (2 vol.; Tübingen: Ernst Wasmuth, 1987).

Bash, A., *Ambassadors for Christ: An Exploration of Ambassadorial Language in the New Testament* (Tübingen: Mohr/Siebeck, 1997).

Benjamin, A.S., "The Altars of Hadrian in Athens and Hadrian's Panhellenic Program", *Hesperia* 32 (1963) 57–86.

Bienkowski, P., *De simulacris barbararum gentium apud Romanos* (Cracow: Gebethner, 1900).

Birley, A., *Hadrian: The Restless Emperor* (London: Routledge, 1997).

Breytenbach, C., *Versöhnung. Eine Studie zur paulinischen Soteriologie* (Düsseldorf: Neukirchener, 1989).

Carr, W., *Angels and Principalities: The Background, Meaning and Development of the Pauline Phrase hai archai kai hai exousiai* (Cambridge: Cambridge University Press), 1981.

Dixon, S., "The Sentimental Ideal of the Roman Family," in B. Rawson (ed.), *Marriage, Divorce, and Children in Ancient Rome* (Oxford: Clarendon, 1991, 99–113

Ehrenberg, V./A.H.M. Jones, *Documents Illustrating the Reigns of Augustus and Tiberius* (Oxford: Clarendon, 1983²).

Ehrhardt, A.A.T., "Imperium und Humanitas. Grundlagen des römischen Imperialismus", *Studium Generale* 14 (1961) 646–64.

Franke, P.R./M.K. Nollé, *Die Homonoia-Münzen Kleinasiens und der thrakischen Randgebiete* (Saarbrücken: Saarbrücken Verlag, 1997).

Halfmann, H., *Itinera principum: Geschichte und Typologie der Kaiserreisen im Römischen Reich* (Stuttgart: Steiner, 1986).

Hölscher, H., "Images of War in Greece and Rome: Between Military Practice, Public Memory, and Cultural Symbolism", *JRS* 93 (2003) 1–17.

– *The Language of Images in Roman Art*, A. Snodgrass (trans.) (Cambridge: Cambridge University Press, 2004).

Jatta, M., *Le rappresentanze figurate delle Provincie Romane* (Rome: Loescher, 1908).

Klingner, F., "Humanität und Humanitas", in *Römische Geisteswelt. Essays zur lateinischen Literatur* (Stuttgart: Reclam, 1979⁶).

Koester, H., *Introduction to the New Testament. Volume Two: History and Literature of Christianity* (Philadelphia: Fortress, 1983).

Kümmel, W.G., *Introduction to the New Testament*, H. Clark Kee (trans.) (Nashville: Abingdon, 1975).

Kuttner, A.L., *Dynasty and Empire in the Age of Augustus: The Case of the Boscoreale Cups* (Berkeley: University of California Press, 1995).

Levi, A. C., *Barbarians on Roman Imperial Coins and Sculpture* (Numismatic Notes and Monographs 123; New York: The American Numismatic Society, 1952).

Macdonald, D. J., "The Homonoia of Colossae and Aphrodisias", *Jahrbuch für Numismatik und Geldgeschichte* 33 (1983) 25–27.

Martin, T., "The Skythian Perspective in Col. 3.11", *NovT* 37 (1995) 249–61.

Mattern, S. P., *Rome and the Enemy: Imperial Strategy in the Principate* (Berkeley: University of California Press, 1999).

Pflaum, H-G., *Les Carrières Procuratoriennes Éqestres sous le Haut-Empire romain* (2 vol.; Paris: P. Geuthner, 1960).

Pollini, J., "The Gemma Augustea: Ideology, Rhetorical Imagery, and the Construction of a Dynastic Narrative", in P. Holliday (ed.), *Narrative and Event in Ancient Art* (Cambridge: Cambridge University Press, 1994) 258–98.

Price, S. R. F. *Rituals and Power: the Roman Cult in Asia Minor* (Cambridge: Cambridge University Press, 1984).

Rose, C. B., *Dynastic Commemoration and Imperial Portraiture in the Julio-Claudian Period* (Cambridge: Cambridge University Press, 1997).

Sebesta, J. L., "Symbolism in the Costume of the Roman Woman", in J. L. Sebesta/ L. Bonfante (ed.), *The World of Roman Costume* (Madison, Wisc.: University of Wisconsin Press, 2001) 46–53.

Smith, R. R. R., "The Imperial Reliefs from the Sebasteion at Aphrodisias", *JRS* 77 (1987) 88–138.

–   "*Simulacra Gentium*: The *Ethne* from the Sebasteion at Aphrodisias", *JRS* 78 (1988) 50–77.

Toynbee, J., *The Hadrianic School: A Chapter in the History of Greek Art* (Cambridge: Cambridge University Press, 1934).

Vermeule, C. C., *Roman Imperial Art in Greece and Asia Minor* (Cambridge: Belknap Press, 1968).

Winter, B. W., *Roman Wives, Roman Widows: The Appearance of New Women and the Pauline Communities* (Grand Rapids, Mich.: Eerdmans, 2003).

Yates, R., "Col. 2.15: Christ Triumphant", *NTS* 37 (1991) 573–91.

Zanker, P., *The Power of Images in the Age of Augustus*, A. Shapiro (trans.) (Ann Arbor, Mich.: University of Michigan Press, 1990).

Chapter 9

Excavating Epaphras of Colossae

Michael Trainor

Though formal archaeological work at the site of ancient Colossae in the Lycus Valley is negligible, the chapters of this book attest that much has been learnt already about the site. Inscriptional, numismatic and ceramic evidence from the Lycus Valley reveal its importance in the ancient world. Its notation by ancient travelers to Colossae further confirms its significance. Well known are the references of Herodotus (484–c.435 BCE) and Xenophon (444–357 BCE), albeit in the context of the military campaigns of Xerxes and Cyrus, with the latter camping there with his army a few days.[1] A final ancient reference to Colossae by the geographer Strabo (63 BCE–c20 CE) concludes a popular and well-researched inventory of ancient descriptions.

As we continue to construct our picture of Colossae from what seems to be a paucity of material, literary and artefactual, one important resource has been overlooked. This comes from a collection of early Christian writings dated to the middle of the first century CE. These are the writings associated with Paul, a second generation follower of Jesus of Nazareth. From a purely historical, sociological and cultural perspective, these writings are frequently bypassed by researchers of ancient Colossae. The main reason for this avoidance comes from a perception that the Christian evangelising and proselytising intent of his writings rob them of their potential to contribute to the "objective" historical, cultural or sociological reconstruction of Colossae.

Apart from the critique which can be offered about "objectivity," that is, that every piece of archaeological, inscriptional or documentary data can never be neutral-free either in its later interpretation or original construction, it is possible to move underneath Paul's writings to look at the social world out of which they come. In this sense, as with any writings of a certain period, they are a "window" into the world from which they emerge. They reveal invaluable cultural and social insights that can contribute to our interpretative perspective of a place offered by other sources of information.

On the one hand we can acknowledge the theological agenda of Paul's writings and the nature of the addressees of his letters, namely fellow Jesus house-

---

1 On Xerxes, see Herodotos *Hist.* 7.30–31.

holders. On the other hand we can place these householders within a particular geographical and social location.

In the case of our particular geographical focus, the Lycus Valley, two letters are particularly pertinent, the *Letter to Philemon* and the *Letter to the Colossians*. Both letters written in the mid to late first century CE were addressed to people living in the Lycus Valley. While some would claim that both come from Paul himself, I join the growing list of scholars who argue that *Philemon* is from Paul while *Colossians* is from one writing in Paul's name after his death and address- ing local issues never before encountered by the historical Paul. The writer of Colossians acts as Paul's ghost-writer, lifting Paul, as it were, "out of the grave" to address this third generation of Lycus Valley Jesus followers.[2]

Space prevents a thorough sociological study of both letters and their implica- tions for understanding the cultural world of the Lycus Valley. However, a focus on one of the characters that both letters extol can offer an insight into the net- work characteristic of the ancient world evident in the Lycus Valley presumed by Paul (in *Philemon*) and his authoritative representative (in *Colossians*) in their re- spective letters. This character is Paul's companion named Epaphras and men- tioned only three times, once in *Philemon* (Phlm 23) and twice in *Colossians* (Col 1:7–8; 4:12–13).

- In Phlm 23, as he concludes his letter to the household of Philemon located at Colossae, Paul sends greetings from his colleagues; one of them is Epaphras. Paul writes, "Epaphras, my fellow prisoner in Christ Jesus, sends greetings to you."
- At the beginning of Colossians (Col 1:7–8), the writer establishes Epaphras' credentials for the letter's recipients. Writing in Paul's name, the author iden- tifies Epaphras as the authoritative representative and communicator of Paul's teaching to the Colossian Jesus' householders:

This [teaching] you learned from Epaphras, our beloved fellow servant. He is a faithful minister of Christ on your behalf, and he has made known to us your love in the Spirit.

- Finally in the concluding section the writer lists those who send their greet- ings to the letter's addressees. The author uses a style similar to Paul's conclu- sion in Philemon by adding Epaphras' name (Col 4:12–13) but expands on his credentials and emphasizes his role within the other Jesus households of the Lycus Valley in Laodicea and Hierapolis:

Epaphras, who is one of you, a servant of Christ Jesus, greets you. He is always wrestling in his prayers on your behalf, so that you may stand mature and fully assured in

---

2 For a summary overview of scholarship on the authorship of Colossians, see M. Y. MacDonald, *Colossians and Ephesians* (Collegeville, Minn.: Liturgical Press, 2000) and E. Lohse, *Colossians and Ephesians* (Philadelphia: Fortress, 1990).

everything that God wills.[13] For I testify for him that he has worked hard for you and for those in Laodicea and in Hierapolis.

From the study of these references to Epaphras, the literary and geographical context in which they appear and the familial language which the writers uses, it is clear that he belongs to an established network of relationships, domestically constructed, and inserted within the wider social network pattern created by Lycus Valley's three ancient cities of Colossae, Hierapolis and Laodicea.

My central aim in what follows is to excavate Epaphras from these two Pauline letters and show the pattern of relationships in which he was involved. Through social network analysis I shall identify the kind of relationship which Epaphras had with fellow Jesus followers and householders. This relationship, influential and authoritative, built upon the credentials attributed to Epaphras by the historical Paul in *Philemon*. It was foundational for the status that Epaphras holds in *Colossians* even to the point, as I have suggested elsewhere, that he might have been its actual writer.[3]

Social Network Analysis

Network analysis offers a sociological model for understanding Epaphras' web of interconnectivity and pattern of relationships.[4] Network analysis developed in the mid twentieth century in a complex history represented in three traditions:

---

3 M. Trainor, *Epaphras: Paul's Educator at Colossae* (Collegeville, Minn.: Liturgical Press, 2008), 3–4.

4 Any interpretative model must be used cautiously, especially in imposing contemporary theories and abstractions on to an earlier period with little appreciation of cultural difference or social sensitivity. On this see M. I. Finley, *Ancient History: Evidence and Models* (London: Chatto & Windus, 1985), 66. A helpful and pragmatic study of the contribution of social network analysis is found in the works of R. Atkins, *Egalitarian Community: Ethnography and Exegesis* (Tuscaloosa, Ala.: University of Alabama Press. 1991); R. E. Hock, "'By the Gods, It's My One Desire to See an Actual Stoic': Epictetus' Relations with Students and Visitors in His Personal Network", *Semeia* 56 (1991) 121–42; M. L. White (ed.), *Social Networks in the Early Christian Environment: Issues and Methods for Social History*, *Semeia* 56 (1991) 1–202; J. K. Chow, *Patronage and Power: A Study of Social Networks in Corinth* (Sheffield, UK: Academic Press, 1992); E. A. Clark, "Elite Networks and Heresy Accusations: Towards a Social Description of the Origenist Controversy", *Semeia* 56 (1992) 79–117; H. Hendrix, "Benefactor/ Patron Networks in the Urban Environment: Evidence from Thessalonica", *Semeia* 56 (1992) 39–58; R. Stark, *The Rise of Christianity: A Sociologist reconsiders History* (Princeton, NJ: Princeton University Press, 1996); H. Remus, "Voluntary Association and Networks: Aelius Aristides at the Asclepieion in Pergamum", in J. S. Kloppenborg/S. G. Wilson (ed.), *Voluntary Associations in the Graeco-Roman World* (London, UK/New York, NY: Routledge. 1996), 146–75; D. C. Duling, "The Jesus movement and social network analysis (part I: The Spatial Network)", *BTB* 29 (1999) 156–76; D. C. Duling, "The Jesus movement and social network analysis (part II: The Social Network)", *BTB* 30 (2000) 3–15.

sociometric analysis employing graph theory to study small groups, the 1930s Harvard study of interpersonal relations and "cliques"; and the work of Manchester anthropologists who applied sociometric analysis and the Harvard interpersonal analysis to understand the structure of tribal and village communities. These three strands were eventually forged in the 1960s and 1970s into a systematic approach to social network analysis.[5] An early key figure in the promotion and accessibility of network analysis was J. A. Barnes. His fieldwork in a fishing village in south-west Norway helped him highlight the main integrating factors of community life that were independent of the traditional anthropological concepts of geography, economics or politics. These were *kinship, friendship* and *neighbourhood ties*. These three primordial relations established what Barnes called a "network":

> Each person is, as it were, in touch with a number of people, some of whom are directly in touch with each other and some of whom are not.... I find it convenient to talk of a social field of this kind as a network. The image I have is of a set of points some of which are joined by lines. The points of the image are people, or sometimes groups, and the lines indicate which people interact with each other.[6]

Barnes' network presumes personal interactions that create a "social field" of friendship. He images the interactions as lines which lead to points and represent people or groups. The work of Barnes and his Manchester colleagues grew in many and complex directions as social researchers took their basic concepts of network analysis and applied them in the study of social structures, interpersonal networks and structural analysis. Barnes' work had immediate application for European and American urban contexts. It has also been applied to rural and Mediterranean contexts.[7]

When applied cautiously in a descriptive rather than prescriptive manner, two principles of network analysis are especially relevant for appreciating Epaphras' role in the Lycus Valley and at Colossae. These two principles concern the *asymmetrical* nature of network relationships and their *relational structure*.[8] Especially pertinent to the second is Barnes' isolation of the three basic relationships, kinship, friendship and neighborhood. As we continue to "excavate" Epaphras

---

5 For a helpful summary of the history of the development of social network analysis, see J. Scott, *Social Network Analysis: A Handbook* (London: Sage Publications, 2000), 17–37.

6 J. A. Barnes, "Class and Committee in a Norwegian Island Parish", *Human Relations* 7 (1954) 39–58, on pp. 42–43.

7 On the rural application of network analysis theory, see H. Befu, *Hamlet in a Nation: The Place of Three Japanese Rural Communities in their Broader Social Context* (Ann Arbor, Mich.: University Microfilms, 1962); L. Pospisil, *The Kapauku Papuans of West New Guinea* (New York, NY: Holt, Rinehart and Winston, 1964).

8 For the basis for these two network principles see Chow, *Patronage*, 35.

and place him within the context of ancient Colossae, the whole area of the Lycus Valley with its interlocking pattern of city, village and rural grid would equivocate to Barnes' neighborhood tie.

Asymmetric Relationships

First, a network generally develops usually along *asymmetrical* lines. These differ in content and intensity with the reciprocal contents of personal ties (information, goods or power) generally being unequal. This first network principle of asymmetry is seen in Epaphras' relationship to Paul and to the audience addressed by *Colossians*.

Epaphras' presentation in the Pauline letters, especially in his greetings offered through Paul (in *Philemon*) or the author of *Colossians*, reveals him as Paul's close colleague. Epaphras' relationship to Paul is asymmetrical. He is a person of status in the Pauline network of colleagues with rank similar but not equal to Paul's standing. Epaphras' authority and status are unmistakably different. He is Paul's emissary to the Lycus Valley Jesus households founded by Paul himself. A cursory reading of *Philemon* and *Colossians* clearly indicates the centrality of the figure of Paul in both letters: he is their real or implied writer, first named and initial greeter to addressees, his authority and status obvious to all mentioned in both letters.

In terms of network patterns two aspects are clear from this. First, Paul is the centre of the relational network in both letters, though in *Colossians* the centre moves explicitly through the auspices of the Pauline writer from Paul to Epaphras. The "Paul" of *Colossians* appropriately retains overall authority. Second, Paul's authority is explicit because of potential conflict or tension that the letter addresses: *Philemon* is addressing the conflict between members of a Jesus household; *Colossians*, the tension brought about by some ignoring Paul's original teaching in favour of a more local, Phrygian, tribal composite preoccupied with astral angelology. In terms of social network theory, the letters reveal an "Ego-centred network," a relational network that is focused specifically on *one person* ("Ego" in Greek, the English "I"). This network involves those who esteem Paul and over whom Paul has authority (called in network theory, "alters," that is, "the others" in the network). He is depicted as the relational centre of a network in which all relationships radiate out from him in a unidirectional and asymmetrical manner.

This diagrammatic representation of the Ego-centred network is helpful for seeing how Epaphras and the rest of Paul's colleagues relate to him as indicated in *Philemon* and *Colossians*. A parallel pattern emerges historically later when Paul is replaced by Epaphras in the Ego-centred network by the writer of *Colossians*.

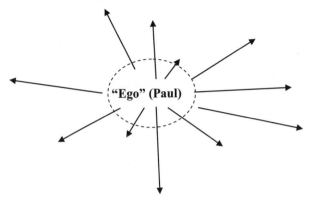

Diag 1a Paul's Ego-centred Network

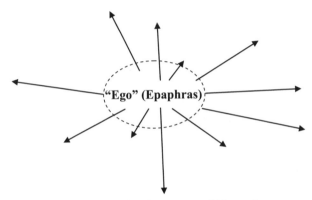

Diag 1b Epaphras' Ego-centred Network

The variations in intimacy of relationship in the Ego-centred network can also be illustrated through a series of concentric circles with each circle representing different orders or zones of intimacy.[9] Three network zones emerge in Paul's Ego-centred ties from one of intimacy, to a zone of network effectiveness through to a broader or more extended network zone.

Epaphras occupies the first *zone of intimacy*. The second zone, the zone of the *effective network*, is occupied by the addressees of the letters. In the *Letter to Philemon*, this is Philemon and his household (Phlm 1b–2); in *Colossians*, "the saints and faithful brothers and sisters in Christ in Colossae (Col 1:2a). A third zone, the *extended network*, is close to this second effective network zone but increas-

---

9 A parallel approach to what I seek to do here in employing the Ego-centred network to Philemon and Colossians is the contribution by Duling, ("Jesus Movement, II", 5) to the Jesus movement.

238

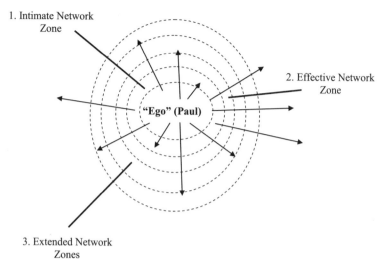

Diag 2 Types of Networks in Paul's Ego-centred Ties

ingly more distant. This zone links Paul to those not directly addressed by the letters and are associates of those addressed.

Network theory further presumes that "the variations in behaviour of people in any one role relationship may be traced to the effects of the behaviour of other people, to whom they are linked in one, two or more steps, in some other quite different relationships."[10]

The zone differentials allow for this variation in behaviour and response to Paul and his authorized collaborator, Epaphras. These variations occur amongst all the auditors of the letters and those outside the immediacy of the letters' intended audience and linked in different ways to those addressed by the letters.

Relational Structured Ties

A second principle of network theory recognizes that participants in a network are linked to each other directly or indirectly by *relational ties* that are voluntary or involuntary understood from the perspective of a broader social or cultural context. When these relational ties are *structured* they create purposeful networks, which form clusters, boundaries and other social links. This second

---

10 J.C. Mitchell, "The Concept and Use of Social Networks", in J.C. Mitchell (ed.), *Social Networks in Urban Situations: Analyses of Personal Relationships in Central African Towns* (Manchester, UK: Manchester University Press, 1969), 1–50, on p. 46.

network principle speaks to Barnes' three core network factors of *kinship, friendship* and *neighbourhood* that have their first century CE Mediterranean expression. These are obvious in the familial-domestic, kinship and network language used by the writers of *Philemon* and *Colossians*.

The Household Kinship Tie

Familial-domestic vocabulary is evident in *Colossians* where the writer presumes a house setting for the reception of the letter (Col 4:14–16). Domestic language also permeates the *Letter to Philemon*. Both letter writers imagine the Greco-Roman household pattern of kinship ties described in terms of domination-subordination/superiority-inferiority. This superior-inferior relationship influenced the management (οἰκονομία of the Greek household described in terms of master and slave, husband and wife, and father and children. These relationships determined the spirit of the domestic network to which Paul and Epaphras belonged. The household's stability reflected the order and stability desired of the wider πόλις, city-state. Order and "partnership" (κοινωνία guaranteed protection and security. This cultural context of the Lycus Valley in south-west Asia Minor demanded that the households of its three major cities, Hierapolis, Laodicea and Colossae, whether Jesus households or not, reflect the kind of stability necessary for social cohesion and defence. This background is presumed in the letter written to Philemon and his "high-context" household at Colossae. It is further explicated in the later Letter to the Colossians, especially in the household code reflected in Col 3:18–4:1.

In the opening lines of *Philemon*, Paul addresses Philemon and all the members of his household. Apphia and Archippus, members of Philemon's household, are called "our sister" and "our fellow soldier." Paul's descriptors reflect the social network pattern indicated by the familial relationship characteristic of the household's fictive kinship, their common bond (which Paul expresses as κοινωνία in the letter), and their role as his missionary companions.[11] The greeting illustrates the Ego-centred network with Paul at its centre. But alongside him is Timothy, Paul's "brother" He is one with Paul in writing to Philemon and his household. Along with Epaphras in *Colossians* Timothy belongs to the first network zone of intimacy.

---

11 B. B. Thurston/J. M. Ryan, *Philippians and Philemon* (Collegeville, Minn: Liturgical Press, 2005), 217. "Fictive kinship" expresses the relationships, obligations and responsibilities between patron and client not based on the natural family relationships. See K. C. Hanson/D. E. Oakman, *Palestine in the time of Jesus: Social Structures and Social Conflicts* (Minneapolis: Augsburg, 1998), 80–1; B. Malina/J. Pilch, *Social-Science Commentary on the Letters of Paul* (Minneapolis: Fortress, 2006), 362–3.

The levels of authority in these opening verses of *Philemon* further reflect the asymmetrical and hierarchical nature of the network in which Philemon's household exist. The terms of address which Paul uses of Philemon and his household companion ("beloved one," "co-worker," "our sister," "fellow soldier") already signal that changing nature of the conventional network pattern and the new criterion for patron-client relations in the Jesus households.[12] This flags the movement of Philemon and his householder to the closer second zone of intimacy in which Timothy already shares.

The Patron-Client Relationship

Epaphras' presentation in both Pauline letters presumes the network pattern and relational tie observable on a macrocosmic level in Epaphras' world mirrored in the patronage system of *clientela* well-known in the Roman world: a person (the "patron," usually though not exclusively a male) used status and power to advance or protect those of lower status ("clients"). This patron-client exchange pattern was the earliest and most fundamental form of human relationship evident in the Roman Empire between 5th century BCE and 5th century CE.[13] It shaped relationships in Asia Minor, including the Lycus Valley and Colossian society, and is presumed in *Philemon* and *Colossians*. The patron-client pattern influenced the way the writers of the letters (Paul and "Paul") related with their addressees, portrayed Paul himself to his audience, and established Epaphras' importance to Philemon's household and his authority amongst the Colossian Jesus followers. When these cultural patterns and insights are placed alongside the neighbourhood network foci first formulated by Barnes, a helpful template emerges.

The Lycus Valley Neighbourhood Pattern

The neighbourhood pattern in each of the Jesus households addressed by the letters would not be limited to one household, but mirror similar patterns in other Jesus households of the Lycus Valley to which all other households were linked. This complex pattern was further influenced by other political, geographical, economic, cultural and political factors that shaped daily life in the valley. The possibility of such complexity points to an "infinite network" where the complexity of relationships between every person in a network is studied from the point of view of a total system (the "total network") and a universal, all inclusive,

---

12 Thurston/Ryan, *Philippians*, 190.
13 T. F. Carney, *The Shape of the Past: Models of Antiquity* (Lawrence, Kansas: Coronado Press, 1975), 171.

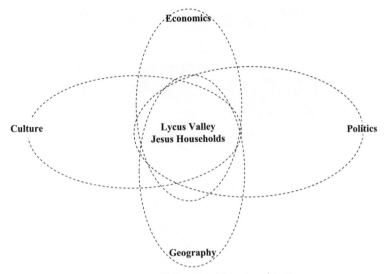

Diag 3 Lycus Valley Neighbourhood Pattern

unbounded network is established.[14] Such a neighbourhood pattern needs acknowledgement as providing the broader cultural and social milieu in which Epaphras' network ties occur. Its adequate study lies beyond the limits of this present chapter. The following diagram seeks to express the interlocking and major overarching societal factors that influenced the network pattern of the Lycus Valley households in which Epaphras was involved.

Colossian Funerary Monuments

The relational ties reflected in the household language evident in *Philemon* and *Colossians* and evident between Epaphras and his fellow Jesus householders are further corroborated by funerary inscriptions. Of particular relevance are those from Colossae.

The present state of research into Colossian inscriptions is in its infancy yet continues to expand as archaeological interest in the site grows.[15] There are two

14 J. A. Barnes, "Graph theory and social networks: a technical comment on connectedness and connectivity", *Sociology* 3 (1969) 215–32; J. Boissevain, "The Place of Non-Groups in the Social Sciences", *Man* 3 (1968) 542–56; J. Boissevain, "Networks", in A. Kuper/J. Kuper (ed.), *The Social Science Encyclopedia* (London, UK: Routledge, 1985), sv.; Mitchell, "The Concept and Use of Social Networks", 1–50.

15 For the inscriptional material here and following I am indebted to the fruits of the research of my colleague A. Cadwallader.

Fig. 1 Funerary stele for Tatianos[16]

funerary inscriptions (out of a possible twenty four) relevant to the present discussion. The first is dated approximately to the same period as the writing of our
two Pauline letters; the second from the third century CE. Though this last one
post-dates the period in which we are most interested, it reflects the relational
spirit evident in the letters memorialized in a later period.

Our first Colossian funerary stele is most significant. Although discovered in
the early twentieth century in modern Honaz, the town closest to ancient Colossae, only recently has its full import been recognized.

The stele depicts a funerary banquet scene with two reclining figures, probably husband and wife, with two small children seated on either side of the table
which contains food. Beneath the table is a dog. The child on the left of the table
is a girl touching bread. The child figure on the right, touching the food on the

16 Photograph by W. Calder which became the plate (pl. 10) supporting *MAMA* VI.48, used
by permission of Manchester University Press.

table, is possibly a boy. The whole scene evokes the kind of household intimacy and relational network which would typify the Jesus households of the Colossian πόλις and reflected in Philemon's household addressed by Paul's letter. An arguable translation of the inscription under the scene reads: "The youngest members of the clan (συγγενικός) [set this up] | for Tatianos son of Tatianos grandson of Artas."[17]

The Greek συγγενικός ("the clan') is a sepulchral term, though not exclusively. It expresses those responsible for erecting the funerary monument, namely the clan or kinship group representative of at least three generations. While the funerary scene and its inscription are not unique in the Greco-Roman world nor for Asia Minor, they are for the Lycus Valley and Colossae. They are contemporaneous with the Pauline letters and underscore the importance of familial intimacy and kinship responsibility for the deceased members of the clan that gets memorialized for those that pass by this funerary monument.

The second funerary stele depicts two standing figures, a male and female, similarly clothed with the woman dressed in an unusual crinkled dress under her outer garment.

The stele's inscription is divided in two, separated by the figures. The text above the figures and the lines beneath them read: "Greetings to those who pass by | The society of friends (ἑταῖροι) honours Gluko."[18]

Though dated to the third century CE, the monument is significant for its description of those who erected the memorial. They are called ἑταῖροι and form an association or "society of friends". The definite article "the" inserted before ἑταῖροι is most noteworthy. In the early Greek period predating the Pauline corpus, ἑταῖροι was well known as a description of friends. By the third century CE and the carving of this inscription, "the" ἑταῖροι became recognized as an association with a corporate identity. This means that the kind of network relationship known in the first century CE and reflected in *Philemon* and *Colossians* was now legally formalized.

These two funerary monuments memorialized the role played by kinship and friendship. Such monuments were also intended to impress those passersby and invite them to consider the role played by honour, status, the domestic setting and the πόλις or *civitas* in constructing the network pattern.[19] All these were powerful social forces and settings. They reflect the kinds of networks that shaped the way people related to each other and Epaphras to his fellow Jesus householders.

---

17 *MAMA* VI.48. The reading used here adopts the corrections made by L. Robert/J. Robert, *BE* 1979.15 (=*SEG* 29.1391).

18 *MAMA* VI.47.

19 On the nature of funerary monuments to "impress", see R. Garland, *The Greek Way of Death* (Ithaca, NY: Cornell University Press, 1985), 109.

Fig. 2 Funerary stele for Gluko[20]

Conclusion

Epaphras is endorsed by Paul in *Philemon* and assumes a status and authority in *Colossians* second to none. He lives within a pattern of social relationships circumscribed by the conventions of the Greco-Roman household. But his relationship to Paul, his authority as Paul's interpreter and the overarching relationship which he has to Jesus, allows him to assist the Lycus Valley Christians reconstruct this pattern. Both letters in which Epaphras appears presume a network pattern that is more than domestic; it is local and universal in scope, concerns at least two generations of Jesus' followers, and straddles geography, different social groups, and even the cosmos.

The Pauline letters to Philemon and Colossae assume a network pattern that is asymmetrical, relational, structured and familial. Epaphras was a key figure

---

20 Photograph by W. Calder which became the plate (pl. 10) supporting *MAMA* VI.47, used by permission of Manchester University Press.

in the social cohesion of the Jesus households of the Lycus Valley. His presentation as an authoritative figure able to present Paul's teaching with authenticity and relevance is best understood within the context of these domestic, geographical, political and economic network patterns revealed within a context of the Graeco-Roman household, patron-client social pattern and supported by recent inscriptional evidence from the Colossae area.

This evidence, gleaned from two Christian documents of the mid to late first century CE, underscores how such documents can contribute in an interdisciplinary manner to the overall picture of life within the Lycus Valley in this Greco-Roman period.

Bibliography

Atkins, R., *Egalitarian Community: Ethnography and Exegesis* (Tuscaloosa, Alabama: University of Alabama Press, 1991).

Barnes, J. A., "Class and Committee in a Norwegian Island Parish", *Human Relations* 7 (1954) 39–58.

– "Graph theory and social networks: a technical comment on connectedness and connectivity", *Sociology* 3 (1969) 215–32.

Befu, H., *Hamlet in a Nation: The Place of Three Japanese Rural Communities in their Broader Social Context* (Ann Arbor, MI: University Microfilms, 1962).

Boissevain, J., "The Place of Non-Groups in the Social Sciences", *Man* 3 (1968) 542–56.

– "Networks", in A. Kuper/J. Kuper (ed.), *The Social Science Encyclopedia* (London, UK: Routledge, 1985) *sv.*

Carney, T. F., *The Shape of the Past: Models of Antiquity* (Lawrence, Kansas: Coronado, 1975).

Chow, J. K., *Patronage and Power: A Study of Social Networks in Corinth* (Sheffield, UK: Academic Press, 1992).

Clark, E. A., "Elite Networks and Heresy Accusations: Towards a Social Description of the Origenist Controversy", *Semeia* 56 (1992) 79–117.

Duling, D. C., "The Jesus movement and social network analysis (part I: The Spatial Network)", *BTB* 29 (1999) 156–76.

– "The Jesus movement and social network analysis (part II: The Social Network)", *BTB* 30 (2000) 3–15.

Finley, M. I., *Ancient History: Evidence and Models* (London: Chatto & Windus, 1985).

Garland, R., *The Greek Way of Death* (Ithaca, NY: Cornell University Press, 1985).

Hanson, K. C./D. E. Oakman, *Palestine in the time of Jesus: Social Structures and Social Conflicts* (Minneapolis: Augsburg, 1998).

Hendrix, H., "Benefactor/Patron Networks in the Urban Environment: Evidence from Thessalonica", *Semeia* 56 (1992) 39–58.

Hock, R. E., "'By the Gods, It's My One Desire to See an Actual Stoic': Epictetus' Relations with Students and Visitors in His Personal Network", *Semeia* 56 (1991) 121–42.

Lohse, E., *Colossians and Ephesians* (Philadelphia: Fortress, 1990).

MacDonald, M. Y., *Colossians and Ephesians* (Collegeville, Minn: Liturgical Press, 2000).

Malina, B./J. Pilch, *Social-Science Commentary on the Letters of Paul* (Minneapolis: Fortress, 2006).

Mitchell, J. C., "The Concept and Use of Social Networks", in J. C. Mitchell (ed.), *Social Networks in Urban Situations: Analyses of Personal Relationships in Central African Towns* (Manchester, UK: Manchester University Press, 1969) 1–50.

Pospisil, L., *The Kapauku Papuans of West New Guinea* (New York, NY: Holt, Rinehart and Winston, 1964).

Remus, H., "Voluntary Association and Networks: Aelius Aristides at the Asclepieion in Pergamum", in J. S. Kloppenborg/S. G. Wilson (ed.), *Voluntary Associations in the Graeco-Roman World* (London, UK/New York, NY: Routledge. 1996) 146–75.

Scott, J., *Social Network Analysis: A Handbook* (London: Sage Publications, 2000).

Stark, R., *The Rise of Christianity: A Sociologist reconsiders History* (Princeton, NJ: Princeton University Press, 1996).

Thurston, B. B./J. M. Ryan, *Philippians and Philemon* (Collegeville, Minn.: Liturgical Press, 2005).

Trainor, M., *Epaphras: Paul's Educator at Colossae* (Collegeville, Minn.: Liturgical Press, 2008).

White, M. L. (ed.), *Social Networks in the Early Christian Environment: Issues and Methods for Social History*, Semeia 56 (1991) 1–202.

Chapter 10

The Silent Witness of the Mound of Colossae: Pottery Remains

Bahadır Duman / Erim Konakçi

Colossae[1] is located on the Lycus Valley to the south of the Büyük Menderes (Maeander) River around 25 kilometres east of Denizli in the southwest of Phrygia *(Fig. 1)*.[2] It is positioned on the roads opening to Ephesus in the west, Uşak in the north and the Lake District in the east providing a geographical transition point between the inner regions and the coast. The city derived its importance from its geographical position and its establishment earlier than other cities in the Lycus valley, such as Tripolis and Hierapolis.[3]

The bi-conical höyük (artificial mound) is the remaining prominent identifying feature for Colossae, but it was located within a larger urban complex. Today, the höyük has a height of approximately 30 metres[4] and lies on an area of 9.24 hectares (280 by 330 metres). Considering the damage caused by agricultural activities around the höyük, it can fairly be calculated that the area of the original mound would have exceeded 12 hectares (*Fig. 2*).

This paper aims to explain pottery finds obtained during a surface survey of Colossae in relation to a relevant historical period, plotting them according to and as they illuminate the unfolding of the historical process. In this respect, all designated periods are given under separate titles and the catalogue of the pottery finds is presented accordingly.[5]

---

1 For general information and references about Colossae, see W. Ruge, "Kolossai", in *Paulys Realencyclopaedie der Classischen Altertumswissenschaft*, XI.1 (Stuttgart: Metzler, 1921) 1119–20 and K. Belke/N. Mersich *Phrygien und Pisidien* (TIB 7; Wien: Österreichische Akademie der Wissenschaften, 1990), 309–11.

2 It is bordered by the mountain Babadağ (Salbakos) in the west, Çökelez in the east, Buldan in the north and the Honaz (Kadmos) mountains in the southwest; its southeastern section is open as far as Lake Acı. Colassae is the current Turkish spelling.

3 During the recent excavations conducted under the direction of Prof. Dr. C. Şimşek in the region defined as Asopos Hill in the ancient city of Laodicea, new data have been found that suggest that the establishment of a settlement dates to the Late Chalcolithic period. Accordingly, the foundation of this city is contemporaneous with that of Colossae.

4 The existing höyük lies on land 453 metres above sea level with a peak at 483 metres high.

5 The "*Cat.No.*" given in each section is linked to the drawings of the pottery listed under each mentioned period.

Fig. 1 The location of Colossae

Fig. 2 The Colossae höyük

The ceramics used in the article as the main database create the most important evidence, thus far explored, for the habitation process, the shaping of chronological development and Colossae's relations with the surrounding cultures and regions. In this regard, even though they seem to be tiny remnants, the pottery finds give crucial information about the socio-cultural structure, commercial relations and nutritional traditions of the population of this ancient city, in direct relationship to the finds in specific *sampling areas* (SAs).

History of Research

Although so far there have been no formal excavations or comprehensive surface surveys focusing on finding the settlement process of the city in Colossae, there have been various researchers who have toured the city and who have published articles that supplement the information provided by ancient sources.

Especially in the nineteenth century, the ancient city was visited by many travellers and introduced in various publications. W. F. Hamilton,[6] G. Weber,[7] W. Ramsay,[8] W. Buckler and W. Calder lead these early researches.[9]

So far, the only archaeological excavation in Colossae was conducted by the Denizli Museum in 1997 at the Necropolis located in the north of the city.[10] Finds of the Hellenistic Period were obtained during the excavations in three

---

6 Hamilton gave detailed information about Colossae, where he traveled in 1836. He stated that its theatre had been ruined and described the rock tombs in the Necropolis. In addition, he described the Lycus and Kadmos Rivers and noted the existence of a number of mills in the vicinity of these two rivers (W. R. Hamilton, "Extract from notes made on journey in Asia Minor in 1836 by W. I. [=J.] Hamilton", *JRGS* 7 (1837) 34–61, on p. 60). In another study, Hamilton recalled that Nicetas Choniates, the Byzantine historian, had taken his name from the city of Chonae, his birthplace, and that Chonos (modern name Honaz) was situated in the immediate vicinity of Colossae, supplanting it after its "destruction" in the Byzantine Period. In reference to the present area of the höyük, he stated that many remains had been located in an area three kilometres north of Honaz: W. J. Hamilton, *Researches in Asia Minor, Pontus and Armenia* (2 vol.; London: John Murray, 1842), 1.508–09.

7 Weber is the primary researcher among the researchers who traveled to Colossae and gave information about the city. In keeping with the investigations he conducted in the Necropolis of the city, he drew some of the tomb types and published some of the specimens that have inscriptions (G. Weber, "Der unterirdische Lauf des Lykos bei Kolossai", *AM* 16 (1891) 194–99, on pp. 198–99).

8 Ramsay addressed the regional geography and the remains of the city in his *Cities and Bishoprics of Phrygia* (2 vol.; Oxford: Clarendon Press, 1895, 1897), 1.208–34.

9 W. Buckler and W. Calder gathered together the tomb stelai with inscriptions and the architectural blocks they found in Colossae, Honaz and Denizli: *Monumenta Asiae Minoris Antiqua Vol VI: Monuments and Documents from Phrygia and Caria* (= MAMA VI) (Manchester: Manchester University Press, 1939), 15–18, Fig. 8–16).

10 H. Yıldız, "Denizli Müzesi Müdürlüğü Lykos Vadisi Çalışmaları", *Müze Kurtarma Kazıları Semineri* 9 (1999) 247–62, on pp. 247–49.

different tumuli. Detailed information was published by Celal Şimşek about the process of urban development, the necropolis and the windmills of the Colossae höyük.[11] Finally, besides the settlement phases of the area and its dispersion area and pottery finds, other small finds such as coins, axes and statues and the architectural block fragments have been evaluated by the present writers.[12]

Colossae in Ancient Sources

Although not absolutely certain as to identification, Colossae is probably the city referred to as Huwalušija, Hu-u-wa-al-lu-ši-ja, Hu-u-wa-lu-ši-ja, Hu-u-wa-lu-ši-ja or Hu-u-wa-lu-ša, in Hittite texts.[13] It is important to corroborate that the city was settled throughout the second millennium BCE; hence new philological and archaeological data become extremely valuable.

The name Colossae was first mentioned by Herodotos in his *Histories*. Herodotos named Colossae as one of the important cities of Phrygia but did not give detailed information. However, he stated that Xerxes crossed a city called Anaua and a lake with the same name while going to the campaign against Greece in 480 BCE and reached Colossae. He held that among the cities through which he passed, this one was a great Phrygian city. He also reported that the Lycus River (Çürüksu) went underground and disappeared around this area and appeared again on the surface around five stadia later to join the Maeander (Büyük Menderes) River.[14]

Another ancient writer who mentioned the city was Xenophon. The writer had participated in Cyrus' campaign in 401 BCE against his brother, the Persian king Artaxerxes. Xenophon related that the army of Cyrus stopped over in Colossae given that the city was large and rich.[15] It is clear that Colossae, described as a *polis*, had been one of the important settlements of the region.[16]

Strabo, when referring to the Phrygian cities, mentioned Colossae among the small cities of the region.[17] In keeping with the information given by Strabo, we conclude that the city, in the first century BCE, was considerably dimin-

---

11 C. Şimşek, "Kolossai", *Arkeoloji ve Sanat* 107 (2002) 3–17.

12 B. Duman/E. Konakçı, "Kolassai: Höyük, Kalıntı ve Buluntuları (Colossae: the Mound, Remains and Findings)", *Arkeoloji Dergisi* 8 (2006) 83–111; E. Konakçı/B. Duman, "Arkeolojik ve Yazılı Kanıtlar Işığında Kolossai (Kolossai with the Light of Archaeological and Historical Evidences)" in *International Symposium on the History and Culture of Denizli and its Surroundings* (2 vol.; Denizli: Pamukkale University, 2007), 2.57–67.

13 G. F. Monte/J. Tischler, *Répertoire Géographique des Textes Cunéiformes* Vol. VI, (Wiesbaden: L. Reichert, 1978), 130–31.

14 Herodotos *Hist.* 7.30.

15 Xenophon *Anab.* 1.2.7.

16 R. T. Marchese, *The Lower Maeander Flood Plain* (Oxford: BAR, 1986), 157.

17 Strabo *Geogr.* 12.8.3.

ished from its old magnificence and size. Pliny, less than a century later, recalled Colossae as one of the most important cities of Phrygia.[18] When the information given by the two ancient writers is considered, it may be said that the city had lost its previous importance in the first century BCE but appears to have revived early in the second century CE and become again one of the significant cities of the region. This change must have occurred through the reconstruction activities supported by the Roman Empire after the great earthquake that demolished Colossae, Laodicea and Hierapolis in 60 CE.[19] Although, as implied by Pliny, Colossae had lost its previous importance in the first century BCE, it must have had a considerable population and continued to play an important role in this region.

In Colossae, which was mentioned in a letter accredited to St Paul, Christianity spread in the first century CE via the activities of Epaphras, one of the friends of St. Paul, an apostle of Jesus. The letter, taken as written to the people of Colossae by St. Paul, contains important information for the history of Christianity in the region.[20] The Church of St. Michael,[21] thought to have originated sometime in the fourth century CE, indicates that Colossae was active within the region in the Late Roman Period.[22] However, no remains of this church have been excavated as yet. The name Colossae was mentioned also in the Second Council of Niceae held in 787 CE. Colossae was damaged considerably in the Arab invasions of the seventh-eighth centuries CE; the city became smaller. Some of the people moved to Chonai (Honaz) established on the lower reaches of Mt. Cadmus.[23] Besides the Arab invasions, the plague outbreak during the reign of Justinian and Constantine V also impoverished many cities and lead to a decrease in population. Sardis, Pergamum, Miletos, Priene and Magnesia, among the key cities in Western Anatolia, became small castle cities. Laodicea was mostly abandoned; Hierapolis became smaller, though it continued to sur-

---

18 Pliny *Nat.* 5.145.

19 Tacitus *Ann.* 14.27 For this great earthquake, which severely damaged the three cities, see E. Guidoboni/A. Comastri/G.Traina, *Catalogue of Ancient Earthquakes in the Mediterranean Area up to the Tenth Century* (Rome: Istituto Nazionale di Geofisica, 1994), 194–95.

20 See generally, M. Trainor, *Epaphras: Paul's Educator at Colossae* (Collegeville, Minn: Liturgical Press, 2008).

21 St. Michael had become a cultic figure within this church; some researchers regard the cult as a continuation of the cult of Apollo thought to have previously existed at Colossae and show the descriptions of Artemis on the coins of the city as the proof of this cult. For the various claims of Michael forerunners at Colossae, see G. F. Hill, "Apollo and St Michael: Some Analogies", *JHS* 36 (1916) 134–62, on p. 156.

22 Ramsay, *Cities and Bishoprics*, 214.

23 Ramsay stated that the city had been destroyed and left during the Byzantine Wars since it had been a defenseless city on an open plain. See Ramsay, *The Historical Geography of Asia Minor* (London: John Murray, 1890), 134–35; George Bean proposed that this movement took place in the 800s CE: G. E. Bean, *Turkey beyond the Maeander* (London: John Murray, 1980), 222.

vive for a while.[24] In 858 CE, Chonai was turned into an archiepiscopal centre, to which episcopacies in the vicinity were affiliated. Colossae therefore had returned to being one of the important cities in the region.[25]

This is the bare sum of textual sources that provides a skeleton historical overview of Colossae. It is against this minimal framework that we propose to present our ceramic findings.

Pottery Finds

The surface survey was conducted across the whole of the höyük and in all the fields in its immediate vicinity (see *Draw. 1*). The site was divided into eight distinct areas consonant with the topographic variations of the land and the resulting material was initially assessed according to the constraints of these divisions. When we allocated the pottery finds of the Colossae höyük in line with the historical process experienced in south-western Anatolia, we observed the presence of settlement from the Late Chalcolithic Period to the Byzantine Period (3500 BCE–1100 CE) *(Graphs. 2.1–8).*[26] In what follows, these finds are given a detailed breakdown of classification at the conclusion of each section of period pottery, providing a description of the pottery sherd, the diameter calculated for the reconstructed pottery piece along with the colour, slip, glaze, temper and firing (all where possible). Although technical minutiae, it must be emphasised that it is precisely this level of systematic evidence that has yielded significant advances in our knowledge of the history of settlement at the Colossae höyük and contributes to our ability to make comparisons between Colossae and other centres in various periods. The drawings of the reconstructed pottery vessels are given at the conclusion of this essay.

Overall, the concentration of pottery groups was particularly marked for the Early Byzantine Period in the majority of sampling areas *(Fig. 3)*.

This advances our sense of the dimension of the settlement in the Early Byzantine Period, even though there is limited written evidence in ancient sources or in previous studies about the settlement on the höyük cone for the Byzantine period. In addition to the glazed potteries of the twelfth century CE, the discovery of a coin dated to the eleventh century CE in our surface survey *(Fig. 4)*[27] confirms that a settlement of some significance continued on and around the höyük long after the Arab invasions tapered off at the end of the eighth century.

---

24 C. Foss, "Archaeology and the 'Twenty Cities of Byzantine Asia", *AJA* 81 (1977) 485–86.
25 Ramsay, *Historical Geography*, 91.
26 We would like to thank M. Bilgin and M. Ok for their help at the drawing stage.
27 Duman/Konakçı, "Kolassai: Höyük", 83ff, Konakçı/Duman, "Arkeolojik", 57 ff.

Fig. 3 Byzantine pottery fragments

Fig. 4 Coin finds from the sampling areas

Fig. 5 Prehistoric pottery

Prehistoric Pottery

The first researcher to mention the prehistoric data of the Colossae höyük was James Mellaart, who carried out surface surveys in the south-western Anatolian Region between 1951 and 1954.[28] Mellaart, Seton Lloyd and Ann Murray indicated Colossae on the maps of south-western Anatolia for the Early Bronze Age,

---

28 J. Mellaart, "Preliminary Report on a Survey of Pre-Classical Remains in Southern Turkey", *AS* 4 (1954) 175–240, on p. 192, map 3. In addition, he mentioned a mouth sherd found in this settlement which was classified within the brown-slipped gray wares group (230–31, No. 346).

Middle Bronze Age and Late Bronze Age in the Beycesultan volumes[29] but gave no further information about the finds on the höyük.[30]

Pottery of the Chalcolithic Period *(Cat. Nos. 1–3)*

It has been asserted that a settlement began on the Colossae höyük in the Late Chalcolithic Period. This has been confirmed by our studies. The potteries dated to the Late Chalcolithic Period (approximately 4000–3000 BCE) were found in SA numbers 1, 2, 4, 5 and 7. The specimens found in 1, 2 and 5 among the sampling areas concerned had a percentage below 10 % among all the potteries collected. Few potteries were found in SA 7, the only sampling area outside the höyük cone in which Chalcolithic pottery was found (amounting to 15 % of the total sample for that SA).

When we evaluated the general qualities of the pottery of the Chalcolithic Period found on the Colossae höyük, we found that they were all handmade. The surface colour is brown, varying in shades from light to dark. The fragments discovered are slipped, and burnish exists on the majority of the specimens. No paint-decorated specimens — a common tradition in south-western Anatolia — were detected. The pottery concerned is intensively sand-, straw- and particularly grit-tempered and had been moderately fired and hard-fired. The fragments found belong to bowls and jars. The pottery of the Late Chalcolithic Period found on the Colossae höyük *(Cat. Nos. 1–3)*[31] follows the general characteristics exhibited by finds from other Late Chalcolithic Period settlements located in south-western Anatolia,[32] most notably specimens from Beycesultan XX–XL,[33] Aphrodisias Chalcolithic I–IV[34] and Kusura A.[35]

---

29 S. Lloyd/J. Mellaart, *Beycesultan Vol I: The Chalcolithic and Early Bronze Age Levels* (London: BIAA, 1962), 196–97, map 6. For the map of Southwestern Anatolia, Early Bronze Age III, see pages 252–53 map 8; S. Lloyd/J. Mellaart, *Beycesultan Vol II: Middle Bronze Age Architecture and Pottery* (London: BIAA, 1965), 76–7, map 1; J. Mellaart/A. Murray, *Beycesultan Vol III, Part II: Late Bronze Age and Phrygian Pottery and Middle and Late Bronze Age Small Objects* (London: BIAA, 1995), 102, maps 2, 4.

30 For new settlements from the Çivril Area see E. Abay/F. Dedeoğlu, "2003 Yılı Denizli/ Çivril Ovası Yüzey Araştırması (Annual Report on Survey Research in the Denizli/Çivril area)", *Araştırma Sonuçları Toplantısı* 2 (2005) 42–50.

31 The following abbreviations are used in the catalogue: Cat No: Catalogue Number; C: Colossae; H: Height; Dm: Diameter; colours (eg YR, R) are from the Munsell Soil Chart; Ref: Reference; EBA: Early Bronze Age; MBA: Middle Bronze Age; LBA: Late Bronze Age.

32 C. Eslick, "The Neolithic and Chalcolithic Pottery of the Elmalı Plain, South-western Turkey". (PhD thesis, Bryn Mawr College, 1978), 166 ff.

33 Lloyd/Mellaart, *Beycesultan Vol I*, 72 ff.

34 M.S. Joukowsky, *Prehistoric Aphrodisias: An Account of the Excavations and Artifact Studies* (Court-St.-Etienne, Belgium: Imprimerie E. Oleffe, 1986), 350–55.

35 W. Lamb, "Excavations at Kusura Near Afyon Karahisar", *Archaeologia* 86 (1937) 1–64, on pp. 15–30. These ancient settlements are within a 120 kilometre radius of Colossae.

Cat. No. 1: C.05.88. *Rim and body sherd of bowl, plain rim, Dm: ?, paste colour 2.5 YR 2.5/1 (reddish black), slip colour 7.5 YR 5/2 (brown), well-burnished, temper: sand, straw, grit. Moderately fired. Chalcolithic.*

Cat. No. 2: C.05.48. *Rim sherd of jar, plain rim, mouth width: ?, paste colour 5 YR 6/8 (light red), slip colour 2.5 YR 5/4 (reddish brown), unburnished, temper: sand, straw, grit. Moderately fired. Chalcolithic.*

Cat. No. 3: C.02.29. *Rim and body sherd of deep bowl, plain rim, Dm: 29, paste colour 7.5 YR 3/1 (very dark gray), slip colour 7.5 YR 4/4 (brown), well-burnished, temper: sand, grit, straw. Hard-fired. Chalcolithic.*

The fact that rather limited numbers of pottery dated to this period were found during our surface surveys prevents us from making comprehensive inferences.

Pottery of the Early Bronze Age I–II (*Cat. Nos. 4–12*)

Pottery specimens dated to periods I, II and III of the Early Bronze Age (EBA) (approximately 3000–2000 BCE) were found during the surface surveys conducted at the settlement. The specimens dated to period I of EBA were found in SA 1, 2, 4, 5 and 7. The specimens found in SA 1 and 4, sampling areas with fewer specimens, were below 10 % of all the potteries collected. EBA specimens reached over 10 % of all the potteries collected in the related south-eastern sampling areas, SA 2, 5 and 7 (14.9 %).

The potteries of EBA periods I and II detected on the Colossae höyük are all handmade and their surface colours are brown, red and black varying in shades from light to dark. The specimens are slipped and the majority of them are burnished. The pottery is straw-, fine sand- and grit-tempered and although the paste structure is not homogeneous, they are black, gray and brown in colour. The specimens had been moderately fired and hard-fired.

The pottery of EBA periods I and II found in Colossae reflects the south-western Anatolian EBA culture and displays characteristics similar to the finds of Levels XVII–XIX[36] and Levels XIIIb–XVI[37] in the Beycesultan excavations.[38] The most densely represented shape in the study for this period is the slightly incurving bowl (*Cat. Nos. 4, 5*). Similar specimens to this type of bowl are encoun-

---

36 Lloyd/Mellaart, *Beycesultan Vol I*, 118–132.

37 Lloyd/Mellaart, *Beycesultan Vol I*, 142 ff.

38 Lloyd/Mellaart, *Beycesultan Vol I*, 138. However, Efe divided western Anatolia into sub-regions in response to the data of pottery of EBA, resulting in a refinement of classification for our study area to "Middle Inner-Western Anatolia"; see T. Efe, "Pottery distribution within the Bronze Age of western Anatolia and its implications upon cultural, political (ethnic?) entities", in M. Özbaşaran/O. Tanındı/A. Boratav (ed.), *Archaeological essays in honour of homo amatus: Güven Arsebük için armağan yazılar* (İstanbul: Ege Yayınları, 2003) 87–104, on p. 91.

tered frequently in Western Anatolia, for example in Level XIX[39] in Beycesultan and from Level I to Level IV in Troy.[40] They also display similarities to Class A wares from Yortan.[41]

Another shape encountered is the jar with an out-turned rim *(Cat. Nos. 7, 11)*. Furthermore, foot sherds of grit-, straw- and lime-tempered and moderately fired cooking pots on tripod feet were found *(Cat. No. 11)*. Such fragments of tripod wares are a common characteristic encountered in almost all western Anatolian EBA settlements.[42] They are similar to the forms C 34, C 35 and D 24 in Troy Levels I, II–III[43], IV and V.[44] Similar ones have also been found in Levels X–XII in Beycesultan.[45]

There is a grooved decoration on two of the handles found *(Cat. Nos. 8, 9)*. Since this decoration type was revealed in Level XVI in Beycesultan, our specimens must have been contemporary to Beycesultan Level XVI and the following levels.[46] In addition, pottery examples with grooved decoration similar to our specimens are comparative to those found in Kuruçay.[47]

Specimens with white paint, groove and white filled incised decoration were detected on EBA II wares found during the surface surveys. Similar examples of the white-painted pottery found at Colossae were discovered in the EBA II levels during the Beycesultan excavations and are regarded as characteristic of the new stylistic properties of this period. *Cat. No. 12,* which shows a mouth fragment with geometric decoration made with white paint on red slip, and a body sherd with white filled incised decoration are distinctive examples.

Specimens with painted decoration have been found at the Yortan necropolis (Group A Wares), in Iasos, Beycesultan XVI, Aphrodisias and Thermi.[48] Incised

39 Lloyd/Mellaart, *Beycesultan Vol I*, Fig.P.14/10–19.

40 Specimens detected are particularly similar to forms A9, A12 and A16 in Troy: see C. W. Blegen/J. L. Caskey/M. Rawson/J. Sperling, *Troy I: General Introduction: The First and Second Settlements* (Princeton, NJ: Princeton University Press, 1950), Figs. 258, 259, 260, 261, 262, 263. C. W. Blegen *et al*, *Troy II: The Third, Fourth and Fifth Settlements* (Princeton, NJ: Princeton University Press., 1951), Fig. 176/32.67, 33.135, 32.103.

41 T. Kamil, *Yortan Cemetery in the Early Bronze Age of Western Anatolia* (Oxford: BAR, 1982), Figs. 23, 24.

42 See, for example, Lamb, "Kasura", fig 7/5a–b.

43 Blegen, *Troy I*, fig. 223b/C34, D24, fig.233/37.1138 for Level I and fig. 59b/D24, C 35 for Level II.

44 Blegen, *Troy II*, Part 2, fig. 243, 35.1090.

45 Lloyd/Mellaart, *Beycesultan Vol II*, fig.P. 49/11–12.

46 Lloyd/Mellaart, *Beycesultan Vol I*, fig 25: 3–4, fig 31: 1, 7.

47 R.Duru, *Kuruçay Höyük II* (Ankara: Türk Tarih Kurumu, 1996), 120/16, 135/8.

48 Kamil, *Yortan*, 18–19; P.E. Pecorella, *La Cultura Preistorica di Iasos in Caria* (Rome: G. Bretschneider, 1984), 84; W. Lamb, *Excavations at Thermi in Lesbos* (Cambridge: Cambridge University Press/New York: Macmillan, 1936), Pl XXX: 1–4, 6, 10. The specimens with painted decoration are dated to EBA II in Aphrodisias: Joukowsky, *Prehistoric Aphrodisias*, 760ff, 398, fig 370: 10.

specimens on which geometrical patterns dominate, can be compared with the finds at Troy, Yortan Cemetery, Beycesultan and Thermi.[49]

Cat. No. 4: *C.02.27. Rim and body sherd of bowl, incurving rim, Dm: 26 cm, paste colour, 5 YR 4/4 (reddish brown) slip colour 5 YR 4/1 (dark gray), particularly well-burnished on interior, sand-, grit- and mica-tempered. Hard- fired. EBA I.*

Cat. No. 5: *C.03.50. Rim and body sherd of incurved Bowl, paste colour 10 YR 4/3 (Brown), slip colour 10 YR 4/3 (brown), burnished, grit- and straw-tempered. Hard-fired. EBA II.*

Cat. No. 6: *C.04.75. Rim and body sherd of jar, excurved rim, squat neck, Dm: 21 cm, paste colour 2.5 Y 5/6 (light olive brown), black core at the centre of the paste, slip colour 2.5 Y 5/4 (light olive brown), unburnished, grit- and straw-tempered. Underfired. EBA II.*

Cat. No. 7: *C.02.10. Rim and body sherd of jar, excurved rim, Dm: 10, paste colour 10 YR 6/6 (brownish yellow), slip colour 2.5 Y 4/4 (olive brown), very well-burnished exterior, grit-tempered. Hard-fired. EBA II.*

Cat. No. 8: *C.02.05. Handle sherd, H: 7 cm, with three vertically grooved ornamentation, paste colour 10 YR 4/1 (dark gray), slip colour 10 YR 7/3 (very pale brown), sand-, grit- and lime-tempered. Hard-fired. EBA II.*

Cat. No. 9: *C.02.99. Handle sherd, H: 5.6, with grooved decoration, paste colour 10 YR 5/8 (yellowish brown), slip colour 10 YR 4/3 (brown), surface burnished, grit-tempered. Hard-fired. EBA II.*

Cat. No. 10: *C.02.14. Body sherd, paste colour 10 YR 4/2 (dark grayish brown), slip colour 2.5 Y 4/4 (olive brown), incised ware white filled, burnished exterior surface, sand-tempered. Hard-fired. EBA II.*

Cat. No. 11: *C.07.75. foot sherd, preserved height, paste colour 2.5 YR 6/6, unburnished, sand-, grit-, lime- and straw-tempered, moderately fired. EBA II.*

Cat. No. 12: *C.02.47. Rim and body sherd of bowl, incurving rim, Dm: 16, paste colour 10 R 4/8 (red), slip colour 10 R 3/6 (dark red), matt white paint, surface burnished, sand-, mica- and grit-tempered, 4 band decorations extending from the upper section of the mouth towards the body. EBA I.*

Pottery of the Early Bronze Age III (*Cat. Nos. 13–14*)

The surfaces of the pottery from EBA III are black, light brown and dark red, and they have red or camel paste colour. These fine sand- and grit-tempered specimens were detected in few numbers in SA 1 and 7. The majority of the pottery sherds were found to be wheel-made specimens *(Cat. Nos. 13, 14)*. The fact that

---

49 Blegen, *Troy I*, 234, 20, 23; Kamil, *Yortan*, fig 26: 26, fig 25:25; Lloyd/Mellaart, *Beycesultan Vol I*, fig 25: 19; Lamb, *Thermi*, fig 35: 19.

on the Colossae höyük EBA III pottery was found is consistent with a number of settlements in south-western Anatolia. It also indicates that settlements of EBA I, II and III are likely to have continued without interruption.

Cat. No. 13: *C.01.33. Rim and body sherd of deep bowl, plain rim, Dm: 24, paste colour 7.5 YR 4/6 (strong brown), slip colour 7.5 YR 2.5/1 (black), mica- and sand-tempered. Hard-fired.*

Cat. No. 14: *C.01.43. Rim and body sherd of jar, rim thickened out, Dm: 32 cm, H: 5.9 cm, pointed knob beneath the neck, paste 7.5 YR 4/1 (dark gray), slip 7.5 YR 4/3 (brown), grit-tempered. Hard-fired.*

Pottery of the Middle and Late Bronze Age
(Cat. Nos. 15–33)

Specimens dated to the Middle Bronze Age (MBA) (approximately 2000–1600 BCE) were found in SA numbers 1, 2, 4 and 7 while the specimens dated to the Late Bronze Age (LBA) (approximately 1600–1200 BCE) were found in SA numbers 1, 6 and 7. The surfaces of MBA specimens detected are dark red, brown and camel. Chaff temper in the paste almost disappeared but a small quantity of plant temper with little intensity exists in the specimens dated to this period. The majority of MBA pottery discovered is composed of red-slipped pottery, characteristic of south-western Anatolia for this period. The shapes found during the surface survey were composed of incurved-rim bowls *(Cat. Nos. 15, 16, 17)*, plain-rim bowls *(Cat. Nos. 19, 18)*, bead rim bowls and bead rim bowls with vertical handle ascending at the rim *(Cat. No. 20)*, carinated[50] bowls with inverted rim, jars with rim thickened out *(Cat. No. 21)*, ring bases *(Cat. Nos. 24, 25)* and body sherds *(Cat. No. 22)*. Very similar specimens of MBA pottery to those from the Colossae höyük have been found at Beycesultan, Aphrodisias and Kusura C.[51]

The specimens dated to the LBA are all wheel-made and burnished. The high quality observed in little-tempered specimens is striking. The forms found are plain-rim bowls *(Cat. No. 32)*, incurved-rim bowls *(Cat. No. 26)* and bead rim bowls *(Cat. Nos. 27, 28, 29, 30, 31)*. The bead rim specimens discovered are very similar to those of Beycesultan.[52] Close parallels to the gold wash ware specimens have been found in Beycesultan I–II–III, Aphrodisias, Bademgediği II–VI,

---

50 The term "carinated" describes the wall of a pottery vessel that has an abrupt change of direction, rather than a continuous curve.

51 Lloyd/Mellaart *Beycesultan Vol II*, Pl 3–4, 31–3, Joukowsky, *Prehistoric Aphrodisias*, 365–66, Lamb, "Kusura", 23 ff.

52 Mellaart/Murray, *Beycesultan Vol III*, fig. P 4.

Panaztepe and Troy VI–VII.[53] Considering the specimens at Beycesultan and Aphrodisias,[54] the numerous examples of gold wash ware on the surface of the höyük confirms that this pottery group was used intensively in south-western Anatolia, particularly during the LBA. On the other hand, in regard to the Early Iron Age, no evidence could be found, apart from two amorphous fragments.

Cat. No. 15: C.03.71. *Rim and body sherd of deep bowl, incurved rim, Dm: 27 cm, H: 7.7 cm, paste colour 5 YR 6/8 (reddish yellow), slip colour 2.5 YR 5/8 (red), mottled slip, slightly burnished, very little small-size mica and chaff plant temper. Hard-fired. MBA.*

Cat. No. 16: C.07.03. *Rim and body sherd of bowl, inverted rim, carinated, Dm: 40 cm, H: 3.9 cm, paste 5 YR 6/8 (reddish yellow), slip 2.5 YR 5/8 (red), little lime and mica temper. Hard-fired. MBA.*

Cat No. 17: C.01.55. *Rim and body sherd of bowl, incurved rim, Dm: 22, H: 3.9 cm, largely abraded slip on the interior and almost completely abraded slip on the exterior, paste 10 R 6/8 (light red), slip 10 R 5/8 (red), abundantly lime-tempered. Hard-fired. MBA.*

Cat. No. 18: C.06.33. *Rim and body sherd of deep bowl, plain white, Dm: 19, H: 6.6 cm, carination from the mouth towards the body, lip thickened out, partially abraded slip on the exterior, paste 10 R 6/8 (light red), slip 2.5 YR 4/8 (red), lime-, chaff- and grit-tempered. Hard-fired. MBA.*

Cat. No. 19: C.01.52. *Rim and body sherd of shallow bowl, plain white, Dm: 21, H: 2.8 cm, thickened lip, slip 5 R 5/8 (red), paste 2.5 YR 6/8, lime- and grit-tempered. MBA.*

Cat. No. 20: C.04.79. *Rim and handle sherd of bowl, bead rim, vertical handle ascending at the mouth, paste 2.5 YR 6/8 (light red), exterior slip 2.5 YR 6/6 (light red), interior slip 2.5 YR 7/8 (light red), slightly burnished, grit- and lime-tempered. Hard-fired. MBA.*

Cat. No. 21: C.03.07. *Rim and body sherd of Jar, rim thickened out, Dm: 32 cm, H: 3.7 cm, paste 2.5 YR 6/8 (light red), slip 2.5 YR 5/8 (red), burnished, small quantity of lime and grit temper. Hard-fired. MBA.*

Cat. No. 22: C.01.11. *Body sherd, horn-shaped knob on the upper section, right section of the horn is broken, 5 rows of groove starting underneath the knob,*

---

53 Mellaart/Murray, *Beycesultan Vol III*, 1–2, 56–7; 99–109; R. Marchese, "Report on the West Acropolis Excavations at Aphrodisias: 1971–1973", *AJA* 80 (1976) 393–412, on p. 407; R. Meriç, "Excavations at Bademgediği Tepe (Puranda) 1999–2002: A Preliminary Report", *Istanbuler Mitteilungen* 53 (2003) 79–98, on p. 88; S. Günel, *Panaztepe II: M. Ö. 2. bine tarihlendirilen Panaztepe seramiğinin Batı Anadolu ve Ege Arkeolojisindeki yeri ve önemi* (Yayınları: Türk Tarih Kurumu, 1999), 84ff; Blegen et al., *Troy III. The Sixth Settlement* (Princeton: Princeton University Press, 1953), 34 ff.

54 Marchese, "Aphrodisias", 403.

paste 2.5 YR 6/8 (light red), slip 2.5 YR 6/6 (light red), lime-, mica- and grit-tempered. Hard-fired. EBA III– MBA ?

Cat. No. 23: C.03.01. Vertical handle, paste 2.5 YR 7/8 (light red), slip 10 YR 8/4 (very pale brown), unburnished, small quantity of lime temper. Hard-fired. MBA.

Cat. No. 24: C.01.14. Ring base and body sherd, paste 10 R 6/8 (light red), slip 10 R 7/6 (light red), slightly burnished, grit- and lime-tempered. Hard-fired. MBA.

Cat. No. 25: C.01.28. Elevated ring base and body sherd. Dm: 5.6 cm, H: 1.6 cm, slightly elevated, broken parts on the location of the base. Paste 10 R 6/8 (light red), slip 10 R 5/6, abundant lime and pottery sherd temper. MBA.

Cat. No. 26: C.02.12. Rim and body sherd of bead rim bowl, Dm: 20, H: 2.7 cm, slip 7.5 YR 6/3 (light brown), paste 7.5 YR 4/4 (brown), very little lime temper. LBA.

Cat. No. 27: C.01.38. Rim and handle sherd of bowl, bead rim and vertical handle, finger print on the joint of handle and mouth, paste 2.5 YR 6/8 (light red), slip 2.5 YR 7/6 (Light red), unburnished, little grit, mica and lime temper. Hard-fired. LBA.

Cat. No. 28: C.01.53. Rim and body sherd of bead rim bowl, carinated, gold wash ware, Dm: 26 cm, H: 3.3 cm, two wide grooves on the section from underneath the lip to the carination, paste 2.5 YR 6/8 (light red), slip 2.5 Y 8/4 (pale yellow), very little lime temper, hardly fired. LBA.

Cat. No. 29: C.01.05. rim and body sherd of deep bowl, bead rim, carinated. Dm: 39 cm, H: 4.5 cm, gold wash ware, two wide grooves from underneath the lip to the carination, paste 2.5 YR 7/6 (light red), gold wash 2.5 Y 8/3 (pale yellow), lime- and grit-tempered. Hard-fired. LBA.

Cat. No. 30: C.01.36. Rim and body sherd of bead rim bowl, Dm: 30 cm, H: 4.1 cm. Hardly fired. LBA.

Cat. No. 31: C.04.68. Rim and body sherd of bowl, inverted flattened rim, Dm: 15, H: 4 cm, slip 5 YR 6/1 (gray), paste: 7.5 YR 4/1 (dark gray), mica- and lime-tempered. LBA.

Cat. No. 32: C.01.54. Rim and body sherd of bowl, plain rim, Dm: 22 cm, H: 2 cm, gold wash ware, 2.5 YR 6/8 (light red), interior and exterior slip 2.5 Y 7/3 (pale yellow), burnished, chaff plant temper. Hard-fired. LBA.

Cat. No. 33: C.02.02. Rim and body sherd of bowl, inverted rim, Dm: 24 cm, H: 3.8 cm, paste 2.5 YR 6/8 (light red), slip 10 R 5/8 (red), burnished, knob decoration beneath the mouth, mica-tempered. Hard-fired.

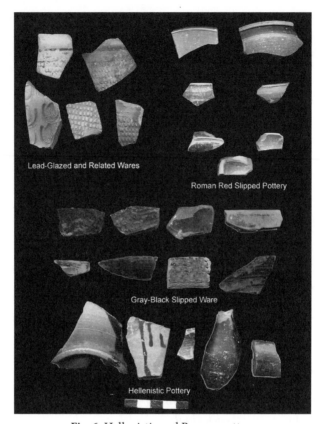

Fig. 6 Hellenistic and Roman pottery

Hellenistic and Roman Pottery

The majority of the finds detected on and around the höyük date to the Hellenistic, Roman and Late Antique periods *(Fig. 6)*.

The specimens of pottery will be dealt with according to the following groups.

Incurved-rim Bowls *(Cat. No. 34–37)*

Incurved-rim bowls constitute another group of wares quite widely used in the Mediterranean Basin.[55] A number of sherds of this group were found in the stud-

---

55 Tarsus: H. Goldman, *Excavation at Gözlü Kule, Tarsus; The Hellenistic and Roman Periods. Vol. I* (Princeton, New Jersey: Princeton University Press, 1950), 157; Cyprus: O. Vessberg/A. Westholm, *The Swedish Cyprus Expedition Vol. IV. Part 3, The Hellenistic and Roman*

ies conducted in Colossae as well. Incurved-rim bowls are dated between the early phases of the third century BCE and the first half of the first century BCE. However the specimens found at Colossae can be dated to the second or first century BCE. We can divide such pottery ware into two groups: deep and shallow bowls.

The fragments in Colossae are mainly comprised of deep incurved-rim bowls. Their rim diameters generally range between 13 and 14 centimetres, except for a few specimens. The rim diameters of these few exceptions can reach up to 25 centimetres. The shallow wide-rim bowls of the second group were fewer in number. Their diameters are larger than the first group and range between 15 and 20 cm.

Cat. No. 34: C.04.60. Dm: 17 cm. H: 1.9 cm. Rim and body sherd of incurved-rim shallow bowl. Hard textured paste, large pores, sparsely lime-tempered, 2.5 YR 5/6 (red), matt and coarse slip 7.5 YR 5/3 (brown).

Cat. No. 35: C.01.58. Dm: 13 cm. H: 2.7 cm. Rim and body sherd of incurved-rim deep bowl. Soft textured paste, large lime and sparse grit temper, 7.5 YR 6/6 (reddish yellow), matt and coarse slip 7.5 YR 7/4 (pink) on exterior and 2.5 YR 6/8 (light red) on interior.

Cat. No. 36: C.01.59. Dm: 14 cm. H: 2.3 cm. Rim and body sherd of incurved-rim deep bowl. Hard and densely textured paste, densely micaceous and sparse pottery sherd temper 5 YR 6/8 (reddish yellow), brilliant, high gloss slip 2.5 YR 5/8 (red) on interior, 5 YR 6/8(reddish) yellow on exterior.

Cat. No. 37: C.01.22. Dm: 25 cm. H: 2.9 cm. Rim and body sherd of incurved-rim deep bowl. Soft textured paste, sparsely mica-tempered 7.5 YR 7/6 (reddish yellow), matt and coarse slip 7.5 YR 6/3 (light brown) on exterior and 5 YR 7/4 (pink) on interior.

Periods in Cyprus (Stockholm: Swedish Cyprus Expedition, 1956), 57–58, 76; Samaria: J.W. Crowfoot/G.M. Crowfoot/K.M. Kenyon, *Samaria-Sebaste. Reports of the Work of the Joint Expedition in 1931–1933 and of the British Expedition in 1935, No. 3, The Objects from Samaria* (London: Palestine Exploration Fund, 1957), 248–251; Palestine: P.W. Lapp, *Palestinian Ceramic Chronology, 200 B. C.–A. D. 70* (New Haven: American Schools of Oriental Research, 1961), 18–19, 172; Stobi: V.R. Anderson-Stojanovic, "The University of Chicago Excavations in the Rachi Settlement at Isthmia, 1989", *Hesperia* 65 (1996) 57–98, on pp. 65, 73, 74; Pergamon: J. Schafer, *Hellenistische Keramik Aus Pergamon* (Berlin: Walter de Gruyter, 1968), 37, 38, 43; W. Radt/G. de Luca, "Grabungen im Fundament des Pergamonaltars. Grobe Keramik – Graue Sondergruppe-Lampen", in C. Abadie-Reynal (ed.), *Les Céramiques en Anatolie aux Époques héllenistique et romaine* (Varia Anatolica XV) (Istanbul: Institut français d'études anatoliennes, 2003), 3–8, on p. 4; Eretria: I. Metzger, *Die Hellenistische Keramik in Eretria* (Bern: Francke, 1969) 15; Salamis: C. Diederichs, *Salamine De Chypre IX, Céramiques hellénistiques, romaines et byzantines* (Paris: E. de Boccard, 1980), 27, 65–72; Athens: S.I. Rotroff, *Hellenistic Pottery: The Plain Wares* (Princeton, NJ: American School of Classical Studies at Athens, 2006), 115, 277.

Mold-made Relief Bowls *(Cat. Nos. 38–41)*

The mold was produced on a wheel and the wet clay was engraved with decorative patterns, after which the mold was fired. The wet pot was placed into the mold and pressed strongly, in order to have the decorations on the mold copied to the pot. The details were added after the pot was taken out of the mold.

Bowls with a semi-globular body constitute the majority of the wares in this category. Such bowls were widely produced and used in the Hellenistic period.[56]

The decoration on these bowls can generally be divided into four groups for analysis: plant decoration, knobs in imitation of a pine cone, overlapping patterns and figures.[57] Also known as Megarian Bowls, the pottery sherds in this group are composed of ten fragments collected from SA 1 (3 pieces), 4 (3 pieces), 6 (3 pieces) and 8 (one example). The sherds obtained all belong to bowls with semi-globular bellies. Some of them have gray paste and are slipped in shades of dark gray and black on the exterior. The sherds in the second group (the "pine cone" group) have colours of yellowish red and shades of red and brown; their constituent clays are creamy red, light red and other reddish shades. The sherd with brownish bright red slip and dark gray paste is distinguished from the others by these features *(Cat. No. 39)*. Since the sherds gathered in this category are rather small in size, only three of the ten specimens have sufficient ornamentation to give a slight idea of what their intact appearance would have been. Some of these sherds are ornamented with overlapping leaves with rounded edges[58] whereas on some other examples the edges of the leaves are pointed.[59] Cross-hatching decoration formed by rows of dots is observable on some of the specimens.[60]

---

56 For mold-made bowls, see G.R. Edwards, *Small Objects From The Pnyx: II, Hellenistic Pottery* (Princeton, NJ: American School of Classical Studies, Athens, 1956), 83–85, *Corinthian Hellenistic Pottery* (Corinth Vol. VII.3; Princeton, NJ: American School of Classical Studies at Athens, 1975), 151–153; S.I. Rotroff, *Hellenistic Pottery: Athenian and Imported Moldmade Bowls, Agora XXII* (Princeton, NJ: American School of Classical Studies at Athens, 1982), 2–3.

57 Rotroff, *Hellenistic Pottery*, 15–24.

58 For similar specimens among finds from Ephesus, see S. Ladstätter/C. Auinger, "Zur Datierung und Kunsthistorischen Einordnung einer Apollon Kitharodos-Statuette", in F. Krinzinger (ed.), *Studien zur hellenistichen Keramik in Ephesos* (Wien: Österreichisches archäolog. Inst., 2001) 71–81, on p. 79, Taf. 48.6; E. Dereboylu, "Weissgrundige Keramik und hellenistische Reliefbecher aus dem Hanghaus 2 in Ephesos", in Krinzinger (ed.), *Studien* 21–44, on p. 32, Taf. 15.89.

59 For similar specimens found at Hierapolis, see G. Semeraro, "Hiérapolis de Phrygie. Les ceramiques á reliefs hellénistiques et romaines", in Abadie-Reynal (ed.), *Les Ceramiques en Anatolie*, Fig. 6–7.

60 For similar specimens, see Edwards, *Corinthian Hellenistic Pottery*, 179–182, Fig. 79.920 and Fig. 80.919; U. Hausmann, *Hellenistische Keramik, Eine Brünnenfüllung Nördlich von Bau C und Reliefkeramik Verschiedener Fundplatze in Olympia* (Berlin/New York:Walter de Gruyter, 1996), 92–93, Taf. 39.199–202.

All the sherds come from the upper half of the body and rim. The series of ornamentations observed on the rim of the unclassifiable sherds are composed of egg-arrow, pearl-paillette and three-leaf olive wreath. This and the sheer presence of mold pieces provide a clue to possible local production in Colossae. The general production[61] of relief bowls, spans from the late 3rd century BCE until the early phases of the 1st century BCE.[62] The specimens found in Colossae can generally be dated to the 2nd – 1st centuries BCE.

Cat. No. 38: C.04.66. Dm: 11.6 cm. H: 3.4 cm. Rim, body and handle sherd of a skyphos. On the exterior, overlapping pine cone ornamentation placed side by side and one under another. Dense and hard textured paste, sparsely lime-tempered, 7.5 YR 7/6 (reddish yellow), bright and coarse surface slip 10 R 4/8 (red).

Cat. No. 39: C.07.20. Dm: 12 cm. H: 4.5 cm. Rim and body sherd of a skyphos. There is a single row of circular ornamentation at the junction of the rim and the upper section of the body, and there is a body and arm depiction likely to belong to a figure on the belly. Hard and densely textured paste, dense lime temper gley 2 4/5 PB (dark bluish gray). Bright and coarse exterior slip 2.5 YR 3/3 (dark reddish brown).

Cat. No. 40: C.06.43. Dm: 12 cm. H: 3.5 cm. Rim and body sherd of a skyphos. A single row of "S" sequence on the upper section of the body with an overlapping pine cone ornamentation immediately underneath, hard and densely textured paste, micaceous 5 YR 6/8 (reddish yellow). Semi-matt and semi-gloss slip 2.5 YR 5/8 (red).

Cat. No. 41: C.06.45. H: 3.1 cm. Rim and body sherd of a skyphos. Relief dot ornamentation on the exterior. Paste: hard and densely textured, lime-tempered 7.5 YR 7/4 (pink). Exterior slip flaked off, matt and coarse interior slip surface 5 YR 4/2 (dark reddish gray).

Semi-Glazed Bowls (*Cat. Nos. 42–43*)

Semi-glazed bowls became very common across a wide geographical area after the beginning of the production of glazed pottery in the Hellenistic period.[63] They were cheap and easier to manufacture.

---

61 Rotroff, *Hellenistic Pottery*, 1.

62 F. O. Waage, *Antioch On The Orontes IV. I: Ceramics And Islamic Coins* (Princeton, NJ: Princeton University Press, 1948), 30; Edwards, *Corinthian Hellenistic Pottery*, 152.

63 For semi-glazed specimens, see S. I. Rotroff, *Hellenistic Pottery. Athenian And Imported Wheelmade Table Ware And Related Material.* (The Athenian Agora Vol. XXIX; Princeton, NJ: American School of Classical Studies at Athens, 1997), 159–60, 337, Fig. 61.950–959. These type of specimens were found in Corinth as well as the Athenian Agora: see Edwards, *Corinthian Hellenistic Pottery*, 28–29, Fig. 1, Fig. 43.2, 6, 11, 15. During the Knidos excavations,

Wares of this type are half glazed and half unglazed. The glaze starts at the rim and is applied up to the middle of the body. In addition, it is sometimes observed that the glaze that ended in the middle of the body dripped paint towards the base. Two of the three specimens of this type found in SA 4 and 1 in Colossae are base sherds while the other one is a body sherd. Among the specimens, the sherds *Cat. No. 42* and *Cat. No. 43* have a dark brownish-red bright interior slip, whereas the colour of the exterior is dark brownish-black on a camel slip decorated with dripped paint marks from the upper body down to the beginning of the base.

Specimens similar to fragment *Cat. No. 43* of this group, which had started to be produced in Anatolia in the early phases of the third century BCE,[64] were found in the Athenian Agora. They were included in the class of wide-scale bowls and dated between 70 BCE and the early phases of the first century CE.[65] This type of ware has been found in Tarsus-Gözlükule. F. F. Jones classifies it under the heading "Local Hellenistic" and a number of examples were found there in levels dated to the Hellenistic and Roman periods.[66] A bowl from Tarsus decorated with drip paint markings similar to the specimens of Colossae has been dated to the Middle Hellenistic period.[67] Also, one of four sherds similar to our specimens, was found in a datable context at Sardis and belongs to the late Hellenistic period.[68]

Cat. No. 42: C.04.71. H: 2.7 cm. Drops of paint on the external surface of the base and body sherd of a ring-base bowl, 2.5 YR 5/8 (red), semi-brilliant and coarse interior slip 10 R 4/4 (weak red), 7.5 YR 7/3 pink on the exterior, hard and densely textured paste, sparsely lime-tempered 7.5 YR 7/4 (pink).

Cat. No. 43: C.04.31. H: 2.4 cm. Base sherd of a body of a high ring-base dish. Medium-hard paste, densely textured, lime-tempered 5 YR 7/6 (reddish yellow). Slip is semi-matt and slip- on the interior and exterior, 2.5 YR 4/4 (reddish brown) on the interior, 7.5 YR 8/4 (pink) on the exterior. Bright, high gloss slip 2.5 Y 2.5/1 (black).

---

semi-glazed unguentarium specimens were found in the cistern and were dated between the 2nd century BCE and the last quarter of the 1st century BCE: see E. Doksanaltı, "Knidos-Kap Krio Helenistik Sarnıç Buluntuları", in Abadie-Reynal (ed.), *Les Ceramiques en Anatolie*, 31, 33, Fig. XXI.5. For specimens of Sardis, see S. Rotroff/A. Oliver/I. Hanfmann/G. Hanfmann, *The Hellenistic Pottery from Sardis: The Finds through 1994* (Cambridge: The Archeological Exploration of Sardis, 2003), 31, Fig. 7–14.

64 Rotroff et al., *Hellenistic pottery from Sardis*, 24.

65 Rotroff, *Athenian And Imported Wheelmade Table Ware*, 337.

66 F. F. Jones, *Excavations at Gözlükule, Tarsus, Vol.1: The Hellenistic and Roman Periods: The Pottery*, H. Goldman (ed.) (Princeton, NJ: Princeton University Press, 1950), 215, Fig. 122.70–71, 80, Fig. 123. 83, 92.

67 Jones, *Excavations at Gözlükule*, Fig. 123.83.

68 Rotroff et al., *Hellenistic pottery from Sardis*, Fig. 7.33, Fig. 8.37, Fig. 9.43, Fig. 12.63 – see at page 24.

Gray-Black Slip-Ware (*Cat. Nos. 44–47*)

Gray-paste wares, plain black slip-ware on the interior and exterior and produced by reducing air during firing, constitute a group frequently encountered in the whole Mediterranean and in Anatolia.[69] A total of 13 sherds were found in SA numbers 1, 2, 4 and 6 in Colossae. The potteries of this group are all body and border sherds. They have bright and matt slip in shades of black and brown on the interior and exterior surfaces and their paste colours are gray in a variety of shades.

The specimens examined can be divided into two groups. The three sherds in the first group are lustrous black-slipped ware and have fine paste of good quality. Ten sherds of the second group have hard and porous paste and their slip varies between shades of matt black and light brown.

Bright black slip is observed in the early specimens of the gray-paste pottery sherds produced from the Hellenistic Period to the Early Roman period while the later specimens are slipped in shades of black.[70] Thus, we can date the fragments in the first group to the beginnings of the Hellenistic Period and in the second group to the late phases of the same period.

Cat. No. 44: C.04.55. Dm: 13 cm. H: 0.6 cm. sherd of a thin convex-rim lid. Hard and densely textured paste, densely lime- and sparsely mica-tempered 5 YR 6/1 (gray). Bright, high gloss slip 2.5 Y 2.5/1 (black).

Cat. No. 45: C.02.24. Dm: 18 cm. H: 4.1 cm. rim and body sherd of a deep bowl with a grooved rim. Soft-textured paste with large pores, very little mica and lime temper with large particles 5 Y 5/1 gray. Bright, high gloss slip, gley 1 6/N (gray) on the interior, gley 1 2.5/N (black) on the exterior.

Cat. No. 46: C.06.28. Dm: 17.5 cm. H: 2.2 cm. rim body sherd of a wide dish with a thin convex rim. Hard and densely textured paste, densely micaceous 5 Y 6/1 (gray). Bright, high gloss slip, gley 1 2.5/N (black).

Cat. No. 47: C.03.17. Dm: 20 cm. H: 2 cm. Rim and body sherd of a deep bowl with a slightly incurved convex rim at the top and lip thickened out. Soft-textured porous paste, sparse mica, lime and pottery sherd temper 5 Y 7/1 light gray. Bright, high gloss slip, gley 1 2.5/N (black).

---

69 For gray-paste pottery, see Rotroff, *Athenian And Imported Wheelmade Table Ware*, 232–33, Rotroff *et al.*, *Hellenistic pottery from Sardis*, 31–32.

70 Rotroff *et al.*, *Hellenistic pottery from Sardis*, 31.

Lead-Glazed Pottery (*Cat. No. 48–49*)

From the excavations carried out to date, lead-glazed pottery is considered to have been of eastern Mediterranean origin. This type of pottery includes the group of wares which are yellow-glazed on the interior, green-glazed on the exterior and have various relief ornamentations.[71] In Turkish excavations till the present, lead-glazed pottery sherds have been found in Tarsus, Smyrna, Perge, Sardis, Arykanda and Laodicea.[72]

In surveys conducted in Colossae, four rim and body sherds were found in SA numbers 4 and 6 that can be tied to the lead-glazed pottery due to their ornamentations.[73] Dot rows, made as relief and which covered the whole body, are observed on these sherds (*Cat. Nos. 48–49).*[74] Besides these, a lead-glazed pottery mold with a negative pine cone decoration was found in SA 1,[75] a clear indication of local production.

These sherds have camel, light red and reddish brown pastes. All four fragments are slipped in shades of brown and red on the interior and exterior. The fact that no glazing was encountered on the sherds may indicate that these wares were broken before being glazed, also a further indication of local production.

The presence of this group, produced in a short period of time between 50 BCE and 50 CE, in Colossae as well, provides us with clues that not only had the type dispersed on the axis of western Anatolia but also had been produced in the southwestern section of Phrygia.

Cat. No. 48: C.06.90. Dm: 12 cm. H: 2.6 cm. Body and base sherds of skyphos. Relief dot rows on the whole body. Soft and densely textured paste 7.5 YR 7/4 (pink). Matt and coarse slip 5 YR 7/6 (reddish yellow).

---

71 For further information about lead-glazed pottery, see Jones, *Excavations at Gözlükule*, 191–96, K. Greene, "Late Hellenistic and Early Roman Invention and Innovation The Case of Lead-Glazed Pottery", *AJA* 111.4 (2007) 653–671.

72 For specimens of Tarsus, see Jones, *Excavations at Gözlükule*, 260–64; for Smyrna: Rotroff *et al.*, *Hellenistic pottery from Sardis*, 171; for Perge: N. Atik, *Die Keramik aus den Südthermen von Perge* (Tübingen: Ernst Wasmuth, 1995), 18–58; for Sardis: Rotroff *et al.*, *Hellenistic pottery from Sardis*, 169–73; for Arykanda: A. Oransay, "Arykanda'dan Bir Grup Kurşun Sırlı Seramik", in C. Özgünel/O.Bingöl (ed.), *Gün Işığında Anadolu, Cevdet Bayburtluoğlu İçin Yazılar* (İstanbul: Homer Kitabevi, 2001), 171–78. Information on Laodikeia has been supplied by the leader of the current excavations, Professor Celal Şimşek.

73 Compare Rotroff *et al*, *Hellenistic pottery from Sardis*, 170–71.

74 For the lead-glazed pottery, on which relief dot rows are described, see Jones, *Excavations at Gözlükule*, Fig. 153.660; Atik, *Die Keramik*, Abb.22.58; Oransay, "Arykanda'dan", 25, 26; Rotroff *et al.*, *Hellenistic pottery from Sardis*, Fig. 131.743, 744.

75 For a similar mold and specimens of lead-glazed pottery observed to have such a decoration, see Jones, *Excavations at Gözlükule*, Fig. 153.665, 151.635, 152.640, 152.655, 153.669; Rotroff *et al.*, *Hellenistic pottery from Sardis*, Fig. 131.745, Atik, *Die Keramik*, Abb. 17.19, 23.70.

Cat. No. 49: C.06.45. Dm: 14 cm. H: 3 cm. Rim and body sherd of skyphos. Relief dot rows on the whole body. Soft and densely textured paste 10 YR 8/3 (very pale brown). Matt and coarse slip 2.5 YR 5/4 (reddish brown).

Roman Red-Slipped Pottery (*Cat. Nos. 50–57*)

While there are various discussions about the manufacturing centres of red-slipped pottery, it is agreed that the type is of eastern Mediterranean origin. Available information about its dispersal is increased regularly by on-going archaeological excavations and surface surveys.

Sherds of a number of red-slipped pottery groups were found in our surveys at Colossae. Fragments of the Sagalassos Red Slip (SRS) ware are numerous among the sherds obtained from the SAs; additionally several sherds of the groups *Eastern Sigillata A* (ESA) and *Eastern Sigillata B* (ESB) are also among the finds.[76] A number of the fragments in question obtained from different sampling areas are bowl and dish shapes. The red-slipped pottery in this group are dated between 1st century BCE and 1st century CE.

Cat. No. 50: C.04.65. Dm: 24 cm. H: 2.5 cm. Rim and body sherd, thin rim flat at the top, wide shallow dish. Soft and loose textured paste 10 YR 8/4 very pale brown. Partially flaked bright slip, 10 R 4/8 (red) on the interior and exterior; 5 YR 3/3 (dark reddish brown) on the exterior rim. ESB.[77]

Cat. No. 51: C.04.64. Dm: 24.5 cm. H: 2.4 cm. Rim and body sherd. Rim thickened out, wide and shallow dish channeled at the top. Soft and densely textured paste, untempered 10 YR 8/4 (very pale brown). Bright, high gloss slip 2.5 YR 6/8 (light red). ESB.[78]

---

76 Sigillatas are pottery ware of fine material, and often pale in colour. For information about the origin of Eastern Sigillatas and groupings, see K.M. Kenyon, "Roman and Later Wares", in J.W. Crowfoot/G.M. Crowfoot/K.M. Kenyon, *Samaria-Sebaste III. The Objects from Samaria* (London: Palestine Exploration Fund, 1957), 281–284; Ch. F. Johansen, "Les terres sigillées orientales", in A.P. Christensen/Ch. F. Johansen (ed.), *Hama Fouilles et Recherches de la Fondation Carlsberg 1931–1938, III 2: Les poteries hellénistiques et les terres sigillées orientales* (Copenhague: Fondation Carlsberg,1971), 55–208, on pp. 55–57; J.W. Hayes, "Sigillate Orientali", in *Enciclopedia dell'arte antica, classica e orientale, Atlante delle forme ceramiche II. Ceramica fine romana nel bacino mediterraneo* (Rome: Istituto della Enciclopedia italiana, 1985) 1–96, on pp. 9–28. For the primary centres of finds in Anatolia, see L. Zoroğlu, "Samsat'da Bulunan Doğu Sigillataları İlk Rapor", *Selçuk Üniversitesi Fen-Edebiyat Fakültesi Edebiyat Dergisi* 3 (1986) 64–68.

77 Hayes, "Sigillate Orientali", Tav. XIII. 16. Form 53.

78 Hayes, "Sigillate Orientali", Tav. XII. 5. Form 13B.

Cat. No. 52: *C.04.49. Dm: 9 cm. H: 1 cm. Body and base sherd of low-base shallow dish. Soft and densely textured paste, sparsely mica- and lime-tempered 5 YR 7/6 (reddish yellow). Bright, high gloss red slip 2.5 YR 5/8 (red). ESB.*

Cat. No. 53: *C.01.44. Dm: 18.8 cm. H: 2.5 cm. Rim and body sherd. Slightly convex rim at the top, lip thickened out, incurving deep bowl. Hard and densely textured paste, lime tempered with large particles 2.5 YR 6/8(light red). Bright, high gloss slip 2.5 YR 5/8 (red). SRS.[79]*

Cat. No. 54: *C.06.73. Dm: 10.5 cm. H: 3 cm. Rim and body sherd, deep bowl with thin rim. Hard and densely textured paste, sparsely lime-tempered 5 YR 6/8 (reddish yellow). Semi-bright and gloss slip 2.5 YR 5/8(red). SRS.[80]*

Cat. No. 55: *C.04.72. Dm: 10 cm. H: 1.7 cm. Rim and body sherd. Rim convex at the top, lip thickened out. Hard and densely textured paste, sparsely lime-tempered 2.5 YR 7/6 (light red). 5 YR 4/6 (yellowish red) on the exterior of brilliant slipped-rim; 2.5 YR 4/8 (red) on the interior and exterior. SRS.[81]*

Cat. No. 56: *C.04.20. Dm: 9 cm. H: 1.8 cm. Body and base fragment, high ringbase, wide and shallow dish. Soft and densely textured paste, sparsely lime-tempered 5 YR 7/6 (reddish yellow). Bright, high gloss slip 5 YR 7/8 (reddish yellow).*

Conclusion

The pottery found at Colossae establishes that there was continuous settlement at the site from the Late Chalcolithic to the Byzantine periods. Although a considerable amount of pottery of the Roman and Late Antique periods was found in sampling areas outside the höyük cone (SA numbers 6–8), the concentration of finds and the indications of continuity (back to two specimens from the Late Bronze Age) show that settlement was concentrated at the mound. The continuity and occasional direct evidence (such as pottery molds) also establishes that there was extensive pottery production at Colossae, albeit directly influenced by styles and types from elsewhere in Anatolia and the Mediterranean.

The agricultural activities carried out on and around the höyük cone have led to considerable destruction of artefacts particularly in the northern and southern sections of the settlement. Besides modern destruction, it is clear that the settlement fabric has also been damaged during constructions at some time or times in the periods under review. The best example of this is observed in SA 5, where the theatre cavea is located. The fact that the majority of the pottery we found during our surveys in and around the theatre belongs to the EBA shows

---

79 J. Poblome/R. Degeest/M. Waelkens/E. Scheltens, "The Fine Ware", in M. Waelkens (ed.), *Sagalassos I* (Acts Archaeologica Lovaniensia Monographiae 5; Leuven: Leuven University Press, 1993), Fig. 96, 1C 170.

80 Poblome, *et al.*, "The Fine Ware", fig. 96, 1C 120.

81 Poblome, *et al.*, "The Fine Ware", fig. 94, 1B 190.

that this section of the höyük had been heavily re-shaped during the building developments, probably during the Roman Period.

This later incision into a prehistoric settlement at Colossae has an interesting parallel at Aphrodisias where a similar formation was substantially quarried out for the construction of the theatre there.[82] Given the extent of the prehistoric materials detected on the höyük as a whole, the settlement appears to have been substantial and considerably built up in the third and second millennia BCE.

Only two amorphous sherds from the Early Iron Age were found at Colossae compared with widespread findings elsewhere in south-western Anatolia. This suggests that the settlement had lost considerable influence at the end of the Late Bronze Age and become weaker with the advent of the Iron Age. However, because it was located on the main trade route that linked to the Euphrates via Iconium and extended from Sardis to Kelanai, Colossae held a geographical advantage at least until the Late Roman period.

Although the centre of the city had largely shifted to Chonai in Late Antiquity, the coins and pottery found during our surveys indicate that the settlement in the area of the höyük continued for some time through the Byzantine period.

The glazed potteries of the Byzantine Period dated to the 12th century CE, the fact that a coin dated to the 11th century CE was found during the surface surveys indicate that significant levels of settlement continued on the höyük cone after the Arab invasions. All this strengthens the assertion that the history of Colossae is extensive and continuous.

---

82 B. Kadish, "Excavations of Prehistoric Remains at Aphrodisias, 1967", *AJA* 73 (1969) 49–65, on p. 51, ill. 2; only a few steps have been recovered so far from the cavea section of the theatre which was constructed by carving out the main rock about 100 metres northeast of the acropolis.

Figures and drawings referred to in the text

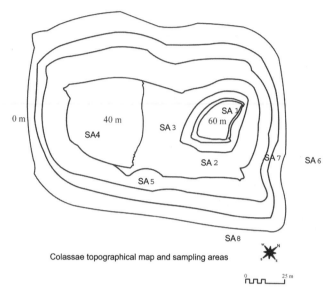

Drawing 1 The sampling areas

Graphs. 2.1–8 *General results from each pottery sampling area*

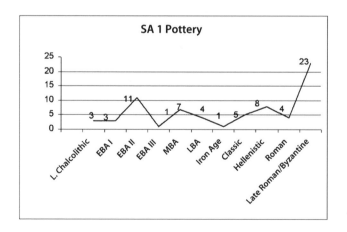

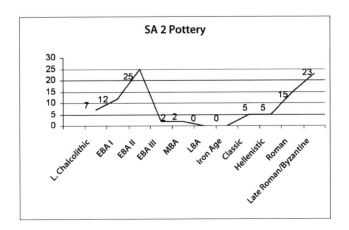

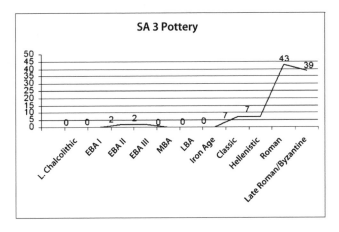

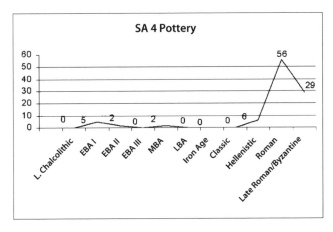

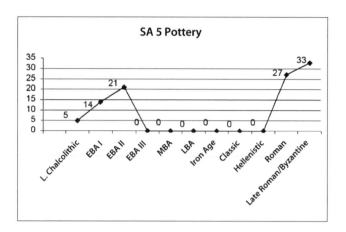

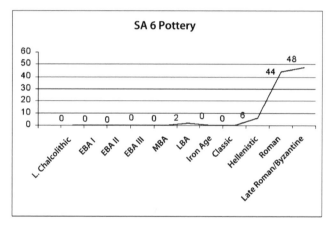

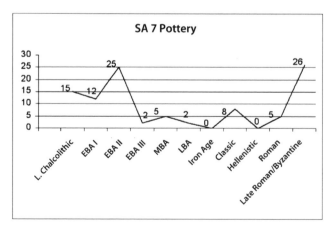

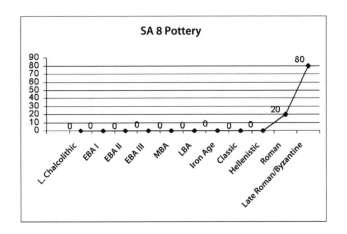

Catalogue drawings

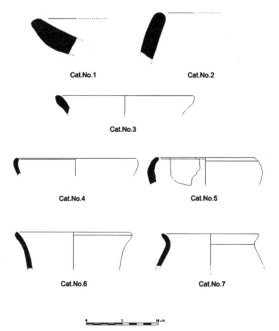

Cat.No.1   Cat.No.2

Cat.No.3

Cat.No.4   Cat.No.5

Cat.No.6   Cat.No.7

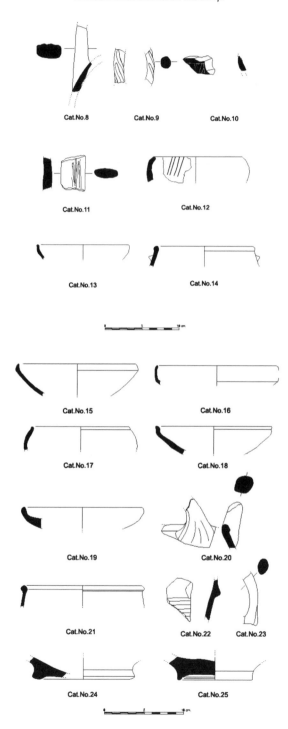

Cat.No.8   Cat.No.9   Cat.No.10

Cat.No.11   Cat.No.12

Cat.No.13   Cat.No.14

Cat.No.15   Cat.No.16

Cat.No.17   Cat.No.18

Cat.No.19   Cat.No.20

Cat.No.21   Cat.No.22   Cat.No.23

Cat.No.24   Cat.No.25

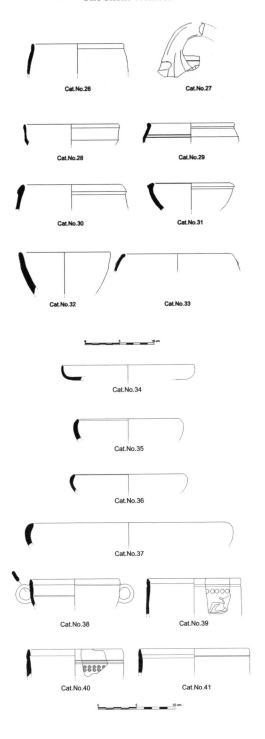

Cat.No.26

Cat.No.27

Cat.No.28

Cat.No.29

Cat.No.30

Cat.No.31

Cat.No.32

Cat.No.33

Cat.No.34

Cat.No.35

Cat.No.36

Cat.No.37

Cat.No.38

Cat.No.39

Cat.No.40

Cat.No.41

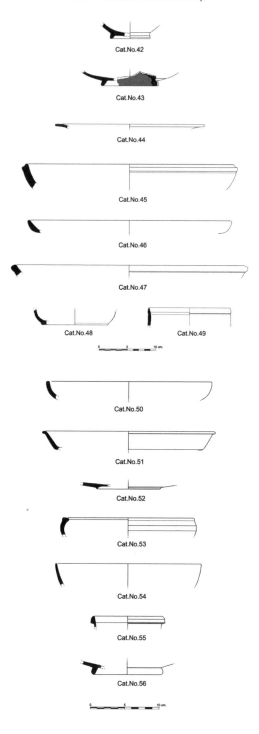

Cat.No.42

Cat.No.43

Cat.No.44

Cat.No.45

Cat.No.46

Cat.No.47

Cat.No.48   Cat.No.49

Cat.No.50

Cat.No.51

Cat.No.52

Cat.No.53

Cat.No.54

Cat.No.55

Cat.No.56

Bibliography

Abay, E./F. Dedeoğlu, "2003 Yılı Denizli/Çivril Ovası Yüzey Araştırması (Annual Report on Survey Research in the Denizli/Çivril area)", *Araştırma Sonuçları Toplantısı* 2 (2005) 42–50.

Anderson-Stojanovic, V.R., "The University of Chicago Excavations in the Rachi Settlement at Isthmia, 1989", *Hesperia* 65 (1996) 57–98.

Atik, N., *Die Keramik aus den Südthermen von Perge* (Tübingen: Ernst Wasmuth, 1995).

Belke, J./N. Mersich, *Tabula Imperii Byzantini Bd 7: Phrygien und Pisidien* (Vienna: Österreichische Akademie der Wissenschaften, 1990).

Blegen, C.W./J.L. Caskey/M. Rawson/J. Sperling, *Troy I: General Introduction: The First and Second Settlements* (Princeton, NJ: Princeton University Press, 1950).

– *Troy III. The Sixth Settlement* (Princeton: Princeton University Press, 1953).

Crowfoot, J.W./G.M. Crowfoot/K.M. Kenyon, *Samaria-Sebaste. Reports of the Work of the Joint Expedition in 1931–1933 and of the British Expedition in 1935, No. 3, The Objects from Samaria* (London: Palestine Exploration Fund, 1957).

Dereboylu, E., "Weissgrundige Keramik und hellenistische Reliefbecher aus dem Hanghaus 2 in Ephesos", in F. Krinzinger (ed.), *Studien zur hellenistichen Keramik in Ephesos* (Wien: Österreichisches archäologisches Institut, 2001) 21–44.

Diederichs, C., *Salamine De Chypre IX, Céramiques hellénistiques, romaines et byzantines* (Paris: E. de Boccard, 1980).

Doksanaltı, E., "Knidos-Kap Krio Helenistik Sarnıç Buluntuları", in C. Abadie-Reynal (ed.), *Les Céramiques en Anatolie aux Époques hellénistique et romaine* (Varia Anatolica XV; Istanbul: Institut français d'études anatoliennes, 2003) 27–33.

Duman, B./E. Konakçı, "Kolossai: Höyük, Kalıntı ve Buluntuları (Colossae: the Mound, Remains and Findings)", *Arkeoloji Dergisi* 8 (2006) 83–111.

Duru, R., *Kuruçay Höyük II* (Ankara: Türk Tarih Kurumu, 1996).

Edwards, G.R., *Small Objects From The Pnyx: II, Hellenistic Pottery* (Princeton, NJ: American School of Classical Studies, Athens, 1956).

– *Corinthian Hellenistic Pottery* (Corinth Vol. VII.3; Princeton, NJ: American School of Classical Studies at Athens, 1975).

Efe, T., "Pottery distribution within the Bronze Age of western Anatolia and its implications upon cultural, political (ethnic?) entities", in M. Özbaşaran/O. Tanındı/ A. Boratav (ed.), *Archaeological essays in honour of homo amatus: Güven Arsebük için armağan yazılar* (İstanbul: Ege Yayınları, 2003) 87–104.

Goldman, H., *Excavation at Gözlü Kule, Tarsus; The Hellenistic and Roman Periods. Vol. I.* (Princeton, NJ: Princeton University Press, 1950).

Göney, S., *Büyük Menderes Bölgesi* (İstanbul: İstanbul Üniversitesi Edebiyat Fakültesi Matbaası, 1975).

Grene, D. (trans.), *The History of Herodotus* (Chicago/London: University of Chicago Press, 1987).

Günel, S., *Panaztepe II: M.Ö. 2. bine tarihlendirilen Panaztepe seramiğinin Batı Anadolu ve Ege Arkeolojisindeki yeri ve önemi* (Yayınları: Türk Tarih Kurumu, 1999).

Hamilton, W.J., "Extracts from Notes made on a Journey in Asia Minor in 1836", *JRGS* 7 (1837) 34–61.

– *Researches in Asia Minor, Pontus and Armenia* (2 vol.; London: J. Murray, 1842).

Hausmann, U. *Hellenistische Keramik, Eine Brünnenfüllung Nördlich von Bau C und Reliefkeramik Verschiedener Fundplätze in Olympia* (Berlin/New York: Walter de Gruyter, 1996).

Hayes, J. W., "Sigillate Orientali", in *Enciclopedia dell'arte antica, classica e orientale, Atlante delle forme ceramiche II. Ceramica fine romana nel bacino mediterraneo* (Rome: Istituto della Enciclopedia italiana, 1985) 1–96.

Hill, G. F., "Apollo and St Michael: Some Analogies", *JHS* 36 (1916) 134–62.

Johansen, Ch.F., "Les terres sigillées orientales" in A. P. Christensen and Ch. F. Johansen (ed.), *Hama Fouilles et Recherches de la Fondation Carlsberg 1931–1938, III 2: Les poteries hellénistiques et les terres sigillées orientales.* Copenhague: Fondation Carlsberg, 1971, 55–208.

Jones, F. F., *Excavations at Gözlükule, Tarsus, Vol.1: The Hellenistic and Roman Periods: The Pottery* (edited by H. Goldman) (Princeton, NJ: Princeton University Press, 1950).

Joukowsky, M. S., *Prehistoric Aphrodisias: An Account of the Excavations and Artifact Studies.* (Court-St.-Etienne, Belgium: Imprimerie E. Oleffe, 1986).

Kadish, B. "Excavations of Prehistoric Remains at Aphrodisias, 1967", *AJA* 73 (1969) 49–65.

Kamil, T., *Yortan Cemetery in the Early Bronze Age of Western Anatolia* (Oxford: BAR, 1982).

Konakçi, E./B. Duman, "Arkeolojik ve Yazılı Kanıtlar Isığında Kolossai", in *International Symposium on the History and Culture of Denizli and its Surroundings* (2 vol.; Denizli: Pamukkale University, 2007) 2.57–67.

Ladstätter, S./C. Auinger, "Zur Datierung und Kunsthistorischen Einordnung einer Apollon Kitharodos-Statuette", in F. Krinzinger (ed.), *Studien zur hellenistichen Keramik in Ephesos.* (Wien: Österreichisches archäologisches Institut, 2001) 71–81.

Lamb, W., *Excavations at Thermi in Lesbos* (Cambridge: Cambridge University Press/ New York: Macmillan, 1936).

–   "Excavations at Kusura Near Afyon Karahisar", *Archaeologia* 86 (1937) 1–64.

Lapp, P. W., *Palestinian Ceramic Chronology, 200 B. C. – A. D. 70* (New Haven: American Schools of Oriental Research, 1961).

Lloyd, S./J. Mellaart, *Beycesultan I: The Chalcolithic and Early Bronze Age Levels* (London: BIAA, 1972).

–   *Beycesultan Vol II: Middle Bronze Age Architecture and Pottery* (London: BIAA, 1965).

Marchese, R. T., "Report on the West Acropolis Excavations at Aphrodisias: 1971–1973", *AJA* 80 (1976) 393–412.

–   *The Lower Maeander Flood Plain. A Regional Settlement Study (British Archaeological Reports International Series* 292[i]) (Oxford: BAR, 1986).

Mellaart, J., "Preliminary Report on a Survey of Pre-Classical Remains in Southern Turkey", *AS* 4 (1954) 175–240.

Mellaart, J./A. Murray, *Beycesultan Vol III, Part II: Late Bronze Age and Phrygian Pottery and Middle and Late Bronze Age Small Objects* (London: BIAA, 1995).

Meriç, R., "Excavations at Bademgediği Tepe (Puranda) 1999–2002: A Preliminary Report", *Istanbuler Mitteilungen* 53 (2003) 79–98.

Metzger, I., *Die Hellenistische Keramik in Eretria* (Bern: Francke, 1969).

Monte, G. F./J. Tischler *Répertoire Géographique des Textes Cunéiformes* Vol. VI (Wiesbaden: L. Reichert, 1978).

Oransay, A., "Arykanda'dan Bir Grup Kurşun Sırlı Seramik", in C. Özgünel/O. Bingöl (ed.), *Gün Işığında Anadolu, Cevdet Bayburtluoğlu İçin Yazılar* (İstanbul: Homer Kitabevi, 2001) 171–78.

Pecorella, P. E., *La Cultura Preistorica di Iasos in Caria* (Rome: G. Bretschneider, 1984).

Poblome, J./R. Degeest/M. Waelkens/E. Scheltens, "The Fine Ware", in M. Waelkens (ed.), *Sagalassos I* (Acts Archaeologica Lovaniensia Monographiae 5; Leuven: Leuven University Press, 1993) 113–30.

Radt, W./G. de Luca, "Grabungen im Fundament des Pergamonaltars. Grobe Keramik-Graue Sondergruppe-Lampen", in C. Abadie-Reynal (ed.), *Les Céramiques en Anatolie aux Époques hellénistique et romaine* (Varia Anatolica XV: Istanbul: Institut français d'études anatoliennes, 2003) 3–8.

Rotroff, S. I., *Hellenistic Pottery: Athenian and Imported Moldmade Bowls, Agora XXII* (Princeton, NJ: American School of Classical Studies at Athens, 1982).

– *Hellenistic Pottery. Athenian And Imported Wheelmade Table Ware And Related Material.* (The Athenian Agora Vol. XXIX: Princeton, NJ: American School of Classical Studies at Athens, 1997).

– *Hellenistic Pottery: The Plain Wares* (Princeton, NJ: American School of Classical Studies at Athens, 2006).

Rotroff, S./A. Oliver/I. Hanfmann/G. Hanfmann, *The Hellenistic Pottery from Sardis: The Finds through 1994* (Cambridge: The Archeoloogical Exploration of Sardis, 2003).

Ruge, W., "Kolossai", in G. Wissowa (ed.), *Paulys Real-Encyclopädie der Classichen Altertumswissenschaft* (Stuttgart: J. B. Metzlersche, 1921) Vol 11.1.1119.

Schafer, J., *Hellenistische Keramik Aus Pergamon* (Berlin: Walter de Gruyter, 1968).

Semeraro, G., "Hiérapolis de Phrygie. Les ceramiques á reliefs hellénistiques et romaines", in C. Abadie-Reynal (ed.), *Les Céramiques en Anatolie aux Époques hellénistique et romaine* (Varia Anatolica XV; Istanbul: Institut français d'études anatoliennes, 2003) 83–89.

Şimşek, C., "Kolossai", *Arkeoloji ve Sanat* 107 (2002) 3–17.

Vessberg, O./A. Westholm, *The Swedish Cyprus Expedition Vol. IV. Part 3, The Hellenistic and Roman Periods in Cyprus* (Stockholm: Swedish Cyprus Expedition, 1956).

Waage, F. O., *Antioch On The Orontes IV. I: Ceramics And Islamic Coins* (Princeton, NJ: Princeton University Press, 1948).

Weber, G., "Der unterirdische Lauf des Lykos bei Kolossai", *Ath.Mitt.* 16 (1891) 194–99.

Yıldız, H., "Denizli Müzesi Müdürlüğü Lykos Vadisi Çalışmaları", *Müze Kurtarma Kazıları Semineri* 9 (1999) 247–62.

Zoroğlu, L., "Samsat'da Bulunan Doğu Sigillataları İlk Rapor", *Selçuk Üniversitesi Fen-Edebiyat Fakültesi Edebiyat Dergisi* 3 (1986) 61–100.

Chapter 11

A stratigraphy of an ancient city through its key story: the archistrategos of Chonai

Alan H. Cadwallader

The Story of St Michael the Archangel

The discrete tellings of the story

The story of St. Michael the archangel of Chonai is known through a number of sources, both textual and visual. Visual representations are found in icons, frescoes, gems, enamelled craft and seals. These all focus on what has become the climax of the story in the textual narratives — the funnelling of a deluge of water as a massive act of deliverance by the archistrategos of the heavenly host, Michael the archangel.

The literary telling occurs in a number of genres: a popular narration with two refined literary recensions, panegyric sermons, a complex epigram, liturgical summaries, occasional brief notices, even an inscription on a reliquary.[1] It

---

1 See Theodoret of Cyrrhus (c. 430 CE), *Interp. ad Ep Col.* (PG 82.613B, 620D–621A); W. Lueken, *Michael: Eine Darstellung und Vergleichung der jüdischen und der morgenländisch-christlichen Tradition vom Erzengel Michael* (Göttingen: Vandenhoeck & Ruprecht, 1898), 75 (11th century); Constantine Porphyrogenitus, *Them.* 3.36, (edition: A. Pertusi, *Costantino Porfirogenito De Thematibus* (Vatican: Biblioteca Apostolica Vaticana, 1952), 68 (ninth-tenth century); panegyrics by Pantaleon the Deacon (*PG* 98. 1264A, 12th century), Nicetas the Paphlagonian (Cod. Paris. Gr. 1180) described by Ehrhard and Halkin as much mutilated (A. Ehrhard, *Überlieferung und Bestand der hagiographischen und homiletischen Literatur der griechischen Kirche* (3 vol.; Leipzig: J.C. Hinrichs, 1937–1939), 2.239–40, F. Halkin, *Bibliotheca hagiographica graeca* (3 vol; Brussels: Societé des Bollandistes, 1957), 2.119) and one accredited to John of Damascus but of considerably later date, judged by Nau as of no value (F. Nau, "Le Miracle de Saint Michel a Colosses", *PO* 4 (1908) 542–62, on p. 545 n2); Nicetas Choniates, *Chron.* 178.19–22 (J. L. van Dieten, (ed.), *Nicetae Choniatae Historia* (Berlin: Walter de Gruyter, 1975) (12th century), Michael Choniates *Encom. Nic.* 95 (S. P. Lampros, Μιχαὴλ Ἀκομινάτου τοῦ Χωνάτου τά σωζόμενα (2 vol.; Groningen: Bouma, 1968 [1879]), 1.56, lines 12–18)) (12th century); Manuel Philes, *Carmina* 226 (E. Miller (ed.), *Manuelis Philae carmina ex codicibus Escurialensis, Florentinis, Parisinis et Vaticanis* (2 vol.; Paris: Imperial Printers, 1855–1857), 1.23) (13th century); Symeon Metaphrastes, *Menologion* (10th century) (see generally, Halkin, *Bibliotheca*, 2.118–121); for the early 11th century reliquary, see S. Werner, "Das Reliquarkreuz des Leon 'Damokranites'", in W. Hörander *et al* (ed.), *Byzantios: Festschrift für Hubert Hunger zum 70 Geburtstag* (Vienna: E. Becvar, 1984) 301–10.

was translated into Latin in the eleventh century.[2] This range of literary genres and material representations combined with the prevalence of the image (often with inscription) on the seals of Metropolitan bishops of Chonai[3] testify to the popularity of the story and the importance of the associated site.[4] For this essay, I wish to focus on the anonymous popular narration.[5]

The story in brief

The story focuses on the rescue of a shrine and its surrounds by the archangel Michael, the archistrategos and taxiarch. The shrine is marked as a place of healing from apostolic times but even then had come as the fulfilment of a promise from the archangel wedded into the apostolic mission from Hierapolis into Phrygia by St John and St Philip. It is specifically recognised by a pagan who approaches from Laodicea for the restoration of his mute daughter. In gratitude for her healing, he provides for the building of a shrine which is later attended by a custodian named Archippos. Its christian fame threatens other religious devotion, especially associated with Artemis-Echidna and the Great Mother. Consequently, a militant force, fired up by the devil, gathers at Laodicea to plot its destruction. The initial conspiracy — to commingle the sacred healing water with that of a primeval river, the Chruses, miraculously comes to naught. The next plan, prodigious in its scope, is to dam the flow of two rivers, the Lykokapros and the Koufos, until a huge flood pours down for the destruction of the shrine, its custodian and devotees. As Archippos prays for redemption, Michael descends, shatters an impenetrable monolith to forge a shaft to evacuate the deluge into an

---

2 See Nau, "Le Miracle", 545.

3 See, for example, the seal of Metropolitan Konstantinos (c. 1050 CE): J. Nesbitt/N. Oikonomides, *Catalogue of Byzantine Seals at Dumbarton Oaks and in the Fogg Museum of Art III: West, Northwest and Central Asia Minor and the Orient* (Washington, DC: Dumbarton Oaks Publications, 1996), § 12.1; *cf* § 99.7, § 2.30.

4 It may also be a means of cementing the Metropolitan's authority in his new position: see J. Cotsonis, "Saints and Cult Centers: A Geographic and Administrative Perspective in Light of Byzantine Lead Seals", *SBS* 8 (2003) 9–26, on p. 23.

5 The standard edition is that of M. Bonnet, *Narratio de Miraculo a Michaele Archangelo Chonis Patrato* (Paris: Librairie Hachette, 1890) and references herein rely upon his text and apparatus. Nau provided a number of adjustments to the critical Greek text (not always to be uncontested however): "Le miracle", 546. A translation into French was provided by B. Bouvier/F. Amsler, "Le Miracle de l'Archange Michel à Chonai: Introduction, Traduction, et Notes", in D. H. Warren/A. G. Brock/D. W. Pao (ed.), *Early Christian Voices: in texts, traditions and symbols: Essays in Honor of François Bovon* (Boston/Leiden: Brill Academic Publishers, 2003) 395–407. See my English translation in the appendix to this collection. Bonnet's edition also contains the edition of Simeon Metaphrastes. For that of Sisinnius, see J. Stiltingo/C. Suyskeno/J. Periero/J. Cleo (ed.), *Acta Sanctorum: September* (Paris/Rome: Victor Palmé, 1869 [1762]), volume 8, 41C–47C.

underground chasm. The enemies are defeated, Archippos' devotion is vindicated and the shrine becomes an even more famous healing centre. In references to the story that follow, see the translation in the appendix to this paper. Chapters have been divided into verse sections for ease of reference.

Assessments of the story

Philip Schaff impugned the story as resting "on no doctrine and no facts, but on the sandy foundation of miraculous legends"[6] When William Mitchell Ramsay first began to investigate the Byzantine period of Asia Minor, he held out high hopes that the various lives of saints would yield much important data about local history.[7] The anticipation was short-lived, at least as far as the story of St. Michael of Chonai is concerned. By 1890, he was writing, "The published versions … are late and topographically absurd, but must be founded on an original of good character, full of local colour."[8] In 1893 the document "is a very late fabrication, probably not earlier than the ninth century. … a curious mixture of knowledge and ignorance"[9] Two years later in the two volume expansion of his earlier articles, *The Cities and Bishoprics of Phrygia*, he bluntly held "no *Acta* of any value connected with the valley or with S. W. Phrygia have been published"[10] The story was written by a person who had not seen the locality and the form in which we have the story was not earlier than the ninth century. But he left open, almost wishfully, that there were earlier forms of the story and that a geological explanation might lie at the root of the story.[11] He was disappointed with what he saw as historical ineptitudes in the story — the confusion of the city of Chairetopa with the site of the shrine at Colossae/Chonai, the etymological pull of the river Lykos over the mountain ridge to the province of Lycia.[12] He was more interested in the pagan mythology behind the story, though he jumped from the Phrygian fertility god Mên Karou to the Greek Zeus.[13] Apollo was

---

6 *History of the Church: Medieval Christianity* (2 vol.; Edinburgh: T & T Clark, 1885), 2.4446.

7 "Cities and Bishoprics of Phrygia II" *JHS* 8 (1887) 461–519, on p. 473. Ramsay began his on-the-ground investigations in Turkey in 1881 – see "Studies in Asia Minor", *JHS* 3 (1882) 1–61.

8 Ramsay, *Historical Geography of Asia Minor* (London: John Murray, 1890), 19.

9 Ramsay, *The Church in the Roman Empire* (London: Hodder and Stoughton, 1903 [1893]), 468, 470.

10 Ramsay, *The Cities and Bishoprics of Phrygia* (2 vol.; Oxford: Clarendon Press, 1895, 1897), 512.

11 Ramsay, *Cities and Bishoprics*, 215.

12 *Church in the Roman Empire*, 463–79.

13 Mên has been defended as the most likely candidate by E. Lucius, *Die Anfänge des Heiligenkults in der christlichen Kirche* (Tübingen: J.C.B. Mohr, 1904), 268, A.L. Williams, "The Cult of the Angels at Colossae", *JTS* 10 (1909) 413–38, on p. 437 and O. Meinardus,

added to his list as a possibility by G. F. Hill,[14] Dionysos by A. B. Cook,[15] Attis by F. Trombley[16] and Herakles by Mina Martens.[17]

Émile Le Camus and F. Nau interpreted the miraculous story as, in origin, the account related by Herodotos about the disappearing Lycus, simply dressed up in Christian pilgrimage garb.[18] Andrew Bennet tried to accumulate the literary references to the story, including some unsubstantiated citations, as argument for the historical basis for a miracle possibly in the third century.[19] The methodological confusion between literary, etymological and historical interests undermines a sincere desire to gather all available evidence. Clive Foss and Speros Vryonis were interested in sifting the story for evidence of Chonai as an important pilgrimage site and station in Byzantine times.[20] Johannes Rohland sees the popular story as sixth century in origin, possibly earlier in regard to the emphasis on healing and the fight with paganism, but passing through a number of developments over time, all configured around the portrayal of various problems for Christians as the work of the devil — disease, opposition, pagan beliefs.[21] His recognition that the historical value of the story is tangential to its specific content has been taken up in perhaps the most creative assessment of the story to date.

Glenn Peers, possibly in an allusion to the impasse into which Ramsay had wandered, is clear that the "aim of the miracle story of Chonai was not to provide a topographical survey or an historically accurate document."[22] He argued that the reworking of the story was occasioned by one particular crisis through which the church had passed, namely the iconoclastic insurgency of the eighth

---

"St Michael's Miracle of Khonae and its Geographical Setting", *Ekklesia kai Theologia* 1 (1980) 459–69, on p. 466.

14 "Apollo and St Michael: Some Analogies", *JHS* 36 (1916) 134–62; compare M. Simon, *Verus Israel: Étude sur les relations entre chrétiens et juifs dans l'empire romain (135–425 ap. J-C.)* (Paris: de Boccard, 1948), 430.

15 A. B. Cook, *Zeus: a Study in Ancient Religion* (3 vol.; Cambridge: Cambridge University Press, 1940), 2.1.114–15.

16 F. Trombley, *Hellenic Religion and Christianization* (2 vol.; Leiden: Brill, 1993), 2.101; see also C. A. Mango, "St Michael and Attis", *Deltiôn tês Christianikês Archaiologikês Hetaireias* 12 (1984–86) 39–62.

17 M. Martens, "L'Archange Michel et l'Héritage eschatologique pré-Chrétien", in A. Destrée (ed.), *Mélanges Armand Abel* (3 vol.; Leiden: Brill, 1978) 3.141–59, on pp. 151–53, 157–58.

18 Herodotos *Hist.* 7.30; Nau, "Le Miracle", 542–43; E. le Camus, "Colosses", in F. Vigouroux (ed.), *Dictionnaire de la Bible* (5 vol.; Paris: Letouzey et Ané, 1899) 2.861–62.

19 A. L. Bennett, "Archaeology from Art: Investigating Colossae and the Miracle of the Archangel Michael at Kona", *NEASB* 50 (2005) 15–26.

20 C. Foss, "Pilgrimage in Medieval Asia Minor", *DOP* 56 (2002) 129–51; S. Vryonis, *The Decline of Medieval Hellenism in Asia Minor and the Process of Islamization from the Eleventh through the Fifteenth Century* (Berkeley: University of California Press, 1971), 20, 33.

21 J. P. Rohland, *Der Erzengel Michael: Arzt und Feldherr* (Leiden: E. J. Brill, 1977), 115–17.

22 G. Peers, *Subtle Bodies: Representing Angels in Byzantium* (Berkeley: University of California Press, 2001), 151.

and ninth centuries. His earlier interpretation deemed that the story owed a considerable debt to the iconoclast position that the ethical life of the humble devotee is the only acceptable image of God.[23] He has modified this a little but maintains that Archippos remains the model template for Christian imitation, an imitation that could be invigorated by a pilgrimage to the site of his devotion to St. Michael.[24] He rejects the guidance and assistance of the archangel as the emphasis of the story, though those elements are present and claims that debates about idolatry and iconophilic devotion do not figure in it.[25] There is a suggestiveness in Peers' insights that I wish to take further even if I demur from his fundamental interpretation.

The Method for Investigating the Story

In his lengthiest treatment of the story, Ramsay was prepared to speak of the author as a redactor fashioning a foundation story of a tale of an apparition of Michael.[26] It was as if the story, not unlike the archangel himself, was subject to protean changes that reflected various pressures upon Christians in this part of the world. The transmission of the manuscript tradition testifies to this: the popular narrative shows a remarkable propensity to tolerate/exhibit changes. In a sense, the presence of completely separate re-tellings is in this same continuum. The assertion of a succession of revisions has been repeated by almost every writer visiting the sacred story, but without detailed or critical exposition. Rather, the story is approached in one-dimensional terms, cherry-picked for various purposes: evidence of pilgrimage, sacred sites, iconoclasm, religio-historical parallels. Text and interpretation remain flat, subsuming the whole to a single all-determining perspective. Even Glenn Peers, whilst recognising there is more to the story than the climactic rescue, does not allow the early chapters of the story to afford their witness. Archippos, the keeper of the healing shrine of

---

23 G. Peers, "Holy Man, Supplicant, and Donor: On Representations of the Miracle of the Archangel Michael at Chonae", *Mediaeval Studies* 59 (1997) 173–82, on pp. 176, 178.

24 Peers, *Subtle Bodies*, 143–154. Compare the argument that attention to the icon alone might qualify as a pilgrimage: A. W. Carr, "Icons and the Object of Pilgrimage in Middle Byzantine Constantinople", *DOP* 56 (2002) 75–92. One can readily see the importance of the story in a similar light as providing the opportunity for movement in devotional practice through meditation upon the narrative (heard or read): see M. L. Ehrenschwendtner, "Virtual Pilgrimages: Enclosure and the Practice of Piety at St Katherine's Convent, Augsburg", *JEH* 60 (2009) 45–73.

25 For a criticism of Peers' position, see my "The Inversion of Slavery: The Ascetic and the Archistrategos at Chonai", in G. D. Dunn/D. Luckensmeyer/L. Cross (ed.), *Prayer and Spirituality in the Early Church V: Poverty and Riches* (Strathfield, NSW: St Pauls Publications/ Virginia, Qld: Centre for Early Christian Studies, 2009) 215–36. See further below.

26 Ramsay, *Church in the Roman Empire*, 468, *Cities and Bishoprics*, 215.

St Michael does not enter the story until chapter 4. The first three chapters are not mere introduction but, as part of the whole story, indicate the battles of the early Christian movement, the means of triumph and the spoils, all of which characterise the heritage upon which the on-going church can profitably draw. And this is not restricted to the Christian heritage. The subtle shift from "Greek" to "pagan/heathen" as the term for the enemies of the site is particularly significant.[27] Not only is it a clue to a seam in the story reflecting the traditional sources that have been drawn into the final narrative; it also indicates that matters "Greek", having been conquered by the apostolic mission, are now themselves part of the heritage upon which Christians can draw. Quite apart from the traces of Hellenistic imagery and stories in the text, there is an overt indication of this in the hastening of both Christians *and* Greeks to the sacred spring for healing, once Archippos, the one trained in the angelic ascesis of the Christians, is established as its guardian (5.1 *cf* 3.1).

This is one of several indications that the story has been worked over many times. There are isolated vignettes, seams between and within stories that are ill-sewn and intertextual links that are ill-fitting, seemingly designed more to allay concerns about orthodoxy than to provide illumination of meaning. These elements invite a tradition-historical methodological application, more familiar to New Testament and Homeric studies.

The Indications of Tensions in the Story

Apart from Ramsay's identification of historical non-sequiturs — the supposed geographical anomaly of Chairetopa, the flow of the Lycus over the Taurus mountains into Lycia, the inappropriate use of a noxious watercourse for healing — there are a series of tensions within the story and between the story and its wider ecclesiastical context that can be briefly listed:
- the use of "Greeks" as the designation of pagan opponents to the Christians at a number of decisive moments in the early chapters of the story (1.2; 3.1,2,6; 5.4) though this gives way to the more general "idolaters" and "heathen" in the latter part of the story;
- the establishment of the healing spring at Colossae/Chonai, which had been prophesied after prayer by the apostles Philip and John as a specific gift of the archangel Michael yet bursts into life seemingly without intervention by the archangel (2);

---

27 On the distinction of Greek and pagan see A. Kaldellis, *Hellenism in Byzantium: The Transformations of Greek identity and the Reception of the Classical Tradition* (Cambridge: Cambridge University Press, 2007), 327. This derives from an earlier period: see J. W. McCrindle (ed.), *The Christian Topography of Cosmas, an Egyptian Monk* (New York: Burt Franklin, 1897), xi.

- the timidness of the story, compared to iconographic representations, in the circumlocutory manner of referring to the hands and lance of the archangel St. Michael (12.3, 4);
- the antipathy towards Laodicea, early a metropolitical diocese, as both the source of paganism and the gathering point of opponents to the shrine at Colossae, whereas Hierapolis is portrayed as early cleansed of pagan influence, the source of apostolic proclamation to the people of Colossae/Chonai and the origins of the shrine's guardian (1:3; 3.2, 6; 4.1; 7:4);
- the apostolic parousia is restricted to Philip and John (1); neither Paul nor, it would seem, the letter to the Colossians have any influence on the narrative;
- the extolling of the majesty of St. Michael, including a consistent mention of his name as a quaternitous collaborator with the father, son and spirit, as the authoritative focus of prayer (3.3, 4; 5.1 cf 12.4), is suddenly and briefly curtailed when Michael, who has stretched himself between earth and heaven, designates himself as a nothing compared to the "awesome and unfathomable glory of divinity" (1.6);
- the use of a direct Moses' allusion to the parting of the waters at the Red Sea (Ex 14:16ff) not in the story of the first deliverance of the shrine by the division of the waters of the Chruses river into two but rather at the execution of a shaft to drain the water away to a subterranean sump (12.3). Not even the striking of the impregnable monolith draws comparison with Moses striking the rock (Ex 17:6–7), even if it would require a contrast to the flow of water.
- There are manifold descriptions of Michael and of the rescue of the shrine that acquire their vividness from allusions that owe more to pre-christian myth than to judeo-christian resources, though the latter is also present.

These seams become the more obvious with their disappearance in the two, more refined re-tellings of the story by Sisinnius and Simeon Metaphrastes in the tenth century. Metaphrastes for example, obviously uneasy about the negative attitude towards Laodicea, makes it the name of another "village" (κώμη) removed from Phrygia altogether, over the mountain range in Lycia.[28]

Layers of traditions making up the story

Without going into detail, these notices of inner tensions, isolated vignettes and patchy seams indicate several layers of tradition that have become part of the on-going shaping and revising of the story. They follow here.

---

28 Metaphrastes § 7. Bonnet (26 n1) simply asserts that the writer seems astonishingly ignorant of location and details, hardly likely for a former high-ranking Byzantine bureaucrat. Rather ecclesiastical niceties were afoot.

1. The sacralizing of a fresh-water spring by crediting it to the intervention of Zeus Katabaites/Bronton (with perhaps other admixtures with older Phrygian deities, such as Mên Karou). The story itself hints at this pre-existence in a number of ways: the absence of an epiphany of the archangel Michael to initiate the healing spring (2.1, 2); the reference to the "discovery" (εὕρεσις) of the spring (3:1);[29] the implication in the attack upon Archippos and in the importance attached to the divine address when bathing in the spring (3.3) that there is a battle over (divine) ownership of the sacred site (note 8:4).

2. The christianisation of an older sacred site by supplanting the powerful figure accredited with its existence by Michael the archangel who nevertheless attracts characteristics of those previous divinities to his epiphany. The most obvious one is Zeus Katabaites and Zeus Bronton (note 11.2) but there are, at least, elements of divinities interwoven as well, especially in their Phrygian permutations.[30] In this aspect, it is significant that attention is deflected in the story from these male divinities by explicit focus on an unholy trinitarian complex of named female divinities: Artemis, Echidna and the Great Mother (1.1–2). The devil appears to have a relationship with these three in counterpoint to Michael's relationship to the Father, Son and Holy Spirit (9.1). The foregrounding of idols and idolatry as having feminine features allows for the appropriation of masculine features from pagan divinities.

3. The theological defence of the site against the hegemonic pressures of a metropolitan overlord by establishing firstly an apostolic line of authority and an exemplar of veneration (2.1–2),[31] secondly, a trinitarian formulation attached to its benefits (3.3, 4; 5.1, 12.4) and thirdly, a counter-accusation of pagan inspiration as lying behind the antagonism (3.2; 7.4). Competition between neighbouring cities had been a characteristic of Roman Imperial polity and this continued into ecclesiastical arrangements. John Cotsonis has suggested that this competition was the reality characterising the relationship between metropolitan and suffragan bishoprics. Local bishops claimed the patronage of a local saint rather than imitate that of their metropolitan.[32] Until Colossae/Chonai itself became a metropolitanate, the city had been subject to the

---

29 A problem recognised by one scribe who changed the word to ῥεῦσιν (Codex A).

30 I develop the details of these elements in my "St Michael of Chonai and the Tenacity of Paganism", in S. Hathaway/D. Kim (ed.), *Intercultural Transmission in the Medieval Mediterranean* (London/NY: Continuum 2012) forthcoming.

31 The tombs of John and Philip were already established sites of devotion and the two had been utilised as the authorities behind other church practices, such as by Polycrates of Ephesus to defend the celebration of Jesus' passion on the 14th Nisan: see Eusebius *Hist. eccl.* 5.19. Their connection in the *Acts of Philip* §§ 128–131 may well have provided the inspiration for this part of the Michael story: Ramsay, *Church in the Roman Empire*, 469, Hill, "Apollo and St Michael", 156.

32 Cotsonis, "Saints and Cult Centers", 17, 19.

ecclesio-political jurisdiction of Laodicea.[33] Canon 35 of the Council of Laodicea (approximately 361 CE) condemned the invocation of angels. There
is little doubt that Colossae was in view.[34] What is significant is that the
Canon anathematises such practices as "idolatry" (εἰδωλολατρεία – twice),[35]
the very description, *inter alia*, used in the story of those from Laodicea who
opposed over a considerable period of time the shrine and its operations
(5.4, 7.3, 9.1 *cf* 3.2).[36] The charge re-gathered potency in the iconoclast conflict and, as we shall see, afforded the opportunity for the story to be interpreted as a criticism of the iconoclasts, ironically, early in the ninth century,
in official control of the church at Chonai.

4. The justifying of the establishment of a permanent fixture and attendants at
the site by reference to a proven and world-renowned track-record of healings
and associated conversions and baptisms (3.1, 2; 5.1) the sanctity of life of its
archetypal persevering custodian, Archippos (4.2–8; 9.1–2, 11.1) and an over-
whelming miracle of deliverance (11.2–12.2). The mention of exorcisms into
the final endorsement of the site and its function by the archangel Michael
(12.4) may be related to the accent on idolatry in the story but both this, and
possession, are notably muted in the description of the Devil in 7.2. It is as
likely a trace of a particular aspect of healing connected with the site through
the ministry of St. Peter of Atroa, who, in a pilgrimage to the shrine early in
the ninth century, performed noteworthy exorcisms that were somehow considered the result of the conjunction of the holy man and the holy site.[37] The
demonstration of permanence is a critical element in the story for the demonstration of the worthy recognition of the site (9.2; 12.4). The ongoing witness
to the power of the site in the addition of a reference to exorcisms testifies to
this longevity. Thereafter, the fantastical realm of the demonic will feature
more prominently in the story's re-tellings.[38]

---

33 See M. Le Quien, *Oriens Christianus in quatuor Patriarchatus digestus; quo exhibentur
Ecclesiae, Patriarchae, caeterique Praesules totius Orientis ... Opus posthumum* (3 vol.; Paris:
Ex Typographia Regia, 1740), 1.813–14.

34 This was made explicit by Theodoret of Cyrrhus (c. 430) in his comment on Col 2:18: *Interp. ad Ep Col.* (*PG* 82.613B, 620D–621A) and a scholion on one manuscript of the Council's
decisions names Colossae in the margin to Canon 35: see Lueken, *Michael*, 75.

35 G. D. Mansi, *Sacrorum Concilium Nova et Amplissima Collectio* (31 vol.; Florence: 1759–
98), 2.569. Later church modulation of this canon interpreted the meaning as "improper worship" of angels, one instance of which was the conferring of names upon the angels other than
those authorised (as by Scripture). See C.J. Hefele, *A History of the Councils of the Church*
(3 vol.; Edinburgh: T & T Clark, 1876), 317.

36 There is a suggestive punning variant in 7.4 where "the lawless mob" (ὁ λαὸς τῆς ἀδικίας)
becomes "the people of Laodicea" (ὁ δὲ λαὸς τῆς Λαοδικίας) who join forces with those who
have gathered at Laodicea, presumably, in this reading (Codices D, V, A) from elsewhere.

37 *Vita* 13.20, E.V. Laurent (ed.), *La vie merveilleuse de Saint Pierre d'Atroa* (Brussels:
Society of Bollandists, 1956).

38 Sissinius § 4.

5. The defence of the site, its management and infrastructures, and its devotional focus in the battle for survival during the iconoclastic controversies. This layer will be dealt with in more detail below.

6. The use of the site and its story as a narrative of defence against Arab and then Turkish military incursions. This layer is less obvious in the popular story,[39] which appears to reach the zenith of its interaction with its context in the second iconoclast controversy (813–843). The ready application of the story to the pressure of the Seljuk encroachment is apparent in, for example, Michael Choniates' encomium on Metropolitan Nicetas of Chonai. Nicetas is cast as an imitator of Archippos standing against the threatening flood of Moslem "barbarians".[40] However, the lack of the familiar language of "barbarian" in all three versions suggests that this "layer" is not so much in the text(s) as indicating the *terminus ad quem* of its recensional development. As regards the anonymous popular story, this may be tightened even further. The outbreak of renewed anti-semitic activity in the Byzantine empire in the tenth-eleventh century[41] is *not* reflected in the story. Given the antagonism to Jews of the renowned Metropolitan Nicetas of Chonai,[42] one would expect some trace of this in the story, but this is clearly later. What remains a puzzle, given the frequent assertion of Jews at Colossae from the pre-Christian period,[43] is the absence of any such evidence in the story.

Such a stratigraphy is not open-ended nor segmented; the story is not an ever-expanding loose-leaf folder. The work of a series of redactors ensured that elements of these (at least) six layers were worked through the story at different periods under different ecclesial and political pressures and with at least some knowledge of the received traditions that formed the cultural heritage of the area. However, the identification of these layers as a justifiable working hypothesis explains the variations in narrative quality, brevity of some stories compared to expansiveness of others, the faulty seams and misplaced scriptural allusions. And it supports the dating of a fifth even fourth century *beginning* to the story. It possibly began in oral form but retained its narrative liveliness even in the later writ-

---

39 But see the variants to the description of the Devil in Codex P for 7.2.

40 Michael Choniates, *Encom. Nic.*, 44 (Lampros, 1, 38).

41 See M. Angold, *Church and Society in Byzantium under the Comneni 1081–1261* (Cambridge: Cambridge University Press, 2000), 509.

42 Michael Choniates, *Encom. Nic.* 88 (Lampros 1.52).

43 See W. M. Ramsay, *The Letters to the Seven Churches. And their place in the plan of the Apocalypse* (London: Hodder and Stoughton, 1904), 420; H. W. Attridge, "On Becoming an Angel: Rival Baptismal Theologies at Colossae", in L. Bormann/K. del Tredici/A. Standhartinger (ed.), *Religious Propaganda and Missionary Competition in the New Testament World* (Leiden: Brill, 1994) 481–98, on p. 497. It should be noted that the actual evidence of a significant Jewish demographic at Colossae is lacking but, rather, is surmised from evidence that explicitly mentions Laodicea.

ten text. No doubt the redactors had an eye towards the shaping of a pilgrim's consciousness if not the retention of her/his interest on the journey and during the days of the festival.

Each of these layers can be linked with a known historical detail associated with Colossae/Chonai and with wider turmoils in the political and religious unfolding of the area over a millennium. To one of these I now turn for illustration.

The iconophilic quality of the story
of St. Michael the Archistrategos

One notable detail in the history of Colossae and Chonai provides the impulse to concentrate on the impact the iconoclastic controversies had on the story of St Michael. Glenn Peers has argued that the theological emphases of iconoclasm — that ethics rather than material witness is to be favoured in christian life and practice — has influenced the shaping of the story. Certainly iconoclasm did have a particular impact on Colossae and Chonai during the second iconoclastic crisis early in the ninth century. The iconomachian emperor, Leo V, had appointed a sympathetic bishop to the diocese, sympathetic that is in his iconomachian, or war-on-icons, opinions. So-called secular appointments seemed to go hand-in-hand with ecclesiastical positions in the Byzantine career path. Accordingly, we find the *strategos* or commander of the province was also a vehement iconoclast. Michael Lakododrakon was far more than a mere white-washer of icons. He set himself on a vicious and murderous program of destruction of any elements as betokened, in his opinion, a deflection from a true spiritual devotion; everything from monkish outfits to heretical teachers came under his notice. One seat of his authority was Chonai. If not the capital,[44] it was at least a *topoteresia* or military headquarters in the Byzantine province of Thrakesion,[45] the mid-sixth century successor in part to the late Roman province of Phrygia Pacatiana. The war over icons was fought on a number of fronts, but one of the most important related to the question of angels. In distilled expression, the angel was asomatic, incorporeal, without body. Accordingly, so the argument ran,

---

44 The thirteenth century Arabic geographer, Yakut, preserves ninth-tenth century Arabic material and names the capital of the Thrakesion theme as Kaniyus, very likely the Arabic form of Chonas. In any case, it does preclude Ephesus: see E. W. Brooks, "Arabic Lists of the Byzantine Themes", *JHS* 21 (1901) 67–77, on p. 74.

45 C. Foss, *Ephesus after Antiquity: A late antique, Byzantine and Turkish City* (Cambridge: Cambridge University Press, 1979), 195–96. He repeated the deduction in his dictionary article on "Chonai", in A. P. Kazhdan (ed.), *The Oxford Dictionary of Byzantium* (Oxford: Oxford University Press, 1991) 427, and has been followed by K. Belke/N. Mersich, *Tabula Imperii Byzantini Bd 7: Phrygien und Pisidien* (Vienna: Österreichischen Akademie der Wissenschaft, 1990), 49. Ramsay had hesitantly raised the possibility: *Historical Geography*, 134–35, 151.

how was it possible to circumscribe, that is to put into material representation, that which is asomatic?

As one of the great pilgrim sanctuaries, Chonai was at the heart of this crisis, renowned for its icon of St Michael the taxiarch.[46] The connection between the archangel and icons goes back at least to the seventh century and probably earlier.[47] More significantly perhaps, the notion that the material world might receive and bear witness to the transformative power of the asomatic, enabled an embrace by improvisation of millennium-long traditions that expressed the numinous experiential quality of certain parts of the earth where the divine seemed to draw close. The ability of the asomatic Michael to leave a visual impact in an icon was therefore nothing more than a microcosm of the impression he had left and could leave on the wider material world.

The iconoclastic struggle was not just a theological debate or a contest over the validity of spiritual experiences. There were real-politik dimensions of long-lasting consequence however much they might be dressed in terminological finery. In Constantinople in 1066 CE, an illuminator working on a newly copied Psalter, painted a pertinent commentary on Ps 25 (26):5 (LXX) "I abhor the assembly of evildoers and with the ungodly I will not take my seat."[48]

The illumination works with visual representations that had established a certain pattern by this time[49] and recalls in two conjoined cameos in the footer margin the iconoclastic struggles of two centuries before. The first has two standing haloed clerics admonishing a crowned but orb-less emperor beneath the red-inked words: ὁ σοπῆρ ἐλέγχων μετὰ τοῦ πῑάρχου τὸν εἰκονομάχ: "The holy father, with the patriarch, refutes the iconomachian". The ecclesial figures are Patriarch Nicephorus and Theodore of Studios, the latter elevated, as Igor

---

46 *Vita S. Cyril. Phileotes* 18 (edition: E. Sargologos, *Vie de S. Cyrille le Philéote* (Brussels: Société des Bollandistes, 1964)). This life belongs to the tenth century, after the iconoclastic fights were over but would appear to reflect a triumphal restoration of what had previously existed rather than an initiation of a memorial of that triumph.

47 The obscure seventh century figure who goes under the name of Eustathius, bishop of Thrace, recounted in an encomium on Michael, the story of a woman, Euphonia, who was shortly to be widowed. She asks her husband, "I wish that thou wouldst command a painter to paint for me the picture of the holy Archangel Michael upon a wooden tablet [that he might] become my guardian and deliver me from every evil thought of Satan." E. A. T. W. Budge, *St Michael the Archangel: three encomiums by Theodosius Archbishop of Alexandria, Severus Patriarch of Antioch and Eustathius, Bishop of Trake* (London: Kegan Paul, 1894), 78.

48 British Library Add 19352 f. 27v. A substantial number of illuminations for the manuscript are reproduced in S. Der Nersessian, *L'Illustration des psautiers grecs du moyen âge, II* (Paris: Klinksieck, 1970). Psalm 25/26 is alluded to directly ("as said by the divine David") in Simeon Metaphrastes version of the St Michael of Chonai story (§ 6).

49 See I. Ševčenko, "The Anti-Iconoclastic Poem in the *Pantocrator* Psalter", in his *Ideology, Letters and Culture in the Byzantine World* (London: Variorum Reprints, 1982 [1965]), XIII. 39–60.

Ševčenko points out,[50] into a position of prominence. The secular leader is likely to be the emperor Leo V, but may in fact be one of his most destructive deputies, Michael Lakododrakon. The significance of the first cameo draws its weight from the contrasting figures of the second cameo. There are three bishops, solidly grouped together though with only one seated. They form "the assembly of evildoers", strikingly without nimbuses given the clerics' haloes of the first cameo. They direct their attention to whitewashing an icon through the use of a long staff reminiscent of the lance thrust into the side of Jesus on the cross.[51] The staff connects all three across their bodies, though it is handled only by the right hand figure.[52] The red-inked text simply names them in the plural:"οἱ εἰκονομάχοι"— "the icon slashers". But their bishops' robes convey something of the battle that beset the church in the eighth and ninth centuries.

What makes this illuminated Psalter so significant for Chonai is the presence of Theodore. From his writings comes the information that the struggle over icons was fought on two fronts: the political and the ecclesial. He combines the two in a single instructional letter.[53] Chonai is specifically mentioned as the seat of an iconoclastic bishop whom Theodore visited in 819 CE and with whom he disputed.[54] Although Theodore does not name the bishop,[55] he does call him the leader of the heretics (αἱρεσιάρχης). Given the imperial support for the iconoclastic destruction and persecution, the conjunction of an iconomachian bishop and a strategos or exarch adds a potency to the St Michael story. The placement of these two leaders at Chonai was nothing other than a direct attack on one of the most powerful sites of iconographic presence and devotion. This is not to be reduced to a single icon in a grand church. Indeed, as Glenn Peers accents, the story of St Michael says nothing directly about painted wood.

But, what Peers does not recognise is that the icon and the debates about icons generally, were directly linked with the recognition, appreciation and veneration *of a holy place*, a place where the material realm was yet infused with the

---

50 *Ibid.* 58.

51 This express association is found in a juxtaposition of images of the two scenes (whitewashing an icon and lancing Jesus) in the Chludov Psalter f. 67r (State Historical Museum, Moscow); see R. Cormack "Painting after Iconoclasm" in A. Bryer/J. Herrin (ed.), *Iconoclasm* (Birmingham: Centre for Byzantine Studies, 1977) 147–63, on pp. 149, 152.

52 I cannot help but wonder whether the impulse to literalise the "as if" of Michael's staff from the popular St Michael story (12.3) to the standard iconography was assisted in any way by the desire to form a counterpoint to this iconomachian representation.

53 Ep.2.63 (to Naukratios, his "child") (*PG* 99.1282).

54 For an analysis of the *modus operandi* of both parties to the dispute at the elite level, see P. J. Alexander, "Religious Persecution and Resistance in the Byzantine Empire of the Eighth and Ninth Centuries: Methods and Justifications", *Speculum* 52 (1977) 238–41.

55 There developed a reticence to name, or at least name correctly, those church leaders who had supported or sponsored the iconoclastic revolt: see Ševčenko, "Anti-Iconoclastic Poem", XIII.44.

power of the immaterial, where the distance between the natural and the super-natural seemed to contract. This is precisely what lies behind Theodore's answer to the objection that angels, being incorporeal, cannot be circumscribed. Theodore agrees with his opponents that the nature (φύσις) of an angel is incorporeality, but he goes on to argue that angels are located by reference to place. He demonstrates his argument by the appearance of the angel to Mary *at Nazareth* (drawing on Luke 1:26).[56] Accordingly, the argument runs, if an angel can be circumscribed by an earthly place, such as Nazareth or Chonai, then an angel can be circumscribed by an icon. Icon *and* site become a crucial combination for the defence of the visual representation of angels. This is why the story of the archangel Michael of Chonai becomes a crucial player in the crisis. It explains why there is such a terminological accent in the story on "this place, that holy place, this land". As the archistrategos says to the custodian, "If you believe, O holy one, that he is able to safeguard this land from the floodtide, come, so that you may witness his power." (11.5). It also helps to explain that even though there is a lengthy description of the piety of the model suppliant Archippos, there is an equally lengthy description of the massive impact that the archangel had on the landscape — the splitting of a river even from its primeval foundation, the heaping up of flood waters into an estopped wall, the fracturing of an impenetrable rock, the rupture of the earth's casing to capture a deluge and turn it to a renewed servant of healing. All this shows emphatically that the asomatic can impact the material realm; what's more, it leaves a permanent testimony to that impress.

Hence, the story, as it developed through this period, incorporated language that was critical for the defence of icons, even as that language was applied to a privileged geographical location. The irony was that the story was not spawned by the iconoclastic controversy. It simply received a further refining revision from an earlier battle with at least one council (Laodicea c. 361CE), a theologian (Theodoret c 420CE) and one might dare to suggest another from the apostolic period — a perhaps pseudonymous Paul — who similarly had extreme concerns about the attention given to angels. But, as Otto Meinardus quipped, "as it occurs so often, that which was once called idolatry was afterwards reckoned as piety."[57]

---

56 Theodore Studios *Antirrh. III.* 47 (*PG* 99.411B).
57 Meinardus, "St Michael's Miracle", 463.

Bibliography

Alexander, P. J., "Religious Persecution and Resistance in the Byzantine Empire of the Eighth and Ninth Centuries: Methods and Justifications", *Speculum* 52 (1977) 238–41.

Angold, M., *Church and Society in Byzantium under the Comneni 1081–1261* (Cambridge: Cambridge University Press, 2000).

Attridge, H. W., "On Becoming an Angel: Rival Baptismal Theologies at Colossae", in L. Bormann/K. del Tredici/A. Standhartinger (ed.), *Religious Propaganda and Missionary Competition in the New Testament World* (Leiden: Brill, 1994) 481–98.

Belke, K./N. Mersich, *Tabula Imperii Byzantini Bd 7: Phrygien und Pisidien* (Vienna: Österreichische Akademie der Wissenschaften, 1990).

Bennett, A. L., "Archaeology from Art: Investigating Colossae and the Miracle of the Archangel Michael at Kona", *NEASB* 50 (2005) 15–26.

Bonnet, J., *Narratio de Miraculo a Michaele Archangelo Chonis Patrato* (Paris: Librairie Hachette, 1890).

Bouvier, B./F. Amsler, "Le Miracle de l'Archange Michel à Chonai: Introduction, Traduction, et Notes", in D. H. Warren/A. G. Brock/D. W. Pao (ed.), *Early Christian Voices: in texts, traditions and symbols: Essays in Honor of François Bovon* (Boston/Leiden: Brill Academic Publishers, 2003) 395–407.

Brooks, E. W., "Arabic Lists of the Byzantine Themes", *JHS* 21 (1901) 67–77.

Budge, E. A. T. W., *St Michael the Archangel: three encomiums by Theodosius Archbishop of Alexandria, Severus Patriarch of Antioch and Eustathius, Bishop of Trake* (London: Kegan Paul, 1894).

Cadwallader, A. H., "The Inversion of Slavery: The Ascetic and the Archistrategos at Chonai", in G. D. Dunn/D. Luckensmeyer/L. Cross (ed.), *Prayer & Spirituality in the Early Church V: Poverty and Riches* (Strathfield, NSW: St Pauls Publications/Virginia, Qld: Centre for Early Christian Studies, 2009) 215–36.

– "St Michael of Chonai and the Tenacity of Paganism", in S. Hathaway/D. Kim (ed.), *Intercultural Transmission in the Medieval Mediterranean* (London/NY: Continuum, 2012) forthcoming.

le Camus, E., "Colosses", in F. Vigouroux (ed.), *Dictionnaire de la Bible* (5 vol.; Paris: Letouzey et Ané, 1899) 2.861–62.

Cook, A. B., *Zeus: a Study in Ancient Religion* (3 vol.; Cambridge: Cambridge University Press, 1940).

Cormack, R., "Painting after Iconoclasm", in A. Bryer/J. Herrin (ed.), *Iconoclasm* (Birmingham: Centre for Byzantine Studies, 1977) 147–63.

Cotsonis, J., "Saints and Cult Centers: A Geographic and Administrative Perspective in Light of Byzantine Lead Seals", *SBS* 8 (2003) 9–26.

Der Nersessian, S., *L'Illustration des psautiers grecs du moyen âge, II* (Paris: Klinksieck, 1970).

van Dieten, J. L. (ed.), *Nicetae Choniatae Historia* (Berlin: Walter de Gruyter, 1975).

Ehrenschwendtner, M. L., "Virtual Pilgrimages: Enclosure and the Practice of Piety at St Katherine's Convent, Augsburg", *JEH* 60 (2009) 45–73.

Ehrhard, *Überlieferung und Bestand der hagiographischen und homiletischen Literatur der griechischen Kirche* (3 vol.; Leipzig: J. C. Hinrichs, 1937–1939).

Foss, C., *Ephesus after Antiquity: A late antique, Byzantine and Turkish City* (Cambridge: Cambridge University Press, 1979).

- "Chonai", in A. P. Kazhdan (ed.), *The Oxford Dictionary of Byzantium* (Oxford: Oxford University Press, 1991) 427.
- "Pilgrimage in Medieval Asia Minor", *DOP* 56 (2002) 129–51.

Halkin, F. *Bibliotheca hagiographica graeca* (3 vol.; Brussels: Societé des Bollandistes, 1957).

Hefele, C. J., *A History of the Councils of the Church* (3 vol.; Edinburgh: T & T Clark, 1876).

Hill, G. F., "Apollo and St Michael: Some Analogies", *JHS* 36 (1916) 134–62.

Kaldellis, A., *Hellenism in Byzantium: The Transformations of Greek identity and the Reception of the Classical Tradition* (Cambridge: Cambridge University Press, 2007).

Lampros, S. P., Μιχαὴλ Ἀκομινάτου τοῦ Χωνιάτου τὰ σωζόμενα (2 vol.; Groningen: Bouma, 1968 [1879]).

Laurent, E. V. (ed.), *La vie merveilleuse de Saint Pierre d'Atroa* (Brussels: Society of Bollandists, 1956).

Le Quien, *Oriens Christianus in quatuor Patriarchatus digestus; quo exhibentur Ecclesiae, Patriarchae, caeterique Praesules totius Orientis ... Opus posthumum* (3 vol.; Paris: Ex Typographia Regia, 1740).

Lucius, E., *Die Anfänge des Heiligenkults in der christlichen Kirche* (Tübingen: J. C. B. Mohr, 1904).

Lueken, W., *Michael: Eine Darstellung und Vergleichung der jüdischen und der morgenländisch-christlichen Tradition vom Erzengel Michael* (Göttingen: Vandenhoeck & Ruprecht, 1898).

Mango, C. A., "St Michael and Attis", *Deltiôn tês Christianikês Archaiologikês Hetaireias* 12 (1984–86) 39–62.

Mansi, G. D., *Sacrorum Concilium Nova et Amplissima Collectio* (31 vol.; Florence: 1759–98).

Martens, M. "L'Archange Michel et l'Héritage eschatologique pré-Chrétien", in A. Destrée (ed.), *Mélanges Armand Abel* (3 vol.; Leiden: Brill, 1978, 141–59).

McCrindle, J. W. (ed.), *The Christian Topography of Cosmas, an Egyptian Monk* (New York: Burt Franklin, 1897).

Meinardus, O. F. A., "St Michael's Miracle of Khonae and its Geographical Setting", *Ekklesia kai Theologia* 1 (1980) 459–69.

Miller, E. (ed.), *Manuelis Philae carmina ex codicibus Escurialensis, Florentinis, Parisinis et Vaticanis* (2 vol.; Paris: Imperial Printers, 1855–1857).

Nau, F., "Le Miracle de Saint Michel a Colosses", *Patrologia Orientalis* 4 (1908) 542–62.

Nesbitt, J. and N. Oikonomides, *Catalogue of Byzantine Seals at Dum,barton Oaks and in the Fogg Museum of Art III: West, Northwest and Central Asia Minor and the Orient* (Washington DC: Dumbarton Oaks Publications, 1996).

Peers, G., "Holy Man, Supplicant, and Donor: On Representations of the Miracle of the Archangel Michael at Chonae", *Mediaeval Studies* 59 (1997) 173–82.

- *Subtle Bodies: Representing Angels in Byzantium* (Berkeley: University of California Press, 2001).

Pertusi, A., *Costantino Porfirogenito De Thematibus* (Vatican: Biblioteca Apostolica Vaticana, 1952).

Ramsay, W. M., "Studies in Asia Minor", *JHS* 3 (1882) 1–61.

- "The Cities and Bishoprics of Phrygia II", *JHS* 8 (1887) 461–519.

- *Historical Geography of Asia Minor* (London: John Murray, 1890).

- *The Cities and Bishoprics of Phrygia* (2 vol.; Oxford: Clarendon Press, 1895, 1897).
- *The Church in the Roman Empire* (London: Hodder and Stoughton, 1903 [1893]).
- *The Letters to the Seven Churches. And their place in the plan of the Apocalypse* (London: Hodder and Stoughton, 1904).

Rohland, J. P., *Der Erzengel Michael: Arzt und Feldherr* (Leiden: E. J. Brill, 1977).

Sargologos, E., *Vie de S. Cyrille le Philéote* (Brussels: Société des Bollandistes, 1964).

Schaff, P., *History of the Church: Medieval Christianity* (Edinburgh: T & T Clark, 1885).

Ševčenko, I., "The Anti-Iconoclastic Poem in the *Pantocrator* Psalter", in his *Ideology, Letters and Culture in the Byzantine World* (London: Variorum Reprints, 1982 [1965]), XIII. 39–60.

Simon, M., *Verus Israel: Étude sur les relations entre chrétiens et juifs dans l'empire romain (135–425 ap. J-C.)* (Paris: de Boccard, 1948).

Stiltingo, J./C. Suyskeno/J. Periero/J. Cleo (ed.), *Acta Sanctorum: September* (Paris/Rome: Victor Palmé, 1869 [1762]).

Trombley, F., *Hellenic Religion and Christianization* (Leiden: Brill, 1993).

Vryonis, S., *The Decline of Medieval Hellenism in Asia Minor and the Process of Islamization from the Eleventh through the Fifteenth Century* (Berkeley: University of California Press, 1971).

Werner, S., "Das Reliquarkreuz des Leon 'Damokranites'", in W. Hörander *et al* (ed.), *Byzantios: Festschrift für Hubert Hunger zum 70 Geburtstag* (Vienna: E. Becvar, 1984) 301–10.

Williams, A. L., "The Cult of the Angels at Colossae", *JTS* 10 (1909) 413–38.

Appendix 1a

A Chronology of Colossae/Chonai

Prepared by Alan H. Cadwallader

Introduction

The reading of nineteenth and early twentieth century reports of Colossae is more characterised by inventiveness in recycling than contribution of anything new. The biblical commentators J. B. Lightfoot and Ernst Renan, the archaeologist William Mitchell Ramsay and the Byzantine textual editor, Max Bonnet between them were responsible for harvesting the modicum of knowledge about Colossae and Chonai that we have. They at least took our knowledge beyond the endless repetitions of Herodotos, Xenophon and Strabo but they did not shake off the persistent judgement of the "destruction" and/or "decline" of Colossae, a judgement that rests on very slim evidence. In a period of European history when the monumental, classical remains were prized, the (re-)discovery of Colossae was singularly disappointing. Whereas almost every European scholar and traveller wanted to go to Lycia where the Xanthus marbles had caused such a storm of interest, those prepared to tread the Lycus Valley were far fewer in number. And of these, there appears to have been an invisible wall just east of Denizli, so that Laodicea received far more eye-witness accounts than Colossae or Honaz. The resilient independence of the population of Honaz, especially when encouraged by a local aga preoccupied with his own importance, may have helped discourage European travel and when the British-funded Ottoman railway went through the area towards the end of the nineteenth century, the discouragement was sealed: Honaz was by-passed.

The effort then in the following chronological chart has been to draw together as many of the trigonometric points that can assist in developing a lineal appreciation of Colossae and Chonai both for their own sakes and as a means of re-installing them into the larger history of Phrygia and Asia Minor. There is also an effort to include the engagement of travellers and scholars with the site, at least in terms of their contact with the area. Perhaps the singular omission is the detail of persons and offices that are yielded by coins and some inscriptions. The dangers in their inclusion are that a chronology would turn into a prosopography. That task deserves to be treated separately. Even so, the material that has been able to be amassed through a careful sifting of secondary and primary literature is salutary. There is in fact far more material directly connected with the area than a dictionary article or historical or biblical introduction would lead one to expect. Moreover, there is a remarkable continuity in the site that runs from the period of the Achaemenid dynasties to the present; it is a quite different impression from what one might gather from the literature about the site, not least from Western biblical scholars and archaeologists.

There is perhaps some justification required for combining Colossae and Chonai into a single chronology. The relationship between the two names is disputed, with some taking the names as indicating two separate sites while others understand the names as a sequential change for basically the same site. However, all are agreed that Colossae and Chonai are so strongly related that one cannot be understood without reference to the other. Accordingly, the modern town of Honaz becomes the inheritor of a long history of the site and area that bears both names, as reflected in this table. The crucial element of the table however has been to extend the line of the site (and perhaps the linkage between the two) into the Ottoman period and beyond. Ramsay's ambitions declared that "Everything that fell between the dawn of history and the final conquest by the Turks lay within my period."[1] In this statement Ramsay's commitment to the classics and to Christianity, a personal determination that mirrored Europe and especially Great Britain in the nineteenth century, shows through and arbitrarily takes the passing of Constantinople into the hands of Sultan Mehmet II in 1453 as the end of worthy notice.[2] The value of extending the chronology is that the site can readily be seen to have value beyond a Eurocentric focus. This awakens the sense that the site today has a great significance to both local people and to wider Turkish intellectual and cultural endeavours. Archaeology is a thriving Turkish enterprise and brings welcome perspectives that frequently have not been entertained by European and American scholars.

With all such macrocosmic surveys, there are limitations. Colossae and Chonai were obviously affected by numerous changes within the Lycus Valley, Phrygia and Asia Minor though these are not always mentioned in the documentary evidence (whether textual or material). Everything from Hittite imperial policy for the area to the influence of Montanism on/in Christian congregations at Colossae can be rightly suspected but the explicit data is still desperately lacking. The information here is frequently fragmentary and invites linkages and leaps that imagination rather than hard evidence can supply. There are some clues however within the outline of where substantial new work is promising to add to the picture. Although Ottoman record-keeping for the area never adopted the scale of a Byzantine or Arab chronicle, there was quite meticulous attention to tax

---

1 W. M. Ramsay, *The Bearing of Recent Discovery on the Trustworthiness of the New Testament* (London: Hodder and Stoughton, 1915), 35.

2 Ramsay's attitude shows itself explicitly in his identification of Turkish interests with the English in his *The Revolution in Constantinople and Turkey: A Diary* (London: Hodder and Stoughton, 1909).

returns, as for the various districts of the empire. These returns have begun to supply important data for demographic and economic understandings of the area, at least from the late fifteenth century onwards, data that no orientalising anecdotes from European visitors can match. Furthermore, the late-nineteenth and twentieth centuries have become a particular focus of cultural history research undertaken by universities (especially Pamukkale University) and the local department of the TC, Denizli Valiliḍi, Kültur ve Turizm Müdürlüḍu, Il Halk Kütüphanesi (Turkish Ministry of Culture). A significant archive of material and analysis has resulted.[3] For the earlier epochs, the beginnings of archaeological surveys of the area, especially as lead by the archaeological department of Pamukkale University have begun to raise hopes that a new era of research on Colossae and Chonai is dawning.

The effort to supply as full a collation as possible for Colossae/Chonai provides a corrective to a comparative archaeological/historical approach. Such an approach was championed rightly by the celebrated French archaeologist, Louis Robert, as a means of identifying the distinctive similarities of cultural artefacts from the Lycus Valley. This carries certain advantages in that prognoses can be formulated for one site from neighbouring sites when the required evidence is lacking. However, there is always the danger that the distinctive marks of a competitive autonomous city, even (or especially) in Roman times, can be lost.

So then, this chronological table provides the latest and fullest anatomical schema of Colossae/Chonai in the hope that it will provide a useful structure on which to build a keener sense of the city across its many epochs. The editions and references that have been consulted in order to build the table are listed at the end of the table for quick and ready reference.

The Table

DATE	PERSONS AND EVENTS	SOURCES
Chalcolithic Age	Possible foundation of Colossae	Bahadır/Konakçi 87
Bronze Age	Bronze Age mound at Colossae.	AS 4 (1956) 230–31
C5–4th BCE	Colossae key station on the Royal Road; royal estates in surrounding country; Lycus river flows through the city; Persian settlers.	Sekunda 113
481	Xerxes rests his army at Colossae en route to battle the Greeks.	Herodotos Hist. 7.30
401	Colossae described as a large, prosperous and established city.	Xenophon Anab. 1.2.6

---

3 See, for example, the two volume work, International Symposium on the History and Culture of Denizli and its Surroundings (2 vol.; Denizli: Pamukkale University, 2007).

401	Cyrus 7 day stopover on journey to Babylon with 10,000 Greek mercenaries to ill-fated battle (of Cunaxa) with Artaxerxes II Mnemon.	Xenophon *Anab.* 1.2.6
395/6	Tissaphernes, Persian satrap (appointed 414 BCE) captured at Colossae baths and assassinated.	Diodoros Siculus 14.80.8
	Araios, an accomplice in the assassination, holds estates at Colossae.	Polyaenus 7.16
	Mardonios, a Persian noble family, holds estates at Colossae	Sekunda 117
	Colossae makes a name beyond the region for the colour of wool produced.	Pliny *Nat.* 21.51
133	Lycus Valley bequeathed by Attalus III to Rome	Ramsay *CBP* 341
51	Cicero, governor of Cilicia, stays at Laodicea and, perhaps, Colossae.	Cicero *Att.* 5.20 *conj*; Winstedt *cf* Hunter 82
23	Strabo the geographer groups Colossae with, *inter alia*, Aphrodisias as significant second-rank cities behind Laodicea and Apameia.	Strabo *Geogr* 12.8.13
50s CE	Christian community established at Colossae (by Epaphras?).	Paul *Phlm* 23; 'Paul' *Col* 1:7,4:12
c. 56	Onesimus, a runaway slave from Colossae, restored to his owner Philemon by Paul of Tarsus, leader in a new religious movement.	Paul *Phlm*
60/1	Severe earthquake in Lycus Valley generates significant need for aid. Laodicea declines imperial support, but Colossae and Hierapolis?	Tacitus *Ann.* 14.27.1, Dio Cassius 54. 30.2–5, Eusebius *Chron* 183.21, Ororios 7.7.12
	Legendary story of visit of Philip, early of Bethsaida, later of Hierapolis.	*AASS* 8 § 1
c.70	Korumbos honoured for repair of the baths at Colossae.	Cadwallader *infra*
129	Visit to area by Emperor Hadrian on pan-Hellenic tour.	*IGR* iv.869
	Local pugilist carries off boxing honours in games held at Tripolis.	*JHS* xviii (1898) 90, § 26
177–180	Colossae enters into *homonoia* relationship with Aphrodisias during the reign of Commodus.	Franke/Nollé pl.47
Late C2	Food shortages impact the city's life.	*IGR* iv.870, Robert *Laodicée* 269, 277–278
c. 220	Colossian athletes enter the athletic games held at Tripolis.	*BCH* XI (1887) 353 § 11.

305	Emperors Constantius I, Diocletian (?) and Maximian (?) honoured at Colossae.	*MAMA* VI.38
Late C4	Philemon claimed as the first bishop of Colossae	*Apost. Const.* 7.46.12
C4–5	Some church teachers (such as Theodore of Mopsuestia and Theodoret) consider the spurious Epistle to the Laodiceans contains some reflections on the church at Colossae. Shrine to St. Michael established at or near Colossae.	*PG* 66.932B, *PG* 82. 625–26D Theodoret *Comm. Ep. Col.* (*PG* 82.613B)
c.430	Theodoret warns against contemporary devotion to angels; draws on canon 35 of the Council of Laodicea (C4) which forbade offering of prayer to angels; applies canon to shrine to Michael the Archangel at Colossae. Theodoret claims Philemon's house still a displayed site at Colossae.	*PG* 82.613B, 620D– 621A *PG* 82.871–72A.
451	Epiphanius, bishop of Colossae, listed at the Council of Chalcedon.	Le Quien 815, Bonfrere 232
C5–6	Church of St Theodore operating at Colossae.	Cadwallader *GBRS* 334–37
530	Colossae listed as a polis of Phrygia Pacatiana	Hierocles *Sunekdemos* § 666.1
c.530	Rhodians said to designate themselves "Colossians" from the time of the construction of the Colossus.	John Malalas *Chronicle* 5.73
692	Kosmas, bishop of Colossae, attends the Quinisextine Council.	Le Quien 815
C7–8	Colossae renamed Chonai?	Peers 163
787	Dositheus bishop of Chonai/Colossae attends the Second Council of Nicea. First notice of change of name of see.	Le Quien 815–16, *AASS* Sept. Vol. 8, p. 39 et 4; cf Constant. Porphyr. *Them.* 1.3
c.815	St Peter of Atroa (Theophylact) performs exorcisms at Chonai.	*Vita* 13.20
819	Iconoclastic antagonism espoused by bishop of Chonai in meeting with Theodore of Studios.	Theodore of Studios *Ep* 2.63.
858	Chonai church becomes an archbishopric. Archbishop sent to Rome as patriarchal envoy.	*Vita Ign* (*PG* 105.516B)
C9th	Chonai becomes the key fortress defence for the valley, the capital or military centre of the theme of Thrakesion, with 10,000 troops under its direction.	Al Fakih (Brooks 74), Yakut VI.864, Constant. Porphyr. *Them.* 1.3, Foss 196, Belke/Mersich 49.

866	Samuel, archbishop of Chonai, attends Council of Constantinople.	Le Quien 815–816. *Vita Ign.* (*PG* 105. 516B)
mid–C10th	Chonai church becomes a metropolitanate with a suffragan at Chairetopa	Belke/Mersich 133; *Notit. Episc.* 150.
	Prokopios, first metropolitan of Chonai (?)	Lauxtermann 100
	Icon at Church of St. Michael object of veneration by pilgrims.	*Vita S. Cyril. Phileotes* 18.1
	Cross supposedly from St. Michael, credited with miraculous powers, perhaps located at Chonai	Hamilton, J. 218n10
	Kyriakos of Chonai, epistolographer and poet, succeeds Prokopios as metropolitan of Chonai	Lauxtermann 100
c.985	Menologion (Synopses and Propers for *inter alia* Saints' Lives) of Basil II includes St. Michael of Chonai (Sept. 6th).	*PG* 117:33CD
c 985	Leon of Magnesia on the Maeander (=St Lazaros of Mt Galesion) rests at Chonai on pilgrimage to and from (in c. 1010) Jerusalem; prays at church of St. Michael. Other pilgrims from Cappadocia, Paphlygonia, Ephesus.	*Vita Lazaros* §§ 6–8, 29
1028	Constantine, metropolitan of Chonai.	Le Quien 816 Nesbitt/Oikonimides III, § 12.1
C11th	The city of Gangra in Paphlagonia sends gold to the shrine of St. Michael.	*Miracula S Georgii* 107–113
1057–58	Patriarch Michael Cerularius commissions, as commentary on his own day, a cross recalling deeds of St Michael the Archangel. It includes the miracle of Chonai.	*DOC* Acc. No 64.13, Class. No. 110.2058–61
1066	Nicholas, metropolitan bishop of Chonai. Constantinopolitan Psalter includes miniature of icon of miracle of St Michael of Chonai.	Le Quien 816 *BL* Add 19352 f. 125r (der Nersessian 46)
c. 1067	Michael Psellos writes letter of introduction (and other letters) for Elias the monk to Sergios (or Xeros), civilian judge of the Thrakesion theme, based (?) at Chonai — "not yet under siege".	Psellos *Ep.* 1 (Dennis)
1070 (6579 a.c.)	Turks under Sultan Alp Arslan, attack township of Chonai; allegedly turn church of St. Michael into a stable.	Jeru. Hag. Savvas ms 697 ff 116–117 (Schreiner); John Scylitzes *Chron* II. 686–87 (*PG* 122. 415–16); Attaliates 140–41; Bar Hebraeus 1.220

1070	Emperor Romanos IV Diogenes receives report that Chonai taken by the "barbarians"	John Zonaras 18.12.18 (Dindorf)
1075	John, metropolitan bishop of Chonai	*BZ* 100.1119 § 2369 Nesbitt/Oikono-mides III, § 99.6, 7
1075	St Cyril Phileotes exalts the icon of St. Michael at the church at Chonai.	*Vita* 18.1.
1081	Chonas, the key fortress town for the control of the Lycus Valley; passes between Seljuk and Byzantine control over the next century.	Pitcher 27; Vryonis ch.3.
c. 1100	Epiphanios, governor of Thrakesion — based at Chonai?	Nesbitt/Oikonmides III, § 2.6
c. 1140	Birth of Michael Choniates, later archbishop of Athens.	
1143	Nicetas, metropolitan bishop of Chonai, eunuch and seer, later to be godfather of Nicetas Choniates	Nic Chon *Chron.* 219.71–5 (van Dieten)
c.1150	Birth of Nicetas Choniates, brother of Michael, later imperial court secretary.	
c.1150	Nicetas, metropolitan of Chonai, refuses to readmit Jews to Chonai.	Mich Chon *Encom.* 88 (Lampros 1.53), Vryonis 52, Laurent § 1590
1176	Byzantine Emperor Michael Comnenos visits church of St Michael to pray before the battle of Myriokephalon. He lost.	Nic Chon *Chron.* 219. 78–80 (van Dieten)
1189	Laodicea and Chonai plundered by Theodore Managaphas. Church of St Michael severely burnt (though perhaps church at Aphrodisias).	Nic Chon *Chron.* 400.88–96 (van Dieten)
1190	Frederick Barbarosa of Prussia, the Holy Roman Emperor, on the way to the Third Crusade, stops in Laodicea and Chonai after ravaging Konya, and is received kindly. He drowned before he reached his destination.	*Ep Frid* 173–178 (Chroust)
1193	Church of St Michael at Chonai ransacked by Pseudo-Alexis.	Nic Chon *Chron.* 422.85–90 (van Dieten)
C12th	Christians along with Seljuk Turks from Konya make pilgrimage and/or mercantile travel to Festival of St. Michael.	Mich Chon *Encom.* 95 (Lampros, 1.56)
c. 1205	Manuel Maurozomes, a claimant to be Byzantine Emperor, formally is granted control of Chonai and Laodicea and the Maeander Valley in a complex treaty arrangement between Theodore (Laskaris) I and Sultan Kay-Khusraw I (Manuel's son-in-law).	Ibn Bibi 23–26; Nic Chon *Chron.* 638.62–69 (van Dieten), Geo Akrop 69 (Macrides)

1206	Theodore I's defeat of Maurozomes hands Chonai and Laodikeia to Sultan Kay-Khusraw I as means of securing his throne.	Skout 531.4–7 (Heisenberg I.295), Nic Chon *Chron.* 638.65–8 (van Dieten), Korobeinikov 106
c. 1253	Karasungur bin Abdullah builds "Ak Han" caravanserai (travellers' hostel) near Honaz on road to Denizli; Colossae the quarry (?).	Arundell 162, Lyle 48
1257	Chonai returns to Byzantine control.	Geo Akropolites 69 (Macrides)
1259–61	Chonai passes into Turcoman control.	Skout 531.8–9 (Heisenberg I.295)
C13th	River valley just west of Chonai becomes known as "Türkmenova".	Wittek 1–2, "CB 847B" 449, Philippson 95 + map
C13–15th	Some by punning allusion, some literally begin to identify Colossians with Rhodians by connection with the most famous Colossus.	Philes *Carmina* 44; Suidas *Lexic.* ss. 314–15. George Monachus *Short Chronicle* (*PG* 110.340B); Cristoforo Buondelmonti (van der Vin 655)
c. 1320	Manuel Philes composes an honorific epigram drawing a spiritual lesson from "the Miracle at Chonai".	Philes *Carmina* 226
1333	Ibn Battuta, pursuing a Mecca-vow 'to travel throughout the earth', passes through the area.	*TIB* 2.425–28
1370	Control of church metropolitanate of Chonai passes to Cotyaeum.	*Acta* I.539
1384	Control of church metropolitanate of Chonai passes to Laodicea (reaffirmed 1394).	*Acta* II.88, 210
C15th	Metropolitical dioceses of Hierapolis, Laodicea, Synnada and Cotyaeum along with their dependencies disappear from episcopacy lists.	Vryonis 297
c.1440	Foundation of Murat Mosque at Chonai, under Sultan Murat II, reputedly on site of chapel of St. Archippos.	Amir 42–44
1522	Two night stay at Honaz (plus 1 night at Denizli) by Ottoman Sultan, Süleyman the Magnificent, on his journey for the breaking of the siege at Rhodes.	Yerasimos 151

	Sultan Süleyman, also called "Kanuni" (institute-maker), revamps bureaucracy inducing great prosperity and administrative accuracy. Honaz a town like Lazkiye (Denizli), of about 1500–2000 people, sizeable by European standards of the time.	Erder/Faroqhi 266–67, 273
1668	Paul Rycaut, English consul at Smyrna, asserts that Honaz previously known as Passas. Notes that the Greeks have become Turkophone.	Arundell 168, Rycaut 58,
	John Luke reports thirty Greek families at "Honíz/Hona", and ten churches, two still "in repair", though no priest resident. Control under the Metropolitan of Smyrna.	*BL* Harl. 7021 ff. 354a, 377b, 378a
1670/71	Turkish traveller, Evliya Çelibi stays at Honaz as part of his wide-ranging description of Turkey; gives positive report of the town.	Çelibi 26, 38, 191
1671	Thomas Smith joins growing band of explorer visitors from European businesses newly stationed at Smyrna interested in visiting "The Seven Churches of Asia" and side-interests, such as Colossae; scathing report on Honaz.	Smith 206
	Classical texts begin to guide (and gather support from) geographical cartography and epigraphical evidence, notably Xenophon and Strabo.	Rennell, Ainsworth
1705	Antonio Picenini notices many columns and fragments with inscriptions, as well as a complicated water-canal system at "Colossas, Chonos"; about 40 Greek families at Chonos. Church near fortress castle on mountain slopes.	*BL* Add 6269 ff. 48– 49, Chandler (1775) 240
1714	The adventurous and impressionable French explorer, Paul Lucas, ranges along the mountains to the south and east of Denizli, noting medieval castles and fortifications.	Lucas 232–34
c1715	Severe earthquake devastates the town of Denizli.	*BL* Add 22998 f.88 (Pococke)
1730s	Soley Bey Ogle, the rebel Aga of Chonai lives in fortified residence protected by 11 cannons.	Pococke 78, Milner 357, Chandler (1775) 240
1740	Pococke reports the death of Soley Bey (1739) but states the area around "Demizely" "so much damaged by the rebellion".	*BL* Add 22998 f.88
1745	Richard Pococke begins process of search for and description of ancient site of Colossae; European cartography of area begins to gain in accuracy.	Pococke 72–74

1750	Robert Wood passes a (mile?)stone near ancient Laodicea; surmises from it that Colossae was nearby.	Wood *Journal* 6 f.67
1764	Society of Dilettantes in London commission Richard Chandler to explore south-west Turkey.	Chandler vi
1763–4	First collectors' publication of coins from Colossian mint.	Pellerin 3.147–48
C18–19	Substantial commercial use of water-mills along Lycus River, west of site of Colossae.	Ainsworth 16, Davis 117
1813–14	Captain Kinneir travels through area, refining maps and taking bearings for a catalogue of longitudes at Greenwich.	Kinneir x
1816	Louis Corancez reports that the general region heavily controlled by local agas.	Corancez 428–31
1826	Francis Arundell provides first recorded inscription from Colossae. Mentions the remains of three churches in vicinity of site.	*AS* 56 (2006); Arundell *Discoveries* 169–70
1826	Letter to Francis Arundell mentions the church of St. Pantaleon at the foot of the mountain just outside of Honaz, along with caves and rock inscriptions.	Arundell *Seven* 318–19
1826	John Hartley finds almost no Greek spoken at 'Konos', even amongst Christians, who live in a total of 30 houses compared with 500 houses inhabited by Turks; 3 mosques, 1 church and remains of monastery of the holy taxiarch Michael.	Hartley 49, 264
1832	J. A. Cramer estimates about 200 Greek families in "Chonos". T. Milner figures the Greeks as living in 50 houses and worship in a room, more like a cellar than a church.	Cramer 2.45, Milner 360
1833	M. J. Cohen estimates the population of Chonai as 1500, living in 300 houses	Kiepert 164
1836	William Hamilton claims to have clarified site of ancient Colossae; sees seats and part of wall of theatre.	Hamilton 60–61
1840	Murray's *Handbook for Travellers* (along with Usborne's, Reidecker's and Macmillan's) point to a growing European tourist interest in the area; Murray retains medieval castle above Honaz as evidence of the site of Colossae.	Murray 274
1842	Edward T. Daniell discovers inscription from principate period at Balbura, for a woman who came from Colossae.	Spratt/Forbes II.289
	Augustus Schönborn, Hermann Loew and Jens Pell cross from Denizli to Tavas and Karajuk Bazaar via "Chonosdagh".	Schönburn 16

1851	Henry Christmas reports remains of two churches and being directed to the site of St. Michael the Archangel's cavity in the earth.	Christmas 300–01
1864	Conybeare and Howson mark substantial change from dogmatic or moral commentary on the New Testament to archaeologically informed details: including coins, inscriptions and etchings of sites. Colossae however left without data.	Conybeare & Howson
1868	Ottoman officials visit Honaz to collect coins for the newly inaugurated Ottoman Imperial Museum.	Davis 121
1869	Ernest Renan incorporates epigraphy and numismatics into studies of Paul's life and letters but considers Colossae necropolis "bizarre et anépigraphes".	Renan 362–65, 358n1
1870	Edmund Davis sketches of the höyük (artificial mound) and a gravestone betray English forms. Reports a number of mills in the district.	Davis 117
1881	William Mitchell Ramsay makes his first surface archaeological foray into area of Colossae.	"Studies" 1–2, "Cities" 371, *Bearing* 36
1884	A. H. Smith discovers "another" disappearing stream, the Tchukur Tchai, in the Khonasdagh pass and takes it to be Strabo's "Cadmus" river.	*JHS* 1887.224, *cf JHS* 1897.406–408
1885	The evangelical Glasgow minister, Rev. W.F Somerville, spends an hour and a half at the site and fancies Philemon's house atop the mound.	Somerville 78
c. 1890	M. Henri Cambournac takes earliest known photographs of Colossae site.	*DB* sv. Colossae
1887–8	Ottoman Railway from Smyrna, begun 1856 with British funding, finally passes near Colossae (Bujali station).	*NID* 243
1893	G. Weber finally puts to rest the efforts to find Herodotus' disappearing river.	*Ath Mitt* 16.194–99
1895	W. M. Ramsay estimates the population of Honaz as half Christian, half Turk. No evidence provided.	*CBP* 216
1897	J. G. C. Anderson discovers further inscriptions from Colossae.	*JHS* 1898.90
1899	P. Gaudin discovers near Smyrna a (third century?) memorial to a student, Diodotos, from Colossae.	*IK* 23.440
1900	A. Philippson reports 500 houses at Honaz.	Philippson 97

1907	Gertrude Bell passes Colossae by rail on way to meet William Mitchell Ramsay at Bir Bin Kalisi.	GBA Diary 25/4/1907
1908	After 70 years of travellers' guides listing Colossae, Macmillan's advises "nothing much to see".	Macmillan 195
1909	G. Lampakis records two nineteenth century epitaphs written in Turkish with Greek letters	Lampakis 455
1920	K. Yalçin writes of 1000 Greeks and 1000 Turks in Honaz	Yalçin, Emanet Çeyiz
1923–4	Repatriation of Greeks at Honaz to northern Greece.	Lausanne Convention
1933	Buckler and Calder visit Colossae and Honaz in search of inscriptions.	MAMA VI
1963	Small ceramic and glass collection from site by J. McDonald.	BIA Pottery Room, Region 20
1976	Harold Mare photographs heavily worn inscription.	PNEAS 1976.50
1976	Otto Meinardus and Klaus Siefer find capitals with cross-designs.	Meinardus 469
1998	Flinders University begins collaborative research on "Colossae: Digging Up the Past".	Trainor
2001	Celal Şimşek, Professor of Archaeology at Pamukkale University, takes aerial survey of site of Colossae, begins investigation of necropolis.	Şimşek
2004–06	Erim Konakçi and Bahadır Duman conduct surface survey of ceramics.	Konakçi/Duman
2005	Plans for the archaeological tourist development of Colossae by the Honaz Municipality.	

Abbreviations

AASS	Acta Sanctorum
AB	Analecta Bollandiana or Bollandiensis
Acta	Acta et diplomata graeca medii aevi sacra et profana
AS	Anatolian Studies
Ath Mitt	Mitteilungen des deutschen archäologischen Instituts, athenische Abteilung
BIA	British Institute in Ankara
BL	British Library
BZ	Byzantische Zeitschrift
CBP	Cities and Bishoprics of Phrygia (Ramsay)
CIG	Corpus Inscriptionum Graecarum
CSHB	Corpus Scriptorum Historiae Byzantinae

DB　　　　　*Dictionnaire de la Bible*
DOC　　　　Dumbarton Oaks Collection
Ep.Att.　　　*Letters to Atticus* (Cicero)
GBA　　　　Gertrude Bell Archives (University of Newcastle-on-Tyne)
GRBS　　　*Greek, Roman and Byzantine Studies*
IGR　　　　Inscriptiones Graecae ad res Romanas pertinentes
IK　　　　*Inschriften Griechischer Städte aus Kleinasien*
JHS　　　　Journal of Hellenic Studies
MAMA　　　*Monumenta Asiae Minoris Antiqua*
NicChon　　Nicetas Choniates
NID　　　　(British) Naval Intelligence Division Manual
NH　　　　　Natural History *(Pliny the Elder)*
Notit. Episc.　Notitiae Episcopatum
PG　　　　　*Patrologia Graeca* (Migne)
PNEAS　　　Publication of the Near Eastern Archaeological Society
Skout　　　Theodore Skoutariotes *Synopsis Chronike*
TIB　　　　Travels of Ibn Battuta

References and Editions referred to in the table

Agir, M., *Honaz: doğa harikası* (İzmir: Nesa, 1994).

Ainsworth, W. F., *Travels in the Track of the Ten Thousand Greeks; being a Geographical and Descriptive Account of the Expedition of Cyrus and of the Retreat of the Ten Thousand Greeks as related by Xenophon* (London: John W. Parker, 1844).

Anderson, J. G. C., "A Summer in Phrygia I", *JHS* 17 (1897) 396–424.
"A Summer in Phrygia II", *JHS* 18 (1898) 81–128.

Arundell, F. V. J., *A Visit to the Seven Churches of Asia Minor with an excursion into Pisidia.* (London: John Rodwell, 1828).

– *Discoveries in Asia Minor; including a Description of the Ruins of Several Ancient Cities and especially Antioch of Pisidia* (2 vol.; London: Richard Bentley, 1834).

Aufhauser, J. B. (ed.), *Miracula S. Georgii* (Leipzig: Teubner, 1913).

Bekker, I., *Constantinus Porphyrogenitus: de Thematibus et de Administrando Imperio* (*CSHB* III; Bonn: Weber, 1840).

Belke, K./N. Merisch, *Tabula Imperii Byzantini Bd 7: Phrygien und Pisidien* (Vienna: Österreichischen Akademie der Wissenschaft, 1990).

Berger, A./S. Güntner/R. Tocci, "Bibliographische Notizen und Mitteilungen", *BZ* 100 (2008) 899–1190.

Boeckh, A., *Corpus Inscriptionum Graecarum* (4 vol.; Berlin: Officina Academica, 1828–1877).

Bonfrère, J., *Onomasticon Urbium et Locorum Sacrae Scripturae* (Amsterdam: Wettstein, 1711).

Bonnet, M., "Story of St Michael of Chonas", *AB* 8 (1889) 289–307 and 308–316.

Buckler, W. H./W. M. Calder, *Monumenta Asiae Minoris Antiqua Vol VI: Monuments and Documents from Phrygia and Caria* (Manchester: Manchester University Press, 1939).

Cadwallader, A. H., "Revisiting Calder on Colossae", *AS* 56 (2006) 103–111.

"The Reverend Dr. John Luke and the Churches of Chonai", *GRBS* 48 (2008) 319–338.

Cagnat, R. *et. al.*, *Inscriptiones Graecae ad res Romanas pertinentes* (Paris: E. Leroux, 1906–1927).

"CB 847B", *Handbook of Asia Minor* (UK: Naval Staff Intelligence Department, 1919).

Chandler, R., *Travels in Asia Minor and Greece or An Account of a Tour made at the Expense of the Society of Dilettanti* (London: J. Booker, 1775, 1817).

Christmas, H., *The Shores and Islands of the Mediterranean, including a visit to the Seven Churches of Asia* (3 vol.; London: R. Bentley, 1851).

Chroust, A., *Quellen zur Geschichte des Kreuzzuges Kaiser Frederichs I* (Berlin: Weidmannsche buchhandlung, 1928).

Conybeare, W. J. and J. S. Howson, *The Life and Epistles of St. Paul* (2 vol.; London: Longman, Green. Longman, Robert and Green, 1864).

Corancez, L. A. O., de *Itinéraire d'une partie peu connue de l'Asie Mineure* (Paris: Renouard, 1816).

Cramer, J. A., *A Geographical and Historical Description of Asia Minor* (2 vol.; Oxford: Oxford University Press, 1832).

Darrouzès, A., *Notitiae episcopatum ecclesiae Constantinopolitanae (Géographie ecclésiastique de l'empire byzantin 1)* (Paris: Institut Français d'Études Byzantines, 1981).

Davis, E. J., *Anatolica: or The Journal of a Visit to Some of the Ancient Ruined Cities* (London: Grant, 1874).

Dennis, G. T., "Elias the Monk, Friend of Psellos", in N. Oikonomides/J. W. Nesbitt (ed.) *Byzantine Authors: Texts and Translations Dedictaed to the Memory of Nicolas Oikonomides* (Leiden: Brill, 2003) 43–62.

Dindorf, L. A., *Ioannis Zonarae: Epitome historiarum* (Leipzig: B. G. Teubner, 1868).

Duman, B./E. Konakçi, "Kolossai: Höyük, Kalıntı ve Buluntuları", *Arkeoloji Dergisi* 8 (2006) 83–109.

Erder, L. T./S. Faroqhi, "The Development of the Anatolian Urban Network during the Sixteenth Century", *Journal of the Economic and Social History of the Orient* 23 (1980) 265–303.

Franke, P. R./M. K. Nollé, *Die Homonoia-Münzen Kleinasiens und der thrakischen Rangebeite.* (Herstellung: Saarbrücker Druckerei und Verlag, 1997).

des Gagniers, J. *et al* (ed.), *Laodicée du Lycos: le Nymphée, Campagnes 1961–1963* (Quebec: L'Université Laval, 1969).

Gaisford, T. and G. Bernhardy, *Suidae Lexicon* (Halle: C. A. Schwetschke, 1853).

Gibbs, H. A. R. (ed.), *The Travels of Ibn Battuta* (Cambridge: Haklyut Society, 1956–).

Greenfield, R. P. H., *The Life of Lazaros of Mt Galesion: An Eleventh Century Pillar Saint* (Washington, DC: Dumbarton Oaks Research Library and Collection, 2000).

Hartley, J., *Researches in Greece and the Levant* (London: Seeley, 1833).

Hamilton, J. and B., *Christian Dualist Heresies in the Byzantine World c. 650 – c. 1450* (Manchester: Manchester University Press, 1998).

Hamilton, W. H., "Extracts from Notes Made on a Journey in Asia Minor in 1836 by W. I. Hamilton", *Journal of the Royal Geographic Society of London* 7 (1837) 34–61.

Heisenberg, A. (ed.), "Theodori Scutariotae Additamenta ad Georgii Acropolitae Historiam" in *Georgii Acropolitae Opera* (Leipzig: B. G. Teubner, 1903), 1.277–302.

Hill, R. C., *Theodoret of Cyrus: Commentary on the Letters of St Paul* (Brookline, Mass: Holy Cross Orthodox Press, 2001).

Houtsma, M. T. (ed.), *Histoire des Seldjoucides d'Asie Mineure, d'après l'abrégé du Seldjouknâmen d'Ibn -Bībī: texte persan* (Leiden: Brill, 1902).

Hunter, L. W., "Cicero's Journey to His Province of Cilicia in 51 BC", *JRS* 3 (1913) 73–97.

Jeffreys, E./M. Jeffreys/R. Scott, *The Chronicle of John Malalas* (Melbourne: Australasian Association of Byzantine Studies, 1986, 2004).

Jenkins, R. J. H., "A Cross of the Patriqarch Michael Cerularius" with "An Art-Historical Comment" by E. Kitzinger, *DOP* 21 (1967) 233–249.

Kiepert, H., *Memoir über die construction der karte von Kleinasien und türkisch Armenien.* (Berlin: Simon Schropp, 1854).

Kinneir, J. MacD., *Journey through Asia Minor, Armenia and Koordistan in the Years 1813 and 1814 with Remarks on the Marches of Alexander and Retreat of the Ten Thousand* (London: John Murray, 1818).

Konakçi, E./B. Duman, "Arkeolojik ve Yazılı Kanıtlar Işığında Kolossai (Kolossai with the Light of Archaeological and Historical Evidences)" in *International Symposium on the History and Culture of Denizli and its Surroundings* (2 vol.; Denizli: Pamukkale University, 2007,) 2.57–67.

Lampakis, G., Οἱ ἑπτὰ ἀστέρες τῆς Ἀποκαλύψεως ἤτοι ἱστορία, ἐρείπια, μνημεῖα καὶ νῦν κατάστασις τῶν ἑπτὰ ἐκκλησίων τῆς Ἀσίας, Ἐφέσου, Σμύρνης, Περγάμου, Θυατείρων, Σάρδεων, Φιλαδελφείας καὶ Λαοδικείας, παρ᾽ ἢ Κολοσσαὶ καὶ Ἱεράπολις. (Athens: 1909).

Lampros, S. P. (ed.), Μιχαὴλ Ἀκομινατοῦ τοῦ Χωνιατοῦ τὰ σῳζόμενα (2 vol.; Groningen: Bouma, 1968 [1879–80]).

Laurent, E. V. (ed.), *La vie merveilleuse de Saint Pierre d'Atroa* (Brussels: Society of Bollandists, 1956).

Laurent, V., *Le Corpus des Sceaux de l'Empire byzantin Vol .2 L'Église* (Paris: Publications de l'institut francais d'Études Byzantines, 1965).

Lauxtermann, M. D., *The Spring of Rhythm: An Essay on the Political Verse and other Byzantine metres* (Vienna: Austrian Academy of Sciences, 1999).

Le Quien, M., *Oriens Christianus in quatuor Patriarchatus digestus; quo exhibentur Ecclesiae, Patriarchae, caeterique Praesules totius Orientis ... Opus posthumum* (3 vol.; Paris: 1740).

Lightfoot, J. B., *Epistles of Saint Paul: Epistle to the Colossians* (London: Macmillan, 9th Ed., 1890).

Lucas, P., *Voyage du Sieur P. Lucas fait en 1714 dans la Turquie, l'Asie, Sourie, Palestine, Haute et Basse Égypte*, A. Banier (ed.) (3 vol.; Rouen: 1719).

Lyle, E., *The Search for the Royal Road* (London: Vision Press, 1966).

Macmillan & Co. *Guide to Greece, the Archipelago, Constantinople, the Coasts of Asia Minor, Crete and Cyprus* (London: Macmillan, 1908).

Macrides, R. J., *George Akropolites: the history* (trans./comm.) (Oxford/New York: Oxford University Press, 2007).

Magdalino, P., *The Empire of Manuel I Komnenos, 1143–1180.* Cambridge: Cambridge University Press, 2002.

Mare, W. H., "Archeological Prospects at Colossae", *Publication of the Near East Archeological Society* 7 (1976) 39–59.

Meinardus, O. F. A., "St Michael Miracle of Khonae", *Ekklesia kai Theologia* 1 (1980) 459–469.

Mellaart, J., "Preliminary Report on a Survey of Pre-Classical Remains in Southern Turkey", *AS* 4 (1954) 175–240.

Miklosich, F./J. Müller, *Acta et diplomata graeca medii aevi sacra et profana* (Vindobonae: C. Gerold, 1860–90).

Miller, E. (ed.), *Manuelis Philae carmina ex codicibus Escurialensis, Florentinis, Parisinis et Vaticanis* (2 vol., Paris: Imperial Printers, 1855–1857).

Milner, T., *History of the Seven Churches of Asia* (London: Holdsworth and Ball, 1832).

Murray, J., *Handbooks for Travellers in the Ionian Islands, Greece, Turkey, Asia Minor and Constantinople, including a description of Malta with maxims and hints for Travellers in the East; with index, plans and maps* (London: J. Murray, 1840).

Nersessian, S. der, *L'Illustration des psautiers grecs du moyen âge, II* (Paris: Klincksieck, 1970).

Nesbitt, J. and N. Oikonomides, *Catalogue of Byzantine Seals at Dum,barton Oaks and in the Fogg Museum of Art III: West, Northwest and Central Asia Minor and the Orient* (Washington DC: Dumbarton Oaks Publications, 1996).

Peers, G., *Subtle Bodies, Representing Angels in Byzantium* (Berkeley: University of California Press, 2001).

Pellerin, J., *Recueil de Médailles de Rois/de peoples et de villes* (Paris: H. L. Guerin & L. F. Delatour, 1762–1767).

Pertusi, E. (ed.), *Constantino Porfirogenito De thematibus* (Città del Vaticano: Biblioteca apostolica vaticana, 1952).

Petzl, G. (ed.), *Die Inschriften von Smyrna I–II* (*Inschriften Griechischer Städte aus Kleinasien* 23–24; 2 vol.; Bonn: Habelt, 1982, 1990).

Philippson, A., *Reisen und Forschungen im westlichen Kleinasien IV: Das östliche Lydien und südwestliche Phrygien* (Gotha: J. Perthes, 1914).

Pitcher, D. E., *An Historical Geography of the Ottoman Empire* (Leiden: E. J. Brill, 1972).

Pococke, R., *Description of the East and Some Other Countries* (London: W. Boyer, 1745).

Ramsay, W. H., "Studies in Asia Minor", *JHS* 3 (1882) 1–68.

– "Cities and Bishoprics of Phrygia I", *JHS* 4 (1883) 370–436.

– *Cities and Bishoprics of Phrygia* (Oxford: Clarendon Press, 1895, 1897).

– *The Bearing of Recent Discoveries on the Trustworthiness of the New Testament* (London: Hodder & Stoughton, 1915).

Renan, E., *Histoire des Origines di Christianisme* (6 vol.; Paris: Michel Lévy Frères, 1869).

Rennell, J., *Illustrations (Chiefly Geographical) of the History of the Expedition of Cyrus From Sardis to Babylonia* (London: W. Bulmer, 1816).

Rycaut, P., *History of the Turks 1679–99* (London: Thomas Basset, 1700).

Sargologos, E., *Vie de S. Cyrille le Philéote* (Brussels: Société des Bollandistes, 1964).

Sathas, K. N. (ed.), Μεσαιωνικὴ Βιβλιοθήκη (Paris: 1894 repr. Hildesheim: George Olms, 1972).

Schoenborn, C., "The Life of the Late Augustus Schoenborn", in M. Schmidt, *The Lycian Inscriptions after the accurate copies of the late Augustus Schoenborn* (Jena: Mauke's, 1868).

Schreiner, P., *Die Byzantinischen Kleinchroniken* (Wien: Österreichische Akademie der Wissenschaften, 1979).

Sekunda, N., "Achaemenid Settlement in Caria, Lycia and Greater Phrygia", in H. Sancisi-Weerdenburg/A. Kuhrt (ed.) *Achaemenid History VI: Asia Minor and Egypt: Old Cultures in a New Empire* (Leiden: Nederlands Instituut voor het Nabije Oosten, 1991) 83–143.

Şimşek, C., "Kolossai", *Arkeoloji ve Sanat* 107 (2002) 3–16, 33.

Smith, A. H., "Notes on a Tour in Asia Minor", *JHS* 8 (1887) 216–267.

Somerville, W. F. (ed.), *The Churches in Asia* (Paisley: J & R Parlane, 1885).

Spratt, T. A. B.,/E. Forbes, *Travels in Lycia, Milyas and the Cibyratis in company with the late Rev E. T. Daniell* (2 vol.; London: John van Hoorst, 1847).

Thurn, I. (ed.), *Ioannis Scylitzae Synopsis Historiarum* (Berlin: de Gruyter, 1973).

Trainor, M., "Unearthing Ancient Colossae in Southern Turkey: Theology and Archaeology in Dialogue", *Compass* 36 (2002) 40–46.

Vigouroux, F. (ed.), *Dictionnaire de la Bible* (5 vol.; Paris: Letouzey et Ané, 1899).

van Dieten, J-L. (ed.), *Nicetae Choniatae Historia*. Berlin: Walter de Gruyter, 1975.

van der Vin, J. P. A., *Travellers to Greece and Constantinople: Ancient Monuments and Old Traditions in Medieval Travellers' Tales* (2 vol.; Istanbul: Nederlands Historisch-Archaeologisch Instituut, 1980).

Vryonis, S., *The Decline of Medieval Hellenism in Asia Minor and the Process of Islamization from the Eleventh through the Fifteenth Century* (Berkeley: University of California Press, 1974).

Weber, G., "Der unterirdische Lauf des Lykos bei Kolossai", *Ath. Mitt* 16 (1891) 194–99.

Winstedt, E. O. (trans.), *Cicero: Letters to Atticus* (LCL; London: Heinemann, 1912).

Wittek, P., *Das Fürstentum Mentesche. Studie zur Geschichte Westkleinasiens im 13.–15. Jh.* (Amsterdam: Oriental Press, 1967).

Wood, R., "Journals" 1750. Manuscripts held by Joint Library of the Hellenic and Roman Societies, University of London.

Yacut, *Geographisches Wörterbuch* (edited by F. Wüstenfeld) (Leipzig: F. A. Brockhaus, 1867).

Yalçin, K. *Emanet Çeyiz: Mübadele Insanlari* (Istanbul: Birzamanlar Yayıncılık, 2005).

Yerasimos, S., *Les Voyageurs dans l'Empire Ottoman (XIVᵉ – XVIᵉ siècles: Bibliographie, Itinéraires et Inventaire des Lieux Habités* (Ankara: La Société Turque d'Histoire, 1991).

Appendix 1b

Colossae (Chonai) 'Nin Kronolojìk Tarihçesi

Derleyen: Alan H. Cadwallader
Çeviri: Umut Özgüç ve Sarp Kaya

TARİH	KİŞİ VE OLAYLAR
Bronz Çağı	Colossae'nln muhtemel kuruluş dönemi.
Millattan once 4–5. yüzyıl (yy)	Colossae'nln Kraliyet Yolu üzerinde merkez konum halini alması, çevre arazilerdeki kraliyet toprakları, Lycus nehrinin şehrin içinden geçmesi ve Persli yerleşimciler.
481	Serhas (Kserkses)'ın Yunanistan'a giderken ordusuyla birlikte Colossae'da konaklaması.
401	Colossae'nın zengin,büyük ve yerleşik bir şehir olarak tanımlanması.
401	Kiros'un 10.000 Helen askeri ile birlikte Artakserkses ile girişeceği talihsiz Kunaksa(Cunaxa) Savaşı için yöneldiği Babil yolculuğu sıra- sında Chonai'da yedi gün konaklamaları.
395/6	Milattan önce 414 yılında atanmış olan Pers valisi Tissaphernes'in Colossae hamamlarında yakalanması ve suikasta uğraması. Suikast ortaklarından Araios'un Colossae'da mülk edinmesi. Colossae'nın bölgede ürettiği yün boyası ile ününü sınırları ötesine taşıması.
133	Likos Vadisinin 3. Attalus tarafından Roma'ya miras bırakılması.
51	Kilikya valisi Cicero'nun Laodikya'da ve muhtemelen Colossae'da konaklaması.
23	Coğrafyacı Strabon'un Afrodisias'la birlikte Colossae'yı, Laodikya ve Apameia'dan sonra, önem derecesi açısından ikinci grup şehirler arasında göstermesi.
50s CE	Muhtemelen Ephahras tarafından Colossae'da Hristiyan cematinin kurulması.
56 civarı	Colossae'dan kaçan bir esir firarisi olan Onesimus'un, yeni bir din hareketinin öncüsü olan Aziz Pavlus (Paul of Tarsus) tarafından, sahibi Philemona'ya iade edilmesi.
60/1	Likos vadisinde gerceklesen şiddetli depremler sonucu meydana gelen acil yardım ihtiyacina karşın Laodikya'nın imparatorluktan ge- len desteği geri çevirmesi. Colossae ve Hierapolis' in imparatorluktan gelen yardımı kabul edip etmedikleri bilinmemektedir. Philip'in önce Bethsaida'ya sonra da Hierapolis'e gerçekleştirdiği efsanevi ziyareti.
66/7	Korumbos'un Colossae'daki hamamları onarmasından dolayı onurlandırılması.

129	İmparator Hadrian'ın pan-Helenik turu sırasında bölgeyi ziyaret etmesi.
	Yerel boksörlerin Tripoli'de gerçekleşen Olimpiyatlarda ödül kazanmaları.
177–180	Commodus'un hükümdarlığı sırasında Colosae'nın Afrodisyas'la birlik oluşturması.
2.yy sonu	Kıtlığın şehir hayatı üzerinde olumsuz etki yaratması.
220 civarı	Colossae'li atletlerin Tripoli olimpiyatlarına katılması.
305	İmparator Konstantius ve muhtemelen Diocletianus ve Maximian 'ın Colossae'da onurlandırılması.
4.yy sonu	Philemon'nun Colossae'nın ilk piskopozu ilan edilmesi.
4–5.yy	Yakapınar'lı Theodor ve Theodore gibi bir takım kilise eğitmenlerinin Laodikya'ya gönderilen mektubun içeriğinde Colossae'daki kilise hakkında bir takim bilgilerin olduğunu belirtmeleri.
	St. Michael tapınağının Colossae'da veya Colossae yakınlarında kurulması.
430 civarı	Theodoret'un, meleklere dua edilmesini yasaklayan Laodikya konsülünün 35. maddesinden yola çıkarak, meleklere tapınılmasına karşı uyarıda bulunması. Theodoret, Laodikya konsülünün bu maddesinin aynı zamanda Colossae'daki Michael tapınağı için de geçerli olduğunu savunmuştur.
	Theodor'un Philemon'un konutunun Colossae'da bulunduğunu iddia etmesi.
451	Colossae piskopozu Epiphanius'un Kalkedon Konsül'unde (Kadikoy Konsili) yeralması.
5–6. yy	St Theodore kilisesinin Colossae'da faaliyet göstermeye başlaması.
530	Colossae'nın Frigya'nın bir şehri (polis) olarak gösterilmesi.
530 civarı	Colossus'un (Rodos Heykeli) dikilmesi ile birlikte Rodosluların kendilerini "Koloselikler" (Colossians) olarak adlandırmaya başlamaları.
692	Colossae piskopozu Kosmas'in Trullo (Quinisextine) Konsülüne katılması.
7–8. yy	Colossae'nın adının muhtemelen Chonai[1] olarak değiştirilmesi.
787	Chonai/Colossae' lı piskopoz Dositheus'un İkinci İznik (Nicaea) Konsülüne katılması. Bölgenin isminin değişmesine dair ilk bildiri.
815 civarı	Atroa'lı Aziz Peter'ın (Theophylact) Chonai'da şeytan çıkarma ayinleri düzenlemesi .
819	Chonai piskopozunun, Studios Manastırı rahibi Aziz Theodore ile olan görüşmesi sonucunda Ikonoklast hareketini benimsemesi.
858	Chonai kilisesinin başpiskopozluğa dönüştürülmesi. Başpiskopozun patriyarkal temsilci olarak Roma'ya gönderilmesi.
9. yy	Chonai'nin 10.000 kişilik ordusu ile vadideki en önemli savunma kalesi ve Thrakesion Teması'nın başkenti veya bir askeri merkezi haline dönüşmesi.
866	Chonai başpiskopozu Samuel'in Konstantinopolis Konsülüne katılması.

---

1 Bugünkü Honaz.

10.yy ortaları	Chonai kilisesinin yardımcı piskopos ile birlikte Chairetapa'da metropolit haline gelmesi.
	Prokopios'un Chonai'ın muhtemel ilk metropoliti olması.
	St. Michael kilisesindeki haçın ibadet nesnesi haline gelmesi.
	St. Michael (Mikhail)'e ait olduğu düşünülen ve bir olasılıkla Chonai'da bulunan haçın mucizevi özelliklerinin olduğuna inanılması.
	Epistolog ve şair olan Chonai'li Kyriakos'un Prokopios'tan sonra Chonai metropoliti konumuna gelmesi.
985 civarı	Basil II Menologion'un Chonai St. Michael festival tarihini (6 Eylül) içermesi.
985 civarı	Maender[2] üzerindeki Magnesia'lı Leon'un (=St Lazaros of Mt Galesion) Kudüs'e olan hac ziyareti sırasında Chonai'da konaklaması (1010 civarı) ve St. Michael kilisesinde ibadet etmesi. Kapadokya, Efes ve Paflagonya'dan bir grup hacı da Chonai'a gelmişlerdir.
1028	Konstantin'in Chonai metropoliti haline gelmesi.
11. yy	Paflagonya'daki Gangra şehrinin St. Michael tapınağına altın göndermesi.
1057–58	Patrik Mihael Kerularios'un döneminin bir şerhi olarak, St. Michael'e adadığı ve Chonai mucizesini de sembolize eden bir haç siparişi vermesi.
1066	Nicholas'ın Chonai metropolit piskopozu olması.
	Psalter'in St. Michael'in mucizesini tevsir eden minyatürünü içermesi.
1067 civarı	Michael Psellos'un, Sergios (Xeros) keşişine Thrakesion Teması'nın sivil yargıçı olan ve muhtemelen Chonai'da ikamet etmekte olan Elias'ı tanıtan bir takım mektuplar göndermesi.
1070	Sultan Alparslan komutasındaki Türklerin, Chonai'a saldırıp St. Michael kilisesini ahıra çevirmeleri.
1070	İmparator IV. Romanos Diogenes'in, Chonai'ın "barbarlar" tarafından ele geçirildigi öğrenmesi.
1075	John'un Chonai metropolit piskopozu olması.
1075	St Cyril Phileotes'in Chonai'da bulunan St. Michael kilisesindeki haçı yüceltmesi.
1081	Likos Vadisi'nin kontrolü için esas savunma şehri görevi gören Chonas'ın bir yüzyıl boyunca Selçuklu ve Bizans İmparatorluğu arasında el değiştirmesi.
1100 civarı	Thrakesion valisi olan Epiphanious'un muhtemelen Chonai'da yaşaması.
1140 civarı	Gelecekte Athena başpiskopozu olacak olan Michael Choniates'in doğumu.
1143	Harem ağası ve kain olan, ve gelecekte Nicetas Choniates'in vaftiz babası olacak olan Nicetas'ın Chonai pizkopozu olması.
1150 civarı	Gelecekte imparatorluk mahkemesi sekreteri olacak olan, Michael'in kardeşi Nicetas Choniates'in doğumu.
1150 civarı	Chonai'i metropoliti Nicetas'in Yahudilerin Chonai'e girmelerini reddetmesi.

---

2 Bugünkü Büyük Menderes Nehri.

1176	Bizans İmparatoru Michael Komnenos'un yenilgiye uğrayacağı Miryakefalon Savaşı öncesinde St. Michael kilisesi'nde dua etmesi.
1189	Laodikya ve Chonai'ın Theodore Managaphas tarafından yağmalanması. St. Michael kilisesinin yanması (bazı düşünürler Laodikya ve Chonai' ın degil Afrodisyas'daki kilisenin yandığını iddia etmektedirler).
1190	Kutsal Roma Cermen İmparatoru Prusya'lı Frederik Barbaros'un 3. Haçlı Savaşı'na giderken, Konya'yı tahrip ettikten sonra misafirperverlikle karşılanacağı Laodikya ve Chonai'da konaklaması. Ancak Frederik Barbaros, 3. Haçlı Savaşı'nda hedefine ulaşamadan boğularak ölmüştür.
1193	Sözde Alexis (Pseudo-Alexis)'in Chonai'daki St. Michael kilisesini yağmalaması.
12. yy	Hristiyanların Konya Selçuklu Türkleri ile birlikte St. Michael kilisesi'ne hacca gitmeleri ve/veya ticari bir yolculuk yapmaları.
1205 civarı	I. Theodor (Laskaris) ile Manuel'in damadı olan Sultan I. Keyhüsrev arasında imzalanan bir anlaşma sonucunda, Manuel Mavrozomes'in Chonai ve Laodikya'nın kontrolünü resmi olarak eline geçirmesi.
1206	I. Theodor'un Mavrozomes'i yenmesi sonucunda tacını güvence altına almak için Chonai ve Laodikya'yı Sultan Keyhüsrev'e devretmesi.
1253 civarı	Karasungur bin Abdullah' ın Honaz yakınlarındaki Denizli yolu üzerinde Ak Han Kervansarayı'nı inşa etmesi. Bu kervansarayın Colossae taşlarından yapıldığı düşünülmektedir.
1257	Chonai'ın tekrar Bizans kontrolüne geçmesi.
1259–61	Chonai'ın Türkmenlerin kontrolüne geçmesi.
13. yy	Chonai'ın hemen batısındaki akarsu vadisinin 'Türkmenova" olarak adlandırılmaya başlanması.
13–15.yy	Kimilerinin kinaye yoluyla, kimilerinin ise ünlü Colossus (Rodos Heykeli) ile olan isim benzerliğinden dolayı Colosyonları Rodoslular ile ilişiklendirmesi.
1320 civarı	Manual Philes' in Chonai'daki mucizeyi konu alan epiği kaleme alması.
1333	İbn-i Batuta'nın Mekke adağını gerçekleştirmek amacıyla çıktıgı ve tüm dünyayı dolaştığı yolculuk sırasında Chonai bölgesinden geçmesi.
1370	Chonai metropolit kilisenin kontrolünün Cotyaeum'a[3] geçmesi.
1384	Chonai metropolit kilisenin kontrolünün Laodikya'ya geçmesi (Bu durum 1394'te tekrar teyid edilmiştir).
15. yy	Piskopozluk bölgesi olan Hierapolis, Laodikya, Synnada[4] ve Cotyaeum'un sömürgeleri ile birlikte piskopozluk listesinden silinmeleri.
1440 civarı	Sultan II. Murat'ın hükümdarlığı sırasında, Chonai'daki Murat Türbesi'nin Aziz Arkipost tapınağı bölgesinde inşa ettirilmesi. Türbenin Arkipost tapınağı bölgesinde inşa edildiği kesin bir veriden çok rivayete dayanmaktadır.

---

3 Bugünkü Kütahya şehri.
4 Bugünkü Suhut kasabası.

1522	Osmanlı İmparatoru Muhteşem Süleyman'ın, Rodos seferi sırasında iki gece Honaz'da ve bir gece de Denizli'de konaklaması. Kanuni olarak da bilinen Sultan Süleyman'ın Osmanlı bürokrasisini geliştirerek ülkenin refahını ve yönetim kapasitesini arttırması. Bu dönemde Lazkiye (Denizli) gibi bir şehir olan Honaz'ın nüfusu 1500–2000 olup zamanın Avrupa şehirleri büyüklüğündedir.
1668	Smyrna'da[5] İngiliz konsolosu olan Paul Rycaut'ın Honaz'ın daha önceki çağlarda "Passas" olarak bilindiğini öne sürmesi. Rycaut ayrıca Yunanlar'ın türkmenleştiğini belirtmiştir. John Luke'un "Honiz/Hona'da" 30 Yunan ailenin yanı sıra ikisi hala onarımda olan ancak herhangi bir papazın yaşamadığı on kilisenin bulunduğunu belirtmesi. Bu dönemde Honiz/Hona, Smyrna kontrolü altında bulunmaktadır.
1670/71	Bir Türk gezgini olan Evliya Çelebi'nin Honaz'da konaklaması. Çelebi'nin bu gezisi sonrası yöre hakkındaki gözlemleri olumlu yöndedir.
1671	Thomas Smith'in, o dönemde sayıları gittikçe artmakta olan ve Smyrna'da konaklayarak Asya'daki Yedi Kilise'nin yanı sıra Colossae ile de ilgilenen Avrupalı gezgincilerin arasına katılması. Smith bu dönemde aynı zamanda Honaz ile ilgili bir rapor da yazmıştır. Özellikle Ksenofon ve Strabon'a ait klasik metinlerin coğrafi kartografiye ve epigrafik bulgulara klavuzluk etmeye ve bu alanlardan destek almaya başlaması.
1705	Antonio Picenini'in üzerinde yazıtların bulunduğu kolonlar ve parçaların yanı sıra " Colossas, Chonos'da" gelişmiş bir su kanalı sistemini ve Chonos'da yaşamakta olan 40 Yunan aileyi keşfetmesi. Picenini ayrıca dağ yamacındaki kale yakınlarında bulunan bir kilisenin varlığını da belirtmiştir.
1714	Maceracı ve duyarlı kişiliği ile tanınan bir Fransız araştırmacı olan Paul Lucas'ın Denizli'nin dağlarından güneyine ve doğusuna doğru seyahat ederek bir takım antik kaleleri ve istihkam bölgelerini keşfetmesi.
1715 civarı	Şiddetli bir depremin Denizli bölgesini enkaza çevirmesi.
1730 civarı	Chonai'lı isyancı ağa Soley Bey'in[6] 11 savaş topu ile korunan bir konutta yaşaması.
1740	Pococke'un Soley Bey'in ölümünü (1739) bildirmesi. Pococke aynı raporda ayrıca "Demizely" bölgesinin Soley Bey isyanları nedeniyle oldukça hasar gördüğünü belirtmiştir.
1745	Richard Pococke'un Colossae antik sitesini ve yazıtlarını araştırmaya başlaması. Bu dönemde ayrıca Avrupa kartografisi önem kazanmaya başlamıştır.
1750	Robert Wood'un Laodikya antik kenti yakınlarındaki kayadan geçtigi sırada Colossae yakınlarında olduğunu düşünmesi.
1764	Londra'daki Dilettantes Sosyetesi'nin (society of Dilettantes) Richard Chandler'ı Türkiye'nin güneybatısını araştırmak için görevlendirmesi.

---

5 Bugünkü İzmir şehri.
6 Avrupa'daki bazı dokümanlarda "Sole Bey Ogle" olarak geçmektedir.

1763-4	Colossia darphanesine ait madeni paraların kolleksiyoncular tarafından ilk defa sergilenmesi.
18-19.yy	Colossae'nın batısında bulunan Likos Nehri üzerindeki su değirmenin ticari amaçlarla kullanılması.
1813-14	Kaptan Kinneir'in bölgeye yolculuğu, haritaları geliştirmesi ve Greenwich boylamı için konum açılarını hesaplaması.
1816	Louis Corancez'in bölgenin ciddi bir şekilde ağalar tarafından kontrol edildiğini bildirmesi.
1826	Francis Arundell'in Colossae'a ait antik yazıtın ilk kopyasını yayınlaması. Arundell ayrıca üç kilisenin kalıntılarının Colossae civarında olduğunu gözlemlemiştir.
1826	Denizli'de yaşayan bir Yunan kişiden Francis Arundell'e gönderilen mektupta, St. Pantaleon kilisesinin yanısıra kaya ve mağara yazıtlarının da, Honaz'ın hemen dışında bulunan dağın eteklerinde olduğunun belirtilmesi.
1826	John Hartley'in "Konos'da" bulunan 500 Türk evine karşılık toplam 30 Yunan evinde ikamet etmekte olan Hristiyanlar arasında bile Yunanca konuşan hiç kimseye rastlamaması. Hartley ayrıca bölgede 3 caminin, 1 kilisenin ve kutsal taksiark Michael manastırının kalıntılarının bulunduğunu belirtmiştir.
1832	J. A. Cramer'in Chonos'da tahminen 200 Yunan ailenin yaşadığını iddia etmesi. T. Milner ise Yunanların toplam 50 hanede yaşayıp, kiliseden çok mahzene benzeyen bir odada ibadet ettiklerini belirtmiştir.
1833	M. J. Cohen'in, Chonai'ın nüfusunun tahminen 1500 civarında olduğunu belirtmesi. Cohen'e göre bu nüfus toplam 300 evde barınmaktaydı.
1836	William Hamilton'ın, Colossae antik tiyatrosunda gördüğü duvarların ve bir takım koltuk kalıntılarının Colossae antik şehrinin varlığına dair bir kanıt teşkil etme ihtimalinin bulunduğunu belirtmesi.
1840	Murray, Usborne ve Reidecker'in yazdığı "Gezginin Elkitabı" adlı kitapta Avrupa'lı turistlerin bölgeye olan ilgilerinin arttığının belirtilmesi. Murray ayrıca Honaz'ın tepesinde bulunan ortaçağa ait kalenin Colossae antik şehrinin varlığına dair bir kanıt teşkil ettiği konusundaki iddiasını sürdürmüştür.
1842	Edward T. Daniell'ın Balbura'da principate dönemine ait ve Colossae'dan gelmiş bir kadına adanmış olan bir yazıt keşfetmesi. Augustus Schönborn, Hermann Loew ve Jens Pell'in "Chonosdahg" üzerinden Denizli-Tavas ve Karacık pazarından geçmesi.
1851	Henry Christmas'ın iki kiliseye ait kalıntıları anlatması ve kendisine Archangel Michael oyuğunun yerinin gösterilmesi.
1864	Conybeare'in ve Howson'ın Yeni Ahit'in yorumlanmasına antik kiliselerde bulunan madeni paralar, yazıtlar ve çizimleri de içeren arkeolojik ayrıntıları dahil etmeleri sonucu, o döneme kadar dogmatik ve manevi bir şekilde yorumlanan Yeni Ahit'e yönelik yaklaşımların radikal bir değişime uğraması. Ancak Conybeare ve Howson Colossae'yı incelememişlerdir.
1868	Osmanlı yetkililerinin Honaz'ı ziyaret ederek, yeni kurulan Osmanlı İmparatorluğu müzesinde sergilenmek üzere madeni para toplamaları.

1869	Ernest Renan'ın Paul'ün yaşamı ve mektupları konusundaki bilimsel çalışmalara epikrafi ve nümizmatiği dahil etmesi. Ancak Renan çalışmasında Colossae mezarlıklarını "bizarre et anépigraphes" olarak yorumlamıştır.
1870	Edmund Davis'in resmettiği höyüklerin ve mezar taşlarının orijinalinden daha çok İngiliz höyüklerine ve mezar taşlarına benzemesi. Davis aynı zamanda bölgede bir çok değirmenin bulunduğunu da belirtmiştir.
1881	William Mitchell Ramsay'nin Colossae'da ilk arkeolojik kazısını başlatması.
1884	A. H. Smith'in Honaz dağında kaybolan Strabo'un "Cadmus" nehrini bulduğunu düşünmesi.
1885	Glasgow Protestan rahibi Rev. W.F Somerville'in Colassae höyüğünde bir saat oturarak Philemon'un evini gördüğünü hayal etmesi.
1890 civarı	M. Henri Cambournac'in Colossae antik sitesinin bilinen ilk fotoğraflarını çekmesi.
1887–8	1856'da başlayan ve finansal olarak İngilizlerin destekleği Osmanlı demiryolu projesinin Colossae'nın yakınlarından geçmesi (Bujali İstasyonu).
1893	G. Weber'in Herodot'un bahsettiği nehrin gerçekte varolmadığını, dolayısıyla nehrin bulunması için yapılan çalışmaların anlamsız olduğunu belirtmesi.
1895	W. M. Ramsay'nin Honaz'ın nüfunun yarısının Hristiyan, yarısının Türk olduğunu iddia etmesi. Ramsay bu iddiasını herhangi bir kanıta dayandırmamıştır.
1897	J. G. C. Anderson'ın Colossae'da başka yazıtları keşfetmesi.
1899	P. Gaudin'in Smyrna yakınlarında Colossae'lı bir öğrenci olan Diodotos adına adanmış, 3. yüzyıla ait olduğu düşünülen bir yazıt bulması.
1900	A. Philippson'ın Honaz'daki 500 eve dair bulguları açıklaması.
1907	Gertrude Bell'in Bir Bin Kalısı'nda Willam Mitchell Ramsay ile buluşmak için çıktığı yolculukta Colossae'dan trenle geçmesi.
1908	Colossae'nın 70 yıldan beri gezi klavuzlarında yer almasına rağmen, Macmillan'ın Colossae'da görmeye değer çok fazla birşey bulunmadığını belirtmesi.
1923–4	Honaz'da yaşayan Rumların Kuzey Yunanistan'a iadesi.
1933	Buckler'ın ve Calder'in yazıtları araştırmak amacıyla Colossae ve Honaz'ı ziyaret etmeleri.
1963	J. Mcdonald'ın kazı alanında küçük bir seramik ve cam kolleksiyonu bulması.
1976	Harold Mare'in yıpranmış yazıtların fotoğraflarını çekmesi.
1976	Otto Meinardus'un ve Klaus Siefernz'in üzerinde haç desenlerinin bulunduğu çeşitli sütun başlarını ortaya çıkarmaları.
1998	Flinder Üniversitesi'nin Türk akademisyenleri ile ortaklaşa olarak "Colossae: Geçmişin derinliklerine bir kazı" adlı projesini başlatması.
2001	Colossae'yi havadan tetkik eden, Pamukkale Üniversitesi Arkeoloji bölümü profesörü olan Celal Şimşek'in necropolis araştırmasına başlaması.
2004–06	Erim Konakçı'nın ve Bahadır Duman'ın yüzey seramiklerini incelemesi.
2005	Honaz Belediyesi tarafından Colossae'nın arkeolojik turistik gelişimini amaçlayan programların başlatılması.

Appendix 2

The Story of the Archistrategos, St Michael of Chonai

Translation by Alan H. Cadwallader[1]

"The recounting and revelation about our holy father
Archippos and his custodianship of the sacred house of
the Archangel Michael at Chonai."

Chapter One

1. Here begins the story of the healings, gifts and favours bestowed upon us by God through the grace and courage of the archistrategos Michael, from the beginning proclaimed by the holy apostles Philip and John the theologian. Saint John, who had driven foul Artemis from Ephesus, ventured up to Hierapolis to Saint Philip, for he was himself battling against the serpent. When they had greeted one another, Saint Philip said, 'What are we going to do, brother John, because I am not able to root out this foul and filthy serpent from this city? She is absolutely abominable, the epitome of all creeping, unclean things.'

2. She was draped with snakes over her whole body with a python encircling her head and another coiled around her neck. She was astride two serpents — every unclean, creeping thing surrounded her. To put it in simple terms, she was decked out like a queen. The Greeks even esteemed her as the Great Goddess. They all used to prostrate themselves before her and offer sacrifice to her.

3. Often, when Saint Philip was seated and teaching, she would set the snakes/creeping things to turn upon the holy one in order to kill him. And she repeatedly said to him, 'Get out of this city, Philip, before I utterly destroy you.' But Saint Philip continued to preach the word of truth and faith. So, having offered up a prayer, the apostles drove her from Hierapolis.

1 Sincere thanks are due to the members of the Greek Reading Group at Flinders University with whom I worked over this text and who provided insights, questions and connections that enrich the resulting translation. The members were Rosemary Canavan, Emily Harding, Margaret Hokin, Julie Hooke, Nicoly Moyse, Joan Riley, Cameron Doody and Fr. Silouan Photineas. An annotated version is in preparation.

Chapter Two

1. After these things happened, the celebrated preachers of truth left and settled at a place called Chairotopa. There the favour, beneficence and wonders of the holy and glorious archistrategos Michael were poised to be unveiled. Having offered up a prayer, the apostles signalled to the people and spoke, 'The mighty taxiarch and archistrategos of the Lord's power is about to come down here and perform dazzling wonders.'

2. Then the apostles departed and were teaching in other cities. And straightaway, water that could effect healings gushed forth in that spot.

Chapter Three

1. After the holy apostles went to their rest, the Greeks again began to roar and rage against the Christians. After many years elapsed following the discovery of the holy water, a report had spread through all the earth, since those who retreated to that place with any and every disease that afflicted them, were being healed. Many of the Greeks who came and saw the healings started to believe in the Lord Jesus Christ and were being baptised.

2. A certain godless idolater in the city of Laodikeia had an only-begotten daughter who had been dumb from the day she was born. Many times, her father, with others who sympathised with him, wanted to go and disturb that holy water, since many of the Greeks who rushed there, were healed from their infirmities and began to believe on our Lord Jesus Christ.

3. On the first day of the week, as if in a vision of the night, the taxiarch of the Lord, Michael the archistrategos, stood before him, telling him, 'Go forth with your child to where the holy water has appeared. Mark my name, if you believe, you will in no way leave disappointed.' So the man rose and went with his daughter. And he beheld the gift of God and believed. He said to those who were healed, 'On whom do you call when you bathe this water upon your bodies?' They replied, 'We appeal to the Father, Son and Holy Spirit and Michael the archistrategos.'

4. Then he lifted up his eyes and his hands toward heaven and said, 'The Father, the Son and the Holy Spirit, O God, through the intercessions of Michael the archistrategos, help me, a sinner.' And scooping up water, he trickled it into the mouth of the child. At that instance, the child let out a cry and shouted, saying, 'God is truly of the Christians, great is your power O Michael, archistrategos.' And he was baptised along with his entire household.

5. Then, to the name of Michael the archistrategos he erected there a small shrine and made a shelter for the holy water. And so, he departed with his daughter glorifying God.

6. But the Greeks continued to roar against the Christians and the holy spring there, wanting to crush it and make it disappear from that land.

Chapter Four

1. Ninety years after the shrine was built above the spring, a child, ten years old, came from Hierapolis. His name was Archippos, the child of faithful, Christian parents and he was the first to be established as custodian there. What follows tells of his life.

2. He lived seventy years after he began to serve the shrine of God; for sixty of them he lived without tasting bread, meat or wine; nor did he wash. And this was all the nourishment he had: he used to eat wild plants boiled up without salt. The blessed man used to prepare this on the first day of the week. And on that day he would sprinkle his honourable soul three times with a third of a measure of water. This the blessed one would do for the refreshment of his body.

3. For clothing, he used to have two rough sackcloth coats. The blessed man vested in one and did not remove it from his flesh until it was completely worn out; then, similarly, he tossed the other coat around him. His bed was pitted with sharp stones. A goat's hide covered the stones so that the shards would not be visible to those who entered. A sackcloth stuffed with thorns was laid under his esteemed head.

4. So these things were the bed on which the blessed one used to lay for rest in the hour when he slept. Each and every night the slave of God lay down on the stones and the thorns and exact a most keenly alert sleep. For the slave of God did not risk any indulgence, training his body and guarding his soul unsoiled from the snare of any alien presence, through the mediation of the archistrategos Michael.

5. He used to say, as he was walking the straight and narrow way, "O Lord, do not make me, a sinner, to be joyful on this earth; do not allow any of the good things of this world come into my humble situation, or implore my sight. O Lord let there not be for me, even for one day of the year, any goodly attraction, nor cause my eyes to stray through the irreverence of this age. But fill my eyes, O Lord, with spiritual tears, and enlighten my heart with insight into your laws and grant to me the gift which you are to present to those who are well-pleasing to you as of old.'

6. 'For why is this body of clay lumbered upon me save that such a stinking mire, this adornment is the training for the incorruptible soul? By contrast, the garment of the soul is a faithful orthodoxy before God, and exercise is about indifference to the flesh — hunger and thirst and angelic asceticism, sleeplessness and watchfulness, prayer and tears, groanings and conversions, silences and mercies and all things pleasing to God. For by all these beautifications the soul glows.'

7. 'For what does the soul desire from the body? Not one thing, except merely each act of righteousness and piety. However the body hankers after *these* things — all-consuming gluttony and profligacy, avarice and every defilement, spectres and evil, wicked desires and all those things which are not pleasing to God. The body delights in such things and the aggrieved soul is taken prisoner.'

8. 'But wretched sinner that I am. What shall I do? Help me O Lord my God and dissolve my body as a grain of mustard, break my heart and make me contrite, so I may not be confounded before you. For, my Lord God, I flourish early like a shoot of grass but, come evening, I flag and slacken. But even so, I will not resile until I have mortified my members from every evil attraction.'

Chapter Five

1. Archippos, the slave of God, was refining these things and mastering the angelic ascesis. Each day he glorified God, the one who furnished him with such endurance. Multitudes of Christians and Greeks hastened to that place. And such as came in fear and faith, were blessing the Trinity, saying, 'O Father, Son and Holy Spirit, one God, have mercy on us through the mediation of Michael the archistrategos.' As they uttered this, they bathed the holy water on their afflictions and they were healed.

2. But those who were unbelievers and enemies of the truth did not want to contemplate the glory of God. Even hourly they snarled like lions wanting to bring the sacred spring to an end and at the same time destroy the slave of God. Many times the ungodly came and scourged him; others seized crosses from the shrine and smashed them over the head of the holy man. Yet others clawed his hair and dragged him outside. Still others yanked hairs out of his beard and tossed them to the ground.

3. Then they hurtled upon the sacred spring to shut it down. Immediately, their hands were restrained. Others who approached it saw a fiery flame leap out from the water onto their faces. Thus they were repulsed and the heathen put to shame.

4. But some began to say to one another, 'If we do not stop this spring and destroy this piddling hermit, all our gods will amount to nothing by the healings here.' In addition, they began to torment the slave of God every day. The blessed one had immeasurable terrors from the idolatrous Greeks, but he endured these things and unceasingly glorified God day and night.

Chapter Six

1. In that place, there was a river flowed past from the west. It was called the Chruses, and, from the beginning of time, it had meandered near the altar of

God. Many times the enemies of the truth conspired to mingle the river with that sacred site but they could not succeed; when they tried, the water of the river fled from the holy place and was divided into two. The river-water cut back into the territory to the right of the sanctuary. And thus it remains to this day.

Chapter Seven

1. In those days, two other rivers began their downward course near that holy place, about three miles to the east. One was called the Lykokapros and the name of the other was the Koufos. These merged together at the spur of the great mountain and coursing back to the right hand side they wandered into Lycian territory.

2. The Devil from the beginning was the accursed one. He is the one who plants seeds of wickedness into people's hearts. He is the one who aids and abets evildoers. He maligns God and loathes the angels. It is he who is the murderer of saints and persecutor of divine churches, the terminator of wellbeing and tempter of the weak. He is the one who deceived the world and refused to be sated, who detests heaven and earth and lusts after everlasting darkness. He is the antagonist of those yearning to be saved and adversary of those straining after salvation. He is the despiser of beauty; he is the antichrist.

3. This is the one who, having engineered darkness and ruin, did not restrain himself from inciting the idolators to suppress the sanctuary of God. Even moreso, he put into their hearts that they divert the rivers against God's holy place, in order that the shrine might be plunged beneath the water, for the place was ideally situated to be engulfed by a flood.

4. In addition, the heathen were advancing from all those towns, some 5000 men. The lawless mob joined forces and came to Laodikeia and devised plans against the incorporeal archistrategos Michael, plans that would prove ineffectual. The leaders of the ungodly began to speak to the crowds, 'The location is susceptible to a watery inundation; for the rivers pour down from the great mountain. Even now, let us divert the riverflows against the one who has spellbound our gods, who has nullified their divine powers through those who are healed there. Since we ourselves cannot kill him nor eradicate this bog, perhaps that place might be destroyed by the reckless intensity of the floods, the sheer volume of water and the force of our gods.'

Chapter Eight

1. Very near the holy shrine was an impregnable monolith of massive breadth and length; its depth was beyond measure. This crag extended about seventy cubits in front of the sanctuary and for a similar distance at the rear.

2. To compound everything, the heathen, the enemies of truth came and arrayed themselves from the promontory of the stone all the way to the spur of the great mountain where the rivers Koufos and Lykokapros begin to flow. And they quarried out and made a channel for the water in order that they might alter the course of the rivers there and so swamp the shrine of God. For the murderous Devil was agitating them.

3. When they completed the ditch for the water, they blocked up the rivers for ten days to harness a huge body of water for the inundation of that holy place. And behold the rivers were swollen with an immense amount water and the mountain torrents were bursting.

Chapter Nine

1. But the slave of God, the custodian Archippos, perceiving the schemes of the Devil and the befoulments of the idolators, cast himself to the ground as if dead. He poured out his supplication to God and Michael the holy archistrategos that they might protect that holy place without harm from the deluge of water. And he did this for ten days. He neither ate nor drank nor rose up from the ground.

2. Rather, glorifying God, he began to speak in this way, 'Blessed be God, I will by no means leave this shrine nor flee. I would rather perish from the flood. For I believe in my God, the one who saves me from despair and hysteria through the intercessions of the incorporeal Michael the archistrategos; for he will never desert his sacred house nor this earth until the end of time.'

Chapter Ten

1. When the ten days were over, the heathen came to unleash the deluge against the archistrategos. The enemies of truth began to say to one another, 'Let us open the floodgates and scamper and perch opposite and view the storming of the place.' Moreover, they conspired together and let loose the torrents during the first hour of nightfall. Then they fled immediately so that they would not perish beneath the tide.

2. And so, having said, 'Let us scamper and perch opposite and view the storming of the place', they stood across to the left. They signalled to one another about the water to the south rushing down from the craggy heights and roaring violently.

3. And they began to feel most uneasy.

Chapter Eleven

1. Meanwhile, the slave of God, the custodian Archippos, was lying at the front of the shrine, drenching the ground with tears and unceasingly beseeching God. Suddenly, he was uplifted by the Holy Spirit and began to sing this song: 'The floods have lifted up, O Lord, the floods lift up their clamour. The floods will mount their poundings from the thunders of many waters. Wondrous may be the heavings of the sea; the Lord is wonderful in the heights. Your testimonies are exceedingly sure. Sanctity becomes your house, O Lord, throughout the sum of days.'

2. Once he concluded the psalm, there was an almighty thunderclap and the holy archistrategos descended and took up a position at the prow of the impenetrable rock. And he addressed the slave of God in a booming voice, 'Come away from the shrine, O custodian, before the flood engulfs you.' When the blessed Archippos advanced and saw the blazing vision of his glory he collapsed to the ground as if dead.

3. Again, a second time, the archistrategos Michael, called out, saying, 'Arise, righteous soul; come with me.' But Archippos, the slave of God, answered in trepidation, 'O Lord, I am not worthy enough to approach you; for I shudder at the sight of you.' Then the mighty taxiarch of the Lord said, 'Do not be alarmed or afraid, but stand upright.' Again, the blessed one was roused, only to flee inside the shrine and scramble under the holy table, terrified and renouncing his own life.

4. Nevertheless, the holy archistrategos, Michael, continued to speak to him, 'Take courage and come with me, because the floods are roaring, surging against you.' But Archippos, the slave of God, said to him, 'I do believe, O my Lord, that mighty is the power of our God and of Michael the archistrategos, and there is no way he would allow this holy place to be destroyed before the endtime.'

5. Then the archistrategos moved from the shrine, saying to him, 'If you believe, O holy one, that he is able to safeguard this land from the floodtide, come, so that you may witness his power.' At last, the slave of God departed the shrine and took up a position at his left side.

6. Archippos heard the rumble vent from him and beheld the immensity of his majesty, a pillar of fire ignited from earth to heaven. And Michael the archistrategos said to him, 'Do you recognise who I am, given that you tremble at the sight of me?' He replied, 'No, my lord, I do not know.' The great taxiarch said to him, 'I am Michael, the archistrategos of the power of the Lord; I am the one poised at the ready before God. Yet even I am not strong enough to gaze upon the awesome and unfathomable glory of divinity, the untouchable furnace of immeasurable power emanating from his countenance. You are not to cower at my countenance; rather, you are to tremble at the mere form and power of the slave. For how are mortals going to see God, the one beside whom I stand with trepidation?'

7. And the archistrategos spoke to him again, 'Do you see the torrent rushing down from the heights of the mountains?' And he replied, ' I do not, my lord, but

I hear with my ears the tumult of much water.' The archistrategos said to him, 'Do not be afraid; just stand firm'.

Chapter Twelve

1. And behold the water surged down from the heights of the mountains right up in front of them. But the archistrategos raised his voice and addressed the floods, 'Do you come against just anyone, O Koufos and Lycokarpros? Who enticed you into leaving your appointed path to come here?'

2. So saying, he made the sign of the cross at the wall of water and said, 'Stand where you are.' And immediately the waters halted and piled up in a great heap as high as ten men. The archistrategos said to the slave of God, Archippos, 'Do you, O holy one, see the power of God?' He answered, 'Yes my lord.' Then the archistrategos said to him, 'Holy one, do not be afraid of the threat from the flood.'

3. And just as Moses at the Red Sea extended his hand with the staff and divided the sea, even so the great taxiarch Michael, the archistrategos, extended his right arm as if controlling a staff in the manner just described. And he struck the top of the impregnable monolith. Immediately the solid stone split from side to side and from top to bottom. The reverberation of the rock's fracture sounded like thunder and all the land was shaken. The archistrategos said to the slave of God, 'Do you see, holy one, the power of God?' He answered, 'Yes my lord, I do see the wonder and the power of God working with you.'

4. Then extending his right arm again he sealed the chasm below with the sign of the cross and blessed it saying, 'In this place every disease, every sickness and spell and incantation and every contrivance of the evil one will be shattered. Here those who are in chains will find release and those who are tormented by unclean spirits and those who are sick will be restored. Anyone at all who seeks sanctuary at this place in faith and fear, calling on Father, Son and Holy Spirit and the archistrategos, Michael, indeed on the name of God and of me, will in no way leave disappointed. The grace of God and my power will continue to overshadow this place, making holy by the name of Father, Son and Holy Spirit. As for our enemies, those who are standing and staring at us, let them be turned to stone right there until the waters should swamp my sanctuary.'

5. Finally, he said to Archippos the slave of God, 'Come, holy one, to my right side.' And immediately, he took up a position at his right. Then the archistrategos raised his voice and addressed the floodwaters, 'Be flung into this crevice; you are to be funnelled into this cavern, roaring until the end of time, the reward for having been readied against me. And the glory of this site will go everywhere through Jesus Christ our Lord, to whom be glory and might now and always and to the ages of ages. Amen.'

Zaman ve Mekanda Colossae: Antik Kentle Bağlar Özetler

Çeviri: Ayse Ercan

1. Zaman ve Mekanda Colossae: Yanlış Konumlandırılma, Unutulma ve Tarihsel Hatalarla Karşı Karşıya

Alan H. Cadwallader ve Michael Trainor

Bu tarihsel inceleme Colossae kentini zamansal ve mekansal bağlamda kurgulama amacı taşıyan denemeler dizisinin bir başlangıç noktası niteliğini taşır. Söz konusu çalışma Colossae'ı konu alan bütünsel bir akademik incelemenin eksikliğini sorgular. Osmanlı yönetimi etkisiyle, Avrupalıların bölgeye duydukları ilgi ve tasarıları doğrultusunda, antik kentin bir anlamda yeniden keşfinin yarattığı memnuniyetsizliğin arkasında yatan temel nedenleri inceler. Erken dönem Avrupa haritacılığında Colossae, mevcut kent kalıntılarından kopuk, gerçekte sahip olduğu coğrafi pozisyonla bağlantısız, Avrupalı araştırmacıların klasik Yunan ve Roma metinlerinin yanısıra İncil ve ekklesiastik geleneklerle bağdaştırılma düşünceleri nedeniyle, tarihsel uyuşmazlık taşıyan yorumlamaların tam ortasında yer alır. Burada sunulan inceleme, Avrupa düşünce dünyasının Colossae'yı gerçeklikten uzak bir şekilde canlı tutma endişesini ortaya koyarak, kentin Rodos adasında konumlandırılmasını, geç Bizans döneminde yerel açıdan önemli bir merkez olması nedeniyle bu kente yönelen Osmanlı ilgisini tartışır. Yerleşime duyulan Avrupalı ilgisinin yeniden canlanması, bir anlamda kentin tanımlanmasına ilişkin yapılan yanlışlıkları da beraberinde getirir. Söz konusu hatalardan en belirgin olanları özellikle kalıntıların az sayıda oluşunun sebep olduğu, kentin günümüz Honaz ya da çok daha görkemli kalıntılara sahip komşu Hierapolis ve Laodikeia antik kentleriyle karıştırılması gibi yanlışlıklardır.

2. Helenistik ve Akhaemenid Dönemlerde Büyük Frigya Eyaleti'nin Güneybatı Sınırlarındaki Topraklarda Değişen Toprak Sahipliği Modeli

Nicholas Sekunda

Colossae antik kenti hakkındaki bilgilerin yetersizliği bizi Kelainai, Apollonia, Hypaipa, Laodikeia, Tabai ve Aphrodisias gibi 'antik Frigya bölgesinin güneybatı sınırlarında uzanan topraklarda' yer alan komşu kentlerle ilgili genel bir resim oluşturmaya yönlendirir. Tarihsel kaynaklar Anadolu'daki Pers hakimiyeti döneminde toprak sahipliği, müdahil olan kişiler ve dinamikler hakkında, Lydialı Pythes'in kendi toprak mülkiyetini korumak amacıyla sonuçsuz kalmış çabaları gibi, eşsiz bir çıkış noktası sunar. Yazıtlarda adı geçen kişilerin isimleri hakkında yapılan incelemelerin yanısıra, mezar buluntuları da antik metinlerden elde edilen verileri destekler. Tüm bu veriler Frigya'daki Pers yerleşimlerinin temelde Pythes'in arazilerinin bir uzantısı olduğunu işaret eder. Bu araziler kuşkusuz bölgedeki refahın başlıca kaynağı olup, aynı zamanda Lydialı ve Pers sefahatı (avlanma) için de önemli mekanlar olup ordunun da (ve isyancıların) başlıca ikmal deposudur. Tithraustes, Ariaios ve Pasiphernes gibi Pers varlığının önde gelenlerinin bölgede çeşitli araziler edindikleri bilinir. Çeşitli veriler Pers soylularının özellikle iki yerleşim tercih ettiklerini kanıtlar ki bunlar Kelainai ve Colossae'dır. Ayrıca onomastik incelemeler toprak hakimiyetinin odak noktasının değiştiğini gösterse de gerek etnik alanda, gerek esirlerle bağlantılı olarak gerekse evlilik ilişkilerinde Helenistik dönem de dahi Küçük Asya'da İran etkisinin sürmeye devam ettiğini gösterir.

3. Lykos Vadisi Dilleri

Rick Strelan

Bu makale Lykos Vadisi'nde M.S. 1. yy'ın erken yıllarında varlık gösteren karmaşık, muhtelif ve akışkan dil dünyasını yeniden inşaa eder. Bölgedeki Yunan hakimiyetini yadsımayarak, bu hakimiyetin sınırlarını konuşulan Yunanca lehçelerinin çeşitliliğini göz önünde bulundurarak sorgular. Yazıtlardan elde edilen kanıtlar bölgesel imla farklılıklarının yanısıra muhtemel telaffuz farklılıklarını gözler önüne serer. Fakat söz konusu yazıtlar dilin kullanımında sadece tek bir alana açıklık getirir ve bu alan dışında kalan dil farklılıkları ancak öneri niteliğinde kalır. Yazıtlar aynı şekilde çokdilli Lykos Vadisi ve Küçük Asya edebiyatı ile bilgi sunmaktan da uzaktır. Örneğin Frigce dönem boyunca devam ederken, Lidce, Karyaca ve Likçe M.S. 1. yy'da artık unutulmaya başlamıştır. Bu yerel dillerin unutulması konusunda başka bir kanıt ise Yunanca'nın (ve Latince) baskın dil olarak etki alanını genişletmesidir. Hristiyan topluluklar arasında ise bir dizi yerel dil gerek dua formunda, gerekse törenler sırasında İncil okumalarında kullanılmaya devam edilmiştir. Çevrelerinde yaşamakta olan topluluklar gibi, Hristiyan topluluklar da çok dilli olmasalar da en azından çift dilli karakterlerini korumuşlardır.

4. Yünlü Dokumalar: Antik Çağ'da Lykos Vadisinde Uluslararası Bir Ticari Malzeme

Hatice Erdemir

Söz konusu çalışma Lykos Vadisi'ndeki başlıca şehirler için koyun ürünleri endüstrisinin ekonomik açıdan ne kadar önemli ve yaygın olduğunu ortaya koyar. Roma döneminde tekstil ürünlerinin vergiden muhaf tutulan lüks tüketim ürünleri haline gelmesinde gerek hayvan otlatmada yaşanan sezonluk sıkıntılar, gerekse eski Avrupalılar'ın katma değerli koyun ürünlerine olan önemli ölçüdeki talebinin payı oldukça yüksektir. Tarım ürünleriyle karşılaştırıldığında bir anlamda 'yükte hafif pahada ağır' olarak değerlendirilebilecek hayvancılık çok daha kazançlı ürünler ortaya koyar. Bu bağlamda hayvancılıkla ilişkili olarak sayısız meslek çeşitliliği ve bunlarla bağlantılı olarak zanaat örgütlenmeleri meydana gelir. Koyun ürünlerine ekonomik açıdan bağımlılık benzer şekilde Lykos Vadisi sınırında bulunan Trapezopolis, Tripolis, Attouda ve Aphrodisias gibi diğer şehirlere de yayılır. Roma döneminde, Asya eyaletinde doğu-batı güzergahında uzanan son derece korunaklı ana yol, ticari ürünlerin taşınması için nehir ve deniz taşımacılığının yanısıra çok yoğun olarak kullanılmaktaydı. Ticarette ihracat kentler arasında ekonomik ilişkilerin yanısıra güçlü kültürel ve sosyal ilişkilerin geliştirilmesini mümkün kılıyordu. Batı Avrupa'ya dek uzanan denizaşırı ticaret ise; Küçük Asya'nın bereketli toprakları yanısıra, bu coğrafada bulunan kentleri refaha kavuşturan, yeni imparatorluk düzenlemelerininin, değişen ticaret yollarınının ve bölge insanının girişimci faliyetlerinin arkasındaki temel sebeplerden biriydi.

5. Hierapolis ve Laodikeia'da Roma Devleti'nin
Sosyal Etkisi Üzerine Epigrafik Kanıtlar

Rosalinde A. Kearsley

Helenistik ve İmparatorluk dönemi süresince Menderes Nehri Havzası'nda yaşamakta olan sosyal açıdan örgütlü toplulukların yayılımı oldukça iyi belgelenmiştir. Laodikeia ve Hierapolis'den elde edilen epigrafik ve arkeolojik verilerin de doğruladığı üzere, Lykos Vadisi bu toplulukların refahı ve yayılımı açısından önemli bir noktaydı. Söz konusu kanıtlar Colossae'da ele geçmesi muhtemel gelecekteki buluntuları değerlendirmek açısından da önem taşır. Temel yapıların inşaası yayılmakta olan Roma dönemi sosyal hayat geleneğinin de bir uzantısıydı. Laodikeia'da ele geçen üç yazıt söz konusu kentlerde yaşayan halkın bu etkilere ne şekillerde maruz kaldığını da açıklar niteliktedir. İlk ikisi özgürlüğü bağışlanmış imparatorluk hizmetindeki, yerel yönetim kadrosundaki iki bireyin ne şekilde sosyal, dini ve dilsel öğeleri kendi yerel özellikleriyle harmanladıklarına ışık tutar. Üçüncüsü ise varlıklı ve soylu bir kadının sosyal hayata nasıl katıldığını anlatır. Küçük Asya'da imparatorluk hizmetinde bulunan kişilerin ve soylu ailelere mensub kadınların sosyal rolü özellikle önem taşımakta fakat hiçbir edebi eserde bu konulara yeterince değinilmemektedir. Burada sunulan epigrafik veriler, Doğu Roma kentlerindeki toplum yapısına olan geleneksel yaklaşımı, bu kentlerdeki sosyal ve siyasi hayatın zenginliğini ve çeşitliliğini sunarak tartışır.

6. Colossae Araştırmalarına Yeni Bir Bakış:
Eski ve Yeni Yazıtların Sunduğu Yeni Katkılar

Alan H. Cadwallader

Gerek incil yorumları etkisinde olsun, gerek arkeolojik keşiflerle ya da turistik amaçlarla ortaya konmuş olsun, Colossae kenti üzerine bugüne kadar ortaya konulmuş çalışmaların büyük bölümü, Laodikeia'nın kuruluşunu takiben Lykos Vadisi'ni ciddi şekilde etkileyen M. S. 60/61 yılındaki depreme dek, kentin zamanla boyutlarının küçülüp, öneminin azalmış olduğunu ifade eder. Bu bölüm eleştirel bir bakışla söz konusu değerlendirmenin dayandığı kanıtları tekrar ele alarak, kanıtların değerlendirmesinde yanıltıcı olabilecek faktörleri ortaya koyup, sonuçta varılan yargılara daha önce yapılmamış saptamalarda bulunur. J. B. Lightfoot ve W. M. Ramsay gibi ondokuzuncu yüzyılın iki önemli akademisyeninin Colossae konusunda yapılan araştırmalarda bugün dahi nasıl etkilerinin sürdüğünü gösterir. Yeni keşfedilmiş olan yazıtlar ve sikkelerden elde edilen kanıtların yanısıra uzun süredir bilinen yazıtların tekrar değerlendirilmesi de kentten elde edilen verilerin bu aksiyomlardan çok dağa sağlam veriler sunduğunun bir kere daha altını çizer.

7. Lykos Vadisi'nde Hristiyanlar:
Efes ve Küçük Asya'nın Batısından Bir Görünüm

Paul Trebilco

Colossae'da yaşayan erken Hristiyan toplulukla ilgili doğrudan bilgiler bir anlamda 'Colossaelılar'a Mektup' ile sınırlıdır. Bu durum Lykos Vadisi'nde yaşamakta olan diğer erken dönem Hristiyan topluluklar için de geçerlidir. Tüm bu kısıtlı bilgiler göz önünde bulundurulduğunda bu makale çok daha geniş bir yaklaşımla ele alınır. Efes'te yaşanan erken Hristiyanlık pratikleri ile ilgili elimize birçok kaynaktan bilgi ulaşır. Söz konusu erken Hristiyan toplulukların hareketliliği, Lykos Vadisi'nde görülebilecek olası bir etkiyi de anlaşılır kılar. Dolayısıyla Efes'te yaşamakta olan Hristiyanlar konusunda geçerli olan bilgiler aslında Lykos Vadisi'ndeki Hristiyanlık konusunda da bize ışık tutar. Ayrıca erken ikinci yüzyılda Küçük Asya'da varolan Hristiyanlık konusunda da kayda değer bilgiler söz konusudur. Peki tüm bu genel resim Lykos Vadisi'ne ne şekilde yansır? Küçük Asya'nın batısında ve muhtemelen Lykos Vadisi'nde süre gelmekte olan yoğun bir Aziz Paulus ve Aziz Johh etkisi olduğu genel olarak kabul edilir. Bu noktada bu makalede Walter Bauer'ın bu yaygın görüşü tartışılarak, Lykos Vadisi'nde Hristiyanlıkla ilgili sonuçlar ortaya konacaktır.

8. Kalıntılardan Colossaelıları Okumak:
Roma Imparatorluk İkonografisi, Ahlaki Değişim ve
Lykos Vadisi'nde Hristiyan Kimliği Oluşturmak

Harry O. Maier

'Colossaelılar'a Mektup' İsa'nın herkesin birgün tanrıya inanacağı ve böylece uzlaşma ve kurtuluşun gerçekleşeceği bir geleceğe yönelik bir tasavvurunu ortaya koyar. Geleneksel olarak yorumcular Paulus'un bu polemik dolu retorik durumundaki teolojik ısrarının temel nedenini muhalifleri ve onların aracı kozmik güçlere zorunlu bir şekilde yönelttiği dini ve münzevi pratiklerinin bir uzantısı olarak var sayarlar. İmparatorluk ikonografyası ve ideolojisine daha dikkatli bir bakış, Paulus'un emperyal Hristiyanlığını algılamak için de daha geniş ve ikna edici bir zemin oluşturur. Aphrodisias Sebasteion'daki anıtsal mimari de olduğu gibi sikkelerde de görülen Küçük Asya'nın imparatorluk kültürüne bakış, aynı zamanda Colossaelılar'a Mektup'da yapılan vurguları da yorumlamayı kolaylaştırır. Bunların başında; İsa'nın huzur dolu hakimiyeti aracılığıyla canlanacak etik ideal, erdemsel ve ahlaki yenilenmenin değerlenmesi, sosyal ve politik değişimler ve son olarak şiddetin değil sevgi ve adaletin hüküm sürdüğü armoni içinde bir Hristiyan dünyasıdır.

9. Colossaelı Epaphras'ı Kazmak

Michael Trainor

M. S. birinci yüzyılın sonlarında İsa'nın iki halefi tarafından kaleme alınmış iki mektup Lykos Vadisi ve Colossae kentini değerlendirmek açısından dönemin kültürel ve sosyal hayatıyla ilişkili önemli veriler sunar. İki mektubun da överek andığı bir karakter yakından bakıldığında Paulus'un (Philemon'a Mektup) ve yetkili temsilcisinin (Colossaelılar'a Mektup) bahsettiği karakteristik ilişkilere ışık tutar. Kendisi Paulus'un yoldaşlarından Epaphras'dır. Bu kişiden bir kere Philemon'da (Phm 23), iki kere de Colossaelılar'a Mektup (Col 1:7–8; 4:12–13) da olmak üzere sadece üç kere bahsedilir. Burada temel amacım 'Paulus mektupları'nda, Paulus'un izini sürerek, dahil olduğu ilişkileri sergilemektir. Sonuçta 'Paulus mektupları' asimetrik, ilişkisel, düzenli ve ailevi bir ilişkiler bütününü ortaya koyar. Epaphras da bu ilişkiler bağlamında Lykos Vadisi'nde İsa'ya inananların sosyal uyumunda anahtar bir rol üstlenir. Epaphras en iyi biçimiyle, Yunan ve Roma yaşamını etkileyen domestik, coğrafi, politik, sosyal ve ekonomik ilişkiler ağı kontekstinde anlaşılır. Bu veriler Colossae civarında bulunan yazıtlardan elde edilen bilgilerle de desteklenir.

10. Colossae Höyüğü'nün Sessiz Tanığı: Seramik Buluntular

Bahadır Duman ve Erim Konakçı

Colossae kenti ile tarihsel bilgilere Herodotos, Xenophon, Strabon ve Plinius'un yanı sıra Hitit ve Bizans kaynakları gibi çeşitli kaynaklardan ulaşılır. Kentle ilgili bu bilgiler genel itibariyle oldukça kısadır ve yerleşimin coğrafi yapısı ve gelişimiyle ilgili ancak genel bir fikir edinmeye yarar. Kentin Aksu nehri yakınında yer alması, Ephesus'dan Sardis'e uzanan ticaret yolu üzerinde bulunuşunun yarattığı stratejik konum, Pers dönemlerindeki askeri ve ticari öneminin, Bizans dönemleriyle mukayese edilebilecek seviyede olduğunu, sadece yüzey araştırmalarında dahi ele geçen ve pek çok veri sunan seramik toplulukları sayesinde ortaya koyar. Bu çalışmanın temel amacı söz konusu seramik buluntuları tarihlerine, kil ve perdah özelliklerine, üretim tekniklerine göre sistematik olarak sınıflandırarak, kentin bilinen tarihiyle bu buluntuları karşılaştırarak yeniden değerlendirmektir. Söz konusu araştırma kentin tanımlanmasında önemli bilgiler sunarak yerleşim evrelerini, yerel üretim sahasını ve seramik üretimindeki olası etkilerin yanı sıra ticaretini de açıklar. Çalışma bu bağlamda Geç Kalkolitik Dönem'den Bizans Dönemi'ne uzanan kesintisiz bir yerleşim kullanımına da açıklık getirir.

11. Temel Hikayeden Yola Çıkarak Eski Bir Kentin Stratigrafisi: Khonae Archistrategosu

Alan H. Cadwallader

Khonae'ın mucizevi kurtuluşunun anlatıldığı hikayenin çevirisi (ki Appendix 2'de sunulmuştur) son ürünü oluşturan geleneği sorgulamak için iyi bir fırsat sunar. Hikaye tümüyle Colossae'da ve Khonae'da yaşayan insanların hayatıyla ilgili tarihsel gerçeklik sunması açısından bir hayal kırıklığı olarak değerlendirilmiştir. Söz konusu tartışmalara girmeksizin, bu makale geleneksel tarihçi bir yaklaşımla hikaye içindeki katmanları inceleyerek, bir anlamda bunları Küçük Asya kilisesi ve toplumu arasında yaşanan meseleleri açıklamak için kullanır. Hikaye içinde yatan tutarsızlıklar ve gerginlikler de bu hikayenin incelenen katmanlarını oluşturur. Kullanılan yaklaşım Colossae/Khonae'da yaşayan hristiyan topluluğun ne şekillerde pagan mirası ile yüzleştiğini, komşularıyla rekabetlerini, İkonoklazma dönemini, Arap ve Türk akınları gibi bir bin yıla yayılan sürece ışık tutar.

Abbreviations

AA	Archäologischer Anzeiger
AAAS	American Association for the Advancement of Science
ABD	Anchor Bible Dictionary
AC	L'Antiquité Classique
AE	L'Année épigraphique
AJA	American Journal of Archaeology
AJP	American Journal of Philology
AJS	American Journal of Sociology
AM	Mitteilungen des Deutschen Archaeologischen Instituts, Athenische Abteilung
ANRW	Aufstieg und Niedergang der römischen Welt
AS	Anatolian Studies
Ath Mitt	Mitteilungen des Deutschen Archäologischen Instituts (Athenische Abteilung)
BA	Biblical Archaeologist
BAR	British Archaeological Reports
BARev	Biblical Archaeology Review
BCH	Bulletin de Correspondance Hellénique
BE	Bulletin épigraphique
BL	British Library
BMGS	Byzantine and Modern Greek Studies
BMPR	Biosocial Mechanisms of Population Regulation
BR	Biblical Research
BS	Bibliotheca Sacra
BTB	Biblical Theology Bulletin
BZ	Biblische Zeitschrift
CIG	Corpus Inscriptionum Graecarum
CP	Classical Philology
CQ	Classical Quarterly
CRAI	Comptes-rendus de l'Académie des inscriptions et belles lettres
DHA	Dialogues d'histoire ancienne
DOP	Dumbarton Oaks Papers
EA	Epigraphica Anatolica
FGrH	Fragmenta der griechischen Historiker
GRBS	Greek, Roman and Byzantine Studies
HTR	Harvard Theological Review
IEph	Die Inschriften von Ephesos
IG	Inscriptiones Graecae
IG²	Inscriptiones Graecae (editio minor)
IGR	Inscriptiones Graecae ad res Romanas pertinentes

IHierapJ	Jewish Inscriptions from Hierapolis
IJO	Inscriptiones Judaicae Orientis
IK	Inschriften griechischer Städte aus Kleinasien
JECS	*Journal of Early Christian Studies*
JESHO	Journal of the Economic and Social History of the Orient
JEH	Journal of Ecclesiastical History
JETS	Journal of the Evangelical Theological Society
JHS	Journal of Hellenic Studies
JJS	Journal of Jewish Studies
JMA	Journal of Mediterranean Archaeology
JRA	Journal of Roman Archaeology
JRAS	Journal of the Royal Asiatic Society
JRGS	Journal of The Royal Geographical Society
JRS	Journal of Roman Studies
JTS	Journal of Theological Studies
LGPN	Lexicon of Greek Personal Names
MAMA	Monumenta Asiae Minoris Antiqua
MBAH	Münstersche Beiträge zur Antiken Handelsgeschichte
NEASB	Near East Archaeological Society Bulletin
NovT	Novum Testamentum
NTS	New Testament Studies
OGIS	Orientis Graeci Inscriptiones Selectae
PG	Patrologia Graeca
PL	Patrologia Latina
PNAS	Procedings of the National Academy of Sciences
PO	Patrologia Orientalis
RBN	Révue Belge de Numismatique et de Sigillographie
RE	Real-Encyclopädie der classischen Altertumswissenschaft
REA	Revue des études anciennes
RevExp	Review and Expositor
RIC	Roman Imperial Coinage
SBS	Studies in Byzantine Sigillography
SEG	Supplementum Epigraphicum Graecum
SIG	Sylloge Inscriptionum Graecum
TAM	Tituli Asiae Minoris
TB	Tyndale Bulletin
TIB	Tabula Imperii Byzantini
TTK	Türk Tarih Kurumu
TÜBİTAK	Türkiye Bilimsel ve Teknik Araştırma Kurumu
VC	Vigiliae Christianae
WuD	Wort und Dienst
ZPE	Zeitschrift für Papyrologie und Epigraphik

List of Figures

All photographs and diagrams have been taken and executed by the editors or the authors of individual chapters, except where otherwise credited.

Chapter One

Chapter Two

Chapter Four

Chapter Five

Chapter Six

Figure 1 An early reproduction of the famous Colossian quadriga coin
Figure 2 An honorific inscription for Markos, Colossae's head translator and interpreter
Figure 3 An honorific bomos for Korumbos, repairer of Colossae's baths
Figure 4 Detail from the honorific bomos for Korumbos
Figure 5 The incised reliefs of the Korumbos bomos

Chapter Eight

Figure 1 Armenia's integration into the Empire, from Tier 1 of the Aphrodisias Sebasteion
Figure 2 The Ethnos of the Piroustae
Figure 3 Ethnos with a bull
Figure 4 Imperator with Roman People or Senate
Figure 5 Augustus by Land and Sea
Figure 6 Claudius and Agrippina
Figure 7 Nero and Agrippina
Figure 8 Germanicus with a Captive

Chapter Nine

Diagram 1a Paul's Ego-centred Network
Diagram 1b Epaphras' Ego-centred Network
Diagram 2 Types of Networks in Paul's Ego-centred Ties
Diagram 3 Lycus Valley Neighbourhood Pattern
Figure 1 Funerary stele for Tatianos
Figure 2 Funerary stele for Gluko

Chapter Ten

Figure 1 The location of Colossae
Figure 2 The Colossae höyük
Figure 3 Byzantine pottery fragments
Figure 4 Coin finds from the sampling areas
Figure 5 Prehistoric pottery
Figure 6 Hellenistic and Roman pottery
Drawing 1 The sampling areas
Graphic 2 General results from each pottery sampling area
Catalogue drawings

Contributors

Alan H. Cadwallader is Senior Lecturer in Biblical Studies at the Australian Catholic University. He has worked for several years with Michael Trainor on the Colossae Project which has lead to collaborative relationships with Pamukkale University in Turkey. He has published several new inscriptions from Colossae and is author of the award winning, *Beyond the Word of a Woman* (Adelaide: 2008).

Bahadır Duman completed doctoral research under Professor Dr. Celal Şimşek at Pamukkale University and, with Erim Konakçi has conducted the first extended ceramic survey of the site of Colossae, which has lead to a number of publications. He has worked extensively on the site of Laodiceia and, with Professor Şimşek, has published "Ampullae Finds at Laodikeia", *Olba* 15 (2007) 73–101 and "Late Antique Unguentaria Found at Laodikeia", *Adalya* 10 (2007) 285–99.

Hatice P. Erdemir is Associate Professor in the History Department on Ancient History at Celal Bayar University, Manisa. After completion of her PhD in the University of Wales, Swansea, she has pursued her interest in a variety of issues of ancient history, from Roman administration and economy to gender issues, family and health and is especially interested in comparative studies of them. She has produced, with Professor Halil Erdemir, a guide to Sardis and, most recently, *Economic Management of Cilicia in the time of Cicero* (Olba: 2009).

Rosalinde A. Kearsley is an Honorary Senior Research Fellow in the Department of Ancient History at Macquarie University. Her research into the Graeco-Roman cities in Asia Minor has included asiarchs and archiereis of Asia; bilingualism and acculturation; and the role of women in public life. Recent publications: 'Women and Public Life in Imperial Asia Minor: Hellenistic Tradition and Augustan Ideology', Ancient West and East 4.1 (2005) 98–121; contributions to G. H. R. Horsley (ed.), The Greek and Latin Inscriptions in the Burdur Archaeological Museum (Ankara: 2007); "Octavian and Augury: The Years 30–27 B. C.", CQ 59 (2009) 97–116.

Erim Konakçi has completed doctoral research under Professor Dr. Celal Şimşek at Pamukkale University and, with Bahadır Duman has conducted the first extended ceramic survey of the site of Colossae. He has been involved at excavations on a number of sites: Bayraklı Smyrna, Ulucak Höyük and Laodicea. He has published a number of archaeological articles including, with M. B. Baştürk, "Settlement Patterns in the Malatya-Elazığ Region in the IVth & IIIth Millennıum BC", *Alt Orientalische Forschungen* 32 (2005) 97–114 and "Military and Militia in the Urartian State", *Ancient West & East* 8 (2009) 169–201.

Harry O. Maier is Professor of New Testament and Early Christian Studies at Vancouver School of Theology and an Alexander von Humboldt Research Fellow. He is author of the award-winning *The Social Setting of the Ministry as Reflected in the Writing of the Shepherd of Hermas, Clement and Ignatius* (Kitchener: 1991, 2002) and *Apocalypse Recalled: The Book of Revelation after Christendom* (Minneapolis: 2003). He is currently completing a book on Roman imperial iconography.

Nicholas Sekunda is Professor of Ancient History at the University of Gdansk and a principal of its Institute of Archaeology, with particular involvement in field research in Macedonia. He is a major contributor to *The Cambridge History of Greek and Roman Warfare* (Cambridge: 2007), *The Children of Herodotus* (Newcastle on Tyne: 2008) and *A Companion to Ancient Macedonia* (West Sussex, UK: 2010).

Rick Strelan is Associate Professor in New Testament & Early Christianity in the School of History, Philosophy, Religion and Classics at The University of Queensland. His specialist research area is the cultural world of Luke-Acts, and his recent publications include Luke the Priest: The authority of the author of the Third Gospel (London: 2008), and "Tabitha: The gazelle of Joppa (Acts 9:36)" Biblical Theology Bulletin 39 (2009) 77–86.

Michael Trainor is Senior Lecturer in New Testament Studies at Flinders University. He has worked for several years with Alan Cadwallader and Professor Claire Smith on the Colossae Project which has lead to collaborative relationships with Pamukkale University in Turkey. He has published several articles on Colossae; his latest book is *Epaphras: Paul's Educator at Colossae* (Collegeville: 2009).

Paul Trebilco is Professor of New Testament Studies in the Department of Theology and Religious Studies at the University of Otago, Dunedin, New Zealand. He is the author of *Jewish Communities in Asia Minor* (Cambridge: 1991); *The Early Christians in Ephesus from Paul to Ignatius* (Tübingen: 2004). He is currently completing a book entitled *What shall we call each other? Self-designation and Identity in Earliest Christianity.*

Index of Ancient Texts

Index of Biblical References

Index of Inscriptions and Papyri

Modern Author Index

Index of Main Subjects